REGULATING CANNABIS:
Towards a unified market

A 5-year investigation of the implementation of the world's first fully regulated cannabis market for pleasure in Colorado

DR TODD SUBRITZKY, PHD

Cannabis Education Online (CEO)
Sydney, Australia

Published by
Cannabis Education Online
Sydney, Australia
www.cannabis-education.online
ISBN: 978-0-6452418-5-3

Kind words for Regulating Cannabis

Dr Mark Monaghan

Head of the Department of Social Policy, Sociology and Criminology University of Birmingham

"This book clearly demonstrates authority in the field of international drug policy and draws predominantly on the latest evidence in doing so. It is a substantial contribution to an emerging policy issue with a plethora of new knowledge displayed throughout. Overall, I found this to be a vital addition to the canon of knowledge regarding cannabis policy change"

Vendula Belackova, PhD

Drug Policy Researcher & Adjunct Senior Lecturer at the Social Policy Research Centre, University of New South Wales

"The author has broadened the understanding of cannabis regulation when it comes to conflicts between consumer protection, private profit, and public health. He has successfully applied and enriched several theoretical concepts in the context of cannabis legalization, especially when it comes to 'the elephant in the room' - the wellness potential of cannabis on legal markets"

i

About the author – Dr Todd Subritzky, PhD

Todd is an author, social scientist, lecturer and entrepreneur. He completed his PhD with the National Drug Research Institute in Australia where his research included multiple trips to Colorado and interviews with senior regulators, industry executives, and front-line public health professionals, together with analysis of hundreds of government documents and almost a thousand media reports regarding the implementation of the recreational cannabis market in the State.

The research has been published in multiple peer reviewed scientific journals including the International Journal of Drug Policy, Drug and Alcohol Review, and Addiction and had been cited over 220 times at time of writing. He has presented his findings at international drug policy conferences in New Zealand, Australia and the US. Todd is a lecturer at La Trobe University (Sydney campus) on the Health Information Management program. In addition, he is also founder of 5th Dimension Wellness (www.medicalcannabisdoctors.com.au) which advocates for better patient access to medical cannabis for patients in need in Australia.

Stay in the Loop

Scan to Follow our Social Media Channels #COOLHEMPSTUFF

www.facebook.com/todd.subritzky/

www.twitter.com/mjsurveys

www.instagram.com/coolhempstuff/

tiktok.com/@coolhempstuff

www.linkedin.com/in/dr-todd-subritzky-phd/

Acknowledgements

For the most part, the past years of this research project have been an enthralling and immensely satisfying period of my life. My journey would not have been possible without the assistance, guidance, wisdom, and support of a number of people.

First, in general to the Coloradan people with their wonderful hospitality, but specifically to the interviewees who freely gave of their time and openly discussed the issues, thank you. The book has benefited greatly from your experience. Second, to my supervisors Professors Simon Lenton and Simone Pettigrew, both world class academics in their own rights but also quality human beings, thank you. Everything they have said has been for the purpose of improving the research and I have been extremely fortunate to have this level of guidance throughout. As one of the world's foremost minds on cannabis policy, both as an academic and government advisor, the wisdom and knowledge of Professor Lenton in particular has been an invaluable asset and I am grateful for that. To Dr David Baker you have been an inspiration and your friendship, support, and advice have been indispensable and very much appreciated – long may that continue. Fourth, to Professor Beau Kilmer, thanks and acknowledgements for introductions to several study participants, which led to yet further introductions. This access to the highest levels of government in Colorado strengthened the book. Fifth, Jo Hawkins and Paul Jones at NDRI have consistently gone above and beyond to assist me. Penultimately, a big thanks to Drs Mark Monaghan and Vendula Belackova whose comments as examiners of the thesis, on which this book is based, improved the final work. My daughter Jade was the inspiration to be the best I could be, which I hope in turn will inspire her as she heads into the chaos of high school and out into the wider cosmos.

Presentations related to the study

Subritzky, T., (2016). Testing times: issues with potency and pesticides in Colorado's commercial recreational marijuana market – Paper presented at International Society for the Study of Drug Policy (ISSDP 2016) Satellite Conference Auckland, May 11 -12, 2016

Subritzky, T., (2016). Smoke and mirrors: issues relating to data collection and impact assessment in Colorado's recreational cannabis market – Paper presented at International Society for the Study of Drug Policy (ISSDP 2016) Conference Sydney, May 16 -18, 2016

Subritzky, T., (2017). Developing regulations for pesticide usage on marijuana crops in Colorado – Paper presented at the 1st Annual Institute of Cannabis Research Conference at Colorado State University-Pueblo, Colorado, USA, April 28-30, 2017

Subritzky, T. (2018) Cannabis and the spectrum of wellness. Presented at Hemposium Conference, Mardi Grass, Nimbin, NSW May 4, 2018.

Subritzky, T. (2018). The strengths and weaknesses of the Colorado cannabis legalisation scheme – presented at NDRI Annual Symposium Melbourne, November 22, 2018
http://ndri.curtin.edu.au/news-events/ndri-events/2018-annual-symposium

Contents at a glance

Including analysis of hundreds of pages of government documents, almost 1000 media articles, and interviews in the field with over 30 senior government officials, industry executives and front-line public health representatives, together with over 800 academic references, this meticulously researched book is the definitive account of real-world cannabis policy implementation.

At a time when cannabis legalisation is spreading across an increasing number of jurisdictions globally, this book cuts across the noise and presents a factual account of issues faced by regulators in the real-world context of Colorado. It can be read as an evidence-based handbook for regulators and should be a first port of call for anyone interested in the legalisation of cannabis.

In January 2014, Colorado implemented a commercial cannabis market for pleasure - the first jurisdiction globally to implement a regulated, adult-use cannabis supply chain from seed-to-sale. It was reported as an historic occasion that presaged a grand social and economic experiment in drug legalisation.

The cannabis academic public health literature is examined prodigiously including its potential for harm and benefit together with alternative regulatory approaches. The book also features a number of papers published in academic journals based on the PhD research of the author. The commodification of cannabis vs the craft approach together with the entanglement of the medical and recreational markets are two of many topical themes discussed in detail.

Multiple recommendations relevant for other jurisdictions considering the legalisation of cannabis are presented. Recognising the limitations of harm reduction approaches that cannot conceptually conceive beneficial aspects of cannabis consumption, a new framework, the spectrum of wellness is proposed as an alternative in Appendix 1 of the book.

List of Abbreviations

Colorado Government Departments and Divisions

CDA Colorado Department of Agriculture

CDHS Colorado Department of Human Services

CDOR Colorado Department of Revenue

CDPHE Colorado Department of Public Health and Environment

CDPS Colorado Department of Public Safety

CDRA Colorado Department of Regulatory Agencies

CDT Colorado Department of Taxation

COSPB Colorado Office of State Planning & Budgeting

MED Marijuana Enforcement Division

MPG Marijuana Policy Group (government contractor)

OMC Office of Marijuana Coordination (Governor's Office)

United States Government Departments

DEA Drug Enforcement Agency

EPA Environmental Protection Agency

FDA Food and Drug Administration

General

A64 Amendment 64 Ballot measure in Colorado, 2012 (not to be confused with the ballot measure in California of the same name of 2016)

CFS Cannabis fragmentation spectrum

CG Collaborative governance

CRCM Colorado recreational cannabis market

CSA Controlled Substances Act

CSC Cannabis social clubs

GACP Good agricultural and collection practices

IPM Integrated Pest Management

MMC Medical Marijuana Code

NASEM National Academies of Science, Engineering, and Medicine

NORML National Organization for the Reform of Marijuana Laws

RMC Colorado Retail Marijuana Code

SAM Smart Approaches to Marijuana

TA Thematic analysis

UN United Nations

WADA World Anti-doping Agency

WHO World Health Organisation

Common Phyto-cannabinoids and Cannabis Pharmacology

THC Tetrahydrocannabinol

CBD Cannabidiol

CBN Cannabinol

ECS Endocannabinoid System

List of Tables

Table of Contents

"We're making the plane while we're flying it"

Andrew Freedman: Director Office of Marijuana Coordination
(Governor's Office)

Chapter 1: Introduction

In November 2012, voters in Colorado used a direct democracy initiative to legalise a commercial cannabis market for pleasure - thereby ending 95 years of prohibition in the State (Colorado Amendment 64, 2012; House Bill 263, 1917). When the first stores opened 13 months later, following a complex and intense pre-implementation period for regulators, Colorado became the first jurisdiction globally to implement a regulated, adult-use cannabis supply chain from seed-to-sale (Subritzky, Pettigrew, & Lenton, 2016b). According to media reports, it was a historic occasion that presaged a grand social and economic experiment in drug legalisation (BBC, 2014, Jan. 1; CNN, 2014, Jan. 2; Wall Street Journal, 2014, Jan. 2). Further, an article in the Denver Post (2013, Dec. 31) reported history professor Isaac Compos as stating; "It's an enormous change ... what we could be witnessing is the first major, major crack in the whole drug war edifice". This book examines the pre-implementation phase of the Colorado scheme and the first five years of the policy's evolution post-implementation.

Benefits of cannabis prohibition in the US context are said to be higher prices, reduced marketing and lobbying opportunities, and a general inconvenience for buyers, thereby, presumably, reducing the potential for instances of problematic consumption (Caulkins, Kilmer, & Kleiman, 2016; Tate, Taylor, & Sawyer, 2013). The stated aim of the federal drug policy in the US is to reduce "[illicit] drug use and drug-related consequences" (Caulkins et al., 2016, p.107). However, cannabis remained the most consumed illicit drug globally (United Nations Office on Drugs and Crime, 2014), and it has been counterclaimed that negative unintended consequences of prohibition such as creating huge criminal markets, diverting resources away from public health to enforcement, and the marginalisation of people who use cannabis, outweigh any potential benefits of prohibition (Lenton, 2000; Rolles, 2012; Szabo, 2014; Wodak, Reinarman, Cohen, & Drummond, 2002). Prominent cannabis policy scholars Caulkins et al. (2016) have noted that an important variable in calculating the benefits of prohibition is the level of harm caused by using a substance. They contended that the argument for prohibiting cannabis is weakened because while excessive consumption of cannabis can cause harmful outcomes, it has been estimated to be substantially less than that caused by other drugs such as tobacco, alcohol, cocaine, and heroin (Degenhardt et al., 2013; Nutt, 2012). In general, there appears to be broad consensus in the literature that cannabis policy in the US has been disproportionately punitive, politically motivated, and ultimately ineffective in reducing problematic consumption and associated harms (Commission on Marihuana Drug Abuse, 1972; Kleiman, 1992; LaGuardia Committee on Marihuana, 1944; MacCoun & Reuter, 2001; Room, Fischer, Hall, Lenton, & Reuter, 2010). In this book, the focus is on the model of legalisation and how it was implemented in Colorado, as opposed to the debate surrounding the pros and cons of legalisation in general or simply looking at outcomes. This approach is consistent with Pacula et al. (2015), who found that differences in policy implementation can lead to different public health outcomes.

In Colorado, the commercial, for-profit recreational cannabis market was built on the existing medical cannabis market that was implemented in 2000 and regulated and commercialised in 2009/10 (Kamin, 2013)[1]. MacCoun and Reuter (2001, p.5) pointed out that the structure of American society needs to be considered when considering the application of various alternative cannabis regulatory models in the US as it affords commercial free speech protection and permits "large corporate campaign contributions. [So] after a drug is legalised … its promotion and sale are likely to be subject to only modest regulations …". Caulkins et al. (2016, p.170) compared this political culture with more paternalistic philosophies in Europe where it was reported that academics thought it "… obvious that consumers needed protection from exploitation by entrepreneurs seeking to profit from drug abuse and dependence". Indeed, from a public health perspective, one of the major concerns is that a market incentivised by profit has the potential to morph into a 'big cannabis' in the mould of tobacco and alcohol industries whose products have been shown to be responsible for considerable burden of disease (Caulkins, 2014; Caulkins et al., 2015; Kleiman, 2014a; Rehm, Taylor, & Room, 2006; Rolles & Murkin, 2016; Room, 2014). Additionally, lessons from the agri-chemical sector, in many respects the most pertinent cannabis-related public health threat, have shown that unbridled capitalism can have grave consequences (Engdahl, 2007). For example, chemical inputs for cannabis cultivation can impose a serious public health threat from the

---

[1] Professor Kamin was also an interview participant in this study.

potential widespread use of toxic pesticides and fertilisers in the cultivation process (Subritzky, Pettigrew, & Lenton, 2017).

Descriptions of the Colorado model as it was initially conceived are varied. On the one hand, respected scholar Kleiman described the for-profit, commercial model as the second worse outcome behind prohibition. He reportedly stated that "marijuana companies' best customers are the problem [consumers]", and that it is "an industry that flatly contradicts public interest" (Lopez, 2014, December 17). Conversely, as noted by Governor Hickenlooper (2014, p.1), "[Colorado is] working as a convener for all interested parties and experts to shape public policy that utilizes the decades of public health lessons gained from regulating alcohol and tobacco". Unfortunately, given data lag and other factors, it will likely take years or even decades for quality impact assessment data to emerge (Kilmer & MacCoun, 2017; Pacula & Sevigny, 2014), so the "bulk early insights are about regulations and implementation instead of outcomes" (Caulkins et al., 2015, p.10). These early insights are the focus of this book, the objectives of which are outlined below.

Research objectives

The overall objective of the study is to investigate issues that arose during the implementation and evolution of the world's first fully Colorado recreational cannabis market in Colorado (CRCM), primarily from a public health and harm reduction perspective. Specifically, the project aimed to:

- Review relevant peer-reviewed literature, codes of regulations, government publications, and other associated grey literature.
- Identify issues associated with the implementation of the CRCM and investigate how these issues evolved as cannabis was normalised from an illicit drug to a legal commercial commodity.
- Explore inherent tensions in relationships between realms of public health, consumer protection (primarily in terms of quality control), and commercial profit-seeking as Colorado implemented its pioneering cannabis scheme.
- Feedback results from the analysis of government documents and media articles through interviews with key regulatory,

public health, and industry stakeholders in the CRCM to further examine a range of perspectives and future challenges.

- Provide a thick, multi-dimensional descriptive account of issues associated with the implementation of the recreational cannabis policy in Colorado.
- Make recommendations for policymakers in other jurisdictions based on the study findings.

Data corpus

This is a multi-source investigation. Data collected were primarily focused on the period ranging from when recreational cannabis was legalized in the State in November 2012, through to 31st December 2018. This period included the pre-implementation phase (Nov. 2012 – Dec 31st 2013), and the first five years of the market's post-implementation evolution (Jan. 1st 2014 – Dec. 31st 2018). The corpus of data included for analysis consisted of:

- Government documents from pre-implementation phase (n=13) totalling over 600 pages including: Legislative Bills (n=4), Governor Executive Orders (n=2), a federal memorandum (n=1), Task Force and General Assembly reports (n=2), a Constitutional Amendment (n=1), and Codes of Regulations (n=3).
- Media reports including samples from Colorado mass media reports from 2014-2016 (n=521) and niche media reports from 2015 and 2016 (n=448).
- Transcripts from face-to-face interviews with key stakeholders such as senior regulators, industry executives, and front-line public health professionals (n=32). (For full list of interview participants in the study see Table 12 in Appendix 2)
- Colorado Official State Web Portal: a publicly available archive that includes hundreds of government reports, updates, industry bulletins, and information from the Marijuana Enforcement Division (MED), the Colorado Department of Revenue (CDOR), the Colorado Department of Public Health and Environment (CDPHE), Department of Agriculture (CDA), and other related departments.

- 'Permanent' iterations of the Colorado Retail Marijuana Code (RMC) 2013-2018 (Colorado Secretary of State, 2019) (n=10).
- 'Emergency' retail marijuana rules 2013-2018 (n=15).
- Other government documents that continuously emerged, such as House and Senate Bills, Governor Executive Orders, state-mandated impact and task force reports, Legislative Council records, and workgroup meeting minutes.
- Public online records of the Colorado Secretary of State and the Colorado State Legislature (General Assembly).
- Observations from the field from tours of cultivation facilities, dispensaries, trade shows, and policy symposiums (three trips to Colorado in 2015, 2016, and 2017 of 2, 2, and 6 weeks respectively).

Significance

For several decades, the cultivation, sale, and use of recreational cannabis have been prohibited by law in most countries. Since Colorado implemented its pioneering recreational market, multiple states in the US, and countries including Uruguay and Canada have also legalised cannabis for adult-use. As the first US state to implement a recreational cannabis market, Colorado is furthest along the process, and therefore an important example to begin investigating early consequences of specific policy choices (Caulkins et al., 2016; Room, 2014; Subritzky et al., 2016b). Implementation of the Colorado model provides an opportunity to go beyond speculation about what legalised cannabis might look like and what its effects might be to gather evidence on the real-world application of a recreational cannabis policy, thereby potentially informing policymakers and researchers in other jurisdictions about what not to do as well as being a blueprint for other schemes. Caulkins, Lee, and Kasunic (2012c, p.1) contended the Colorado reforms were "unprecedented - no developed polity in the modern era has legalized [non-medical] marijuana". Furthermore, Kilmer and MacCoun (2017) pointed out that the majority of the literature was necessarily forecasting and speculative based on studies of other legal drugs such as alcohol and tobacco, or founded on versions of decriminalisation in the US, and/or the de facto model in the Netherlands that has historically tolerated the retail sale of small amounts of cannabis but has not regulated the cultivation or manufacture of cannabis products (these concepts are described in more detail in Chapter 3).

Thus, this study is significant for the following reasons. First, Colorado was the world's first jurisdiction to implement a legalised commercial cannabis market for adult-use. As such, analysis of its implementation and evolution is important to inform policymakers from other countries and states who may seek to introduce a legal cannabis market. Second, policy impact research on legalised cannabis has been limited by the illegality of the product, which has prevented evidence-based analysis. The present study is an initial step towards rectifying this evidence deficit by examining 'real-world' experience. Third, since Colorado implemented its world-first initiative, multiple North American jurisdictions including California and Canada have reformed their cannabis policy and implemented commercial recreational cannabis markets. Placing the Coloradan model within the context of those markets further increases the significance of the study. Fourth, because it examines a first of its kind legal cannabis market, the study will be of interest to a wide variety of stakeholders including public health researchers, policy and lawmakers, drug policy reform advocates, and the general public both in the US and internationally. It may be of particular interest to regulators in countries such as New Zealand, who have a similar population to Colorado and recently voted on legalising cannabis, Australia where ACT (like Colorado) had legalised small amounts of cannabis (although not a commercial market) in contradiction of federal law in late 2019, Mexico, or others considering non-prohibition cannabis models.

Terminology

Marijuana/ cannabis

In this book, the terms cannabis and marijuana are used interchangeably, although I am cognizant of the potential for controversy. The term marijuana or marihuana, popularised in the US by advocates of prohibition in the 1930s, is said to have been intended as a derogatory slur towards minority groups and Mexican immigrants in particular (Herer, Conrad, & Osburn, 2007; Lee, 2012; McKenna, 2010). However, it is a label that is almost universally recognised, and in Colorado, it is the legal term employed to describe the plant. Therefore, while it is acknowledged that cannabis may be considered a more neutral term, and it is employed where possible throughout the book, it is unavoidable that the term marijuana is also used in the US context.

Retail/ recreational cannabis

Across the data corpus, the academic literature, and in this book, various terms are used to describe the non-medical cannabis market in Colorado. These terms include recreational, retail, adult-use, popular-use, pleasure market, and non-medical (Kamin, 2016; Room, 2014). The term 'recreational cannabis', is not without dispute. For example, long-time cannabis legalisation advocate and entrepreneur DeAngelo (2015, p.66), who considers all moderate consumption of cannabis to be therapeutic, claimed "the term 'recreational' has become the catchall phrase to describe all cannabis use that is not 'medical' ... [and] has ... become a code word to describe 'just getting high'. This is unfortunate, because ... it perpetuates misconceptions about cannabis that have kept it illegal for decades".

Furthermore, the term 'retail' cannabis is employed in the regulations, on state government websites, and by stakeholders, to refer to the non-medical market. For example, the Colorado Retail Marijuana Code (RMC) refers to the code of regulations for the entire recreational market from seed-to-sale (the full supply chain including both production and distribution) as opposed to retail stores (Colorado Secretary of State, 2019). To avoid confusion, when the term retail is used, unless explicitly stated, it refers broadly to the CRCM, as opposed to in the usual sense of retail/wholesale segments of a supply chain. The term adult-use is also a commonly used term to distinguish the market from the medical side, as opposed to insinuating those comparable markets are for children. Where possible the term 'Colorado recreational/retail cannabis market' (CRCM) is used for clarity.

User/ consumer

It has been argued that stigmatising language infuses studies on the consumption of psychoactive drugs, such as cannabis (Global Commission on Drug Policy, 2018). This stigmatism dehumanises people who use cannabis as derelict, or deviant, and as belonging to the margins of society (the so-called 'othering') (Becker, 1963/2008; Lunze, Lunze, Raj, & Samet, 2015). An example of 'othering' is the term 'user', which is perceived as being associated with characteristics such as 'lazy', 'worthless', 'irresponsible', and 'no future' (American Society of Addiction Medicine, 2018; Global Commission on Drug Policy, 2018; International Society of Addiction Journal Editors, 2018). In addition, it has been shown that stigmatising language is not limited to the general public and can directly impact clinical care. For example, a randomised control study provided clinicians with identical case studies where the individual was referred to as either a 'substance abuser' or a 'person with a substance use disorder' and it was found that mental health professionals were more likely to blame the individual as personally culpable and consider that punitive measures were appropriate (as opposed to treatment) when the term abuser was incorporated (Kelly & Westerhoff, 2010).

To avoid using stigmatising language about people who use cannabis, in this book the guidelines presented by the Global Commission on Drug Policy (GCDP) are followed. The guidelines presented in Table 1 below have been modified from the term 'drugs' in the broader context of drug and/ or substance use and specifically applied to cannabis. The term 'people who use drugs' (PWUD) has also been recommended by several scholars (Crofts, Costigan, & Reid, 2003; Lancaster, Seear, & Ritter, 2017). Furthermore, the term 'consumer' is also employed as an alternative to 'user'. This follows Lammers and Happell (2003) in the sense of a person being an active recipient in the consumption of drugs.

Table 1: Modified Global Commission on Drug Policy guidelines to avoid stigmatising language around people who use cannabis.

Recommended terms	Not recommended terms
Person who uses cannabis	Cannabis user
Person with non-problematic cannabis use	Recreational, casual, or experimental user
Person with cannabis dependence, person with problematic cannabis use, person with cannabis use	Addict, cannabis abuser, dope head, druggie, stoner

disorder, person who uses drugs (when use is not problematic)	
Cannabis use disorder, problematic cannabis use	Cannabis habit
Has a cannabis use disorder	Addicted to cannabis
Abstinent, person who has stopped using cannabis	Clean
Actively uses drugs, positive for substance use	Dirty (as in dirty screen)
Respond, program, address, manage	Fight, counter, combat, and other combatant language

Source: (Global Commission on Drug Policy, 2018, p.30)

Medical cannabis

While this book has a primary focus on the recreational cannabis market in Colorado, the foundation of that market on the pre-existing medical cannabis laws in the State meant that it could not be examined in isolation. As such the term medical cannabis is employed throughout the book. However, there is a broad range of definitions for medical cannabis. To avoid confusion the term 'medical cannabis' is used throughout the book in relation to the legal medical cannabis market in Colorado unless otherwise stated.

Dependence/ addiction

It should be noted that the terms dependence and addiction are often conflated. As noted by the Global Commission on Drug Policy (2018), dependence relates to depending on a substance to function, while addiction is more closely aligned with the continuation of compulsive use despite harmful consequences, a crucial distinction. In this regard, the term addiction is avoided.

Australian/ American spelling

While this book is presented primarily in Australian English, to remain true to original media articles, specific journal guidelines, and government documents, American English has been retained in some instances.

Issues

Throughout the book, the term 'issues' is applied regularly. Usage of this word follows the dictionary definition as a broad term generally to describe problems or challenges associated with, in this case, implementing the legal cannabis market. It is not used conceptually.

Theoretical underpinnings

Given the diversity of the book objectives that include the investigation of issues related to the implementation of the CRCM, a combination of three theoretical frameworks underpinned the research to ensure appropriate depth of analysis. These include incorporating a public health and harm reduction perspective as a guiding principle, a collaborative governance framework to examine policy implementation, and Stoa's cannabis fragmentation spectrum to provide nuance to the commercial model incorporated in Colorado. In Appendix 1, the spectrum of wellness is also introduced as an alternative framework for considering the consumption of cannabis.

Public health and harm reduction

The potential public health harms associated with the consumption of cannabis are described in detail in the following chapter. As noted by Fischer, Rehm, and Hall (2009), the public health approach has a general focus on reducing harms as opposed to use *per se,* which is very much aligned with the concept of harm reduction. There has long been ambiguity around the term harm reduction as it relates to drug policy (Wodak & Saunders, 1995). In general the concept encompasses a pragmatic approach of "accepting the reality of substance use behaviour, while directing effort at minimising the harmful consequences" (Crofts et al., 2003; Erickson, 1995, p.283; Szabo, 2014). Goode (2012) noted that, in relation to drug policy, harm reduction aims to minimise the most harmful aspects of drug consumption and emphasise practicality of regulations. Rhodes and Hedrich (2010, p.19) "envisage harm reduction as a 'combination intervention', made up of a package of interventions tailored to local setting and need, which give primary emphasis to reducing the harms of drug use".

Lenton and Single (1998) sought to bring clarity around definitions of harm reduction. In their still relevant paper, they contended that defining characteristics of harm reduction include: (i) the goal of reducing harms associated with drug use as opposed to reducing use *per se*; (ii) strategies to reduce harm for people who use drugs; and (iii) a likely net reduction in drug related harm. The authors provided an overview of four categories of definitions for harm reduction including narrow, broad, hard empirical, and socio-empirical. These are now introduced.

Narrow definitions of harm reduction exclude abstinent-oriented programs and "referred to only those policies which attempted to reduce the risk of harm among people who continue to use drugs" (Lenton & Single, 1998, p.214; Single, 1997). While this category of harm reduction definition is conceptually clear, the authors argued that the removal of abstinence goals is restrictive as it excludes potentially helpful strategies for harm reduction such as custody and court diversion schemes. Furthermore, from a clinical perspective, negotiated abstinence is a valuable tool for reducing harmful patterns of consumption. Indeed, even long-term cannabis advocates recommend periods of 'fasting' when consumption is felt to be problematic to self or others (Dussault, 2017).

According to Lenton and Single (1998), broad definitions of harm reduction include any program with the objective of a reduction of harm caused by drug use. These definitions have the advantage of including policies with a focus on abstinence and the disadvantage of being so broad, they risk ceasing to be useful. Indeed, Wodak and Saunders (1995) noted that broad definitions might also include options to indefinitely incarcerate users under the pretext of limiting harm.

Hard empirical definitions require that the reduction of harm can be measured to demonstrate the usefulness of the policy (Lenton & Single, 1998). This category of harm reduction has the advantage of flexibility in that can be applied to any programme that can be proven to have reduced harm and will appeal to policy makers as cost benefit analyses of the policy could, in theory, be undertaken with relative ease. Disadvantages include 'real world' challenges of impact assessment and the tendency to neglect factoring in the cost of interventions in calculations.

The socio-empirical definition of harm reduction was laid out by Lenton and Single (1998) as their preferred model. Under this definition, harm reduction programmes are required to meet three conditions including: (i) having a primary goal of reducing harm (as opposed to use *per se*); (ii) abstinence focused approaches are included; and (iii) there is a strategy in place to make reasonable judgements on the effectiveness of the programme (challenges associated with impact assessment are addressed in chapter 3 of the Literature review and in Chapter 8 of the Results in the context of youth protection).

Some harm reduction organisations have contended that a universal definition is not viable, however they listed several principles considered central to the practise (e.g. Harm Reduction Coalition, 2017; Harm Reduction International, 2017). As noted harm reduction is incorporated as a guiding principle and as such an overview of these are reproduced in Table 2 below:

Table 2: Principles of harm reduction in practise

1. Acceptance, for better or worse, that licit and illicit drug use is part of our world and working to minimize harmful effects is better than simply ignoring or condemning the behaviour.
2. Understands drug use as a complex, multi-faceted phenomenon that encompasses a continuum of behaviours from severe abuse to total abstinence and acknowledges that some ways of using drugs are clearly safer than others.
3. Establishes quality of individual and community life and well-being – not necessarily cessation of all drug use – as the criteria for successful interventions and policies.
4. Calls for the non-judgmental, non-coercive provision of services and resources to people who use drugs and the

	communities in which they live to assist them in reducing attendant harm.
5.	Ensures that people who use drug and those with a history of drug use routinely have a real voice in the creation of programs and policies designed to serve them.
6.	Affirms people who use drugs themselves as the primary agents of reducing the harms of their drug use and seeks to empower these people to share information and support each other in strategies which meet their actual conditions of use.
7.	Recognizes that the realities of poverty, class, racism, social isolation, past trauma, sex-based discrimination, and other social inequalities affect both people's vulnerability to and capacity for effectively dealing with drug-related harm.
8.	Does not attempt to minimize or ignore the real and tragic harm and danger associated with licit and illicit drug use.

Source: Harm Reduction Coalition (2017)

Use reduction

Caulkins and Reuter (1997) have contended that while use-reduction and harm reduction are often conflated, they are distinct concepts. The objective to reduce cannabis use can be incorporated into the harm reduction framework as a major strategy to reduce harm. The distinction is necessary because different types of drug use are associated with different risks. To illustrate the point Caulkins and Reuter (1997) compared the extremes of harm associated with a pregnant heroin addict using an HIV infected needle, to an adult with no dependents, consuming low potency, organically grown herbal cannabis on a Friday evening to relax after work. In both cases a schedule 1 substance is being consumed, however the former seems, on the face of it, more harmful than the latter. This is where the distinction between use reduction and harm reduction is important.

Caulkins and Reuter (1997) argued that US policy aims to reduce drug use as opposed to minimising drug harm. Use-reduction strategies stem from the pathology model of drug use (Barratt, Allen, & Lenton, 2014; O'Malley & Mugford, 1991).

It has been suggested that historically a large body of drug policy research has been informed by the hegemonic pathology, or 'deficit' model, of drug use (Barratt, 2011; Karlsson, 2010; Moore, 2002; O'Malley & Mugford, 1991). This view "positions [illicit] drug use as inherently aberrant, as destructive to both health and happiness, and as reflecting some kind of deficit in personality or social position" (Southgate & Hopwood, 1999, p.308). On the face of it, international cannabis controls and prohibition in the US and other countries appear to be informed by the deficit model. Extreme perspectives of the deficit model confer the judgement that all non-medicinal drug use is 'bad' (Zinberg, 1986). To illustrate the point, Caulkins and Reuter (1997) noted that according to this view, even if an adult consumed a psychotropic drug that had zero risk of harm to herself or others, that use is seen as unacceptable because it is morally wrong (for a more detailed discussion on this point please refer to Subritzky (2018) provided in full in Appendix 1 of the book).

Caulkins and Reuter (1997) outlined three concepts of drug use relevant to the CRCM, which can be considered as targets for use reduction depending on the goals of policy makers. These include: (i) prevalence of use (how many people use cannabis at the population level); (ii) frequency, or quantity of use (how often and/or much is used in total by the consumer); and (iii) total expenditure on drugs. The authors note different policies will create different outcomes and therefore strategies should be targeted towards specific goals. For example, if reduced prevalence is the objective, they contend there is more chance of helping recreational, or people who use cannabis moderately to abstain, so targeting this group would be most likely to achieve the desired outcome. If an aim is to reduce the overall quantity of cannabis consumed, targeting the frequency of use by people with cannabis use disorder could be a more cost-effective approach. Finally, if the objective is to reduce overall expenditure on drugs by consumers, then increasing prices would be a counterproductive measure to achieving goals, although it may well reduce net quantities consumed. As will be examined in detail in Chapter 8 of the book, in the case of the CRCM it would seem logical that use reduction goals target the most vulnerable people who use cannabis. However, as stated by Caulkins and Reuter (1997, p.1149) "although reducing use is a principal way of reducing harm, it is neither the only way nor a fool proof way".

Controlled use

Alternative strategies than use-reduction to minimise the overall harm of drug use have been provided by Becker (1963/2008), Zinberg (1986), and Grund (1993), who considered the possibility of people who use cannabis learning from peers how to consume cannabis in a controlled fashion. This controlled use of drugs was defined as "regular ingestion ... without escalation to abuse or addiction, and without disruption of daily social functioning" (Waldorf, Reinarman, & Murphy, 1991, p.267). From this perspective, a reduction in the quantity of cannabis consumed (dosage and frequency) is considered secondary to the quality of use. 'Quality' in this sense refers to "the conditions of use, which include the using pattern and the social setting" (how, where, when, and with whom the drug is used) (Zinberg, 1986, p.42). This is in contrast to the public health approach that considers high frequency, regular use from the perspective of amplified risk (Crépault, Rehm, & Fischer, 2016).

The concept of controlled use is built on an understanding of cannabis intoxication through the interaction of drug, set, and setting (Weil, Zinberg, & Nelsen, 1969). According to Zinberg (1986): 'drug' is defined in pharmacological terms relating to its preparation, method of consumption, and user tolerance (as outlined in Chapter 2); 'set' relates to the personality, attitude, and expectations of the person consuming the drug; and 'setting' considers social controls including laws, user rituals, and environment. Earleywine (2002, p.99), reiterating Baudelaire (1860/1998) among others, noted that in practical terms, those who arrange to consume cannabis in a relaxed, safe, and comfortable environment "frequently report positive effects from the drug". While the Zinberg model has been critiqued for being overly reliant on ritual, further refinement has been added to include meaningful social roles, such as secure employment, relationships, and life aspirations as important anchors in controlling drug use (Decorte, 2001; Grund, 1993). Following this, the most vulnerable people who use cannabis are not simply those who consume regularly, but those who frequently consume in a low-quality use environment as outlined above, and who lack stable life structures.

When the concept of controlled use is employed as a harm reduction strategy, education on how to reduce risk when consuming cannabis is paramount. Generally, under the controlled use perspective, education is provided by peers in cannabis ritual situations (Zinberg, 1986). This is due to the theory being largely focussed on illicit drug consumption. In legal markets, as noted by Barry and Glantz (2016b), campaigns educating populations are most effective when they target adult populations as well as youth.

Practical guidelines

Aside from theoretical applications, the harm reduction framework also includes practical guidelines to reduce cannabis related harm. For example Lenton (2016) discussed reforming laws around home grown cannabis as an harm reduction strategy. While noting the ambiguity of the concept, scholars have pointed out that regulating limits to delta 9 tetrahydrocannabinol (THC) potency and predatory marketing strategies, encouraging the cultivation of products with higher cannabidiol (CBD):THC ratios, or funding drug driving education campaigns may be considered as harm reduction in the context of a legal cannabis market (Hudak, 2016; Kamin, 2016; Subritzky, Lenton, & Pettigrew, 2016a).

Specific guidelines to reduce risk among people who intend to continue using cannabis have been put forward by scholars (Fischer et al., 2017; Room et al., 2010). These are paraphrased in Table 3 below (the harms identified in the literature that the guidelines aim to reduce are examined in the following chapter of the book).

Table 3: Guidelines for lower risk cannabis use

Abstinence is the best way to avoid risks associated with cannabis use.
Initiation of cannabis use before reaching the age of 16 carries significantly higher risks.
Low-potency THC and/or balanced THC:CBD ratio products are thought to be less risky.
Use of synthetic cannabinoids should be avoided.

Avoid combusted cannabis inhalation and give preference to non-smoking use methods (such as vaporisation and edibles).
Avoid deep or other risky inhalation practices.
High-frequency cannabis use should be avoided.
Don't drive while under the influence of cannabis.
Populations at higher risk for cannabis use–related health problems should abstain.
Avoid combining risk behaviours such as early initiation and high-frequency use.
Avoid mixing cannabis with tobacco.
Pregnant women should not smoke cannabis.

Source: (Fischer et al., 2017; Room et al., 2010).

Harm reduction is an important analytical framework that moves beyond the pathology model towards pragmatic acceptance of drug use and provides practical guidelines that may reduce the impact of harmful cannabis consumption. A major critique of this approach is that, by accepting and legitimising drug use, harm reduction sends the wrong message by weakening the moral position, which states that all drug use is 'bad' (Barratt, 2011; Zinberg, 1986).

Additionally, the concept is open to critique from cannabis normalization advocates, in that it does not appear to consider cannabis use that has been identified as largely nonharmful. Scholars have long pointed out that, while consuming cannabis is not without risk, when considered in the context of burden of disease, most cannabis use does not constitute a significant threat to public health (Caulkins et al., 2016; Kleiman, 1992; Room et al., 2010). Indeed, statistics indicate that approximately 90% of people who use cannabis will not reach levels of clinically defined dependence (Caulkins, Hawken, Kilmer, & Kleiman, 2012a; Kleiman, 2014b). This vast block of people who consume cannabis in a manner that is not perceived as immediately harmful, appear to be underrepresented in the harm reduction framework.

Despite these limitations, the harm reduction concept is applied primarily as a guiding principle in the analysis of the data corpus in this book as it is relevant in a legal cannabis context. Thus, in the body of work presented in the Results section of this book, the analysis was primarily undertaken from a harm reduction perspective in the sense that policy objectives should prioritise the minimisation of harmful consequences of a legal cannabis market particularly to the most vulnerable including youth and people who depend on the substance. Beyond this, the Coloradan specific public health approach as stipulated by the Colorado Department of Public Health and Environment (CDPHE) is described in Chapter 4.

Collaborative governance

As the name implies, collaborative governance (CG) is a system of governance that draws on the collaboration of multiple stakeholders including government regulators, relevant subject matter experts, and industry to devise regulations and resolve complex policy issues (Ansell & Gash, 2008). Colorado used a collaborative governance (CG) approach to implement the policy in Jan. 2014, just 13 months after it was legalized (Kamin, 2015). The CG process has been described as critical to enabling regulators in Colorado to devise comprehensive cannabis regulations within the tight deadlines stipulated in A64, the constitutional amendment that legalised cannabis in the State (Hickenlooper, 2014; Hudak, 2015b). Indeed, "in a mere three months, the A64 Task Force developed a comprehensive framework for the legislation and regulations needed to implement A64" (Blake & Finlaw, 2014, p.366).

Collaborative governance has a rich theoretical pedigree and this framework is central to Chapter 9 where the theoretical literature is reviewed and applied in practice. Specifically, the Ansell and Gash (2008) contingency theory of CG is outlined and used as a framework to examine the data corpus for examples of benefits and risks associated with CG in the implementation of the CRCM policy. Thus, in Chapter 9 a theoretical framework is applied to real-world qualitative data to grow the evidence base on both CG and cannabis policy implementation.

The cannabis fragmentation spectrum: cannabis as a commercial agricultural commodity

The CRCM is often described as a 'commercial model', however, there is a wide range of approaches contained with that overarching term. The so-called 'cannabis fragmentation spectrum' (CFS) as outlined by Stoa (2017) from an agricultural perspective, delineates several models under the broad rubric of commercial/free-market conceptions. The CFS distinguishes between regulations that encourage the consolidation and commodification of cannabis plantations and sales outlets on the one hand, and the protection of smaller scale farmers and the creation of an artisan industry on the other. The CFS includes three components, namely commodification, vertical integration, and appellation designations. Stoa (2017, p.317) pointed out that "contrary to the views of many prognosticators, the eventual consolidation of the marijuana industry is not a foregone conclusion. In this matter, states and local governments have a choice to make".

The CFS allows for more nuanced discussion around the 'commercial model' than is generally apparent in the cannabis policy literature. It is introduced as a framework for understanding cannabis cultivation, manufacture, and sale within an agricultural framework in Chapter 3. The CFS is then reconsidered in the overall discussion of the book (Chapter 11) in light of the results and in the context of emerging commercial models in the US, which differ greatly from state to state in terms of market structure.

Chapter 2: Defining cannabis, how it interacts with the human body, and laying out its potential for harm and benefit

It is necessary to lay a foundation for the book by introducing the fundamentals and complexity of cannabis, how it interacts with the human body, and what potential harms and benefits are associated with its consumption. This chapter reviews these matters and goes beyond standard public health descriptions of cannabis to provide a level of detail of an order higher than is common in the literature on recreational cannabis. In this way the chapter provides essential background material for analysis of regulatory detail later in the book. This approach relates directly to the following objectives of the book:

- Provide a thick, multi-dimensional descriptive account of issues associated with the implementation of the recreational cannabis policy in Colorado.
- Make recommendations for policymakers in other jurisdictions based on the study findings.

In addition, the official Coloradan definition of cannabis is introduced, which can then be placed into context against broader (and narrower) definitions of the cannabis plant and associated products later in the book and also to introduce a definition that can be used throughout the book without ambiguity.

Introducing cannabis: a complex biological organism

The study of cannabis is multifaceted. Tens of thousands of books, papers, and reports over centuries, even millennia, have been written, verbally handed down or sketched into rock regarding its unique history as a herbal remedy, industrial fibre, religious aid, food, hedonic intoxicant, and weaponised agent of chemical warfare (Booth, 2005; Earleywine, 2002; Estren, 2017; Herer et al., 2007; Herodotus, 440

BC/2016; Jay, 2010; Ketchum, 2012; Lee, 2012; Mills, 2003; Solomon, 1970). Indeed, "it is only in the last century that quality control issues, the lack of a defined chemistry, and above all, politically and ideologically motivated prohibition relegated cannabis as *planta non grata*" (Maccallum & Russo, 2018, p.12). The spectrum of opinion around cannabis appears to range from it being a 'miraculous cure-all' through to being the 'root of all evil' (Abel, 1943/1980; Clarke & Merlin, 2013; Crowley, 2016). This polarising aspect of the plant is a consistent theme that was identified when reviewing the literature on this topic.

There exists enormously diverse material related to cannabis in terms of (in no particular order) cultivation techniques, breeding strategies, pharmacology, ethnopharmacology, botany, religion, entheogens, ethnobotany, neuroscience, molecular biology, biogenetics, history, psychology, psychopharmacology, horticulture, political strategy, public and holistic health, archaeobotany, and cultural impact (Cervantes, 2006, 2015; Chasteen, 2016; Clarke, 1993; Indian Hemp Drugs Commission, 1894/2010; Lee, 2012; Merlin, 1973; Moreau, 1845/1973; Rosenthal, 2010; Shulgin, 1991; Thomas & ElSohly, 2016). Descriptions of cannabis are also prominent in the digital world. For example, a search for cannabis or marijuana in Google Scholar produced half a million results, there were over 200,000 related listings in the Proquest database, and 25,000 relevant titles were found on the topic at PubMed, the online database for the US Library of Medicine. Despite this wealth of material, even more knowledge may have been disposed of for fear of providing incriminating evidence to authorities in the age of prohibition (Brady, 2013; Smith, 2012), and is therefore likely lost to the general public.

The plant itself is a complex biological organism stemming from the hemp or Cannabinaceae family (Rätsch, 2005; Schultes & Hofmann, 1992). It is an annual plant and is classified as a dioecious species in that it largely produces the male and female reproductive organs in separate plants, although hermaphrodites or inter-sex plants do exist (Cervantes, 2015). For those seeking intoxication, female plants are of most interest as they have significantly higher percentages of THC than the males (Rätsch, 2001).

At the core botanic level, the taxonomy of the plant is imprecise. Agreement cannot even be reached as to whether cannabis evolved from one or a multitude of species. For example, Thomas and ElSohly

(2016, p.2) contend that cannabis is "... a single, highly polymorphic species" whereby *cannabis indica* and *cannabis ruderalis* are classified as varieties of *Cannabis sativa* as opposed to separate species (see also Fuchs, 1542/1999; Iversen, 2007; Linnaeus, 1753/2014). Conversely, it is claimed that polytypic categorisations have become the accepted norm with *sativa, indica* and *ruderalis* classified as distinct species (see for e.g. Grinspoon, 1997; Hudak, 2016). McPartland, Clarke, and Watson (2000) identified *cannabis afghanica* as a potential fourth species, while cannabis *Americana* has been posited as a potential fifth species (Houghton & Hamilton, 1908). There is also a dispute regarding whether cannabis and hemp are separate species (Corsi, Pellati, Brighenti, Plessi, & Benvenuti, 2019), which has implications in the US context given that hemp was legalised federally in late 2018. Hemp has traditionally been associated with industrial uses despite containing low concentrations of prominent cannabinoids such as CBD and to a lesser extent THC, which is the cannabinoid responsible for intoxication and can be extracted from hemp to develop high potency cannabis products (Hudak, 2018). Beyond this broad variation in how cannabis is categorised, there exist thousands of varieties (technically chemical varieties or chemovars but commonly called 'strains') within the genus cannabis sativa with distinct cannabinoid and terpenoid profiles that impact consumers in different ways (Cervantes, 2015; Leafly.com, 2018; Lenson, 1999; Werner, 2011). For example, the world's self-reported largest database of cannabis DNA had over 3000 listings at the time of writing (Phylos, 2019), while Schwabe and McGlaughlin (2017) contended there are thousands more with no documented genetic profile. Presently, much cannabis in Colorado is defined simply as *hybrid* (observations from the field). Thus, even within the category of herbal cannabis of the genus cannabis sativa, there is a wide range of potency ratios that impact consumers in different ways. Having a basic understanding of this variation and complexity is an important starting point for regulators and those researching public health impacts related to the consumption cannabis. This is primarily because different varieties can and do impact the body in different ways, with some being viewed more harmful than others (Fischer et al., 2017; Room et al., 2010). Given that the book is guided by public health and harm reduction principles, knowledge of the variety among the broad species of cannabis is essential foundation knowledge for the rest of the book.

Major cannabinoids: THC, CBD, and beyond

The cannabis plant contains over 100 different phyto-cannabinoids and more than 400 non-cannabinoid compounds (Clarke & Merlin, 2013; Russo, 2013; Thomas & ElSohly, 2016). What is known relates largely to two cannabinoids: (i) delta 9 THC, which has been identified as the intoxicating compound within the plant (Gaoni & Mechoulam, 1964a, 1971); and (ii) cannabidiol (CBD), a largely non-psychotropic metabolite first discovered by Adams, Hunt, and Clark (1940).

When cannabis is harvested several chemical reactions take place that transform cannabinoids naturally. For example, under the influence of heat, the process of 'decarboxylation' transforms from its natural acidic form THCA to THC (THCA is non-intoxicating). There are currently two THC chemical classes that have been identified in the plant, namely Delta 8 THC and Delta 9 THC. According to ElSohly and Waseem (2014), these two classes each consist of multiple compounds with Delta 9 THC including 18 separate compounds, while Delta 8 THC has just two. While both THC classes induce intoxication, because Delta 9 THC is much more abundant in the plant, the psycho activity of cannabis has largely been attributed to the effects of Delta 9 THC (Institute of Medicine, 1999). In this book, use of the term THC relates to Delta 9 THC.

In addition to THC, there is also considerable research being conducted into CBD, one of the most prominent (alongside THC) cannabinoids that occur naturally within the genus cannabis sativa. Similar to THC, CBD is a metabolite that requires decarboxylation to transform from its natural state of cannabidiolic acid or CBDA (Russo, 2017). First isolated in 1940 (Adams et al., 1940), over the last couple of decades evidence has been starting to accrue that suggests CBD has medicinal potential for a range of ailments. For example leading cannabis researcher Russo (2017, p.198) has claimed "CBD is a pharmacological agent of wondrous diversity, ... encompassing analgesic, anti-inflammatory, antioxidant, antiemetic, antianxiety, antipsychotic, and anticonvulsant [properties]". This view was reflected by cannabis researchers Mechoulam, Peters, Murillo-Rodriguez, and Hanuš (2007, p.1) who stated in a comprehensive review of the academic literature: "The plethora of positive pharmacological effects observed with CBD make this compound a highly attractive therapeutic entity".

Beyond these two major cannabinoids, it is relevant to provide a brief summary of some cannabinoids of emerging clinical interest to highlight both what is known and not known regarding the pharmacological constitution of the cannabis plant. In addition, outlining these compounds also continues the theme of complexity and is directly related to the two core objectives stipulated at the beginning of this chapter. Furthermore, this text provides context for the potency testing subsection below, which stipulates steps involved in cannabinoid profiling that go well beyond the two major cannabinoids described above.

Cannabinol (CBN) results from the degradation of THC in the presence of oxygen and UV light, whereby the oxidation of THC transforms it into CBN (Meijer, 2014). In general, it has been found that CBN binds less effectively than THC to CB1 receptors in the endocannabinoid system (Pertwee & Cascio, 2014). Nonetheless some therapeutic benefits have been associated with CBN most notably including as a sedative with claims that "2.5 – 5 mg of *CBN* has the same level of sedation as a mild pharmaceutical sedative, with a relaxed body sensation similar to 5mg to 10mg of diazepam" (Steep Hill Labs, 2017), although the clinical evidence on this is far from conclusive with the strongest evidence dating back to the 1970s and 80s.

Cannabigerol (CBG) was the first compound isolated from cannabis resin in a pure form (Gaoni & Mechoulam, 1964b). There remains relatively little research into the therapeutic potential of CBG, however recent research has indicated some promise in regards to the regulation of vomiting and nausea (Rock et al., 2011). Furthermore, it has been suggested that both CBN and CBG are associated with limiting inflammation associated with skin disorders such as psoriasis (Oddi & Maccarrone, 2014). From the limited evidence available on this cannabinoid there is a suggestion that CBG and CBD may oppose each other at specific receptor sites within the endocannabinoid system.

Similar to the other minor cannabinoids described above, there have been relatively few studies with a focus on the pharmacological effects of Cannabichromene (CBC). There is some evidence that CBC has analgesic properties when administered at high doses, although the main therapeutic potential for CBC appears to be when administered in conjunction with other cannabinoids. For example, a possible synergism between CBC and THC has been suggested (Costa & Comelli, 2014).

How these constituents cumulatively interact with the cannabinoid receptors in the endocannabinoid system of humans is known as the entourage effect, of which very little is understood (Mechoulam, 2006; Mechoulam & Hanus, 2000; Russo, 2011). The above sections highlight both the complexity of the plant and how little research has been conducted on individual cannabinoids.

Cannabis preparations and methods of consumption

The three most common types of preparation include: (i) dried cannabis efflorescence (often referred to as herbal or 'whole-plant' cannabis, flower, or bud); (ii) cannabis oil extract; and (iii) edible cannabis products such as cookies. How cannabis is consumed impacts on the pharmacokinetic profile of the drug, which means that there are differences in the rate that cannabinoids absorb into the bloodstream according to how they are consumed. Generally, the method of consumption relates to the preparation type. The following information is drawn from the Israeli Ministry of Health (2018):

Inhalation: Dried cannabis flower is usually inhaled either by smoking or vaporising. When cannabis is inhaled active constituents are absorbed into the bloodstream quickly via the lungs.

Sublingual administration: Cannabis oil extracts are generally intended for sublingual administration in which the substances are absorbed directly from the oral mucosa into the bloodstream. With this method, the process of metabolism in the liver and gastrointestinal tract is bypassed.

Oral administration: Cannabis edible products are intended for oral administration. In this process, cannabinoids enter the bloodstream via the gastrointestinal tract and therefore take longer to activate cannabinoid receptors.

These methods of consumption are described in more detail in Chapters 6, and 7 in the specific Coloradan context, with a particular focus on edible products, vapourisation, and the relatively new phenomenon of dabbing, which is a method of inhaling high potency concentrated cannabis products for fast absorption into the bloodstream.

The Coloradan definition of recreational cannabis

Given the complexity noted above, how cannabis is defined is a fundamental consideration for policymakers in legal cannabis jurisdictions to eliminate ambiguity and reduce the risk potential associated with its consumption, which may evolve from broader definitions of the plant. The following legal definition of cannabis in the CRCM was first stipulated in A64, that is, in the State's Constitution, and remains current in the RMC. While the following definition could be placed in Chapter 4 that outlines the CRCM in detail, it is presented here because this definition from A64 was used to inform how cannabis is broadly defined throughout the book.

"Marijuana or Marihuana [or cannabis] means all parts of the plant of the genus cannabis whether growing or not, the seeds thereof, the resin extracted from any part of the plant, and every compound, manufacture, salt, derivative, mixture, or preparation of the plant, its seeds, or its resin, including marihuana concentrate. Marijuana or Marihuana does not include industrial hemp, nor does it include fiber produced from the stalks, oil, or cake made from the seeds of the plant, sterilized seed of the plant which is incapable of germination, or the weight of any other ingredient combined with marijuana to prepare topical or oral administrations, food, drink, or other product" (Colorado Amendment 64, 2012, p.3).

As noted by Caulkins et al. (2015), having such a broad definition limits policy levers available for regulators to address issues that arise from product diversity. Under the A64 definition, regulators are limited in response options to issues because the broad definition of cannabis does not differentiate between higher and lower risk products. For example, a key challenge with the A64 definition is that it does not distinguish between herbal cannabis (natural plant material) and manufactured products (such as high potency concentrates or edibles), thereby ignoring studies and documented experiences of cannabis consumers with very different outcomes over at least two centuries (Becker, 1963/2008; Indian Hemp Drugs Commission, 1894/2010; Moreau, 1845/1973; Siegel, 1989; Tart, 1971; Weil, 2004). The A64 definition allows for a wide range of product types including marijuana-infused products (MIPs[2]) such as drinks, edibles (e.g. cakes, lollies, chocolate bars), and topicals that are applied to the skin and then absorbed. According to DeAngelo (2015, p.81), there are "... dozens of different kinds of capsules, tinctures, concentrates, extracts, and subliminal sprays". Nonetheless, having noted the diversity that surrounds cannabis, to avoid ambiguity the broad legal definition provided in A64 is used in this book to describe cannabis as opposed to individual products that may be smoked or eaten, unless otherwise specifically stated.

Consumer safety and quality control

A central component of a legalised cannabis market is the ability to provide customers with a (relatively) safe, consistent, and pure product (Pacula, Kilmer, Wagenaar, Chaloupka, & Caulkins, 2014). Product testing should analyse at a minimum potency in relation to THC percentages and THC to CBD ratios, and purity, in regard to harmful pesticides, moulds and other residuals (Kilmer, 2014). However, achieving consistency in testing among cannabis products is not straight forward because the process requires that a clear set of analytical procedures is followed. Different methodologies can and do produce different outcomes. The following sub-section provides a brief overview of the process of testing cannabis for potency. A detailed description of testing procedures is undertaken in Chapter 7, which examines the issue of regulating pesticide usage on cannabis crops in the CRCM.

Potency testing

Testing for potency is an exercise in cannabinoid profiling of a sample. As stated above, understanding the strength of cannabis being consumed is an important public health consideration. It would seem apparent that consumers should be able to make informed purchasing decisions with an expectation of known potency. Concerns relating to variation of testing results have been observed in reports pertaining to

---

[2] Not to be confused with 'Minor in Possession' (MIP) which is the charge for under aged cannabis consumption in Colorado

cannabis testing generally (e.g. Gieringer & Hazekamp, 2011; Thomas & ElSohly, 2016; United Nations Office on Drugs and Crime, 2009). In tests on 75 medical cannabis products from across the US, it was found that in relation to THC content, 17% were labelled correctly, 60% over-labelled (stating higher potency than was identified in tests) and approximately 20% under-labelled (Vandrey et al., 2015). As noted by Unger, Brauninger, Hudalla, Holmes, and Sherman (2014, p.13): "The newness of the industry has encouraged the growth of an amateur ... testing industry". This is particularly concerning with edible products where a clear risk of over intoxication has been noted (MacCoun & Mello, 2015; Subritzky et al., 2016b), and is discussed in more detail in Chapter 6. In regards to potency tests, Thomas and ElSohly (2016) pointed out several aspects that require consideration including consistency between labs (and across batches) and homogeneity in a product, to ensure THC is spread evenly throughout a manufactured product.

The first step for potency testing is collecting a representative sample from raw plant material. However, this is problematic as THC percentages in cannabis vary both within and across plants (Sexton & Ziskind, 2013). Aaron Stancik, the scientific director of a cannabis testing laboratory reportedly stated: "Cannabis is especially varied and individual plants can have a THC gradient of about 15% from the top to bottom flower. Even two choice buds from the same plant can vary by a few percent" (Stancik, 2015, July 20). Attention must also be paid to the age of sample with changes to the chemical structure and ratios occurring throughout the growing and storage processes (Thomas & ElSohly, 2016; United Nations Office on Drugs and Crime, 2009). Furthermore, the rate of oxidative degradation from THC to cannabinol (CBN) is variable and dependent on storage methods whereby the most pronounced rate of decay has been demonstrated in material exposed to light above 22°C and minimal when stored below 4°C in darkness (Trofin, Dabija, Vaireanu, & Filipescu, 2012).

Under optimal circumstances, random selections are made from across a cannabis plant or plants and homogenised through a grinding process to create a uniform sample. According to Sexton and Ziskind (2013), a five-gram representative sample is required to reduce variability in results. Additional steps for potency testing may include weighing the material, extraction, and liquid chromatography analysis (CannLabs, 2015). Unger et al. (2014) have made the following recommendations: (i) labs should be certified to the ISO 17025 standard; (ii) accreditation by an independent third party should be encouraged; (iii) all methods with public health implications should be included in the accreditation; (iv) all labs must pass regular proficiency testing programs; and (v) lab directors must hold a doctorate in a relevant field or years of relevant experience (a similar rule was incorporated in the Colorado regulations as discussed in Chapter 7).

Intoxication

THC was first identified by Gaoni and Mechoulam (1964a). It is known as one of the most prominent cannabinoids in most cannabis strains and is the primary psychoactive ingredient in the plant. A description of THC and how it interacts with the human body is provided later in the Chapter, however, some things clinical science finds hard to describe. When asked if he could explain what it means, biochemically speaking, to be stoned, pioneering cannabis researcher Raphael Mechoulam reportedly suggested to "leave it to the poets" (Pollan, 2001, p.158). Furthermore, Earleywine (2002) has pointed out that attempts to describe the phenomenology of cannabis intoxication stemmed, initially, from subjective accounts in literature as opposed to science. Thus, it is appropriate to briefly consider qualitative literary portrayals of the subjective cannabis consumption experience that produces intoxication.

In the mid-19th century, for example, Baudelaire (1860/1998), Ludlow (1857/2015) and Gautier (1846/1966, p.163), who preferred concentrated preparations of hashish, sometimes in extremely large dosages about "the size of one's thumb", and under the observation of Dr Moreau (1845/1973), described, each with their own particular rhetorical flourishes, deliriant experiences of ecstatic visions, rapture, paranoia, and temporary descents into madness. Indeed, it was this use of hashish as a tool to access these temporary states of insanity that provided the foundation for Moreau's ground-breaking research (Moreau, 1845/1973). While little known, the study on Hashish and Mental Illness, remains relevant and insightful in modern times, perhaps because the scientist included himself in the experiments, an auto-ethnographic methodology that would likely prove difficult for ethics committees to approve in modern research contexts (as a small aside this methodology was the foundation for Freud's experimentation with cocaine (Freud & Byck, 1975)). These portrayals of intoxication illustrate examples of what can be considered in the 'high risk' category of cannabis consumption.

More recently Ginsberg (1966, p.87), not known for concision, said of consuming a likely less potent preparation of cannabis flower: "... the marijuana consciousness is one that, ever so gently, shifts the centre of attention from habitually shallow, purely verbal guidelines and repetitive second-hand ideological interpretations of experience to more direct, slower, absorbing, occasionally microscopically minute engagement with sensing phenomena during the high moments or hours after one has smoked". The key point is that cannabis intoxication is highly subjective, reliant on factors such as preparation, dosage, method of consumption, tolerance, and body type, not to mention the dimensions of set and setting as outlined in the previous chapter, as they relate to 'quality' of the consumption. It has been noted that this variation indicates that no single experience of cannabis intoxication is typical (Earleywine, 2002; Iversen, 2007). Clinical studies that consider cannabis intoxication specifically from a public health perspective as an acute harm are reviewed later in the chapter.

The endocannabinoid system

With the discovery of the endocannabinoid system (ECS) in the 1990s, scientists began to understand how cannabis and specific cannabinoids influence the human body (Mechoulam, 2006). While this point is usually discussed in the context of medical cannabis, it is also relevant to recreational consumption. For example, Solinas, Goldberg, and Piomelli (2008) noted that evidence suggests the ECS plays an important role in signalling reward events in the brain and specifically described the involvement of cannabinoid receptors in this process. This signalling role links directly to previously noted descriptions of the CRCM as a pleasure market and it is therefore presented as crucial foundational knowledge for the present study. Further, as described in more detail below, for various reasons it is not common knowledge that the body naturally produces endogenous cannabinoids and includes a network of receptor sites for cannabinoids (e.g. Allen, 2016). For bureaucrats devising cannabis regulations, having an understanding that cannabinoids naturally occur in the body may be helpful to provide some balance, particularly when considered in the context of nearly a century of prohibition. In addition, whether labelled medical or recreational, cannabis interacts with the body via the ECS, and having a general knowledge of the product and its effects is thus directly related to the book objectives.

Scientists believe that the ECS evolved in primitive animals approximately 600 million years ago and it has been called one of the most significant medical findings in the 20th century (Russo, 2016a). It is an important system of the human body and understanding its functions is central to understanding how and why cannabis can be both an effective medicine and a recreational pleasure. The human endocannabinoid or endogenous cannabinoid system impacts both peripheral processes and the central nervous system (Mechoulam & Parker, 2013).

According to Russo (2016a, p.594), the ECS is "a unique and widespread homeostatic physiological regulator … that performs major regulatory homeostatic functions (principally the maintenance of internal equilibrium) in the brain, skin, digestive tract, liver, cardiovascular system, genitourinary function, and even bone". Other scholars have prescribed even more functionality to the endocannabinoid system such as it being the modulator of fertility, hunger, and aging (e.g. Blesching, 2015; Maccarrone, 2005; Viveros, de Fonseca, Bermudez-Silva, & McPartland, 2008).

The ECS consists of a network of naturally occurring *endogenous* cannabinoids – in other words, the body naturally creates cannabinoids to deal with an imbalance within the human body. In addition to these naturally occurring cannabinoids in the body, the ECS also consists of cannabinoid receptors (known as CB1 and CB2 among others) that respond to cannabinoids within the cannabis plant when consumed. At the most fundamental level, the function of the ECS has been described as 'a lock and key' that modulates internal activity within the body. As explained by Russo (2016a) the ECS consists of three parts, namely cannabinoid receptors, endogenous cannabinoids [or endocannabinoids], and regulatory metabolic and catabolic enzymes. These are now briefly described.

Cannabinoid receptors

Cannabinoid receptors are technically "G-protein coupled receptors where one or another of THC, anandamide, and 2AG bind" (Russo, 2016a, p.2). These receptors are broadly categorized as CB1, CB2, and TRPV1 and have been shown to interact with cannabinoids from the genus cannabis sativa, particularly THC and CBD (Pertwee, 2008).

Recent studies indicate that the behavioural effects of THC are receptor-mediated. More specifically, neurons in the brain are activated when a compound binds to its receptor. Binding to a receptor results in a change in the cell's activity, the regulation of its genes, or the signals that it sends to neighbouring cells. Delta 9 THC most commonly binds with the CB1 and CB2 receptors, which are a core function of the human endocannabinoid system (Szabo, 2014).

CB1 Receptor

"CB1 is the psychoactive, neuro-modulatory, and analgesic receptor" (Russo, 2016a, p.2). It is to be found in relatively low concentrations in some peripheral non-neuronal tissues such as liver, heart, stomach, fat tissue, and testis, although its main localization is in the nervous system (Szabo, 2014).

CB2 Receptor

CB2 has been described as "an anti-inflammatory immunomodulatory receptor" (Russo, 2016a, p.2). Initially, it was thought that the CB2 receptor was limited to peripheral immune-related organs including the spleen, thymus, and tonsils, however current observations indicate CB2 receptors are also present in neurons in the brain. For example, CB2 receptor mRNA or protein has been located in regions such as the hippocampus, cerebral cortex, and spinal sensory neurons (Szabo, 2014). In comparison to CB1 receptors, CB2 receptors have more restricted distribution and much lower density.

TRPV1 or if you prefer, transient receptor potential vanilloid 1.

Transient receptor potential channels such as TRPV1 are ionotropic cannabinoid receptors that regulate temperature and pain responses and can be enriched by standardized cannabis extracts. More research is needed to better understand the therapeutic potential of these receptors with data only starting to accrue.

Endogenous cannabinoids

Two (relatively) well-known endocannabinoids are anandamide (AEA) and arachidonoyl glycerol (2-AG) (McPartland & Russo, 2014; Mechoulam, Fride, & Di Marzo, 1998). Endocannabinoids act as transmitters and AEA and 2-AG bind to and activate multiple receptors including CB1, CB2, and TRPV1 (Russo, 2016a). Endo means within, in this case, the body, so unlike THC, which is a phyto-cannabinoid, endogenous cannabinoids are naturally produced by human cells (Russo, 2016a). Endocannabinoids appear to be made on-demand within the body and used only when needed – nor are they stored in the body for later (Russo, 2016a).

Regulatory metabolic and catabolic enzymes

The third component of the ECS consists of metabolic enzymes that immediately break down endocannabinoids once they have been used, which are employed when necessary but no longer than needed (Russo, 2016a). This is a key distinction between endocannabinoids and other body signals including classic neurotransmitters and hormones that can persist after use and/or be stored for later use. There are over a dozen of these enzymes that have been identified (Russo, 2016a).

Not taught at medical schools

Given the significance of the ECS outlined above, it would seem a logical assumption that it would be widely taught at medical schools, however, this does not appear to the case. For example, Evanoff, Quan, Dufault, Awad, and Bierut (2017) undertook a national survey in the US to identify the percentage of medical schools that included medicinal cannabis in their curriculums and found less than 10% offer content on cannabis in their curricula. This study was supported by independent research from Dr Allen (2016), which asked over 100 accredited American medical schools specific questions relating to the ECS in their curricula. It found only 13% of schools surveyed had the ECS mentioned in any course. This is relevant to the present study because it highlights a knowledge gap that exists not only for regulators in the pioneering Coloradan model but also for doctors and a range of other stakeholders. This knowledge gap is considered in more detail in Chapter 9 within the CG theoretical framework. Having introduced some of the complexities associated with cannabis, potential public health risks associated with its consumption are now reviewed.

Potential public health risks

As noted above, cannabis is associated with serious public health risks. However, there is a spectrum of interpretation (both moral and medical) of how serious the risks are, ranging from social utilitarian perspectives that consider all consumption of cannabis beneficial if consumed with positive intent, through to those who contend any consumption is harmful. For context, it is generally contended that the burden to public health related to the consumption of cannabis is substantially lower than harm associated with other drugs (Bonomo et al., 2019; Fischer et al., 2017). Attempts to quantify and compare the contribution to the total burden of disease relating to cannabis, other illicit drugs, alcohol, and tobacco provided estimates of 0.2%, 1.8%, 2.3%, and 7.8% respectively (Degenhardt, Ferrari, & Hall, 2017; Room et al., 2010). On one hand, cannabis advocates tend to argue that these statistics indicate cannabis is less harmful than other drugs. On the other hand, those who believe that public health could be jeopardised by the legalisation of cannabis may cite the statistics as evidence that prohibition works in keeping these rates low and would likely expect to see significant increases in associated harms in legal markets.

In this sense, the statistics appear to infer, that on the one hand, prohibition was effective in limiting harm compared to legal drugs, yet on the other hand, the statistics do not justify ongoing prohibition due to perceived lack of harm in comparison to licit substances. An important caveat is that the cannabis statistics were calculated before the implementation of legal markets of the drug, which may influence patterns of consumption. While there is an expectation that legalising cannabis use, production, and distribution will result in higher rates of use, it remains unknown how patterns of consumption will evolve, and whether public health will see net benefits or increasing harm (a snapshot of the latest consumption patterns in the Colorado context are presented Chapter 10 of the book).

The diversity in perspectives associated with the harms of cannabis reflects the complexity of the matter. This section of the chapter outlines: (i) the complexity and methodological limitations of conferring causality of harm; (ii) evidence of acute harms; (iii) evidence of chronic harms; (iv) population-level harms; and (v) prohibition.

Complexity and limitations of inferring causation of harm

As noted by Caulkins et al. (2015), quantifying the risks associated with cannabis consumption is complex from a public health standpoint and includes two distinct levels, namely, individual consumption, and patterns of consumption across populations. First, the effects of cannabis consumption on individual health and others *per se* are an important consideration. From this perspective, harms associated with the consumption of cannabis have been systematically reviewed and synbooked by several scholars (e.g. Caulkins et al., 2015; Fischer et al., 2017; National Academies of Sciences Engineering and Medicine, 2017; Room et al., 2010; Szabo, 2014; Volkow, Baler, Compton, & Weiss, 2014). However, it has been noted there are methodological limitations on the study of psychoactive substances such as cannabis and alcohol, which obstruct the ability to make causal inferences (Caulkins et al., 2015; Earleywine, 2010; Iversen, 2007; Zimmer & Morgan, 1997).

For causation to be confidently inferred there must be similarity in control and treatment groups (abstainers and people who consume cannabis) both relating to easily observable variables (e.g., education attainment, age, economic status, gender, etc), and less obvious factors (e.g., propensity to mental health problems, self-control, or maturity). According to Caulkins et al. (2015, p.29), "the vast majority of studies rely on correlational methods because they account for differences only in observable factors between [people who do and do not use cannabis] that the data capture". In this sense, potentially important unmeasured differences, so-called 'residual confounding', may exist between cannabis consumers and abstainers (Hall & Degenhardt, 2015). Caulkins et al. (2015) pointed out that correlational studies are more credible than observational studies (at the individual level) when they include: data from a range of time periods and settings; control variables related to hypo booked unobservable factors; and propensity score methods, that attempt to closely match observable variables among control and treatment groups. Further limitations include: the non-linearity of dose-response effects, which hinder the ability to extrapolate beyond dose range; and ethical barriers, such as restrictions on study designs, settings, and dosage (Caulkins et al., 2015). To provide perspective on the influence of confounding factors, in a review of studies focussed on the association between cannabis use and psychosis for example, it was found that "...10–85% of the observed risk was due to confounding" (Moore et al., 2007; Sommer & Van Den Brink, 2019, p.465).

Second, Caulkins et al. (2015) argued that consideration should also be given to how cannabis policy and laws affect patterns of consumption, and therefore, potentially, health risks to people who use cannabis and others at the population level. Within this perspective, decisions and regulatory choices are optimally informed by data that can provide indications of net consequences around outcome dimensions including road safety, mental health, or dependency. One approach condenses the matter down to a simple equation:

> "Total harm = average harm per dose x number of doses per user x numbers of users, or more simply:
>
> total harm = prevalence x intensity x harmfulness" (MacCoun & Reuter, 2001, p.10).

However, as Caulkins et al. (2015) noted, while this equation is useful to focus measurement instruments, and potentially guide policymaking, there is also ambiguity around data collection from this second perspective of harm measurement. Indeed, the authors pointed out there are minimally four aspects exposed to variation within the framework of the calculation. First, the prevalence of use is considered in light of the age distribution of users. To illustrate the point, Caulkins et al. (2015) compared usage rates between 16- to 20-year-olds with 40- to 44-year-olds. They concluded that, on balance, given concerns relating to the cannabis and brain development of young people (see below), higher prevalence of consumers in the younger age bracket is likely more harmful than larger totals in the older age group. Second, perhaps more importantly, is the frequency (user days), intensity (amount consumed per day), and duration of cannabis use careers (generally years of use since initiation) (Caulkins et al., 2015; Room et al.,

2010). Studies attempting to explore these nuances in cannabis consumption patterns tend to mirror those of alcohol and emphasise "a strong positive correlation between frequency of use and quantity consumed per day of use, suggesting the consumption is skewed towards the minority of heavy users" (Burns, Caulkins, Everingham, & Kilmer, 2013, p.1). Indeed, it is estimated that consumption follows Pareto's law whereby 80% of cannabis consumption stems from 20% of the most frequent consumers (Kleiman, 2014a). Third, according to Caulkins et al. (2015), cannabis regulations may impact both the method of consumption (as outlined in chapter one) and the structure of distribution (e.g. is the drug commercially promoted, and/or is public health information provided at the point of sale?). Fourth, risk patterns may be influenced by controls on, for example, THC potency, outlet density, price, messaging, and quality control.

As noted by Caulkins et al. (2015), raising these concerns around the correlational nature of studies and measurement of harm at the policy level, does not reduce the gravity of cannabis associated risks. The authors argued that, while it remains difficult for causal inferences to be conclusively established, there are strong reasons to believe common causal antecedents (such as personal and emotional traits, the stability of life structures, family relationships, and communities) are associated with both cannabis use and health issues. Indeed, lessons from the tobacco industry indicate that on balance it makes sense to err on the side of caution. "Observing that the evidence is not as strong as it was for tobacco is not, in some sense, terribly reassuring; tobacco use was killing hundreds of thousands of people per year. Harms can reach a threshold for alarm far before reaching that level" Caulkins et al. (2015, p.31).

Having described the complexity and limitations around inferring causation, the literature relating to acute and chronic harms is now examined. In medical terms, toxicity is defined as: "The degree to which a substance (a toxin or poison) can harm humans or animals. Acute toxicity involves harmful effects in an organism through a single or short-term exposure. Chronic toxicity is the ability of a substance or mixture of substances to cause harmful effects over an extended period, usually upon repeated or continuous exposure, sometimes lasting for the entire life of the exposed organism" (MedicineNet.com, 2018, p.1).

Acute harms

It has been noted that cannabis is very safe in terms of the risk of fatal overdose, with no known deaths reported in the epidemiology literature from mere consumption (Hall, 2015; Iversen, 2007). These authors pointed out that, based on animal studies, humans can tolerate dosages 5000 times higher than is required to achieve intoxication. This is because cannabis use does not have a toxic effect on the circulatory system and heart or depress respiration (Gable, 2004; Kalant, 2004). In this manner, acute harms associated with cannabis consumption, in contrast to alcohol, prescription, and other illicit drugs, but similar to tobacco, are not immediately life-threatening. Potential acute harms of cannabis consumption (not exhaustive) addressed in this section include: (i) intoxication and cognitive impairment; (ii) traffic accidents; and (iii) accidental poisoning, particularly to children. These are now briefly examined.

Intoxication and cognitive impairment

In general, studies relating to cognitive impairment during intoxication are inconclusive. For example, while Hall and Pacula (2003) noted associations between cannabis intoxication and short-term memory retention, slowed reaction times, and attention deficit, Earleywine (2002) pointed out these associations are strongest in laboratory settings among naïve consumers. The National Academies of Sciences Engineering and Medicine (2017) identified 94 systematic reviews from 2000 to 2016 regarding cannabis and cognition around the domains of learning, memory, and attention. Of these, five were considered good quality, which included neuropsychological data relating to brain function from functional magnetic resonance imaging (fMRI), which measures brain activity. Three of these reviews considered the cognitive domain of learning. The findings suggested strong support for interference with learning associated with acute cannabis use, however there was mixed, and minimal support for sustained interference with learning, particularly after periods of abstinence (Broyd, van Hell, Beale, Yücel, & Solowij, 2016; Grant, Gonzalez, Carey, Natarajan, & Wolfson, 2003; Schreiner & Dunn, 2012). This is in line with other studies that have suggested, perhaps unsurprisingly, that learning complicated tasks while intoxicated by cannabis may be less effective than non-intoxicated learning (e.g. Iversen, 2007).

In terms of the cognitive domain of memory, only one systematic review was identified that addressed the issue at the acute level. The review included 22 studies using a range of neuropsychological tests that assessed the association between acute cannabis consumption and working memory and concluded there is moderate to strong evidence for cannabis interference on short term memory (Broyd et al., 2016). The same systematic review also considered the cognitive issue of attention using metrics such as continuous task performance, and reaction time. The authors reported findings, based on 17 studies, that there is strong evidence of acute interference of cannabis on attention (Broyd et al., 2016). Limited evidence was identified relating to long-term attention deficit after periods of cessation (Crane, Schuster, & Gonzalez, 2013).

Driving

There is general agreement in the literature that, given the possibility of cognitive impairment during intoxication described above, there are added risks when driving under the influence of cannabis (Asbridge, Hayden, & Cartwright, 2012; National Academies of Sciences Engineering and Medicine, 2017; NORML, 2018; Rogeberg & Elvik, 2016). It was initially suggested by earlier studies that cannabis-impaired drivers may compensate for this by driving slower, taking fewer risks, and keeping more distance between other vehicles (Liguori, Gatto, & Jarrett, 2002; Smiley, 1999). Certainly, there is evidence that college students *perceived* less risk when driving under the influence of cannabis compared to alcohol (McCarthy, Lynch, & Pederson, 2007). However more recent work has demonstrated that impairment cannot be offset by cautious driving (Armentano, 2010; Iversen, 2007; Szabo, 2014). For example, in a review of related research, Room et al. (2010) noted that self-reported cannabis use was associated with double the risk of an accident. Furthermore, in a review of experimental studies, Ramaekers, Berghaus, van Laar, and Drummer (2004) found that risk of accident while intoxicated by cannabis was in the range of three to seven times more likely compared with drivers who had not consumed psychoactive drugs at a dose considered to be equivalent to the alcohol limit on driving. The fine-grained review also concluded that crash risk was more highly associated with automated driving tasks such as road tracking control compared to complex tasks requiring conscious control (such as reversing around a corner).

Regarding traffic fatalities, more research is needed as current research findings in the literature are contradictory. For example, in a study focusing on US states with medical cannabis, Anderson, Hansen, and Rees (2013) found an almost 9% decrease in traffic fatalities, despite increases in the consumption of cannabis. They concluded this was likely the result of cannabis being consumed as a substitute for alcohol. In contrast, Salomonsen-Sautel, Min, Sakai, Thurstone, and Hopfer (2014) examined temporal changes in driver fatalities in Colorado before and after the commercialisation of the medical cannabis market in 2009 and found twice as many cannabis-related traffic deaths compared to the pre-commercialisation period.

In terms of additional risk beyond mere intoxication, Blows et al. (2005) found an almost nine-fold increase in crash risk among habitual cannabis users. Berg et al. (2017) meanwhile, in a multi-level factor analysis that surveyed 1567 people who use cannabis aged 18 – 34 via Facebook in the US, found almost 50% reported past-month driving after consuming cannabis and 75% as passengers of an intoxicated driver. They concluded that correlates of the past month driving while under the influence of cannabis included frequent use, less perception of risk, and being at the younger end of the age sample. According to Caulkins et al. (2016), there seems to be a consensus in the literature that driving while intoxicated by cannabis is riskier than driving having not consumed the drug, but less risky than driving under the influence of alcohol. They further note that driving under the influence of both drugs simultaneously constitutes a higher risk than driving intoxicated by either substance individually. Latest driving while impaired by cannabis statistics in the context of the CRCM are discussed in Chapter 10 of the book.

Accidental poisoning

Caulkins et al. (2015) noted that increases of admissions of young children to emergency departments in Colorado for accidental ingestion of cannabis is particularly concerning. Indeed, case reports have described respiratory failure and coma resulting from cannabis ingestion by children (Amirav, Luder, Viner, & Finkel, 2011; Appelboam & Oades, 2006; Carstairs, Fujinaka, Keeney, & Ly, 2011). Caulkins et al. (2015) cited media stories, which reported that by mid- 2014 in Colorado, child admissions for accidental consumption of cannabis had equalled the total for all of 2013. Wang, Roosevelt, and Heard (2013) considered 1378 Coloradan patients under 12, who were admitted for unintentional ingestion of a substance. They found an increase in admissions for cannabis ingestion by children after the commercialisation of the medical cannabis market in 2009. For perspective, 14 out of the 588 child admissions for unintentional ingestions post-2009 were cannabis-related, or .2% of the total. Data from federal reports also reported increases in hospital admissions for children unintentionally consuming cannabis in the State (Rocky Mountain High Intensity Drug Trafficking Area, 2013, 2014, 2015, 2016). Caulkins et al. (2015) linked these increases to the packaging of cannabis products that may be attractive to children. As stated in the comprehensive National Academies of Sciences Engineering and Medicine (2017) report, limitations in surveillance tools have contributed to a lack of precise data on this issue and more research is needed.

Chronic harms

Dependency

According to the WHO (2016, p.2), "cannabis-use disorders refer to a spectrum of clinically relevant conditions and are defined via psychological, social, and physiological criteria to document adverse consequences, loss of control over use, and withdrawal symptoms". More generally, Room et al. (2010) contended that dependency is distinguished by continued consumption of cannabis despite ongoing distress, and discomfort, resulting from loss of control of cannabis use (as noted in Chapter 1 this definition is more closely associated with the term 'addiction'). Diagnostic criteria for substance dependence can be found in both the Diagnostic and Statistical Manual of Mental Disorders (DSM-5; American Psychiatric Association, 2013), and the International statistical classification of diseases and related health problems (ICD-10; WHO, 1992). While ICD-10 differentiates between dependent and harmful cannabis consumption, DSM-5 classifies the level of dependency and associated damage to health as low, moderate or severe (WHO, 2016). The DSM-5 definition has been critiqued for being unidimensional (MacCoun, 2013b).

Over the last 20 years, evidence has emerged of cannabis withdrawal syndrome (Gorelick et al., 2012; Hall, 2015). Clinical diagnosis of cannabis withdrawal syndrome requires that the person who uses cannabis reports at least two mental symptoms and one physical. According to Volkow et al. (2014), mental symptoms might include difficulty sleeping, restlessness, anxiety, craving, and irritability. Physical symptoms may include headaches, sweating, pain, and/or general discomfort, but are less commonly observed (Vandrey & Haney, 2010). For context, these symptoms, while uncomfortable for potentially up to a week after abstinence, appear to be less severe than effects of withdrawal reported for other substances such as alcohol, tobacco, and opioids (Hall, 2015).

Statistics show that approximately 9% of people who have ever used cannabis will meet the criteria of dependence as stipulated by DSM-5 (Lopez-Quintero et al., 2011). Furthermore, there is a general consensus in the literature that this number increases to one in six when the use career is initiated in adolescence and up to half for youth who consume cannabis on a daily basis (Compton, Dawson, Goldstein, & Grant, 2013; Hall, 2015). It has been estimated that 1-2% of the total adult population is affected by cannabis use-disorders and 2.7 million people in the US, aged 12 and over, reportedly meet the DSM-5 criteria of dependence (Hall, 2015; Volkow et al., 2014). For perspective, this 9% compares with estimates of dependence for people who have ever experimented with nicotine (30%), heroin (23%), and alcohol (15%) (Hall, 2015).

Clinical trials of cognitive behaviour therapy have demonstrated substantial reductions in the frequency of use and severity of health issues associated with cannabis consumption, despite the majority of patients continuing to consume cannabis 12 months after treatment (Danovitch & Gorelick, 2012). Treatment for cannabis withdrawal syndrome has been increasing in recent years (Budney, Roffman, Stephens, & Walker, 2007; Caulkins et al., 2015; Vandrey & Haney, 2010). Based on a study of the Dutch cannabis coffeeshop model, MacCoun (2011) identified an association between increased treatment admissions and higher potency cannabis. Touching (anonymous) real-world accounts of people attempting to break the cannabis habit on the internet seem to confirm the difficulties associated with cessation of dependent cannabis consumption (e.g. CannabisRehab.org, 2018; Marijuana-Anonymous.org, 2018).

Mental health

Illnesses relating to mental health can include schizophrenia and other psychoses, depression, anxiety, and suicidal tendencies. This subsection focusses on reviewing studies relating to the association between cannabis and psychosis generally, due to psychosis having both the widest coverage and the strongest association with cannabis use in the literature (Caulkins et al., 2015; National Academies of Sciences Engineering and Medicine, 2017). However, a key difficulty in assessing associations between mental disorders and cannabis consumption relates to whether cannabis causes the issue, or whether those with an existing mental illness are more likely to seek out cannabis for purposes of self-medication (Caulkins et al., 2015).

According to the NASEM report, psychosis tends to be characterised by three classes of symptoms including: (i) delusions, or unusual motor behaviour; (ii) negative symptoms, such as lack of interest, or motivation; and (iii) cognition impairment. The report concluded there is "substantial evidence of a statistical association between cannabis use and ... schizophrenia or other psychoses" (National Academies of Sciences Engineering and Medicine, 2017, p.295). Such associations have been replicated in multiple studies (e.g. Di Forti et al., 2015; Donoghue et al., 2014; Radhakrishnan, Wilkinson, & D'Souza, 2014). The NASEM report further noted that the magnitude of the association ranges from moderate to large and appears to be dose-dependent, particularly regarding the potency and frequency of consumption (National Academies of Sciences Engineering and Medicine, 2017). These conclusions were based on five systematic reviews and 60 primary articles that were assessed as fair or higher quality. For example, based on studies that included dose criterion and cannabis use before the onset of psychosis, Marconi, Di Forti, Lewis, Murray, and Vassos (2016) found an association between cannabis use and psychosis among the most intense users (odds ratio 3.9%; confidence interval 95%). In other words, the review, which enrolled over 65,000 participants, concluded high use cannabis consumers were almost four times more likely to be associated with psychotic disorders than abstainers.

Limitations in the literature reviewed by NASEM included an over-reliance on self-report data, lack of randomisation, and lack of data on long term use and frequency of consumption (National Academies of Sciences Engineering and Medicine, 2017). As an example, a review of methodological strengths of relevant studies found that while an *association* is supported, *causality* of psychosis that would not otherwise have occurred cannot be conclusively established (McLaren,

Silins, Hutchinson, Mattick, & Hall, 2010). Furthermore, the association itself is weakened when studies attempt to control for common risk factors such as increased familial morbid risk (e.g. Hall, 2015; Proal, Fleming, Galvez-Buccollini, & DeLisi, 2014). In general, Hall (2015) pointed out that at the population level, the effects of cannabis consumption on psychoses is relatively small. Indeed, it is claimed that "thousands of [consumers] would have to be prevented from use for a year to prevent one case of schizophrenia" (Caulkins et al., 2015, p.38; Hickman et al., 2009). However, there appears to be general consensus that risk of association, if not causality, increases several-fold under certain conditions including: (i) early onset of use (Malchow et al., 2013; Schlossarek, Kempkensteffen, Reimer, & Verthein, 2016); (ii) consumption of high THC products, particularly when THC is disproportionately high compared to CBD (Hall & Degenhardt, 2015); and (iii) high frequency and intensity of use (Gibbs et al., 2015). The highest risk is associated with a combination of these three factors (Fischer et al., 2017; National Academies of Sciences Engineering and Medicine, 2017). In general, research indicates there may be an association between high potency (THC) cannabis and increased risk of adverse outcomes, with high THC:CBD ratios thought to be most problematic (Di Forti et al., 2015; Fischer et al., 2017; MacCoun, 2013a; Szabo, 2014). Conversely, high CBD:THC ratios have been connected with antipsychotic effects (Morgan & Curran, 2008; Zuardi, Crippa, Hallak, Moreira, & Guimarães, 2006). This has relevance for the Coloradan definition of cannabis outlined above that allows for a range of products including high potency THC concentrates, and which constitute a higher risk for adverse mental health effects than does herbal cannabis.

Brain development

As has been noted by several scholars, the brain is still developing until approximately the age of 21 (e.g. Gogtay et al., 2004). Thus, prenatal and adolescent exposure to "environmental insults" such as THC, are particularly concerning (Volkow et al., 2014, p.2220). Studies connecting cannabis use and adverse outcomes on the developing brain of humans are strictly correlational due to the range of social and psychological factors involved in the process (Caulkins et al., 2015). That notwithstanding, Volkow et al. (2014, p.2220) have argued that regular consumption of cannabis in adolescence is associated with "impaired neural connectivity" in certain regions of the brain that are involved in alertness, memory, and learning, compared with control groups (Batalla et al., 2013; Filbey & Yezhuvath, 2013; Zalesky et al., 2012).

The complexity of the matter is highlighted by results published by the same authors that appear to reach diametrically opposed conclusions. For example, on the one hand, Meier et al. (2012, p.1) suggested that cannabis consumption resulted in a "neurotoxic effect on the adolescent brain, [with] more persistent use associated with greater decline, [and which] cessation did not fully restore …". On the other hand, Meier et al. (2017, p.257) argued that "short-term cannabis use in adolescence does not appear to cause IQ decline or impair executive functions, even when cannabis use reaches the level of dependence. Family background factors explain why adolescent cannabis users perform worse on IQ and executive function tests". Furthermore, some studies have demonstrated that four weeks of abstinence is correlated with a reversal of any impairment to brain development (Hirvonen et al., 2012), while others argue that cessation does not fully restore impairment to brain development (Meier et al., 2012). A recent prospective longitudinal study of 1000 boys found that use of cannabis in adolescence is not associated with structural brain differences in adults regardless of whether there was no, moderate, or high frequency consumption in youth (Meier, Schriber, Beardslee, Hanson, & Pardini, 2019).

In a recent study based on 4,500 youth and young adults, there were mixed findings. First, people who consumed cannabis frequently, defined as three or more times per week, performed worse on measures of executive control. Second, an association was found between mild cognitive deficit and early initiation of a user career. Third, "occasional cannabis [consumers] displayed equivalent or even slightly better executive control, social–cognitive, and memory abilities compared with [abstainers] (ps < .05), suggesting complex relationships between cannabis use and cognition in youth." (Scott et al., 2017b, p.1). Indeed, a recent systematic review and meta-analysis concluded that "results indicate that previous studies of cannabis in youth may have overstated the magnitude and persistence of cognitive deficits associated with use" (Scott et al., 2018, p.585). Further details on increased risks of early initiation of cannabis use careers are provided in Chapter 8, which examines youth protection in the context of the CRCM (Subritzky, Lenton, & Pettigrew, 2019).

Additional risks

Associations between the consumption of cannabis and several other chronic health risks have been established, although again causality is difficult to prove. This is largely due to numerous limitations identified in studies including: heterogeneity of samples; disparity in dose, frequency, and duration of use; lack of consideration of individual characteristics; reliance on self-report data; no distinguishing between consumer groups or patterns of use; and polydrug use (National Academies of Sciences Engineering and Medicine, 2017). However, despite numerous studies and inconclusive findings, it is worth listing some of the negative outcomes associated with cannabis consumption, which are common in the literature. These include: (i) lower academic achievement; (ii) respiratory disease, particularly symptoms such as phlegm production and chronic cough; (iii) likelihood of people who use cannabis to 'graduate' to other more harmful drug use, the so-called 'gateway effect'; (iv) increased prenatal exposures, which has the been linked to lower birth weights; (v) impaired immunological functioning; and (vi) depression, anxiety, and suicide. Detailed reviews of the literature for these health risks have been published elsewhere (National Academies of Sciences Engineering and Medicine, 2017; Preedy, 2017; Room et al., 2010; Szabo, 2014), and as such are not addressed in this book.

Less studied, but more recent health risks that have appeared in the literature relate to: (i) cannabinoid hyperemesis syndrome, a rare disorder characterised by cyclic vomiting among intense cannabis consumers (Galli, Andari Sawaya, & Friedenberg, 2011; Schreck et al., 2018); and (ii) periodontal gum disease (Meier et al., 2016; Thomson et al., 2008).

Cannabis as a substitute or complement to other drugs

One factor that has the potential to substantially impact public health outcomes at the population level relates to indirect effects, for example, whether cannabis is used as a substitute or a complement to other drugs such as alcohol, prescription drugs, and tobacco. First, regarding alcohol, Caulkins et al. (2015) have argued (hypothetically) that if cannabis consumption was to double in a newly legalised commercial market, this may turn out to be a substantial net gain for public health if those new consumers substituted cannabis use for alcohol, which as noted above has a higher burden of disease than cannabis. Indeed Caulkins et al. (2012a) made the case that a 10% reduction in problem drinking, even when coupled with a two-fold increase in cannabis consumption, will equate to public health benefits at the population level. Conversely, if people who use cannabis consumed it as a complement to alcohol, that is, in addition to it, this would be a net public health loss. At the time of writing it was unclear which is likely to be the case. For example, while Caulkins et al. (2015) noted a strong association between cannabis and alcohol consumption, they could not establish causality. In a systematic review of the related literature, Subbaraman (2016) found mixed results, with a stronger association of substitution in states with more liberal cannabis policy. More recently a study of purchase data found a 13% decrease in alcohol sales in states with medical cannabis laws (Baggio, Chong, & Kwon, 2017).

Second, in relation to prescription opioids, given there is currently an opioid crisis in the US, with over 60,000 overdose deaths in 2016 alone, there is hope cannabis may substitute for abusive consumption (Center for Disease Control and Prevention, 2018; Reiman, Welty, & Solomon, 2017). The idea centres around the notions that: (i) cannabis may be effective for pain relief with fewer side effects and less addictive than opioids for the estimated 100 million Americans who suffer from chronic pain (Institute of Medicine, 2011; Scientific American, 2017); and (ii) could potentially act as an 'exit drug', in assisting people to move away from opioid dependency (Armentano, 2017). Recent studies indicate there may a case for the substitution argument as opioid-related deaths and opioid dependence have been shown to be reduced in states with medical cannabis laws. For example, Bachhuber, Saloner, Cunningham, and Barry (2014) found in a time analysis study ranging from 1999 to 2010, that states with medical marijuana laws had 25% less opioid analgesic overdose mortality rates. In a separate study, Powell, Pacula, and Jacobson (2015) concluded that the effect of fewer opioid deaths in states with medical marijuana laws was confined to those jurisdictions that permit dispensaries (easier access to cannabis). Several other studies have reported findings based on self-report data that cannabis is perceived as an effective substitute for problematic opioid consumption (Lucas & Walsh, 2017; Lucas et al., 2016; Reiman et al., 2017). In response to this still-emerging scientific evidence, US Attorney General Jeff Sessions reportedly stated the notion was "stupid", and that people must be told cannabis consumption would in fact "destroy their lives" (Vox, 2017, Mar. 16). Whilst it is the case that the findings on cannabis availability and opioid overdose statistics is only tentative and is far from established beyond doubt, it remains unclear what evidence AG Sessions based his assessment on. This statement highlights the controversial nature of the study of cannabis and the polarity of debate surrounding the drug noted above. Furthermore, this is a complex subject, and while the weight of emerging evidence seems to indicate an association between less prescribed opioids and legal cannabis, it remains unclear the extent to which harm may be reduced, particularly when considered in the context of the pareto principle for example.

Third, tobacco is seen as potentially having a high degree of complementarity with cannabis consumption (Caulkins et al., 2015). Caulkins et al. (2015) contended that past-month cannabis consumers are three times more likely to smoke tobacco than abstainers and that 95% of people who use cannabis have reported ever smoking a cigarette. In a (hypothetical) calculation, based on figures of 400,000 tobacco-related deaths annually in the US, Caulkins et al. (2015, p.45) noted that even a 1% increase in tobacco consumption may result in "4,000 additional premature deaths per year, an outcome that could outweigh any plausible benefits of marijuana legalization". It is possible that some of this risk may be mitigated by using vaporisers that reduce carcinogenic intake (Subritzky et al., 2016b), however, the extent to which vaporiser use becomes commonplace and what impacts this could have on potential increases in tobacco smoking rates is unclear. This point is discussed in more detail within the Coloradan context in Chapter 6.

Harms of prohibition

The effectiveness of prohibition in reducing cannabis use rates has been questioned (Lenton, 2000, 2005; Room et al., 2010). For example, cannabis policy scholars with a public health focus tend to include a section on the harms of prohibition in chapters discussing the harmful effects of the drug (e.g. Caulkins et al., 2015; MacCoun & Reuter, 2001; Rolles, 2012; Room et al., 2010; Szabo, 2014). In general these scholars have contended that while prohibition *may* reduce cannabis consumption due to making it more expensive, and difficult to access, it also creates a large black-market, prevents effective regulation of aspects such as potency and pesticides, and is probably a driving factor behind the increasing potency of cannabis, which has (arguably) been apparent since the early 1970s (McLaren, Swift, Dillon, & Allsop, 2008; Room et al., 2010). As such it is appropriate that harms associated with the prohibition of cannabis are discussed in this chapter alongside the harms presented above.

Cannabis prohibition laws relate to at least three levels of activity including possession and use; cultivation; and sale of the drug, with punishment increasing in severity for perceived seriousness of the criminal activity. A cannabis conviction in the US results in two categories of punishment, namely: "the punishment directly imposed by the judge; and a range of collateral sanctions that are triggered by the conviction" (Boire, 2010, p.219).

It is widely recognised this approach has resulted in disproportionate incarceration of marginalised groups, particularly people of colour (Alexander, 2012; Erickson, 1993; Golub, Johnson, & Dunlap, 2007; Hart, 2014; Lynch, 2002; Tate et al., 2013). For example, figures from New York circa 2008 demonstrated that while people of colour constituted 26% of the population, they made up 50% of those arrested for cannabis offences (Tate et al., 2013). Latinos (including white Hispanics) were four times more likely than whites to be arrested for cannabis possession (Levine, 2010). On the other hand, white people, who, despite making up 35% of the New York population, were less than 10% of those arrested for possession of cannabis (Levine, 2010).

This racist perception is easily identified in media reports of modern times, which while not definitive, do seem to demonstrate a pattern that has been well documented as above. For example, in January 2018 alone it was reported that: (i) a Kansas State Congressman claimed cannabis was outlawed because the genetics of African Americans caused them to react badly to it (Reason, 2018, Jan.8); (ii) a Kentucky State assistant police chief advised a new recruit to "shoot black kids caught smoking marijuana, and then sexually assault their parents" (Associated Press, 2018, Jan.22, p.1); and (iii) in Georgia over 60 people, predominantly black, were arrested for less than one ounce of cannabis between them (Huffington Post, 2018, Jan.3).

Several sources have highlighted significant harms associated with prohibition, for example, an estimated 26 million people have been arrested on cannabis-related issues since federal prohibition began in 1937 (e.g. Drug Policy Alliance, 2019a; Marijuana Policy Project, 2015; NORML, 2017a; Rolles, 2012). As Caulkins et al. (2015, p.43) pointed out, arrest records "can entail the loss of food assistance, access to public housing, and federal financial aid for postsecondary education". Arrests or citations can also impede employment opportunities and negatively impact on family relationships (Wodak et al., 2002).

However, an arrest or conviction is not necessary for asset forfeiture. "If a police officer simply believes that your cash or property is associated with a crime, that cash or property may be seized [without charge] subject to state and federal laws" (Cannabis Business Law, 2017, Aug. 30). In one famous case in 2003, well-known cannabis advocate Tommy Chong (of Cheech and Chong fame) received a nine-month prison sentence, US$20,000 fine, and $120,000 worth of assets forfeited for selling cannabis paraphernalia such as pipes (not cannabis). "They showed up at my door with a 12 to 15-member armed SWAT team, DEA agents, FBI ... There was a helicopter and Fox News out on the street" (Holland, 2010, p.207). Asset forfeiture laws were recently strengthened in the US (Attorney General Order No. 3946-2017, 2017). Having looked at the range of public health risks associated with cannabis consumption and the difficulties in distinguishing between association and causality, some of the challenges associated with impact assessment are now described.

Impact assessment and challenges to data collection

Given the diversity and complexity outlined above, it is perhaps understandable that there are challenges and gaps associated with data collection around the consumption of cannabis and the impact of cannabis law changes on the prevalence of cannabis use. However, there is a wide range of cannabis statistics being collected in the context of the newly legalised recreational market in Colorado which are likely important markers of impact. These data relate to price, tax revenues, volumes of product sold, seed-to-sale cultivation statistics such as plant yields, employment figures, and arrest rates. Yet data on cannabis consumption by Coloradans since the implementation of the scheme are only starting to accrue. This information is critical for the examination of the public health consequences of such drug policy changes (Kilmer, 2015b). Until recently, data modelling on the public health consequences of legal regulated recreational cannabis markets have been necessarily speculative due to the previously illegal nature of the product (Caulkins et al., 2012a; MacCoun & Reuter, 2001). The implementation of the Colorado scheme provides an opportunity to investigate the effects of a real-world application of a fully commercialised, non-medical cannabis market for adults.

Attempting to measure behavioural cannabis use patterns associated with a commercial recreational cannabis market is problematic due to the number of variables. For example, the previously noted diversity between cannabis strains, preparation, potency, method of consumption, and subjective effects means that data collected may be lacking necessary detail or, if included, would be prohibitively expensive to implement. Although a recent equivalency template has provided greater perspective in regards to production, dosage, and price, and allows for concentrates and infused products to be calculated across a common denominator of cost per unit of THC, the challenge remains significant (Marijuana Policy Group, 2015).

Furthermore, variation in policy between medical and recreational markets in Colorado may result in disparity due to age, possession quantity, and plant limit regulations, which make isolating patterns of consumption specifically for recreational use that are distinct from medical usage challenging (Ghosh et al., 2015). To further confound matters, Pacula, Jacobson, and Maksabedian (2015) demonstrated that cannabis for medical purposes is more likely to be vaporised or consumed in edibles than recreational cannabis, thereby further highlighting the challenges associated with assessing impact of the recreational market independently, which presumably carries higher risk potential for the consumer than its medical counterpart.

Additional challenges include, but are not limited to, federal prohibition and proprietary methods that hinder the establishment of reference labs and development testing proficiency standards (Ghosh et al., 2015), a lack of international disease classification codes for hospital administrators that hinder like for like comparisons, and an inability to accurately compile data relating to suspected and proven cases of driving under the influence of drugs (DUID) (Ghosh et al., 2015;

Ingold, 2014e), with questions remaining over accuracy and delays to blood tests (Squibb, 2015; Wood, Brooks-Russell, & Drum, 2015).

More generally in the US, data systems for measurement of quantity of cannabis consumed by individuals, as opposed to prevalence of use, are insufficient (Caulkins et al., 2016; Kilmer, 2015b, November 25). Additional methodological challenges pertaining to the comparison of results internationally have also been described (Kilmer, Reuter, & Giommoni, 2015). Potential for bias in self-report surveys stemming from, for example, people who lie or are excluded from the sampling frame, has also been noted (Kilmer, 2015b, November 25). In specific regard to Colorado data collection instruments, Ghosh et al. (2015) provided a timely overview of measures implemented to monitor the prevalence of use, public health effects, and challenges associated with assessment. They noted that a problem with using the existing population-based surveys was that they didn't include validated questions addressing issues such as variation in methods of marijuana consumption, home storage, cultivation, and intoxication. This issue is discussed in more detail in Chapter 8 in the context of youth protection. As a result of the limitations of current data collection processes, it may be years or decades before the consequences of newly legalised commercial marijuana markets, such as that in Colorado, are revealed (Pacula & Sevigny, 2014).

Potential benefits of cannabis

The most obvious benefits relating to the consumption of cannabis identified in the literature related to medical applications. As is described in more detail in Chapter 4, the medical and recreational cannabis markets are closely aligned in Colorado. Thus, while the primary focus of this paper is on recreational cannabis it is relevant to briefly review the history of accounts of the benefits of medical cannabis.

Medical cannabis was first introduced to modern western medicine in London by O'Shaughnessy (1843) (based on fieldwork in India), as a treatment for pain, migraines, and morphine withdrawal (see also Mikuriya, 2007; Russo, 2014). Since then, there appears to have been an overlap and apparent inability to disentangle the recreational and medical cannabis within the literature, as was first observed in the comprehensive and still relevant findings of the 3,200 page report of

Indian Hemp Drugs Commission (1894/2010), where the vast majority of interviewees in the study reported at least temporary beneficial health or spiritual effects from moderate non-medical cannabis consumption (Kalant, 1972). Unsurprisingly, perhaps, there are numerous well known modern-day cannabis advocates who concur with this view (e.g. Bello, 2010; DeAngelo, 2015). This leads to a range of definitional considerations regarding the use of cannabis for therapeutic or pleasure purposes, which are outside the scope of the book (Lancaster et al., 2017; Sznitman & Lewis, 2015; Sznitman & Zolotov, 2015).

Due to the historical prohibition of cannabis, research around the effectiveness of consumption for therapeutic purposes is lacking and often conflicting. However, evidence is beginning to emerge that demonstrates cannabis can be effective for numerous conditions. For example a comprehensive review of the medical cannabis literature by the National Academies of Sciences Engineering and Medicine (2017), that built on the work of its predecessor the Institute of Medicine (1999), reported "conclusive evidence" that natural botanical cannabis (as opposed to individual cannabinoids) is effective for the treatment of pain in adults, nausea linked to chemotherapy, and symptoms of spasticity related to multiple sclerosis.

Research continues into the therapeutic potential of THC with new research quickly evolving. According to Carlini (2004), from a clinical point of view, it is beyond reasonable doubt that THC produces some therapeutic benefits with the effects on nausea due to cancer chemotherapy, as an appetite promoter, and reducing symptoms associated with multiple sclerosis are clearly demonstrated. Other areas of potential therapeutic value for THC include heart disease (Blesching, 2015). Indeed, THC is almost certainly the most studied constituent in cannabis, nonetheless this unique molecule continues to surprise scientists as new information emerges relating to its influence on human psychology and physiology (Blesching, 2015).

The theory of clinical endocannabinoid deficiency

There is an emerging literature that documents ECS deficiency syndrome as an etiology (causation or origination) in psychological disorders, irritable bowel syndrome, migraine and other conditions

(McPartland, Guy, & Di Marzo, 2014; Russo, 2008). The theory of ECS deficiency syndrome is that "all humans have an underlying endocannabinoid tone that is a reflection of … the relative abundance and state of cannabinoid receptors … and in certain conditions … the endocannabinoid tone becomes deficient and productive of pathophysiological syndromes" (Russo, 2016b, p.154). The concept has been touted as a possible explanation for why cannabis can be therapeutically beneficial in some chronic diseases that are treatment-resistant and also pleasurable in recreational contexts. Several studies have indicated that the ECS is intimately involved in the processing of pain signals. For example, Russo (2016b) contended that the best evidence supporting CED theory relates to migraine, fibromyalgia, and irritable bowel syndrome. These are briefly addressed in turn below.

According to Greco, Gasperi, Maccarrone, and Tassorelli (2010, p.85), a migraine is a "neurovascular disorder characterized by recurrent episodic headaches and caused by abnormal processing of sensory information". Migraines are highly prevalent in the US impacting an estimated 14% of Americans at an annual cost of $20 billion (Russo, 2016b). While the precise mechanisms underlying migraines are yet to be fully understood, there is strong evidence suggesting that activation of the ECS is a promising therapeutic tool in the reduction of both inflammatory and physiological pain thought to be involved in migraine attacks (Greco et al., 2010).

Fibromyalgia is a chronic musculoskeletal pain that may increase pain response to pressure, enhance pain sensitivity, and is often accompanied by fatigue and problems sleeping (Valença, Medeiros, Martins, Massaud, & Peres, 2009). It is prevalent in approximately 4% of US patients, and like migraines, disproportionately impacts the female population at a ratio of approximately 4-9:1. Cannabis or cannabinoids are often used by fibromyalgia patients and there is some evidence suggesting cannabis may be effective in treating related symptoms including pain and increased sleep quality (Russo, 2016b).

Irritable bowel syndrome relates to a cluster of disorders characterized by abdominal pain, and similar to migraine and fibromyalgia, its underlying mechanisms are yet to be fully understood. Nonetheless, evidence points to the ECS being involved in the regulation of multiple gastrointestinal functions, and activation of CB1 and CB2 receptors under certain conditions has been shown to decrease hypersensitivity in the gut and limit secretion (Storr, Yüce, Andrews, & Sharkey, 2008).

While the evidence is only starting to accrue there are indications that clinical endocannabinoid deficiency is associated with a broad range of ailments from cancer and aging through to motion sickness (Blesching, 2015; Russo, 2016b). More evidence is needed to better understand the clinical efficacy of replenishing naturally occurring endocannabinoids with phyto-cannabinoids to fight multiple chronic diseases.

Pleasure, holistic health, spirituality, creativity, and fitness

"Several scholars have found that the overwhelming reason for consumption provided by people who use cannabis is pleasure (e.g. Duff, 2008; Webb, Ashton, Kelly, & Kamali, 1998). This is perhaps unsurprising given that an often-used description of the effect of cannabis on mood is euphoria (Ashton, 2001). Moore (2008) pointed out that the term pleasure has become marginalised in discourses that seek to understand drug use. It would not seem unreasonable to conclude that many people who use cannabis may do so with the aim of enjoying it" (Subritzky, 2018, p.19).

Throughout the course of this research, numerous accounts of cannabis being perceived as beneficial within holistic health conceptions, spirituality, and fitness were identified in the grey literature and also in interviews conducted with people who use cannabis in Colorado. These potential benefits were discussed in a paper by the author of the book, however, this was deemed to be outside the scope of the primary objectives of the current study. As such the paper '*Considering the spectrum of wellness as an interpretive framework for cannabis consumption*' has been included in Appendix 1 (Subritzky, 2018).

In this chapter, cannabis was defined including the distinction between whole-plant cannabis and extracted cannabinoids, variety of methods of preparation and consumption, and the central role of ECS in modulating cannabis consumption, primarily via CB1 and CB2 receptors. This provided a solid foundation and context for the Coloradan definition of cannabis as stipulated in A64 by demonstrating the complexity of cannabis and comparing it with the generic coverall definition applied to the CRCM. Further context for the CRCM was provided in reviews of the potential harms and benefits associated with the consumption of cannabis. Three main threads were presented throughout the chapter including the polarity of opinion (and clinical evidence) surrounding cannabis, its complexity, and challenges in differentiating between recreational and medical cannabis from an ontological perspective, despite legal distinctions. In Chapter 3, an overview of cannabis reform in the US is introduced together with a brief description of practical regulatory issues, and a summary of cannabis policy alternatives to bring additional context to the CRCM.

Chapter 3: Contextualising cannabis legalisation and stipulating practical regulatory and policy alternatives

The Colorado approach to cannabis regulation is commonly described as the standard commercial approach similar to alcohol (Caulkins et al., 2015). However, the commercial option is just one of a range of policy alternatives available to cannabis regulators. Furthermore, even within the commercial model, there is a spectrum of approaches that will likely result in vastly different outcomes. This chapter moves the book from defining cannabis in the broadest sense to an overview of policy options available to cannabis regulators, which provides further context for the Coloradan approach. The chapter reviews the literature around these issues as follows. First, the CRCM is placed into historical context in terms of international controls on cannabis and a brief overview of cannabis policy reform in the US is presented. This includes highlighting definitional challenges associated with legalisation when compared with terms such as depenalisation, decriminalisation, *de jure,* and *de facto* legalisation. Second, an outline of specific practical issues and options associated with the regulation of recreational cannabis is presented. Third, alternative cannabis regulatory options are described. Incorporating the CFS, these models are then framed in the context of cannabis as a commercial agricultural commodity to allow for the contextualisation of the CRCM next to other commercial cannabis models that have emerged in American markets since 2014 such as Canada and Uruguay. Fourth, a comparison of cannabis regulation with other 'vice' industries including alcohol and gaming is discussed. Fifth, the chapter is rounded off with a review of real-world cannabis policies in other jurisdictions such as the Netherlands, Portugal, and Uruguay.

International controls

Cannabis was first added to the international drug control system in 1925, moved to the strictest prohibition category with no accepted medical or non-medical usage in 1961 (Single Convention on Narcotic Drugs), and explicitly criminalised for non-medical use in 1988 (Convention Against Illicit Traffic in Narcotic Drugs and Psychotropic Substances) (Bruun, Pan, & Rexed, 1975; Mead, 2014; Room et al., 2010; United Nations, 1961, 1988). Increases in arrests and harsher punishments for cannabis use and possession in the 1960s in the US and other countries resulted (Bonnie & Whitebread, 1974).

Internationally there were several large public inquiries into the known harms associated with the consumption of cannabis in the late 1960s and early 1970s including in the UK (Wootton Report), Holland (Baan Commission), Canada (LeDain Commission Report), Australia (Commission of the Australian Government), and the US (National Commission on Marihuana and Drug Abuse) (Iversen, 2007). While acknowledging the serious risk potential associated with cannabis outlined in the previous chapter, these enquires essentially concluded "harms perceived for cannabis use were exaggerated, ... the effects of criminalisation of cannabis were potentially excessive ..., and that lawmakers should drastically reduce or eliminate criminal penalties for the personal use of cannabis" (Room et al., 2010, p.76). These conclusions mirrored those of earlier studies in 1894 (Indian Hemp Drugs Commission), 1925 (Panama Canal Zone Report), and 1944 (LaGuardia Commission Report). These reports did not mean to say there are no risks associated with cannabis, rather it is to highlight that the risks as they have been demonstrated scientifically, have often been presented out of context and exaggerated (Meier et al., 2019). This has been a consistent finding of cannabis policy scholars for more than a century in the US (Iversen, 2007), despite continued reports of statements from politicians indicating harsher penalties are appropriate (e.g. Marijuana Moment, 2020, Feb. 10).

Both the suitability and enforceability of the international drug conventions have been questioned, while the issue of whether Colorado contravenes them was disputed (Hawken & Kulick, 2014; Room, 2014). Internationally, these controls have failed to achieve the main aim of eliminating, or even reducing, illicit cannabis markets. There were an estimated 182.5 million people who used cannabis globally, which consisted of 80% of the estimated total of illegal drug use at the start of this study (Room, 2012; United Nations Office on Drugs and Crime, 2016). At the rhetorical level, cannabis plays an important role in justifying the existence of these drug treaties and conventions. It has been suggested that when cannabis is excluded, "illegal drug use is not a global population-level issue" (Room et al., 2010, p.9). Indeed, there is growing pressure on such institutions to justify the costs and benefits associated with attempts to prevent cannabis consumption, where prevalence has been increasing despite strict controls (Caulkins, Nicosia, & Pacula, 2014; Paley, 2014; Quah et al., 2014).

Consequently, less punitive models of prohibition arose in different countries and states with the aims of complying with international obligations as outlined in drug conventions while attempting to lessen the impact of cannabis controls on citizens. Common conceptions of prohibition with reduced sanctions include: (i) depenalisation; (ii) decriminalisation; and (iii) *de facto* legalisation. These concepts as they are presented in the literature are confusing and have not been clearly defined, with different authors presenting contradictory definitions, for example:

(i)   Depenalisation has been defined on the one hand as relating to any law changes that decrease the severity of civil or criminal sanctions. In this sense, cannabis offences may remain criminalised, albeit with shorter periods of incarceration, fines, or through the administering of caution or diversion for minor offences (Mead, 2014; Pacula et al., 2005; Room et al., 2010). On the other hand, depenalisation may refer to policy that allows for the possibility of a criminal case to be closed without punishment if deemed to be minor or not in the public interest, for example (EMCDDA, 2005).

(ii) Decriminalisation is a contested term commonly employed term that is understood by some authors as a sub-category of depenalisation (Room et al., 2010). It has been argued that the term 'prohibited with civil sanctions' more accurately reflects this level of prohibition (Lenton, 2012). In general, these terms refer to the replacement of criminal sanctions with monetary penalties such as fines. It has been noted that the terms refer to personal possession and use of cannabis as opposed to supply (EMCDDA, 2005).

(iii) *De facto* legalisation is where cannabis use remains prohibited by law but not enforced, such as in the Netherlands (the 'Dutch coffee shop model' is discussed in more detail in later in the chapter).

61

Despite these attempts in some jurisdictions to lessen the impact of cannabis prohibition for possession of small amounts of cannabis, and in many cases cultivation of prescribed small numbers of plants, its cultivation and sale remain punishable by death in several countries in the 21st century (Gallahue et al., 2012). In 2018, the introduction of the death penalty for serious drug offences was reportedly being discussed as a policy option by the US Federal Government, which raised the possibility of the federal government executing owners of licensed state cannabis businesses (Cannabist, 2018, Mar. 22; Office of Attorney General, 2018). Furthermore, in the US, numerous state laws encourage asset forfeiture without conviction and federal penalties can stipulate life imprisonment for cannabis offences deemed serious (NORML, 2017b). These strict penalties provide a stark contrast to a legal cannabis market such as that introduced in Colorado and thereby further highlight both the historic nature of the scheme and the uncertainty that Coloradan regulators faced when they implemented a recreational cannabis market despite the drug remaining illegal at the federal level.

Practical issues for cannabis regulation

Several scholars have mapped out cannabis regulatory options (e.g. Belackova & Wilkins, 2018; Caulkins et al., 2015; Kilmer, 2015a; Room et al., 2010). The majority of these were included in Rolles and Murkin (2016) practical guide to cannabis policy and a comprehensive report on cannabis policy options by Caulkins et al. (2015). In simple terms these authors take the risk reduction guidelines that have been in place for legally available substances such as alcohol and tobacco and applies them to the regulation of cannabis. In doing so, they highlighted regulatory considerations for 11 key issues linked to public health outcomes including: (i) production; (ii) price; (iii) tax; (iv) preparation and method of consumption; (v) potency; (vi) packaging and labelling; (vii) vendor licensing; (viii) purchasers; (ix) outlets; (x) marketing; and (xi) regulating institutions. As the overall objective of the book is to examine issues in the implementation and evolution of a recreational cannabis market, these guidelines provide important context for the analysis in subsequent chapters. While the Rolles and Murkin and are now briefly introduced:

Production. Rolles and Murkin (2016) discussed several aspects of the cultivation and manufacture of cannabis products including licensing, quality control (see the previous chapter), security, and production limits. How production is licensed and linked to supply is a central component of regulatory action. Depending on priorities, regulators may select options ranging from limiting production licenses to one company through to allowing free market participation (this point is further elaborated in the section relating to agriculture and the SFS below). Additionally, the supply chain may be vertically integrated, where the same company both produces and sells products, or these components may be separated. These macro factors can be situated within the CFS and are considered in more detail below. The issue of security, in general, refers to how regulators will monitor production to prevent diversion to black-markets. Limitations on production may reduce risks of both diversion to the black-market and powerful companies with "excessive lobbying power" (Rolles & Murkin, 2016, p.52). The argument from this perspective is that if there is less product there is less likely to be an excess that could spill into the black-market, which is in contrast (and addition) to standard considerations of diversion to black-market due to over-regulation.

Price. Rolles and Murkin (2016) noted three key challenges around the issue of price including how to establish price controls, understanding the impacts of price on patterns of use, and the difficulties of reconciling competing priorities (such as dissuading cannabis consumption, reducing black-market size, and revenue generation for regulatory bodies and public health interventions). Price control is an important regulatory tool that draws on lessons from the alcohol and tobacco industries (Pacula et al., 2014), and has a relationship to both consumption patterns and interstate black-market activity. The price of cannabis products has been predicted to drop substantially if cannabis is legalised at the federal level, largely due to economies of scale (Caulkins, 2017; Oglesby, 2018).

Direct price controls include tax rates or fixed prices, while indirect controls may consist of increased regulatory burden or production limits. A major concern of several scholars is that commercial markets that encourage economies of scale may result in price collapse that could lead to patterns of increased consumption (Caulkins et al., 2015; Pacula & Lundberg, 2014). On the other hand, if prices are kept too high there is the risk that purchasing from the black market will be more attractive (Caulkins et al., 2015).

Taxation. A central argument for legalising cannabis is that it provides the ability for governments to generate revenue that can assist with public health interventions to reduce harmful consumption patterns (Caulkins, 2017; Caulkins et al., 2015). There are several regulatory options relating to the taxation of cannabis products, each with advantages and disadvantages. These options include: (i) a fixed percentage of price; (ii) unit weight, for example per gram; (iii) a progressive tax that increases according to product potency or other variables; (iv) license fees; (v) local tax; (vi) denial of tax deductions for business expenses; (vii) square footage tax base; and (viii) indoor electricity add on base (Caulkins et al., 2015; Rolles & Murkin, 2016). Further considerations involve the point of collection and the ability to adjust taxation models as issues arise (Caulkins et al., 2015).

Preparation and method of consumption. The issue of how to regulate the various preparations and methods of consumption is an important one for rule-makers to consider. As noted in the previous chapter the Coloradan definition of cannabis allows for a wide diversity of products that can be smoked, eaten, or applied topically to the skin. A detailed overview of methods of consumption within the Coloradan context is presented in Chapter 6, which provides a 'snapshot' of the CRCM 18 months post-implementation, so further descriptions are not provided here.

Potency. The challenging nature of potency testing cannabis was described in the previous chapter, and as such is not discussed further here.

Packaging and labelling. Rolles and Murkin (2016) noted challenges for regulators regarding the packaging of retail cannabis products including: (i) childproofing to reduce the risk of accidental ingestion; (ii) labelling, specifically around product contents (e.g. potency) and consumer risk warnings; and (iii) design of packaging that does not encourage consumption (such as plain packaging vs branded packaging).

Vendors. Regulatory challenges related to vendors include aligning licensing requirements with policy objectives, the ability to enforce regulations, and whether online sales should be permitted. Rolles and Murkin (2016) noted three aims that are central to vendor regulation including the promotion of health and wellbeing (such as minimising the harm associated with free-market approaches that incentivise sales growth), protection of youth and other vulnerable people from risks associated with cannabis consumption, and crime prevention. There are several strategies that can be required of retail sellers to achieve these aims including: (i) ensuring legal age limits are adhered to; (ii) educating consumers on the risks associated with cannabis consumption at point of sale; (iii) compliance with quality control regulations; and (iv) the completion of responsible vendor programs that may require additional staff training guided by public health experts. A further point is regarding fitness to hold a vendor licence and whether people with a criminal conviction be excluded. For example, should people convicted of cannabis cultivation under the previous prohibition model be eligible for a vendor license?

Purchasers. Discussion around regulations pertaining to purchasers of cannabis products generally relate to four central challenges: (i) what age restrictions should be established (if the limit is too low, it may encourage problematic consumption among youth, while if it is too high, black-market growth may occur); (ii) how should age limits be enforced to ensure effectiveness; (iii) bulk purchases may need to be limited to prevent resale in non-regulated markets; and (iv) whether or not public consumption should be allowed, and if so, the determination of appropriate locations. The issue is complicated by the enormous variability of locations and situations where people consume cannabis from yoga and hiking to churches to the cinema.

Outlets. There are several considerations relating to the regulation of cannabis sales outlets. These include: (i) density and location of outlets, where there is a need to negotiate competing priorities such as to meet demand, reduce black-market activity, and prevent oversupply, which may increase problematic consumption patterns (lessons from alcohol indicate a greater density of outlets is associated with increased public health risks (Livingston, 2008)); (ii) appearance and external signage restrictions, particularly from the perspective of limitations on marketing; (iii) opening hours; and (iv) restricting the sale of other drugs such as tobacco and alcohol at outlets.

Marketing. Restricting the ability of for-profit companies to promote cannabis products is seen as an important harm reduction tool by public health scholars. While Rolles and Murkin (2016, p.159) contended that a total "ban on all forms of cannabis advertising, promotion, and sponsorship should be the default starting point for any regulatory system", there are a number of legal and political impediments (such as the right to commercial free speech in the US context and constitutional restraints such as those stipulated in Colorado's Amendment 64) that prevent implementing best practise recommendations. Examining the tension between commercial profit seeking (of which marketing is a key aspect) and public health objectives in the CRCM is one of the core objectives of the book.

Regulating institutions. Rolles and Murkin (2016) pointed out that the regulation of cannabis is influenced at international, national, state, and local levels. Internationally, beyond conventions described above, aspects that require consideration include: (i) international trade and transit of cannabis (e.g. via trade agreements); (ii) human rights, with institutions such as the United Nations (UN) transitioning from "overseeing a global prohibitionist system to one more like the UN role with regard to alcohol and tobacco" (Rolles & Murkin, 2016, p.171); and research around public health impacts, perhaps in a manner that the WHO monitors harms associated with tobacco and alcohol. A key challenge facing regulators is managing tensions that arise between various levels in the hierarchy such as federal prohibition and state legalisation in the Colorado context.

Cannabis policy models

Rolles and Murkin (2016), Caulkins et al. (2015), and others have noted the importance of having clear aims when cannabis policy is being developed. Proponents of legalising cannabis generally stipulate goals that include: the improvement and protection of public health; harm reduction; increasing tax revenues; reducing arrests for minor cannabis-related offenses; reduction of black-markets; quality control (potency and adulterants); libertarian philosophies that minimise government involvement for consumer grower systems; protection of human rights; improving public security; cost-effective solutions; and limiting access for youth and other vulnerable people (Caulkins, Kilmer, MacCoun, Pacula, & Reuter, 2012b; Kamin, 2016; Rolles & Murkin, 2016). The ranking of these aims will depend on regulatory objectives.

As public opinion in the US has shifted in the direction of legalising recreational cannabis (CNN Political Unit, 2015), it has been argued that "the [public] debate in the US has focused largely on a false dichotomy: continue to prohibit supply or create a for-profit industry" (Kilmer, 2017, p.8). However, the academic literature includes descriptions of several potential policy alternatives to these approaches. In the US context, where cannabis is simultaneously legalised in some states and federally prohibited, scholars have considered legalisation from the perspectives of cooperative federalism, the rescheduling or de-scheduling of cannabis as a schedule 1 controlled substance, and/or the distinction between medical and recreational cannabis markets (e.g. Chemerinsky, Forman, Hopper, & Kamin, 2015; Kamin, 2016, 2017a; Kleiman, 2013).

From a public health standpoint, a multi-criterion decision analysis matrix has been proposed that applied 27 criteria within seven thematic clusters closely associated with the practical issues of cannabis regulation outlined above (Rogeberg et al., 2018). This approach identified four generic regulatory models including absolute prohibition, decriminalisation, state control, and free market (Rogeberg et al., 2018). Caulkins et al. (2015) detailed additional layers from the perspective of supply, specifically the types of organisations permitted to cultivate, manufacture, and distribute cannabis. In their architecture of supply overview, Caulkins et al. (2015) described two extreme options, two commonly discussed options, and eight middle-road alternatives (see figure 1 below).

Figure 1:

Twelve Supply Alternatives to Status Quo Prohibition

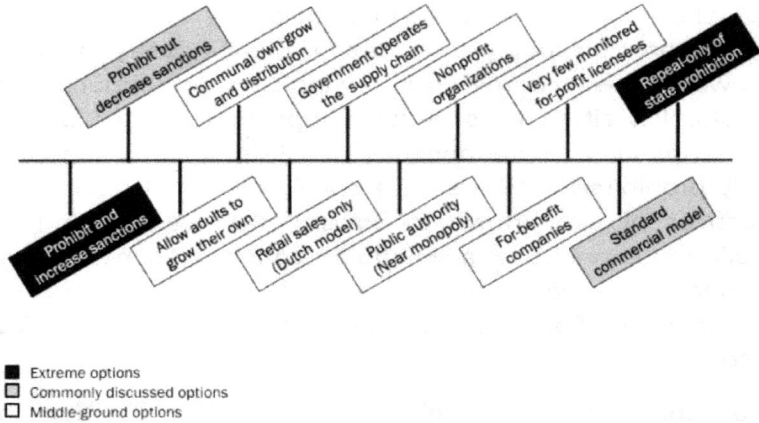

- ■ Extreme options
- □ Commonly discussed options
- □ Middle-ground options

Source: (Caulkins et al., 2015, p.50)

In the following subsection, the most commonly discussed cannabis policy options identified in the literature are described in more detail including home grow, cannabis social clubs/ communal grow, and state monopoly of production.

Home grow

Allowing adults to grow their own cannabis (self-supply) is a policy option that has been applied in various jurisdictions, both in recreational and medical contexts. It has been argued that the home grow approach can reduce public health and social risks by avoiding the ills associated with widespread use in a fully commercial model while giving consumers quality control over the cannabis they put into their bodies (Belackova, Brandnerova, & Vechet, 2018; Decorte, 2010). In the US, Australia, and some other countries, the home production of limited numbers of cannabis plants by adults has been decriminalised (prohibited with civil penalties) since the associated committee findings of these countries in the 1970s as outlined above (Caulkins et al., 2015; Lenton, 2004; Lenton & Allsop, 2010). Home growing cannabis is permitted in some jurisdictions where large scale commercial production is allowed (e.g. Colorado) and not allowed in others (e.g. Washington State). This issue was highlighted In Washington D.C. recently with the example of a legal self-supply policy where commercial production is prohibited. Reports of that market tended to frame home growing negatively with the state being described as a "hotbed for DIY cannabis" (Cannabist, 2017, Nov.24). In an international web survey of 'small-scale' cultivators, approximately 70% supported the notion that adults should be permitted to grow their own cannabis post-prohibition, although support varied according to whether regulations such as restrictions on plant numbers or licences applied (Lenton, Frank, Barratt, Dahl, & Potter, 2015).

As noted by Caulkins et al. (2015), within each approach to cannabis policy there is broad scope for refinement. Regarding the home grow option, examples of variation reflect the diversity of cannabis cultivation described in Chapter 2 of the book and include: limits to the scale of cultivation (by plant numbers allowed for individuals or households, or size of permitted cultivated area); ability to supply or 'gift' cannabis to friends (grow and give), which may act as a social control to protect against black-market risks (Belackova & Vaccaro, 2013); and distinguishing between indoor hydroponic and outdoor growing techniques, which may include aspects such as limits on wattage for grow lights, yield, and plant size (both height and breadth) (Caulkins et al., 2015; Lenton, 2016; Lenton, Bennett, & Heale, 1999).

While the evidence relating to the impacts of the self-supply models is still emerging, there are signals of both beneficial and negative implications from public health and safety perspectives. On the one hand, advantages of this approach include the possibility of moving supply away from both criminal and commercial enterprises that are motivated by profit (Caulkins et al., 2012b; Lenton, 2016). Additionally, there is evidence that self-suppliers perceive self-grown cannabis to be 'healthier' than that purchased on the black-market (Potter et al., 2015). As such, it has been noted that "cannabis cultivation is not [necessarily] an isolated, economically motivated behaviour and that social, psychological and health reasons exist for cannabis self-supply" (Belackova & Wilkins, 2018, p.27). There is no plausible evidence in the academic literature of increased consumption in jurisdictions where homegrown cannabis is permitted (Lenton, 2016; MacCoun, 2013a).

On the other hand, disadvantages appear to include the risk of product diversion to black-market and the potential to weaken regulations in a fully legalised market by, for example, allowing for unregulated cannabis cultivation (Caulkins et al., 2012b; MacCoun, 2013a). Furthermore, allowance of home growing may reduce revenues for governments (since it is difficult to tax) and restrict their ability to enforce labelling or quality control standards (Caulkins et al., 2015). Finally, there have been reports that the grow and give approach can be manipulated, whereby commercial firms may offer everyday goods such as fruit juice at marked-up prices, with small quantities of cannabis then gifted for free (e.g. Associated Press, 2018, Feb.1). It has been suggested that this outcome could be limited if grow and give was restricted to non-commercial entities (Caulkins et al., 2015). Importantly too, home growing currently appears to be limited to a small minority of market share in black, decriminalised, and regulated markets (Belackova, Maalsté, Zabransky, & Grund, 2015; Caulkins et al., 2015; Lenton et al., 1999).

Cannabis social clubs

The communal grow and distribute, or co-op model is a consumer-driven approach that builds on self-supply and provides flexibility that may be absent from strict home grow policies (Belackova & Wilkins, 2018; Caulkins et al., 2015). The best current examples of this approach are cannabis social clubs (CSC) that operate within decriminalisation laws in some countries such as Belgium and Spain, the latter being where the first official CSCs was established in 2001 (Belackova, Tomkova, & Zabransky, 2016; Decorte, 2015; Parés & Bouso, 2015). CSCs are also part of the framework recently implemented in Uruguay as discussed below (Pardo, 2014). From a sociological perspective, CSCs build on the concept of social supply in which sales do not appear to be incentivised by profit motives (Coomber, Moyle, & South, 2016; Scott, Grigg, Barratt, & Lenton, 2017a). Key tenets of CSCs include: being not-for-profit associations; being initiated and regulated by people who use cannabis; having the potential to reduce harm through peer education (such as information sharing about strain-specific effects); and controlled use around restricted and planned supply to members (Belackova & Wilkins, 2018; ENCOD, 2011). In addition to supply, CSCs may provide dedicated spaces for consumption (Decorte et al., 2017). As noted by Belackova and Wilkins (2018, p.27), "CSCs can be seen as a remarkable demonstration of consumer agency in cannabis production and distribution".

As a not-for-profit, consumer-driven model for regulating cannabis, CSCs seem to contain several built-in risk minimisation mechanisms (Belackova et al., 2016). These include: having no incentive to advertise or promote consumption; education being disseminated by peers, which may result in less risky use practises (such as not combining tobacco with cannabis, limiting risks of acute intoxication, and vaporising as opposed to smoking product); perceived higher quality of cannabis; the potential to significantly undercut black-market activity; the possibility to limit price collapse that may eventuate from large scale commercial cultivation through the implementation of a traditional artisanal market; the ability to monitor cannabis consumption patterns; an opportunity to combine and streamline the supply of both recreational and medical cannabis; and reduced risk of arrest, particularly if public consumption is prohibited (Belackova et al., 2016; Belackova & Wilkins, 2018; Caulkins et al., 2015; Decorte, 2015). Another benefit is that because they are limited and non-commercial, CSCs can be wound back if there are public health costs in a way that an established commercial market cannot (Decorte, 2018).

Conversely, as a self-regulatory model, CSCs are limited in a number of areas including: no formal authorisation to supply cannabis (at least in the European contexts); little oversight that formal codes of conduct are being adhered to; lack of anonymity for members who must officially register; increased accessibility may encourage higher consumption rates; an inability to insure against theft or damage to crops; harm reduction measures are implemented at the discretion of CSCs themselves as opposed to an overseeing regulatory body; the potential imposition of restrictive 'top-down' regulation on self-regulatory bodies; the potential for profit-driven clubs to emerge; an apparent lack of transparency in operating procedures; and the superficial nature of quality control methodologies (Belackova & Wilkins, 2018; Decorte et al., 2017).

State monopoly

There are historical precedents of governments controlling the supply of drugs such as opium, alcohol, and tobacco (Caulkins et al., 2015). Several scholars have argued that, from a public health perspective, the state monopoly model is a preferred option for regulating cannabis

(Caulkins et al., 2015; Pacula et al., 2014; Rogeberg et al., 2018; Room, 2014). As speculated by Caulkins et al. (2016, p.181), a state monopoly is more palatable than a commercial approach from a public health perspective, because it "would have a fighting chance of avoiding ... the aggressive marketing efforts that would likely result from commercial legalization". In general this assessment is based on lessons from the historic public health failing of tobacco and alcohol regulations, which suggest better public health outcomes when supply is controlled by governments compared to less regulated free-market approaches (e.g. Babor, 2010; Barry & Glantz, 2016b; Borland, 2003; Pacula et al., 2014; Room, 1987). Potential public health objectives that can be achieved via state control of supply include eliminating or reducing commercial promotion and encouraging the development of less harmful products (Borland, 2003; Rolles & Murkin, 2016).

In the US context, strong protections are afforded to the commercial-free speech of private companies posing challenges for things such as advertising restrictions (Edwards, 2014; Endejan, 2015). However, as noted by Caulkins et al. (2015), enabling the government to control production and distribution could remove this obstacle and allow regulators to implement strict limitations on advertising. When the state controls production, policy levers are available such as overseeing the entire supply chain or limiting government involvement to individual components such as cultivation, manufacture, product testing, and/or sale. An example of this variability might include monopoly of retail sales outlets only, which could provide the ability to manage aspects such as external signage and point of sale promotions (Caulkins et al., 2015).

Further, a state monopoly has the potential to control product innovation both to hinder higher risk product development and as an encouragement to bringing potentially less harmful goods to market. For example, the state could choose to incentivise the cultivation of strains with higher CBD:THC ratios while limiting or prohibiting high THC:CBD products that were shown in the previous chapter to constitute a higher risk. Lower risk products such as these are a feature of the Uruguayan model discussed in more detail below. Additional benefits of the state monopoly approach include the potential to control diversion to the black-market, reverse the policy if it is not effective with relative ease compared to established private businesses with vested interests, and avoid price collapse (Caulkins et al., 2015).

The Regulated Market Model devised by Professor Borland for tobacco demonstrates how these protective elements could function in practice (Borland, 2003). The model proposes the establishment of a regulatory body to act as a bridge between the retail and manufacturing segments of the supply chain (Borland, 2003). Under this approach, the regulatory body has complete oversight of cannabis production as a controlled substance. The overseeing body may stipulate, for example, that products are generic including plain packaging requirements, and public health focussed labelling standards with stringent warning language (Borland, 2003; Caulkins et al., 2015; Rolles & Murkin, 2016). Figure 2 below is reproduced from the Borland Regulated Market Model as it was conceived for tobacco but could be modified to guide cannabis policy (Rolles & Murkin, 2016). This is a blended model whereby free market supply to a government-controlled wholesale organisation that manages product control, packaging, potency, testing, etc, and then sells to commercial retailers. A prominent recent example of this is the proposed Mexican drug policy (Zedillo, Pérez-Correa, Madrazo, & Alonso, 2019).

Figure 2: The Regulated Market Model

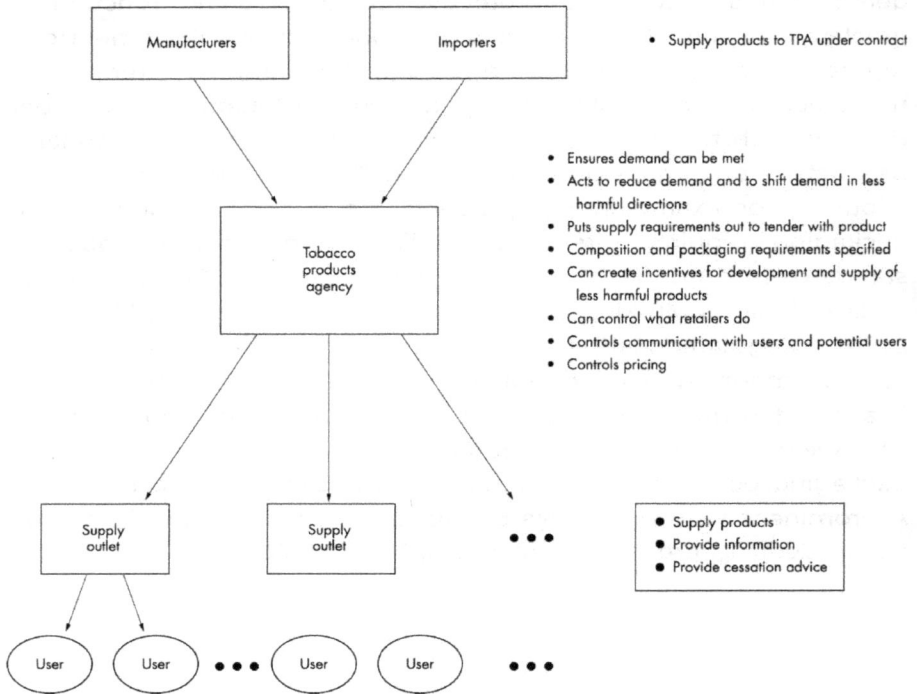

Source: (Borland, 2003)

Conversely, there are some limitations to the state monopoly model. First, particularly in the US context, the state monopoly model is hindered by the notion that state employees could violate federal laws that prohibit the cultivation and sale of cannabis under the Controlled Substances Act (CSA). While there is some debate as to whether states might be exempt from the CSA, it is generally agreed the state monopoly is not a viable option in the US currently (Caulkins et al., 2015; Oglesby, 2015). Second, it has been argued that limiting advertising may be a mixed blessing. On the one hand, reducing exposure to cannabis promotion by youth, for example, is viewed positively from a public health perspective. On the other hand, this may inconvenience consumers by reducing access to product information and price comparisons that can potentially inform safer consumption practices (Caulkins et al., 2015). Third, state monopolies are generally seen as less efficient than free-market models when it comes to production (Caulkins et al., 2015). Inefficiency can lead to higher production costs, inability to meet demand, issues around product quality, and slower response times to public health problems that may arise, which in turn can lead to expansion of the black-market. Fourth, product innovation is driven by demand in a free-market approach. From a consumer perspective, state monopolies may limit product choice, which may, in turn, lead to increased black-market activity if demand is not met in a regulated environment. These macro issues can be drawn together, compared, contrasted, and ultimately best understood with a comprehensive framework.

Agriculture and the cannabis fragmentation spectrum: conceptualising the commercial model

While states in the US have tended to regulate recreational cannabis in a manner more or less similar to alcohol (e.g. Caulkins et al., 2015), it has been argued that this approach "reveals a regulatory blind spot" for an agricultural product that, by some measures, is the largest cash crop in the US (Stoa, 2017, p.297). Indeed, since cannabis was prohibited long before any cultivation regulations, states now face challenges regulating one of the country's largest agricultural industries for the first time (Stoa, 2017). In a comprehensive study that considered the regulation of cannabis first and foremost as an agricultural product, Stoa (2017) made the case that cannabis cultivation is a burgeoning agricultural industry and should be recognised as such by regulators. The study considered elements that appear to be limited in the cannabis-focused public health literature including: (i) the so-called 'cannabis fragmentation spectrum' (CFS), which delineates several models under the broad rubric of commercial/free-market conceptions; (ii) environmental impacts of water quality and allocation, pesticides, energy use, indoor agriculture, certified organic standards, crop insurance, and disaster relief; and (iii) local ordinances versus state regulations (Stoa, 2017). The central focus of this book is the commercial model undertaken by Colorado regulators, and as such, the following subsection focusses on the CFS to illustrate diverse options that exist under the umbrella term 'commercial model'.

The CFS as outlined by Stoa (2017) addresses a fundamental question, namely: should regulations be developed that permit the consolidation and commoditisation of cannabis plantations and sales outlets, or is the protection of small-scale farmers and the creation of an artisan industry a priority? The CFS includes the concepts of commodification, vertical integration, and appellation designations, and these are now briefly described.

First, at one end of the spectrum, cannabis is commoditised as a generic, mass-produced, and inexpensive agricultural product. As noted above, it is generally argued that the commoditisation of cannabis will lead to price collapse (due to economies of scale and technological advance), and by association, higher risk potential from a public health perspective. Additionally, price competition may force smaller farms out of business. Indeed, it has been argued that the 'agribusiness' model of food production in the US, even for non-intoxicating produce, is fundamentally broken, corrupted, and controlled by self-interested corporate influence to the detriment of public health and the environment (Engdahl, 2007; Nestle, 2013). As described in detail in the following chapter, while Colorado initially attempted to limit the impact of commoditisation by restricting out of state investors' access to markets, federal legalisation is seen as a potentially disruptive force, particularly if interstate commerce were to be permitted and banking restrictions removed (Stoa, 2017). A clear example of commodification was reported in the Canadian context where a cultivation facility "the size of 19 football fields ... expected to produce 75,000 kgs of cannabis annually" was approved (Cannabist, 2018, Mar.7).

However, a policy that allows commoditisation does have some advantages from a regulatory perspective. To illustrate the point, Stoa noted that while regulators in States such as California grapple with licensing 50,000 or more farmers, other states including New York, Florida, and Ohio seek to limit cultivation licenses to 20 or fewer. In this sense, regulators may license a handful of large farms, on which they can "lavish regulatory attention ... to ensure compliance" (Stoa, 2017, p.321). Additionally, lower prices may reduce the scope of black-market activity (this aspect is discussed in more detail below in the Uruguayan context).

Second, vertical integration of the supply chain, that is, when the same firm both grows and sells cannabis, occupies a middle position on the CFS. As discussed in the next chapter, the CRCM initially opted for a vertically integrated approach. Regulatory advantages of vertical integration include reduced businesses to oversee; a simplified process to track cannabis from seed-to-sale; reduction of supply chain diversion to the black market; and improved business efficiency, which may lead to increased profitability. Disadvantages include high barriers to enter the market, particularly around significant start-up costs; amplified business risk, whereby failure of any aspect of the business may negatively impact other areas; and the potential to increase market consolidation for large firms (Stoa, 2017).

Third, at the opposite end of the spectrum, cannabis cultivation could be regulated by appellation designations similar to the US vineyard or microbrewery model. "An appellation is a certified designation of origin that may also require that certain quality or stylistic standards be met" (Stoa, 2017, p.325). The appellation model may best be suited to outdoor cannabis cultivation in jurisdictions such as Northern California, which is said to cultivate 60% of the entire US cannabis supply, as it tends to focus on aspects such as climate, soil quality, and aridity that contribute to the overall quality and uniqueness of harvested cannabis (Stoa, 2017). Just as certain grapes thrive in different climatic environments, cannabis seeds are diverse. Indeed, demand appears strong for so-called 'landrace strains', that originate from, and are unique to, geographic locations around the world as can be demonstrated by a popular YouTube channel with almost 100,000 subscribers and views in the 10 of millions (Strain Hunters, 2016). However, the model could be modified to include certified growing standards to incorporate indoor cultivation. This may protect the intellectual property of industries in other jurisdictions. For example, the Netherlands and Colorado have established reputations for cultivating cannabis produce that is apparently well regarded among cannabis consumers (Decorte, 2010; Leafly.com, 2018). Thus, advantages of appellations include: (i) product differentiation that may hinder commoditisation; (ii) protection of local industries' hard-earned reputations; (iii) preventing price collapse; and (iv) consumer protection through the certification of authentic products. Disadvantages include: (i) challenges to enforce at the local level if other jurisdictions are not included; (ii) a lack of regulatory leadership at the federal level; (iii) indoor cultivation techniques may lessen the relevance of geographic appellations; and (iv) there is no guarantee that appellations would prevent consolidation of the market, even if the model allows for product diversity and hinders commodification

(Stoa, 2017). The CFS is returned to in the overall discussion of the book to reconsider these macro factors of the CRCM within its framework five years post-implementation.

Learning from other industries

Alcohol

In general terms, "the guiding spirit of this [regulate like alcohol] approach is to let the market evolve to maximize the efficiency of production, the appeal of products to consumers, and the size, scale, and scope of the market—subject only to remaining within the regulatory parameters" (Caulkins et al., 2015, p.53). As noted, Caulkins et al. (2015) contended that the 'regulate like alcohol' option is essentially the standard commercial model discussed in the Coloradan context. Under this approach, the cultivation, distribution, and sale of cannabis are undertaken by private businesses within the free market that guides the broader economy (Caulkins et al., 2015). As previously described, the 'regulate like alcohol' approach to cannabis regulation is concerning from a public health perspective because it risks over-commercialisation, particularly if advertising and retail sales are inadequately regulated (Rolles & Murkin, 2016).

To address public health concerns within the commercial model as a general rule, more stringent product-specific regulations can be implemented that may include restrictions relating to: age; impaired driving; quality control; packaging; product innovation; advertising; production quantities; and retail stores, such as density, location, operating hours, and separation from convenience stores (that increase risk of exposure to minors) and other drugs such as alcohol and tobacco (Caulkins et al., 2015).

However, simply referring to a 'standard alcohol model' can be confusing for several reasons. First, an immediate complication is that alcohol in the US is partially regulated at the federal level (Alcohol and Tobacco Tax and Trade Bureau, 2006), while cannabis is federally prohibited. As such it would seem not entirely possible to regulate cannabis similarly to alcohol. Second, in Colorado for example, liquor and beer have separate codes of regulations (Colorado Department of Revenue Enforcement Division, 2016). As a point of reference, high potency liquor in Colorado is taxed at a flat rate of US $2.28 per *gallon,* while wine and beer are taxed at $.28 and $.08 per *gallon* respectively (Tax Policy Centre, 2017). Following a similar logic for cannabis, this would seem to infer those separate regulations be crafted relating to, for example, low THC flower and high THC concentrates (as noted these are generally considered low and high-risk products respectively). This would likely be viewed positively from a public health perspective in comparison to the blanket singular definition of cannabis incorporated in Colorado as described in the previous chapter. Third, in a handful of US states, alcohol is supplied via a state monopoly approach, which has been described above as having some advantages from a public health perspective, although not possible under federal prohibition. In these regards, the term 'regulate like alcohol' is not helpful despite its prominence across the literature and related government documents.

As noted above, from a public health perspective, the most beneficial aspect of the standard commercial model is the argument that it is the model most conducive to generating tax revenue for the state that can be used to fund the regulatory mechanism, oversee quality control, and increase services such as drug education, youth prevention, counselling, and treatment programs (Caulkins et al., 2015). Public health lessons from the alcohol model that have been found to decrease harmful consumption patterns include: keeping prices artificially high; adopting a state monopoly approach, or if not possible, establishing a strong licensing system; and placing limitations on types of products and marketing (Pacula et al., 2014).

Gaming

Debate around drug policy in general, and cannabis legalisation specifically, can be informed by other vices such as gambling policies, although the gaming model has received relatively little attention in this context (MacCoun & Reuter, 2001). Similarities between cannabis and gambling include: being seen as pleasurable to significant portions of the population; posing a moral issue; the formation of large illicit markets when prohibited; and being potentially habit-forming and harmful (both are listed in the American Psychiatric Association Diagnostic and Statistical Manual as pathological conditions when perpetrated to excess) (MacCoun & Reuter, 2001). It has been argued that, on the one hand, the regulation of gaming has achieved substantial benefits, most notably the diversion of funds from criminal organisations back to public coffers. On the other hand, there is evidence that "state governments have become greedy boosters of a behaviour that clearly causes problems" (MacCoun & Reuter, 2001, p.142).

In regards to implementing regulations based on gaming, Wilkins (2018) has suggested that the not-for-profit gaming model in New Zealand could potentially be adapted as a framework for recreational cannabis. Under the model, not-for-profit cannabis societies would be required to distribute 40% of sales for community purposes such as drug treatment and prevention. In addition, several public health-focused elements could be factored into the model including local control of outlet density, price controls, restrictions of advertising at the place of sale and on the internet, and the prevention of industry influence. The model has the advantage of being tested and providing promising outcomes regarding problematic gambling habits, and further research will be regarded with interest.

Lessons from other jurisdictions

Throughout the duration of this study, cannabis policy has undergone unprecedented reform in multiple jurisdictions, both in the US and internationally. For example, at time of writing Canada had implemented a commercial recreational cannabis market at the federal level (Fischer, 2017). On the face of it, the Canadian for-profit model appears similar to the Coloradan approach, and as such is not described here, however, emerging observations from that jurisdiction are considered in the overall discussion of the book. The following sub-section outlines real-world cannabis policies, distinct from those theoretical approaches described above, that have been implemented in other jurisdictions. These include models in place in the Netherlands, Portugal, and Uruguay.

The Netherlands

The Netherlands has a well-established policy that tolerates the possession, sale, and open consumption of small quantities of cannabis – this is despite the drug remaining officially prohibited in the country (Room et al., 2010). A key aim of the policy was to "establish a legal and practical separation of cannabis - judged to pose 'acceptable' risks to consumers and society - from hard drugs associated with unacceptable risk" (Grund & Breeksema, 2013, p.11). The so-called 'Dutch coffee shop model' evolved as the Netherlands moved from formalised depenalisation in the mid-1970s to *de facto* legalisation in the mid-1980s (MacCoun & Reuter, 2001). Licenses for these 'coffee shops' are granted under strict conditions that impose age restrictions, bans on the sale of other drugs such as alcohol, limitations to external signage and marketing, and maximum trade stocks of 500 grams (MacCoun & Reuter, 1997; Rolles et al., 2014). MacCoun and Reuter (2001) argued that this gradual evolution from depenalisation towards commercialisation is associated with an increase in levels of consumption. However, the argument is disputed, with other scholars concluding that external social forces and cultural factors, as opposed to cannabis policy *per se,* may have contributed to increases in consumption noted in the early 1990s in Holland and across Europe (Grund & Breeksema, 2013; Korf, 2002; Room et al., 2010).

A defining characteristic of the Dutch model is that the commercial cultivation and wholesale distribution of cannabis remain prohibited, are strictly enforced, and, at least technically, "a matter of organised crime rather than innocent gardening" (Decorte, 2010, p.272). This 'backdoor problem', where cannabis production is not legally endorsed but can be accessed in small amounts via the 'front door' of coffee shops, creates a regulatory void, particularly around quality control issues such as the application of potentially harmful pesticides and product testing, which are not regulated and remain illegal. In this regard, the Dutch cannabis policy is distinct from Colorado, which implemented the world's first fully 'seed-to-sale' regulatory approach. In recent times it was reported that the Dutch government had voted to experiment with the regulation of cannabis cultivation in a handful of local jurisdictions (Dutch Review, 2018, Jan.15; The Telegraph, 2017, Feb.21).

As a real-world example of cannabis policy that has been implemented for three decades, the Dutch coffee shop model has provided some valuables lessons. For example, there is broad consensus, consistent with US and Australian data, that decriminalisation of cannabis in the Netherlands is not associated with increased levels of consumption (as opposed to the commercialisation of the market) (Grund & Breeksema, 2013; MacCoun & Reuter, 2001; Room et al., 2010). Additional lessons include: it cannot be ruled out that *de facto* legalisation may increase consumption rates among youth; the separation of drugs is legally possible and results in less criminalisation, stigma, and more controlled consumption; and cannabis policy crafted with public health objectives can reduce associated harms (Grund & Breeksema, 2013).

Portugal

In 2001 Portugal implemented a policy that decriminalised the personal use of all illicit drugs including cocaine, heroin, and cannabis (Hughes, 2017). Similar to the Netherlands, the commercial cultivation and sale of cannabis remained prohibited under this model. The reform was based on the comprehensive national drug strategy that aimed to develop evidence-based policy (Hughes & Stevens, 2010). According to the European Monitoring Centre for Drugs and Drug Addiction (2017), the strategy is guided by the twin pillars of reduction in both demand and supply. A central tenet of the Portuguese model is the referral system, whereby treatment is offered if the individual is identified as a person with problematic cannabis (or other drug) consumption (Room et al., 2010). Referrals are based around the Commissions for the Dissuasion of Drug Addiction (Comissies para a Dissuasao da Toxicodependíncia - CDTs), which consist of panels of up to three people including medical professionals and social workers (Hughes & Stevens, 2007). The CDTs are designed to guide people with cannabis dependence towards treatment, without imposing strict penalties. While the CDTs were noted as important to the success of the reforms, it has also been claimed that they require substantial resources and are difficult to administrate (Room et al., 2010). In general, it is difficult to draw firm conclusions regarding public health outcomes from the Portuguese decriminalisation approach, both overall and as it pertains to cannabis specifically (Hughes & Stevens, 2007).

Laqueur (2010) noted a problem with the Portuguese model: while the scheme was set up to deal with serious drug problems, primarily associated with the use of heroin and to a certain extent cocaine, most people who appeared before the CDTs have not been people with significant drug problems, but young cannabis consumers not dependent on the drug (in 2009, three quarters of cases before CDTs were people who use cannabis) (Laqueur, 2010). This is an inefficient use of the time and resources of the Portuguese system and puts an unnecessarily onerous burden on these people who use cannabis. Perhaps as a consequence, it has been reported that Portugal was considering distinguishing cannabis from other drugs by legalising the drug from production to sale (Algarve Daily News, 2018, Mar.6).

Not surprisingly, the Portuguese approach is controversial, and "... has been deemed both a 'disastrous failure' and a 'resounding success'" (Greenwald, 2009; Hughes & Stevens, 2012, p.101; Pinto, 2010). The literature relating to the Portuguese drug policy reflected the polarity of opinion outlined in the previous chapter in relation to cannabis in general and the CRCM specifically. Hughes and Stevens (2012, p.109) noted in their review of two supposedly evidence-based yet diametrically opposed assessments, that they found clear proof of "selective use of evidence (focusing on different indicators, choice of years or data sets) and omission or a lack of acknowledgement of other pieces of the puzzle. Both also showed differential appreciations of data strengths and weaknesses. ... In so doing, both provided a version of events that offered certitude and support for opposing 'core beliefs'". While this "promulgation of errors" clearly fuels misconceptions, it was noted that can be beneficial if it leads to increased awareness of policy that may generate further scope for reform, which would seem to an optimistic view (Hughes & Stevens, 2012, p.109).

Uruguay

In 2013 Uruguay legalised the cultivation and sale of cannabis for recreational purposes, becoming the first nation to do so at the federal level (Pardo, 2014). The market was rolled out after an extended three and a half year pre-implementation phase in contrast to the 13 months in Colorado with the first sales reported in mid-2017 (Cannabist, 2017, Jul.18). According to Rolles and Murkin (2016), the approach is a state monopoly on production and supply that is broadly based on the Borland blended model outlined above. The Uruguayan model is distinct from the Coloradan approach in several ways. First, it was driven by the government as opposed to a ballot initiative, with the majority of the public initially opposed to the measure according to polls (Pardo, 2014). Second, the overseeing regulatory body was created specifically to implement the reform, with no existing experience (such as a medical cannabis market in Colorado) to draw on. Third, the model legalised three forms of cannabis production including: a home grow option (of up to 6 plants); a consumer cooperative based on CSCs, with up to 45 members (Decorte et al.,

2017); and the licensing of a small handful of producers who are required to sell to the government only (Queirolo, Boidi, & Cruz, 2016; Room, 2014), which is an example of the state monopoly/ blended model outlined above. Fourth, retail sale is permitted through licensed pharmacies, although it was reported that due to issues with accessing banks, there was a move to dedicated dispensaries (Cannabist, 2017, Sep.14). Fifth, consumers are required to sign up to a confidential registrar and are limited to a quantity of 40 grams per month (Room, 2014). From a public health perspective, several best-practice recommendations are incorporated into the model including a full ban on advertising and limitations on both potency and number of strains in the market. Furthermore, high THC concentrates and infused products such as edibles were not included in the initial regulations (Pardo, 2014; Room, 2014), meaning the Uruguayans had significantly fewer issues to regulate in their pre-implementation phase despite having three times as long as Coloradan regulators.

Conversely, several concerns have been noted regarding the Uruguayan model. First, in line with stated objectives for legalisation, officials aimed to set the price low ($1 per gram) to effectively compete with the black-market (Pardo, 2014). Such a low price point may raise flags from a public health perspective given the links noted above between price and consumption patterns, however, the risks may have been mitigated by defining legal cannabis as a relatively low potency, herbal preparation, which as previously described is generally regarded as a lower risk preparation. Furthermore, the low price may adversely influence the ability of the government to generate sufficient revenue to effectively regulate the market. Second, consumers may have reservations entering their details into a government database that may be leaked to employers or manipulated by future governments potentially opposed to cannabis legalisation (Rolles & Murkin, 2016). Third, quantity and product limitations in Uruguay may be too restrictive for some consumers, who could potentially seek out the black market. Fourth, it was reported that the legalisation process in Uruguay was backed by George Soros, who is a major shareholder in Monsanto, "the world's largest producer of genetically modified seeds" (Engdahl, 2014, Mar.2, p.1). As such, there is a reported concern that despite Uruguay removing the profit motive from sales of cannabis with the state monopoly approach, powerful corporate interests such as Monsanto and Bayer may have the intention of cornering the market with patented GMO seeds in a manner similar to corn and soybeans (Centre for Research on Globalization, 2018, Oct.15).

Chapter summary

This chapter has provided context to the CRCM by placing the scheme within a historical context of cannabis policy reform in the US. Furthermore, it illustrated the importance of considering the Coloradan approach within the broader cannabis policy landscape by contrasting the commercial model to potential non-commercial approaches. In addition, the CFS framework for nuanced analysis of the commercial for-profit approach was outlined with the CRCM situated within it in the middle vertical integration position. Finally, real world policies were reviewed and compared with the Coloradan approach. These issues will be considered again in the overall discussion of the book in light of the results chapters. In the next chapter the book is further funnelled down to the specific Coloradan approach to cannabis regulation.

Chapter 4: The Coloradan model of cannabis regulation

In the previous chapters, context for the study was provided by outlining the complexities associated with defining cannabis and its potential for harm and benefit, together with an overview of alternative cannabis policy models. Furthermore, the CRCM was situated within the CFS in the middle position, which added nuance on the specific nature of the commercial model incorporated by the State. This chapter provides background information relating to the history of cannabis reform in Colorado with a focus on: (i) the progression from decriminalisation to medical cannabis to the recreational market; (ii) a description of the medical cannabis foundation for the CRCM; (iii) the legalisation campaign behind A64; (iv) the formal rulemaking process in the state; (v) the Coloradan collaborative governance approach to policy implementation; and (vi) an overview of the specific detail of the CRCM as it was initially implemented. First, however, fundamental demographic and geographic information on Colorado is provided for insight into the diversity of the State and further perspective for the study.

Colorado is a diverse state

Colorado is a small to medium-sized state with varied geography and population of approximately 5.5 million people. Around half of the population live within the Greater Denver region and the majority of 4.7 million inhabitants reside within the front range urban corridor, a region in the south-east of the Rocky Mountains (Metro Denver, 2017). The State is consistently ranked among the most healthy in the US on multiple public health metrics including lowest prevalence for adult obesity, highest physical activity and fruit intake (Centers for Disease Control and Prevention, 2016a, 2016b), and life expectancy (US Health Map, 2014).

The physical landscape includes flat and arid plains, large rivers and the high peaks of the Rocky Mountains. The climate is predominantly dry with changeable temperatures - an important consideration for both cannabis farmers and regulators looking to develop cultivation standards - with warmer southern regions seemingly more suitable for outdoor cultivation while growers in cooler central and northern regions may find indoor facilities more appropriate.

Colorado incorporates low socio-economic and high crime areas through to extremely wealthy regions. For example, Pueblo County has a reported unemployment rate of 6.3% and average income per capita of US$20,000 per annum, which compares to 3.9% and $67,000 respectively in Aspen, a well-known ski resort town with a reported high density of billionaires (Aspen Journalism, 2017; Best Places, 2017). In addition, Colorado Springs, the second-largest city in the state has a large military base and the economy is heavily reliant on government contracts (Colorado Department of Military and Veterans Affairs, 2015). Consequently, different areas view cannabis legalisation through different lenses. For example, Sal Pace, the County Commissioner in Pueblo County stated that the cannabis industry bought much needed economic benefits to the region through job creation (City of Denver, 2015). In Aspen, on the other hand, the market is often considered in the context of cannabis tourism or protecting the family-friendly brand of the area. Colorado Springs had not legalised non-medical cannabis at the time of writing, although medical cannabis was approved, presumably not wanting to antagonise the federal government with their military base. This geographic and socio-economic heterogeneity is noted as a caveat to the findings of the entire book regarding the ability to make generalised conclusions about the Colorado model even within the state, let alone outside it.

History of cannabis reform in Colorado

Colorado has a long history of pioneering cannabis reforms. As noted by Kamin (2013), the state was among the first in the US to: (i) criminalise the cultivation and sale of cannabis in 1919, and possession in 1929; (ii) decriminalise possession in 1975; (iii) legalise the cultivation and possession of medical cannabis in 2000; (iv) regulate and commercialise medical cannabis in 2009/2010 (Salomonsen-Sautel et al., 2014; Schuermeyer et al., 2014; Wang et al., 2016); (v) legalise the cultivation, manufacture and sale of recreational cannabis in 2012; and (vi) implement a seed-to-sale commercial market for adult use in 2014. Table 4 below, compiled from government and media sources, lists significant events in the history of cannabis reform in Colorado to provide background and perspective on the CRCM.

Table 4: Timeline of significant events in the history of cannabis reform in Colorado

Date	Event
1876	Colorado becomes a state, hemp and cannabis legal.
1917	House Bill 263 criminalises recreational cannabis use in Colorado. "An act to declare unlawful the planting, cultivating, harvesting, drying, curing, or preparation for sale or gift of cannabis sativa, and to provide a penalty therefore".
1929	Colorado legislature makes sale, possession and distribution of cannabis a felony.
1937	Marihuana Tax Act of 1937 prohibits cannabis federally
1968	Opinion poll shows 67% of Colorado university students support marijuana legalisation.
1973	First cannabis relegalization bill in Colorado introduced intending to license growers, wholesalers and retailers. A 35% tax on (then) going rate of $15/ oz proposed. Bill failed to pass.
1975	Based on the National Commission on Marijuana and Drug Abuse Report, Colorado decriminalises cannabis possession (petty offence, $100 fine for possession of 1 oz).

1979	Dangerous Drugs Therapeutic Research Act passed in Colorado and allowed cancer patients to consume medicinal cannabis with doctor prescription. Program dependent on federal approval which did not arrive.
1986 - 2010	Colorado police make an estimated 210,000 arrests for possession of cannabis.
1998	Failed attempt to legalise medical cannabis in Colorado. Votes from ballot were not counted due to a technicality.
2000	Amendment 20 legalises unregulated medical marijuana in Colorado (becoming the only state to legalise medical cannabis in its constitution). For full details please see section 'Medical cannabis, regulation, and commercialisation in Colorado' below.
2005	Mason Tvert who oversaw A64, helped pass resolutions at Colorado University stipulating cannabis penalties be no worse than alcohol for on-campus consumers.
2006	Amendment 44 (Safer Alternatives to Recreational Enjoyment Campaign) to legalise recreational cannabis in Colorado fails, collecting only 40% of the vote.
2009	US Deputy Attorney General Ogden Memo 'The Ogden Memo' inadvertently acts as a catalyst for commercialisation of medical marijuana dispensaries in Colorado.
2010	Colorado Medical Marijuana Code established via HB10-1284. Colorado Department of Revenue oversees the issue of three license types: (i) Medical Marijuana Centres (Dispensaries); (ii) Medical Marijuana Optional Premise Cultivation Facilities; and (iii) Infused Products

	Manufacturers. These become the foundation for the first iteration of retail marijuana code (RMC) released in 2013.
2011	Several competing cannabis legalisation proposals considered in Colorado, including the campaign to legalise cannabis like alcohol (A64).
2012 Nov. 6	A64 is approved by ballot measure legalising commercial production and sale of cannabis for adult-use. A ballot initiative also passed in Washington State (not implemented until mid-2014).
2014 Jan. 1	First recreational cannabis stores open in the State. Colorado becomes the first jurisdiction worldwide to implement a fully seed-to-sale recreational cannabis market.

Sources: (Ballotpedia, 2017b; Colorado State Government, 2017; Open States, 2017; US Department of Justice, 2017; Westword, 2012a, 2012b)

Medical cannabis, regulation, and commercialisation in Colorado

While the focus of this study is on the adult-use component of legal cannabis in Colorado, some background relating to the history of medical cannabis is necessary to provide perspective to the construction of the CRCM. Thus, the following section briefly considers the introduction of medical cannabis to Colorado and the development of the regulations and commercial structure, which later informed the RMC.

It is important to note that in practical terms, the CRCM is built on, and closely related to, the medical cannabis industry of the State. Indeed, the eleven states who had legalised recreational cannabis in the US at the time of writing had first implemented a medical scheme. Kilmer and MacCoun (2017, p.2) made explicit the role of medical cannabis in "facilitating the emergence of both industrial and regulatory structures [of recreational cannabis markets], but more importantly, by enabling the psychological changes needed to destabilize the 'war on drugs' policy stasis". For example, they pointed out that medical cannabis foundations started to build an evidence base that could be used to minimise concerns about legalisation in non-medical markets and established an active and visible cannabis industry for the first time. It is this foundation, laid by the medical cannabis market in Colorado, that is now briefly addressed including the development of initial regulations and the commercialisation of the medical cannabis industry.

As shown in Table 4 above, cannabis for medicinal use in Colorado was legalised by a ballot initiative, namely, Colorado Amendment 20 (2000). The ballot measure authorised "the medical use of marijuana for persons suffering from debilitating medical conditions ... in lawful possession of a registry identification card" (Ballotpedia, 2017d). To access the medical market, patients required a doctor's recommendation to join the medical cannabis registry that issued red cards to those who were eligible. At time of writing the following conditions could qualify a patient for a doctor's recommendation: cancer, glaucoma, HIV or AIDS, cachexia, persistent muscle spasms, seizures, severe pain, and post-traumatic stress disorder (Colorado Department of Public Health and Environment, 2017b).

Aside from requiring a doctor's recommendation, the medical cannabis regulations in Colorado had three key differences to the CRCM, which relate to legal age, price, and allowed (self-grow) plant count numbers. First, medical cannabis is available to qualified patients who are 18 and older, and younger with medical exemption (compared to 21 for CRCM). Second, tax rates are lower in the medical market, which translates to lower prices. Data from 2017 indicated that average retail prices per gram of flower/bud were US$6.95 and $4.07 for recreational and medical respectively (BDS Analytics, 2017). The third relates to cultivation, and plant numbers, which were almost entirely unregulated for the first ten years of legal medical cannabis (Kamin, 2013). The emergence of regulation and the commercial structure, on which the RMC is based, are now described.

Approximately nine years after Colorado legalised medical cannabis, US Deputy Attorney General Ogden (2009) issued a memo that contained formal guidelines for federal prosecutors in states who had at that time enacted some form of legal cannabis for medical use. The

Memo reiterated that "illegal drug manufacturing and trafficking networks continues to be a core priority in the Department's efforts against narcotics and dangerous drugs" Ogden (2009, p.1). However, it also stated in part: "As a general matter, pursuit of [this priority] should not focus federal resources in your States on individuals whose actions are in clear and unambiguous compliance with existing state laws providing for the medical use of marijuana" Ogden (2009, p.2). According to a report in the Marijuana Business Daily (2016, Jul. 27), former Attorney General James Cole clarified that the Memo was intended to portray the message that genuinely sick people and their caregivers would not be a focus for prosecutors, however he stated there was a "misreading" of the intent of the document, which led entrepreneurs to feel free to grow their businesses without threat of enforcement. The period in 2009 was described by Kamin (2013, p.150): "The Wild West attitude that typified the industry during this period led to howls for reform or at least regulation of the booming marijuana industry. Women in bikinis parading on busy boulevards with sandwich boards advertising '$5 joints' and the appearance of 'medical' marijuana dispensaries with names like "Daddy Fat Sacks" and 'DrReefer.com' [were common]".

Kamin (2013) has argued that because of the 'Wild West' attitude, two competing regulatory models were debated in 2010 in the Colorado legislature that aimed, in general, to either ban the dispensaries or legalise the status quo. Heavy lobbying by enforcement, industry groups and drug treatment specialists ultimately saw the passing of House Bill 1284 (2010), a modified version that legalised the dispensaries, thereby officially creating the commercial market, by allowing for-profit sales and relatively easy access (from an outlet density perspective). Kamin (2013, p.151) stated: "In an explicit battle between law enforcement and the nascent commercial drug industry in Colorado, the industry won—the drug-dealers trounced the drug-warriors." Kamin contended in the article that there were three contributing factors that allowed this situation to occur including: (i) the economy was in the doldrums and additional revenue streams were sought by local governments; (ii) pervasive commercial vacancies added to a situation where landlords were more flexible as to whom they would allow as tenants; and (iii) hope for change to federal cannabis policy was prevalent after the election of President Obama. These medical regulations led to the Medical Marijuana Code (MMC), which formed the basis of the RMC that were initially developed in 2013.

To provide some perspective on the surge in registered medical cannabis patients at the time, Figure 3 below shows the increase in applications for medical cannabis cards in 2009/10 that coincided with the regulation and commercialisation of that market. Figure 3 reflects the legal changes described above that explicitly regulated the opening of for-profit dispensaries licensed to sell cannabis to citizens with the appropriate medical card. It seems reasonable to speculate that beyond the structural factors contributing to this surge noted above, patients may have felt more empowered to discuss the use of cannabis with doctors on the one hand, while on the other there is a suspicion that many who consumed cannabis for non-medical purposes sought to obtain medical cannabis cards from doctors by exaggerating or concocting ailments. The latter scenario seems to provide an example of what has been labelled 'the trojan horse', that is, the notion of medical cannabis being legalised as a pretence for recreational cannabis consumption (e.g. Hall & Weier, 2015; PBS Frontline, 1997-1998). The full extent to which this was the case may never be known.

Figure 3: Medical cannabis applications in Colorado 2004 – 2010

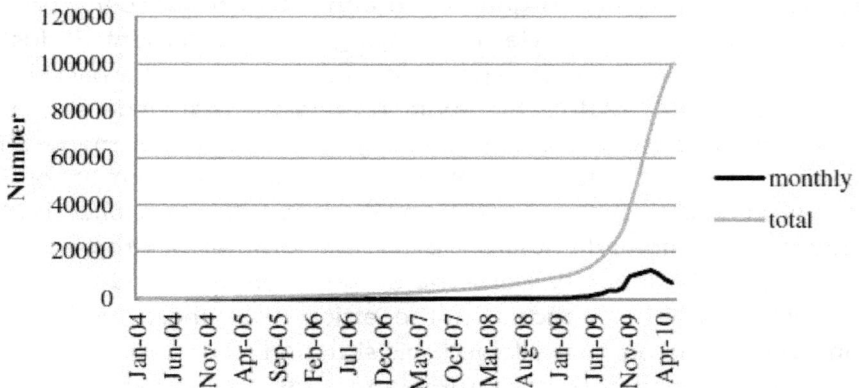

Source: Kamin (2013)

94

A64 background

Having briefly outlined the history and relevance of the Coloradan medical cannabis market to the CRCM, a description of the background to A64 itself follows. As noted by the Commission on Marihuana Drug Abuse (1972, p.146), the distinguishing feature of regulating cannabis is that it "institutionalises the availability of the drug". A64, through which the Constitution in Colorado was amended to legalise cannabis, was among the first to frame this process, and as such, it can be viewed as a historical document of central importance to the CRCM (and beyond). The Campaign to Regulate Marijuana Like Alcohol (2012, p.1) was the driving force behind A64 and self-described as "a locally-based effort being carried out by a broad and growing coalition of activists, organizations, businesses, and professionals throughout the state and across the nation".

The first notable point relating to the document is that it was an initiated constitutional amendment as opposed to legislative change. An initiated constitutional amendment is a form of direct democracy that amends a state's constitution through the ballot initiative process. 24 states in the US have a provision that allows for this (Ballotpedia, 2017e). In Colorado, there are rules that govern the process of initiating a ballot. These include gathering a required number of signatures that is calculated from votes cast at the previous election and a single subject rule among others (Ballotpedia, 2017a, 2017e, 2017f). This differs from legislative change, and its limitations for regulators may have important implications compared to, for example, a public health department designing the regulatory scheme (Caulkins et al., 2012c). The official text of ballot measure that passed on Nov. 6 2012, with 55.3% of the vote follows (Ballotpedia, 2017c, p.1):

Shall there be an amendment to the Colorado constitution concerning marijuana, and, in connection therewith, providing for the regulation of marijuana; permitting a person twenty-one years of age or older to consume or possess limited amounts of marijuana; providing for the licensing of cultivation facilities, product manufacturing facilities, testing facilities, and retail stores; permitting local governments to regulate or prohibit such facilities; requiring the general assembly to enact an excise tax to be levied upon wholesale sales of marijuana; requiring that the first $40 million in revenue raised annually by such tax be credited to the public school capital construction assistance fund; and requiring the general assembly to enact legislation governing the cultivation, processing, and sale of industrial hemp?

As shown in Table 4 above, there is a history of both successful and failed attempts of cannabis law reform in Colorado, which may have been instructive to the authors of the Amendment. Indeed, it appears that little was left to chance. For example, media reports indicated the A64 campaign "was the result of a meticulous, inch-by-inch political strategy that began in 2000 with the passage of a medical-marijuana initiative"(Denver Post, 2012, Nov. 10). In another report, it was claimed that "supporters of marijuana legalization out-planned, outspent and outfoxed marijuana opponents. They capitalized on years of groundwork to re-frame the political debate about marijuana" (Denver Post, 2012, Dec. 28).

In addition, a failed attempt at legalisation in California (Proposition 19, 2010) may have provided lessons. For example, Ethan Nadelmann, former head of Drug Policy Alliance, a national drug reform advocacy organisation that supported the legalise cannabis campaign in Colorado, stated at the International Cannabis Business Conference, that lessons from previous failed campaigns had been learned (fieldnotes, Feb 2015). These lessons included attempting to pass a ballot measure during a non-presidential election cycle, funding, and the wording of the proposed amendment (the latter two are expanded further below).

It was reported that supporters of the initiative began drafting ballot language in January 2011, with fundraising beginning shortly after (Denver Post, 2012, Dec. 28). The 62-page final draft of A64, that included arguments for and against and public comments from interested parties, seemed to indicate that the language of the document was carefully considered. One example related to use of the word tobacco in the document, which was "strongly" opposed by the A64 campaign and removed: "Tobacco use is seriously looked down upon in society and we do not think it is fair to raise the issue of tobacco use in the 'Arguments For' section, creating an association between marijuana and tobacco in the minds of voters" (Amendment 64 Final Draft, 2012, p.19).

A64 was supported (and funded in part) by several national organisations who advocate for drug reform to reduce harms from both drug use and prohibition. For example Marijuana Policy Project

(2017), with the stated mission to "change state laws to reduce ... penalties for the medical and non-medical use of marijuana", was reported to be the biggest donor, with a contribution of approximately US$1.2m (Denver Post, 2012, Oct. 20). Marijuana Policy Project claims to have played a leading role in drafting, funding and staffing the initiative. However, support from national organisations for a state election in Colorado was not without controversy. It has been noted that approximately two-thirds of the campaign funding for A64 came from out of state. The head of the opposition campaign was reported to have said: "We have seen a tidal wave of out-of-state money trying to influence the outcome of our election and seeking to use Colorado as a test case for a national pro-pot agenda" (Westword, 2012, Sep. 25). Table 5 below lists national organisations who supported the A64 campaign.

Table 5: US national organisations that supported the passing of A64

US national organisations supporting A64
Marijuana Policy Project
Drug Policy Alliance
National Organization for the Reform of Marijuana Laws
Students for Sensible Drug Policy
Law Enforcement Against Prohibition
Women's Marijuana Movement
Multidisciplinary Association of Psychedelic Studies

Source: (Campaign to Regulate Marijuana Like Alcohol, 2012)

Table 6 lists a sample of relevant ballot measures, funding and outcomes for perspective. As can be noted, both a previously failed attempt and increased funding are apparent in the successful campaigns listed below. From Table 6 it is apparent that funding in support of legalising cannabis increased significantly over the decade from 2006 – 2016. For example, the failed Ballot measure in Colorado in 2006 was outspent by a factor of 5:1 by the opposition campaigns. This compared to 2016 in California when $25 million was spent in support of the 'Yes' campaign, as opposed to only $2 million by the opposition. It is perhaps not surprising that in the former example the campaign to legalise failed while in the latter it passed. This increase in funding for the Yes campaigns may indicate that the industry is growing in influence.

Table 6: A sample of cannabis ballot initiatives, campaign funding, and outcomes 2006 – 2016

Ballot measures	Yes campaign $	No campaign $	Outcome
Colorado 2006, Amendment 44	$200k	$1m	Failed
California, 2010, Proposition 19	$4m	$300k	Failed
Colorado, 2012, Amendment 64	$3.5m	$700k	Passed
California, 2016, Amendment 64	$25m	$2m	Passed

Source: (Ballotpedia, 2017b; Denver Post, 2012, Oct. 20)

Summary of formal rulemaking process in Colorado

The formal rulemaking process in Colorado is well established and governed by the Administrative Procedure Act (Colorado Secretary of State, 2018a). The process allows for public input and includes a mechanism for swift action when necessary. According to the Colorado Center on Law and Policy (2012), the steps include: (i) an agency determines a rule is needed; (ii) notice of rulemaking hearing is filed; (iii) proposed rules are made available by agency; (iv) rulemaking public hearing is held, with all associated documents and testimony (written and oral) becoming part of public record – rules must be adopted no later 180 days after hearing; (v) review by Attorney General; (vi) review by Office of Legislative Legal Services; (vii) rule filed with Secretary of State. Figure 4 below outlines the formal process for the adoption of permanent rules according to the Administrative Procedure Act.

Figure 4: Colorado State Permanent Rulemaking Process

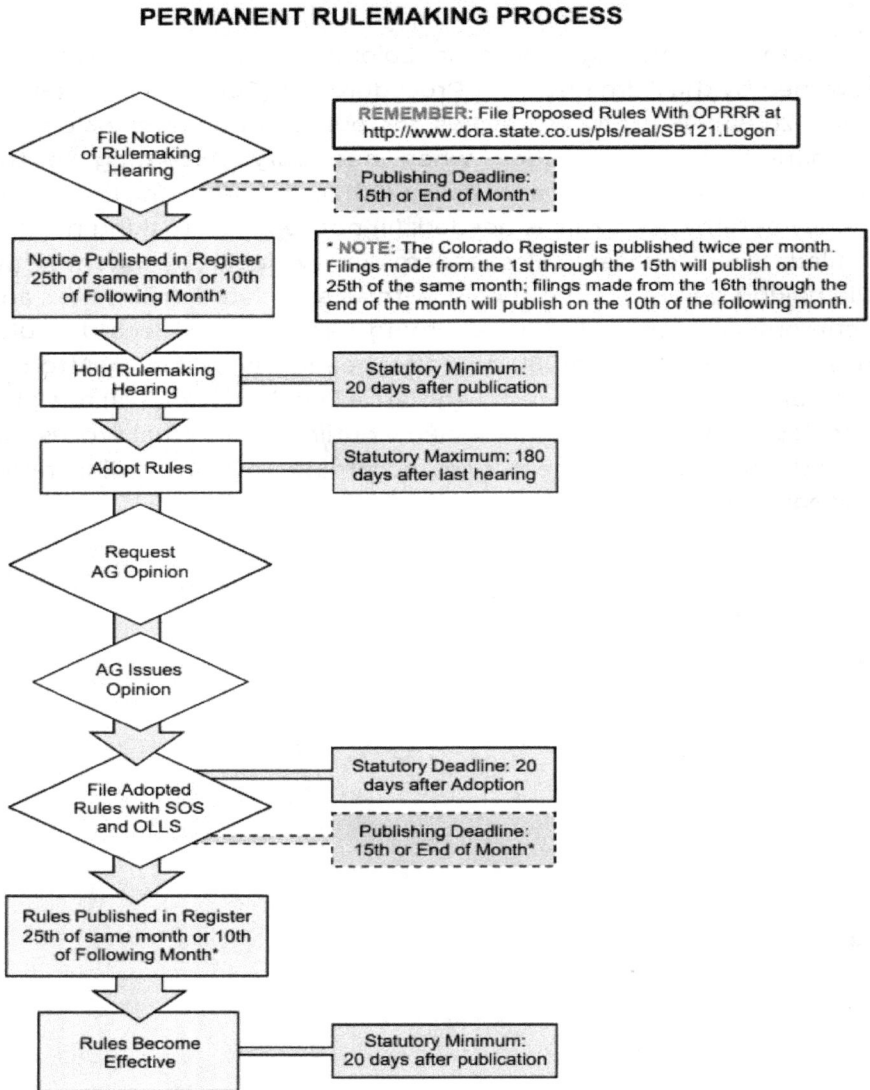

PERMANENT RULEMAKING PROCESS

File Notice of Rulemaking Hearing

REMEMBER: File Proposed Rules With OPRRR at http://www.dora.state.co.us/pls/real/SB121.Logon

Publishing Deadline: 15th or End of Month*

Notice Published in Register 25th of same month or 10th of Following Month*

* NOTE: The Colorado Register is published twice per month. Filings made from the 1st through the 15th will publish on the 25th of the same month; filings made from the 16th through the end of the month will publish on the 10th of the following month.

Hold Rulemaking Hearing

Statutory Minimum: 20 days after publication

Adopt Rules

Statutory Maximum: 180 days after last hearing

Request AG Opinion

AG Issues Opinion

File Adopted Rules with SOS and OLLS

Statutory Deadline: 20 days after Adoption

Publishing Deadline: 15th or End of Month*

Rules Published in Register 25th of same month or 10th of Following Month*

Rules Become Effective

Statutory Minimum: 20 days after publication

Source: (Colorado Secretary of State, 2018c)

In certain situations, a regulating agency may introduce an emergency, or temporary rule within the Administrative Procedure Act framework when "immediate adoption of the rule is imperatively

100

necessary to comply with state or federal law or federal regulations or for the preservation of public health, safety, or welfare" (Colorado Secretary of State, 2018a, Section 24-4-103(6a)). Emergency rules allow for timely adoption of regulations and add an important element of flexibility for cannabis regulators in Colorado, particularly given the potential for unexpected consequences of regulations in a pioneering jurisdiction. Emergency rules expire after 120 days unless it is converted to a permanent rule by following the procedures outlined above. Figure 5 below outlines the process for the adoption of emergency rules according to the Administrative Procedure Act.

Figure 5: Colorado State emergency/temporary Rulemaking Process

EMERGENCY RULEMAKING PROCESS

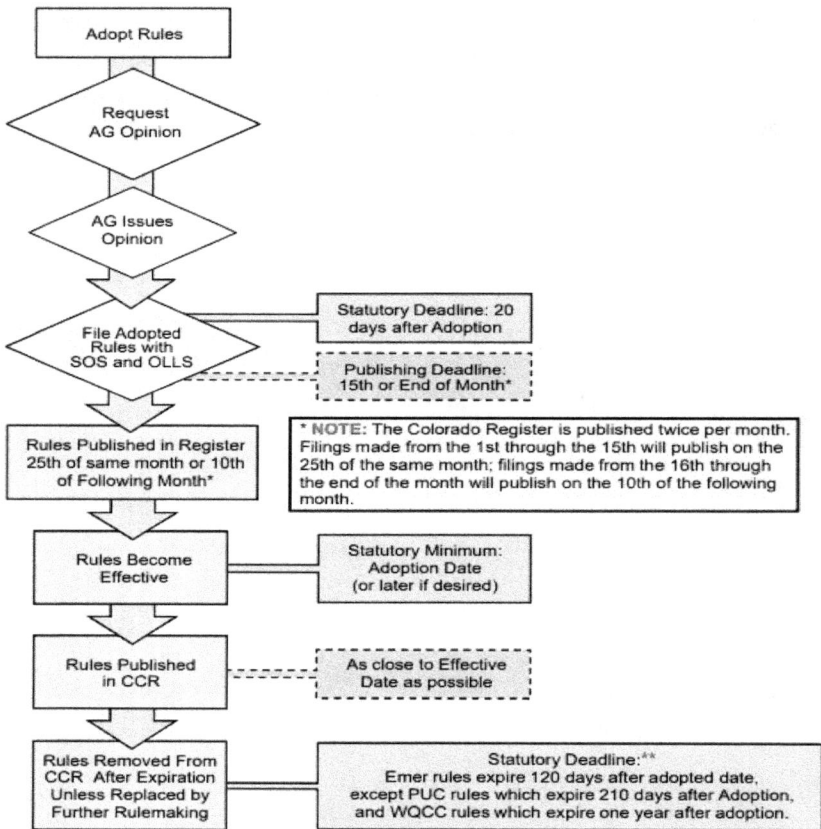

```
┌─────────────────────┐
│     Adopt Rules     │
└─────────────────────┘
          │
      ◇ Request ◇
      ◇ AG Opinion ◇
          │
      ◇ AG Issues ◇
      ◇ Opinion ◇
          │
      ◇ File Adopted ◇──────── Statutory Deadline: 20
      ◇ Rules with   ◇         days after Adoption
      ◇ SOS and OLLS ◇
                     └ - - - - Publishing Deadline:
                               15th or End of Month*
          │
┌───────────────────────────┐   * NOTE: The Colorado Register is published twice per month.
│ Rules Published in Register│   Filings made from the 1st through the 15th will publish on the
│ 25th of same month or 10th │   25th of the same month; filings made from the 16th through
│ of Following Month*        │   the end of the month will publish on the 10th of the following
└───────────────────────────┘   month.
          │
┌─────────────────────┐   Statutory Minimum:
│   Rules Become      │   Adoption Date
│   Effective         │   (or later if desired)
└─────────────────────┘
          │
┌─────────────────────┐   As close to Effective
│  Rules Published    │- -Date as possible
│  in CCR             │
└─────────────────────┘
          │
┌─────────────────────┐   Statutory Deadline:**
│ Rules Removed From  │   Emer rules expire 120 days after adopted date,
│ CCR After Expiration│   except PUC rules which expire 210 days after Adoption,
│ Unless Replaced by  │   and WQCC rules which expire one year after adoption.
│ Further Rulemaking  │
└─────────────────────┘
```

** Emergency Rules will have effect up to 120 days after the Adopted date as per 24-4-103(6) C.R.S.
Statutory authority for PUC exception (up to 210 days) per 24-4-103(6)(b) and 40-2-108(2) C.R.S.
Statutory authority for WQCC exception (up to one year) per 25-8-208 and 25-8-402(5) C.R.S.

Source: (Colorado Secretary of State, 2018b)

Colorado Department of Revenue collaborative governance process

As noted by the Colorado Center on Law and Policy (2012), government departments and agencies have a significant amount of flexibility to craft their own rulemaking process. In the CRCM, the State Licensing Authority (SLA) is the Colorado Department of Revenue (CDOR).

The process of collaboration exists within the wider context of rulemaking as specified on the State government website. This rulemaking process frames the development of all new regulations and is therefore central to developing an understanding not only of the collaborative process but also the CRCM as a whole. For clarity the process is included below in full:

Following the lead of the Governor's Amendment 64 Task Force, the Marijuana Enforcement Division (MED) has adopted a highly collaborative process to develop industry regulations. The Division initially assembles workgroups made up of stakeholders and subject matter experts to deliberate and provide direction and guidance for the proposed language with which to begin its formal rulemaking process.

Once the proposed language has been developed, the SLA issues a Notice of Formal Rulemaking and the Division begins the official rulemaking process as dictated by the Colorado Administrative Procedures Act (C.R.S. 24-4-101 et. seq.). (Colorado Department of Revenue Enforcement Division, 2017). (Colorado Department of Revenue Enforcement Division, 2017)

The initial regulations and market structure of the CRCM

The Colorado approach to cannabis legalisation has been described at various times as public health-focused, harm minimisation focused, entrepreneurial, and collaborative (Ghosh et al., 2016; Hickenlooper, 2014; Kamin, 2016). At its core, however, the CRCM is built around a commercial/free-market structure, broadly based on the commercial distribution of alcohol noted above and in the previous chapter, that incentivises licensed businesses to profit from the cultivation, manufacture, and sale of cannabis (Caulkins et al., 2015). The model is framed and limited by the statuary requirements of A64, that, for example, set deadlines regarding implementation timelines; defined cannabis in the broadest sense (as noted in Chapter 2); and bestowed significant autonomy on local jurisdictions to establish or prohibit businesses operating within its area. Additionally, federal prohibition created numerous regulatory hurdles such as limiting access to resources including the Food and Drug Administration (FDA) and the Environmental Protection Association (EPA) (Subritzky et al., 2016b). Of the 321 local jurisdictions in Colorado, 67 opted initially to allow both medical and recreational dispensaries for the initial roll out with 228 jurisdictions banning both. By 2016, 79 jurisdictions allowed both medical and retail facilities (Colorado Department of Revenue Marijuana Enforcement Division, 2014, 2017).

Considering that the CRCM has only recently been implemented, it is not surprising that nuanced analysis of the Colorado model is scarce as the literature moves from speculative modelling to describing a real-world scenario. Furthermore, as noted by the Blue Ribbon Commission on Marijuana Policy (2015, p. i), cannabis legalisation is not a single event, but rather "a process that unfolds over many years requiring sustained attention to implementation". In this sense, the RMC in Colorado can be seen as a dynamic document that is constantly evolving. However, throughout the course of writing this book, studies have been slowly emerging that provide incremental and time-specific 'snapshots' of aspects of the CRCM (e.g. Hudak, 2015b; Kleiman, 2015; Subritzky, Lenton, & Pettigrew, forthcoming; Subritzky et al., 2016b), and these are reviewed in detail in Chapter 10 as a means of assessing how the CRCM has evolved since its initial implementation. Full licensee information for medical and recreational markets, which is continuously updated, is available at the MED online portal (Colorado Department of Revenue. Enforcement Division, 2016). This section of the chapter introduces core aspects of the regulations initially implemented and lays the foundation for more nuanced analysis later in the book.

As stipulated by A64, the Colorado Department of Revenue (CDOR) was empowered as the State Licensing Authority (SLA) of the CRCM, which is controversial from a public health perspective. As noted by Caulkins et al. (2015, p.102) "One might expect ... that a liquor-control board ... might be more cognizant of ... a dependence-inducing intoxicant than would, say, a department of revenue, as in Colorado, which might be more focused on good governance that is mindful of matters of process and equitable treatment across licensees. One might also expect that neither would necessarily have as much of a proactive focus on protecting public health as a health or child-welfare agency would". Furthermore, as noted above, departments of revenue may prioritise revenue over public health outcomes (the role of the CDPHE in providing a public health framework is described below while their involvement in the regulatory process is analysed in Chapter 9 of the book).

In late 2012, a gubernatorial executive order established a task force with 30 stakeholders including lawyers, public health representatives, consumers, legislators, cannabis industry insiders, and others (Pardo, 2014). The taskforce was guided by nine principles, most notably including ensuring the safety of Colorado youth; that regulation is efficient and not unduly burdensome with the ability to respond quickly to consumer needs; and a predictable funding mechanism under the new law (Hickenlooper, 2014). Operating within the tight deadline set by A64, the Task Force made 58 recommendations relating to issues such as advertising restrictions, driving laws, monitoring public health impacts, and public safety – the majority of which eventually passed into the first temporary and permanent iterations of the RMC released in July and September 2013 respectively (Pardo, 2014). Regarding taxation, a package of measures was implemented after special voter approval including a standard sales tax (2.9%), a 'special marijuana sales tax' (10%), and an excise tax on wholesale marijuana transfers (15%) (Subritzky et al., 2016b).

According to Caulkins et al. (2015), wholesale transactions from the excise tax are in practice based on weight and were described as a de facto weight-based model. These authors explained that the weight-based approach has the disadvantage of providing an incentive to produce higher potency products. The excise tax relates to the first point of sale from the producer, so this would exclude concentrated products that are manufactured. Colorado has taken this further by incorporating an average market rate (AMR) for several products to reduce the possibility of gaming the system by vertically integrated firms (Colorado Department of Revenue, 2019a). This distinction means that the 15% excise tax relates to the AMR price as opposed to actual purchase prices of wholesale transactions. It has been argued that both price and weight revenue collection structures for cannabis are exposed to the risk of lost income in the sense that if the market price drops then government revenue will be directly impacted (Caulkins et al., 2015).

Regarding production, no limits were placed on either the quantity of cannabis that could be produced at the market level or the number of licenses that could be issued, and these were left to the free market mechanism of supply and demand (Kamin, 2015). Vertical integration was a requirement of the initial regulations, which was later removed as discussed below in Chapter 10. As has already been noted this situated the CRCM in the middle of the CFS originally, and this concept is revisited in the overall discussion of the book. Table 7 below is a simplified version from Pardo (2014) and outlines key aspects of the RMC as initially implemented.

Table 7: Key aspects and regulatory detail of the first iteration of the Colorado Retail Marijuana Code

Issue	Regulatory detail
Personal possession quantity	28.5 g (1 oz)
Home grow plant limits	6 plants, only 3 in flower/ person
Minimum age	21
Potency limits	Not specified
Residency requirements	Some for consumption (non-state residents can purchase ¼ amount of residents). Yes for licenses (minimum 2 years)

Public consumption	No "open and public" consumption.
On-site consumption in licensed distributers	Prohibited
Drugged driving standard	New 5 ng THC/ml blood *per se* DUID
Traceability	Yes, seed to sale
Taxes	15% excise tax from cultivation to processing or retail 10% excise tax on sale in addition to any existing local or state sales tax.
Background investigations	Yes, criminal background check and financial information. Fingerprinting required.
Production and distribution limits	Until October of 2014, establishments were required grow at least 70 percent of the cannabis they sell and sell no more than 30 per cent of what they grow to other outlets Producers are capped at three different levels of production: Type 1 is no more than 3600 plants; Type 2 is no more than 6000 plants; Type 3 is no more than 10,200 plants.
General restrictions and local regulations	Local municipalities can prohibit the establishment of cannabis producers, processors, and retailers. Local zoning and health ordinances can further regulate the market.

Hours of distribution	Cannot sell, serve, distribute, or initiate the transport between hours of 12-8AM Mon-Sun.
Packaging and labelling requirements	Yes: quantity, serving size, ingredients, potency.
Product warning labels of health effects	Yes
Child-resistant packaging	Required for the final sale of cannabis retail products.
Quality control and contaminant testing	Yes for retail cannabis.
Free retail samples	Prohibited to give away retail cannabis or retail cannabis products to a consumer for any reason.
Advertising and Promotion	Permitted, but restricted to avoid reaching minors under 21 for retail establishments. Signage permitted at place of business in compliance with local ordinances.
Advertising warnings	No misleading or safety claims can be made
Internet sales	Prohibited
Security systems	Required and detailed

Cannabis club	Not permitted
Medical cannabis	Yes, continuing in existence with new laws and is tax-exempt. Prorated fees when converting medical retailer to non-medical
Tax and fee distribution	First $40 M to Public School Capital Construction Assistance Fund; remainder to General Fund to later be distributed to local governments. The established cannabis Cash Fund will be used to pay for enforcement of regulations.
Sanctions and penalties for violations or noncompliance	Yes, tiered schedule that includes up to $100,000 fines and suspension and/or revocation of license.
Prevention and treatment	Yes, the law mandates that state agency will establish educational materials regarding appropriate retail cannabis use and prevention of cannabis use by those under 21.
Monitoring and evaluation	Yes, required by law for Colorado Department of Public Health and Environment to monitor health effects of law every two years starting in 2015.

Source: Pardo (2014, p.730-732)

Chapter 5: Issues in the implementation and evolution of the commercial recreational cannabis market in Colorado

Subritzky, T., Pettigrew, S., & Lenton, S. (2016). Issues in the implementation and evolution of the commercial recreational cannabis market in Colorado. International Journal of Drug Policy, 27, 1-12. http://dx.doi.org/10.1016/j.drugpo.2015.12.001

Introduction

In 2012, Colorado legalised a commercial, non-medical (recreational) marijuana market for adults via amendment 64 by ballot initiative. The State legislature set up a task force with 30 stakeholders including lawyers, public health representatives, consumers, legislators, cannabis industry insiders and others who produced 58 recommendations for the development of initial regulations (Amendment 64 Task Force, 2013; Colorado Department of Revenue and Marijuana Enforcement Division, 2013). The taskforce was guided by nine principles set out in the amendment most notably: ensuring the safety of Colorado youth; efficient regulation that is not overly burdensome; the ability to respond to consumer needs; and a predictable funding mechanism under the new law (Hickenlooper, 2014).As noted by Governor Hickenlooper (2014, p.1), "We are working as a convener for all interested parties and experts to shape public policy that utilizes the decades of public health lessons gained from regulating alcohol and tobacco". As of September 2015, recreational marijuana licenses have been granted in Colorado to 385 retail stores (dispensaries), 496 cultivators and 141 infused product manufacturers (Colorado Department of Revenue, 2015c). This paper addresses issues stemming from the resulting regulation and considers the regulatory model against the above four main principles.

Background

Existing literature has necessarily been limited to speculation and modelling the implementation and potential implications of a commercial marijuana market (Caulkins et al., 2015; MacCoun & Reuter, 2001; Rolles & Murkin, 2013; Room et al., 2010). A major concern for public health commentators has been that given the widespread use of cannabis (Kilmer & Pacula, 2009; United Nations Office on Drugs and Crime, 2014), small increases in consumption could result in large-scale increases in harm (Lenton, 2013). It has been proposed that regular and heavy cannabis consumers and the young will be particularly susceptible to any increases in cannabis availability occurring as a result of the Colorado scheme (Hall & Degenhardt, 2015). Such risks may be amplified via profit-focused models of recreational marijuana markets (Caulkins, 2014). The implementation of the Colorado model provides an opportunity to go beyond speculation to gather evidence on the real-world application of a recreational cannabis policy, thereby potentially informing policymakers and researchers about what not to do as well as being a blueprint for other schemes. While respected scholar Kleiman has reportedly described the commercial profit driven model as the second worse outcome behind prohibition (Lopez, 2014, December 17), implementation of the Colorado model has reportedly received a self-assessed "A" grade from Colorado's Director of Marijuana Coordination, Andrew Freedman. He explained that they started with no template to guide new legislation and emphasised that from the state's perspective, legislation was driven by public health concerns as opposed to tax revenues (The Cannabist, 2015b, March 27). Unfortunately, given data lag and other factors, it may take years or even decades for the full extent of the scheme's impact on consumption patterns and user initiation rates to become clear (Pacula & Sevigny, 2014). As a consequence, the majority of early insights are likely to focus on regulations and implementation as opposed to outcomes (Caulkins et al., 2015).

As the academic literature on the implementation of the Colorado scheme is only now beginning to emerge, this paper brings together material sourced from peer reviewed academic papers, grey literature publications, along with reports in mass and niche media outlets and government publications. It addresses tension between public health representatives and profit focused firms, the influence of industry and investment, the relevance of the cannabis market as a cash-based economy, politics and public opinion, changes in methods of consumption, testing (in relation to both products and consumers), the definition of the black-market, school funding, drug education programs and staff training and other issues. The remainder of this paper will address each of these in turn after describing the Colorado regulatory process.

Regulatory Process

The legal status of the Colorado CRCM is complex. Labelled "quasi-legal" by (Hawken, Caulkins, Kilmer, & Kleiman, 2013), there is variance in and crossover between international, federal, state, local and tribal jurisdictions. Federally, cannabis remains a prohibited schedule I substance that according to the Drug Enforcement Administration (DEA) (2018) has "... no currently accepted medical use and a high potential for abuse". However, the US Government appears to own a patent for using cannabinoids to treat a variety of diseases (Leaf Science, 2014, July 25). These contradictions impact directly on the Colorado market in several important ways.

The new regulations regarding marijuana policy are important from a public health perspective, with the intention to regulate the availability, supply and promotion of marijuana in order to protect the most vulnerable. The process that governs the recreational marijuana market in Colorado has been described as a "work group model" by Christian Sederberg, an attorney from the cannabis industry who was an integral member of the Amendment 64 campaign (Garcia & Manning, 2015, August 25). General legislation must first pass through the House and Senate, usually with a deadline for final implementation. Once passed, a work group is formed consisting of stakeholders representing industry (including cultivators, product manufacturers, testing facility operators and marketing professionals), public health (including representatives from Children's Hospital, a School Resource Officer and the Department of Health and Environment), law enforcement (including County Sheriff of Colorado and Association of Chiefs of Police), regulators, and so on, who collaborate via work group meetings and public hearings to fine tune the detail (House Bill 14-1366 Edibles Work Group, 2014a). The process in theory leads to a comprehensive regulation when agreement is reached, although in practise it can and has resulted in regulatory paralysis due to lack of consensus (see for example Ingold, 2014b, October 20; Ingold, 2014d, November 17; The Denver Post Editorial Board, 2014, November 22). Opposition groups contend "...promised regulation has been met by an industry that fights tooth and nail any restriction that limit its profitability" (The Gazette, 2015b, March 22).

Nor is the law uniformly implemented across the state, with local areas empowered to a considerable extent and only 67 of 321 jurisdictions opting to allow medical and recreational dispensaries (Brohl, Kammerzell, & Koski, 2015b). Cannabis businesses are subject to regulations from the Colorado Department of Revenue Marijuana Enforcement Division (2015) which stipulate comprehensive licensing criteria, inventory tracking procedures (see Metrc, 2015), a framework for testing compliance, expensive security measures such as 24 hour video on every cannabis plant, restrictions on proximity to schools, and limitations on most forms of advertising such as targeting minors (Endejan, 2015). Initial rules, which have since expired, outlined vertical integration whereby retailers were obliged to cultivate their own product, which essentially outlawed wholesale distribution (Schroyer, 2014, October 1). Since October, 2014, Colorado residents could apply for licenses as standalone wholesale growers or retail only stores with specific regulations for each market segment (Ingold, 2014c, June 30). In addition, requirements of the Colorado Department of Revenue, Department of Public Health & Environment, Fire & Safety and compliance with standard classification of child resistant packages as outlined by American Society for Testing and Materials (ASTM) must be met.

However, federal prohibition means there exist no standards for testing under frameworks established by the Food and Drug Administration (Allen, 2015, April 28). Moreover, there are currently no pesticides registered for cannabis in the US (Stone, 2014) (product testing is discussed further below). Zoning and building codes contribute additional layers of compliance. For the consumer public there are (i) age restrictions, (ii) regulations preventing public consumption and (iii) differences in quantities allowed to be purchased by locals and those from out of town. The regulatory environment, it should also be noted, is extremely dynamic and constantly evolving at state and local levels.

Predictably, the industry has protested that the regulations are too onerous. Thus the term 'regulatory tsunami' has been used by some firms to describe the processes that they claim to restrict cottage growers because of the financial burden that only larger businesses can afford (Johnson, 2015, April 23). One industry insider commented, "This industry has been regulated into absurdity, it's like you're handling nuclear material" (Gilboy, 2014, October 23). Others contend that over-regulation contributes to a larger black-market (discussed below).

Commercialism and Public Health Tension

The commercialised regulatory model of the Colorado cannabis market crystallises tension between industry profit and public health. Researchers have identified high frequency consumers and youth as most vulnerable to the negative consequences of legal cannabis (Caulkins et al., 2012a). A public health approach would aim to reduce cannabis consumption and as far as possible prevent youth from early initiation to cannabis user careers. This is at odds with a profit centric model of distribution that exists to increase sales (Caulkins, 2014). Tobacco and alcohol companies have been drawn on as examples of how "big cannabis" could potentially market products to the detriment of consumers (Room, 2014). According to Ben Cort of the Center for Addiction Recovery and Rehabilitation at the University of Colorado: "Just like Big Tobacco before it, the marijuana industry derives profits from addiction ... and its survival depends on turning a percentage of kids into lifelong customers" (The Gazette, 2015b, March 22).

Commercial entities and public health researchers square off on two main fronts: marketing and lobbying. First, marketing is a critical activity for commercial enterprises and is a key feature of this debate. Research has shown correlations between levels of cannabis consumption and both advertising (D'Amico, Miles, & Tucker, 2015), and number of outlets (Freisthler & Gruenewald, 2014; Room, 2014). A recent study in California showed greater exposure to medical marijuana advertising was associated with higher probability of use among youth (D'Amico et al., 2015). While advertising of marijuana is essentially banned in Colorado regulations, there are exceptions. These include shop front signage and websites limited to those over 21, and marketers have a tendency to find loopholes and engage in guerrilla strategies such as viral internet campaigns or ambush marketing at public events.

Several uncertainties pertain to this issue as demonstrated by recent television advertisements that were subsequently prevented from airing due to legal concerns (Labak, 2015, July 22). For example, do product reviews of different cannabis strains such as those published in The Cannabist (2015d) constitute advertisements? A recent study involving Youtube demonstrated that 34% of captured videos relating to marijuana concentrates included product reviews, promotion, and/or product recommendations (Krauss et al., 2015 , p.3). The study further found that only 20% of the videos under investigation were limited to viewers aged 18 years and over. Questions also remain as to: whether and how cannabis regulations should deal with product placement in movies or interviews; how laws will keep pace with modern technologies such as social media, website advertising, and online sales; and whether celebrity branding should be regulated more explicitly as performers such as Snoop Dog and Willie Nelson take steps to enter the industry (Kedmey, 2015, April 21). Another important question concerns how the right to commercial free speech in the US constitution will impact such matters (e.g. Edwards, 2014; Endejan, 2015).

Second, given the unique regulatory process in Colorado, industry representatives have the ability to exert influence at the work group level before regulations are finalised. In addition, lobbying power has increased within the National Cannabis Industry Association (NCIA), or "big pot" (Kleiman, 2014a) since implementation (Bentsen & Gunton, 2014, July; Caulkins, 2014; National Cannabis Industry Association (NCIA), 2014). As of August 2015, the NCIA consisted of nearly 1000 member legal cannabis businesses (Dowell, 2015, August 4). Although in dollar terms it remains well behind established lobbying groups such as those representing the alcohol industry, growth of lobbies is a concern for public health researchers (Kleiman, 2014a).

Industry and Investment

Cannabis is a profitable commodity, with estimates setting expenditure at €40 – 120 billion globally per annum (Kilmer & Pacula, 2009). The legal US marijuana market, including medical and recreational, was estimated at $2.7 billion in 2014 (Marijuana Index, 2015). Media sources reported that close to US$700 million was spent in the licensed medicinal and recreational markets in Colorado in 2014 (Wyatt, 2015d, February 10), and official statistics showed it brought in almost $70 million in state taxes and licensing fees that year (Brohl et al., 2015b). According to the Colorado Department of Revenue (2015b) , taxes on recreational cannabis include a standard sales tax of 2.9%, a 10% special marijuana sales tax and 15% excise tax on wholesale marijuana transfers. Colorado Cannabis Chamber of Commerce (CCCC) (2015) claims 18,000 direct jobs have been created to further contribute to the economy. In 2015, a venture capital firm with Bob Marley branding rights among its assets raised a record $75 million in a funding round (Shontell, 2014, December 16). Since the Securities and Exchange Commission (SEC) recently approved share registration of a marijuana dealer (Millman, 2015, January 28), Silicon Valley and Wall Street investors appear to have been increasingly active.

Many companies selling marijuana are thriving, with Medicine Man Denver (2015) estimating $12 million in revenues for 2014 (MSNBC, 2014) and Incredibles (2015) producing 40,000 infused candy bars per month (CNBC, 2015, February 26). Moreover, growing demand for supplementary services, such as cartridges for smokeless cigarette devices (vapourisers), means vast profits, with O.penVAPE (2015), for example, distributing 270,000 cartridges in one month and growing exponentially (CNBC, 2015, February 26). In terms of opportunity, cannabis testing has been identified as "the most attractive subsector of the industry", with projections indicating a billion dollar industry testing over 5000 pounds of marijuana by 2020 (Marijuana Stock News, 2015, July 16). Consulting firms have developed training and education programs that are increasingly delivered through marijuana-focused conferences and other events (e.g. International Conferences Group, 2015). In addition, new technologies such as software for tracking and tracing of marijuana plants and products have been developed to meet the new regulatory environment (see Metrc, 2015). A social media company, MassRoots (2015), has developed a self-styled Instagram for cannabis app and recently applied for a Nasdaq listing. With a growing base of 500,000 users currently, the app has been described as a mobilising force for the 2016 elections (CNN Money, 2015a, August 31). Moreover, a host of other industries have emerged around the Colorado CRCM including data mining, security, electrical lighting, law firms, specialist transportation and delivery services such as the recently launched "Uber for weed" as detailed by Mann (2015, April 6). It was claimed that a minimum of $1 million is required to establish a competitive retail marijuana dispensary in Colorado (MSNBC, 2014).

While some have compiled fortunes in quick time, others have lost their investments. Fifty-five marijuana focused companies were publicly traded in the US (Bloomberg, 2015, April 15), with a reported $23 billion lost by naive investors in cannabis penny stock "pump and dump" schemes (Pearson, 2015, February 26). Cautious regulating that requires 24 hour surveillance on every cannabis plant also appears to benefit larger corporations due to considerable set-up costs (Johnson, 2015, April 23). Indeed, long-term advocates such as NORML have pointed out that marijuana legalisation movements appear to be 'losing their innocence' as enterprises focus on profit maximisation (Stroup, 2015, March 16).

A Cash Business

Marijuana transactions have traditionally taken place on a cash-only basis and this aspect is yet to evolve in legalised markets. Banking is an issue that illustrates the operational difficulties of the contradictions between federal and state law in the US. Federally licensed banks have no mandate to take on clients in the cannabis industry. Industry press reported that in 2014, 1292 relationships were terminated by banks who apparently feared accusations of association with money launderers (Olson, 2015, April 27). Despite Colorado senators calling for legislation that ensures access for legal marijuana businesses to basic banking services (Mendoza, 2015, July 9), as recently as August, 2015, an application for a Colorado credit union to join the nation's centralised banking system was denied (Popper, 2015, July 30). In response, a lawsuit has been filed against the Federal Reserve stating the ruling is "anti-competitive [and] ... detrimental to public safety" (CNN, 2015, Jul. 31, July 31). USA Today (2015, Jul. 31, July 31) has observed that, as a result, most marijuana-related businesses in Colorado must operate on a cash only basis and bear the high cost of handling and safeguarding this cash themselves with "the public at risk in having hundreds of millions of dollars of cash flowing about the streets of Colorado". In addition it has been noted that armed guards are required to "escort marijuana business owners when they arrive to pay ... taxes" at the Colorado Department of Revenue (USA Today, 2015, Jul. 31, July 31). Governor

Hickenlooper has reportedly vowed to continue pushing the federal Government for a resolution (CNN Money, 2015b, July 31)

As such, the cannabis lobby, NCIA, is attempting to address the issue by expanding efforts federally. NCIA Deputy Director West reportedly stated "(n)ow is a good time for us to step up to yet another level by expanding that lobbying team…" (Dowell, 2015, August 4). Additionally, Section 280E of the federal tax law prevents cannabis producers, processors and retailers (officially drug traffickers) from deducting business expenses from gross profit (Bentsen & Gunton, 2014, July; Canna Law Blog, 2015, January 30), which is problematic for anyone running a cannabis business. Thus there is a higher likelihood of undeclared transactions in this sector and an accompanying loss of tax revenues for the state (see discussion on black-market below).

Politics and Public Opinion

For at least 2 years surveys have shown that the majority of people in the US favour cannabis legalisation (Galston & Dionne, 2013; Motel, 2015, April 14). Public opinion plays a crucial role in the political process (Lenton, 2004), and politicians and law makers now see cannabis as an issue that must be addressed in election campaigns. Most notably the issue has a clear role in the 2016 presidential election (Hudak, 2015a, March 22). For example, it is claimed that potential Presidential Candidate Chris Christie, who calls state revenue from cannabis "blood money", would clamp down on states operating CRCM (Wood, 2015, March 27). Conversely, Hillary Clinton announced a 'wait and see approach', while "I wasn't a choir boy" Republican Rand Paul is a co-sponsor of a federal CARERS bill aimed at legitimising medical marijuana (Associated Press, 2014, December 6; Kroll, 2015, March 11). Paul recently became the first presidential candidate of a major party to accept campaign funds from the legal marijuana industry, with a $5000 contribution from NCIA's Political Action Committee being one of several donations made at a private fundraiser in Denver. In line with traditional Republican philosophy, Paul has been reported as believing the federal government should stay out of state matters (The Cannabist, 2015c, July 1). Moreover, other candidates such as Jeb Bush and Donald Trump have been forced to state a position publicly on the issue. In contrast, Kleiman (2014a) has observed that "letting legalisation unfold state by state, with the federal government a mostly helpless bystander, risks creating a monstrosity."

Although some polls indicate marijuana legalisation is popular among voters, other data indicate that marijuana *consumers* are viewed less than favourably (e.g.Hatalsky, Trumble, & Diggles, 2014, December 8; Stroup, 2015, March 16) suggesting stigma remains towards this group. Industry representatives are taking steps to reduce this stigma. For example, the replacement of industry icon Tommy Chong (of "Cheech and Chong" fame) by the NCIA seems to be an attempt to strengthen legitimacy via "dehippification" (the authors' term) as "the cannabis industry wants to move past the stoner stereotypes ... to remake itself as a ... respectable segment of the economy" (Burges, 2015, March 31).

Methods of Consumption

The way cannabis is consumed is evolving. The traditional method of smoking via joints, pipes or bongs is being replaced by eating, using a vapouriser for smokeless inhalation or "dabbing" a concentrated form of the flower material. Outcomes including levels of intoxication and long-term health issues such as lung disease and dependency can vary according to how marijuana is consumed.

Edibles

The surprising popularity of marijuana infused products (MIPs), commonly known as edibles, is an issue that has underpinned the regulatory evolution of medical and recreational cannabis in Colorado. Official data indicates approximately 5 million units of edible products were sold in Colorado in 2014, with just over half in the recreational market (Brohl et al., 2015b). MacCoun and Mello (2015) note that the packaging of edibles that appears similar to that of non-infused snacks, has the potential to confuse children. Kleiman has reportedly stated that once regulated correctly, edibles may be the healthiest method to imbibe marijuana (Lopez, 2014, December 17), although the variably delayed impact and level of intoxication after ingestion has the potential for harmful, or at least unpredictable, outcomes. Dr Alan Shackelford, a Denver medical marijuana doctor, stated in an interview: "When marijuana is ingested, the absorption rate is much slower and subject to many variables. The onset of effect is slower, the peak is achieved much more slowly and the effect typically lasts much longer" (Baca, 2014b, December 4). This variability is not helped by the manufacturing process that can involve traditional baking techniques or simply spraying concentrated extracts of marijuana onto normal non-intoxicating candy.

Since the implementation of recreational marijuana reform, there have been reports in the Colorado media of two suicides and one murder claimed to be related directly or indirectly to edibles (Gorski, 2014, July 1). According to statistics reportedly presented by Children's Hospital Colorado, unintentional ingestions of marijuana remain low in comparison to presentations for consumption of other toxic items (McDonough, 2015, March 30) However, Michael DiStefano, medical director of the hospital, was reported to have said hospital admissions doubled for accidental ingestion of cannabis to nine cases in the first six months of 2014 (Ingold, 2014a, May 21). The issue received further attention after an influential New York Times article detailed an uncomfortable experience with a marijuana-infused chocolate bar based on a personal account (Dowd, 2014, June 3).

A response to the potential dangers of consumption has been relatively swift from both advocacy groups and regulators. Public education programs were launched by advocacy groups (Council on Responsible Cannabis Regulation, 2014; First Time 5, 2014; Marijuana Policy Project, 2014).

On the regulatory side, the stated aim of the Marijuana Enforcement Division (MED) is to enact processes and regulatory procedures to provide full transparency in its regulation. In regards to edible marijuana products, two separate bills passed the House and Senate in 2014 (House Bill 14-1366 Edibles Work Group, 2014b; Marijuana Enforcement Division, 2014b). Stakeholder work groups with representatives from industry, enforcement, Smart Colorado, and public health were established (Brohl et al., 2015b). The result has been changes to compliance laws regarding packaging, labelling and potency restrictions that require edibles to be either wrapped individually or clearly marked increments containing a maximum of 10 milligrams of tetrahydrocannabinol (THC) (Baca, 2015e, January 29). Governor Hickenlooper reportedly stated that the bills "are critical to our ongoing goal of making Colorado the healthiest state in the nation and our constant goal of protecting children" (Ingold, 2014a, May 21).

An additional issue is the disparity identified between product labelling and actual THC content that has been blamed on the quality of both manufacturing techniques and testing procedures (Baca, 2014a, March 9). There is, however, apparent evidence of improvement in product compliance with follow up tests by Steep Hill Labs in 2015 reporting a higher degree of reliability between reported and actual THC levels in marijuana edibles, although there remains room to improve (Baca, 2015c, April 12). Similarly, there appears to be room for improvement in the regulatory landscape of Colorado's CRCM generally. In 2015, draft regulations were tabled by regulators recommending edible marijuana be marked with a stop sign shape while use of the word "candy" was also under review (Wyatt, 2015b, August 11). However, manufacturing firms argued that claiming using a symbol that is akin to putting "a skull and cross bones on items" resulted in a watering down of the symbol to a THC symbol which is due for consideration before a public hearing (The Denver Post Editorial Board, 2015, August 22). The new rules must be finalised and implemented in early 2016.

Dabbing

Technological advancements in extraction techniques and a wider selection of concentrates have increased the popularity of dabbing (Chambers, 2013, October 28): "Dabbing is the inhalation of a concentrated THC product [commonly] created through butane extraction" (Stogner & Miller, 2015). More precisely, concentrated forms of cannabis are inhaled through an "oil rig", a type of specialised pipe, that vapourises the product on a hot surface known as the "nail", which is usually made of titanium, quartz or ceramic (Kleiman, 2015; Prichard, 2015a, June 19). The consumer heats the concentrate with a blow torch, although the correct temperature is contested among aficionados, with debate generally centering on flavour maximisation and the reduction of toxin intake: This process has been described in detail by Coffey (2015, August 3).

While sales percentages and market share of concentrates are not publicly available in Colorado (as the authors were informed via email by the Marijuana Enforcement & Taxation Department of Revenue), it appears they account for a substantial though smaller segment of the market behind traditional flower and edible options. In an attempt to map consumer activity, one study drew on a sample frame of 125,000 tweets with available geolocation data. After adjusting for general Twitter use, Daniulaityte et al. (2015) showed that "dab"-related terms were significantly more prominent in Oregon, Colorado and Washington where recreational and medical marijuana have been legalised. Another study looking at Youtube as a potential learning resource for dabbing found high rates of representation (8%) from Colorado channels publishing related videos (Krauss et al., 2015).

In terms of extraction, there is a range of procedures which vary in complexity. To extract Butane Hash Oil (BHO), referred to variously as nectar, moon rock, honeycomb, wax, shatter, crumble, oil or errl, butane is pressurised in a vessel and the plant material is washed over. Additional forms of concentrated THC derive from extraction procedures known as Kief, Water hash, CO2 oil and Rosin (Prichard, 2015b, June 19). The process of BHO extraction, or "blasting", is extremely volatile due to the flammable nature of butane and has been identified as the cause of a number of high-profile home explosions. In Colorado, where more than 30 butane explosions were linked to amateur concentrate manufacturing in 2014, new regulations went into effect on July 1, 2015 outlawing home extraction by non-licensed manufacturers (Moreno, 2015, June 30). It is now a requirement that licensed manufacturers in Colorado purchase specialised equipment such as vacuum ovens and comply with normal fire and safety conventions around dangerous goods (see House Bill 15-1305 Unlawful Manufacture Marijuana Concentrate (CO), 2015). However, given the higher cost of concentrated marijuana in Colorado dispensaries, estimated at $700 per ounce compared to $200 per ounce for standard flower material, and the believed ease of extraction, home manufacture of concentrates is predicted to remain popular (Bell et al., 2015).

While media reports suggest dabbing is riskier than smoking marijuana (see for example Montemayor, 2015, March 26), a recent study involving 357 participants found that using 'dabs' was no more problematic than using herbal cannabis, however participants self-reported a higher tolerance and withdrawal, suggesting a higher dependence potential for dabbing (Loflin & Earleywine, 2014). The same study noted informal claims of THC percentages between 70 – 90%. This potency is specifically linked to BHO extraction, which produces the strongest concentrate on the market today. As a counterpoint, kief extraction, for example, produces a concentrate with THC in the 20 – 60% range (Prichard, 2015b, June 19). The risk of products with higher THC percentages is dependent on a number of variables, not least of which is the ability of the user to titrate the dosage. Discomfort can be experienced from "dabbing" too much too quickly (Prichard, 2015c, June 19). Evidence remains limited regarding potential health benefits of consuming lower quantities of more potent forms of cannabis (Hall & Fischer, 2010). Conversely, a recent study has suggested links between daily use of higher potency cannabis with low cannabidiol (CBD) ratios and schizophrenia (Di Forti et al., 2015). Furthermore, imagery of blow torches and media headlines that present dabbing as the "crack of cannabis" (Dunt, 2015, September 1) have some industry insiders concerned about the image being presented at a time when public support for the scheme is extremely vulnerable to any indication of increasing harm. Whether out of concern or interest, mass media stories certainly provide exposure given that Google searches for the term "dabbing" spiked immediately after the above mentioned article, although searches on the topic have been generally increasing sharply since 2013 (Google Trends, 2015). The issue of dabbing remains an important consideration for future research. Caulkins et al. (2015) contended that tax models may be an area where the question of concentrates could be addressed, perhaps in a manner similar to the comparative taxes applied to beer versus whiskey.

Vapourisation

This is a process where cannabis is heated to allow transmission of cannabinoids without combustion (Gieringer, 2001). As noted above, the manufacturing of vapourisers as a cannabis delivery mechanism is a growing industry in Colorado and nationally, providing consumers with the ability to consume both flower material and concentrates in a more discrete odourless form (Drug Enforcement Administration (DEA), 2017). This is an important consideration in Colorado where public consumption of cannabis remains outlawed as mentioned previously.

Recently popularised by the e-cigarette movement, another perceived advantage of 'vaping' is the potential for harm reduction as the method is designed to "deliver inhaled THC content without carcinogens and toxicants" (Hall & Fischer, 2010, p.241). Many carcinogens present in smoke are related to toxic by-products of the combustion process rather than cannabinoids inherent in the plant. Hall and Fischer (2010) identified a number of studies that indicated a reduced health risk when utilising vapourisers as a cannabis delivery system. Temperature, again, has been mentioned as an important consideration in reducing negative health impacts because different cannabinoids have different boiling points. Insufficient heat does not boil off the pharmacologically active cannabis terpenoids, while extreme temperatures cause combustion and associated carcinogens (Quora, 2013). In contrast, a link has been identified between residual nitrogen and unsafe levels of ammonia in marijuana vapour, so it is recommended to ensure a "clean" plant product that has been "flushed" of residues, something that is done in the final growing stage, before harvest to further reduce respiratory risk (Quora, 2013). Quality testing that aims to identify pathogenic microbes and moulds in cannabis in the Colorado scheme (such as outlined by Daley, Lampach, and Sguerra (2013)) may reduce some, but not all, harmful outcomes associated with vapourised marijuana consumption (see below for a more detailed discussion regarding testing protocols in Colorado).

Testing

Marijuana testing is a complicated process both in terms of scientific methodology and within complex and confusing intersecting frameworks of federal and state laws. In essence, there are two broad areas of relevance to testing: product quality and consumer testing.

Product testing

Firstly, a central component of a legalised marijuana market is the ability to provide customers with a safe, consistent and pure product (Kilmer, 2014). Quality product testing should ensure safety in regards to (i) purity, for example identification of harmful pesticides, moulds and other residuals, and (ii) potency relating to both THC percentages and THC to CBD ratios (Kilmer, 2014). Under the Colorado scheme, mandatory testing for potency began in May 2014, followed by testing for consistency in July 2014 (Marijuana Enforcement Division, 2014a; Rappold, 2015, March 24). However, it has been claimed that the Colorado testing landscape remains immature and displays a number of limitations including: non standardised lab testing, which has led to a wide disparity of results (Allen, 2015, April 28; Green, 2015, March 28; Wyatt, 2015a, March 26); lack of access to testing, particularly from medical caregivers (Kammerzell, 2015); and insufficient testers to deal with the volume of requests (Kammerzell, 2015). As such, the presence of fungus and residues remains problematic in Colorado marijuana (Rappold, 2015, March 24). To date, 16 facilities have been granted general testing licenses in Colorado for recreational marijuana, some of which have further achieved provisional certifications to test for potency/ homogeneity, residual solvents contamination and microbial contamination (Colorado Department of Revenue, 2015c).

Further, as (Stone, 2014) has noted, an emerging concern is how to address pesticide use and abuse in CRCMs. Federal prohibition excludes cannabis specific pesticides from registration within the existing robust regulatory framework of the Environmental Protection Association (EPA) that approves hundreds of agricultural commodities as safe for human consumption and offers guidelines for maximum residue level (MRL) (Daley et al., 2013). Although no pesticides or fungicides have been approved for use on cannabis federally, the Colorado Department of Agriculture (CDA) (2015) lists several criteria and guidelines for compliance that must be followed according to state law. Media reports suggest such concerns led to over 60,000 cannabis plants being quarantined at 11 grow facilities (Hughes, 2015, April 30). Colorado is slowly beginning to enforce the regulatory requirements for pesticide testing of recreational and medical marijuana. In September 2015, Denver officials expanded pesticide inspections to ensure only pesticides allowed by the CDA are used on products (Baca, 2015f, September 7). However, as of September 2015, Gobi Analytical (2015) remained the only lab certified to test for pesticides (Migoya & Baca, 2015, September 7).

Testing consumers for intoxication

Second is the issue of drug testing consumers, which relates specifically to driving under influence (DUI) and employment law. Current methods of testing impaired drivers involve blood or saliva testing and have been noted to lack accuracy in measuring real time levels of intoxication. Traces of fat soluble THC can remain in the body for days to weeks after consumption, which is problematic for DUI testing because a positive test can be triggered despite no current impairment (Wood et al., 2015). In an extreme case in July 2015, a driver with THC levels in the blood 4 times the legal limit was found not guilty (Roberts, 2015, July 22). Studies have shown breath testing for cannabis may offer a viable alternative (e.g. Himes et al., 2013). As such, a number of companies are trying to develop new reliable technology for testing levels on intoxication (see for example Caba, 2014; Cannabix Technologies Inc., 2015; Emerging Growth LLC, 2014; Equities Canada, 2014).

The principal concerns with employment law and marijuana involve testing and contract termination (Klein, 2015). A recent high profile case in the Colorado Supreme Court demonstrated the sensitive nature of this complex matter after ruling a quadriplegic person with a medical marijuana card who consumed off duty to control leg spasms was fired legally after cannabis was identified during a random drug test (Millican, 2015, June 17; Wallace, 2015, June 15). In Colorado, employers have the ability to craft their own policies where surveys indicate that employment levels are having an impact on the rigour of implemented workplace drug testing policy. For example, in early 2014 many firms increased drug testing while a year later, as unemployment rates dropped below 5% and competition increased for identifying skilled labour, a number of companies began omitting THC from a pre-employment drug screen, particularly in the hospitality industry (Wallace, 2015, June 15). An important consideration of good drug testing regimes includes situational clarity, such as determining whether tests will be administered pre-employment, randomly or upon reasonable suspicion of impairment. In addition, employers need to outline types of tests, provide notice, assure confidentiality and uniformity of enforcement and so on (Klein, 2015; Phillips et al., 2015). As the legal marijuana market in Colorado matures, of interest will be the extent to which, if at all, the synthetic cannabis market develops as a potential mechanism to bypass workplace testing.

Defining the Black-market

In an excellent summation of possibilities associated with legalised cannabis markets, Caulkins et al. (2015) described how specific choices by policy makers may determine the extent to which legal marijuana replaces the black-market. Under this framework, price is seen as a major factor contributing to black-market activity encouraged by excessively high taxation, expensive regulatory compliance, variation between medical and recreational costs and lack of ability to deduct legitimate business expenses as outlined above.

Cross-border transactions, such as a recent attempt to fly out 200 pounds of marijuana flower to Kansas (Rizzo, 2015, July 22) or $12 million of medical grade product to Minnesota (Turtinen, 2015, March 26) are clearly black-market activities. However, it is becoming apparent in Colorado that as the regulatory framework evolves, there are definitional challenges regarding what constitutes a black-market, particularly regarding caregiver quotas that until recently were legal although unregulated. For example, do the black-market merchants now consist simply of unlicensed or unregulated growers and distributors selling a no longer illicit product that is untaxed? In Colorado it is legal for anyone over 21 to grow up to 6 plants each in any normal household (Colorado Department of Revenue and Marijuana Enforcement Division, 2013), although regulations are being considered by many jurisdictions at the local level to reduce this limit (Phillips, 2015, July 25).

The matter is further complicated by rules specific to the medical market that were implemented before the legalisation of recreational cannabis. These rules provided a loophole for unregulated cultivators to grow significant sized crops for the sake of medical marijuana patients without obtaining a license (Schrader, 2015, April 14). The establishment of "grow ops" meant thousands of plants were often cultivated legally in single locations creating safety concerns such as overloaded electrical systems, hazardous lighting and chemical use (Watts, 2015, March 10). The recreational marijuana industry complained that such grow operations invited back black-market elements as caregivers were not obliged to comply with residential requirements, background checks or "seed to sale" tracking. To address this, new regulations were passed into law in May 2015 that limited licensed caregivers to 99 plants. According to a sponsor of the bill, the regulation aimed to ensure that caregivers were included within the regulatory system (Wyatt, 2015c, May 18). This has been modified further at the level of local councils, with Denver, for example, imposing limits of 36 plants in one location (Watts, 2015, March 10). Presumably it is also in the industry's interest to limit the capacity for users to grow their own marijuana.

Additionally, long-time marijuana dealers harbour some resentment to being shut out of the legal industry. As one grower/dealer has been quoted as saying "It's kind of like we made all the sacrifices and they packed it up and are making all the money" (Griego, 2014, July 30).

From this perspective, taxation is seen as a blunt instrument forcing the most socioeconomically vulnerable back to the black-market. Yet another consideration is to what extent black-market dealers can translate their skills into the modern industry. "There's no denying that if you've surreptitiously evaded the cops, maintained customer loyalty and kept your business afloat ...you know...something about growing and selling pot effectively" (Hesse, 2015, February 11). In late 2014, it was estimated that 40% of all marijuana transactions in Colorado were undertaken among black and grey segments of the marijuana economy (Bard, 2014, September 3). It remains unclear to what extent black-market dealers have an opportunity to be registered as licensed industry professionals.

School Funding, Drug Education Programs and Staff Training

In specific regard to schools, under the Colorado model a 15% excise tax is earmarked for "Public School Capital Construction Assistance Fund Transfer" (Cannabis Public Media, 2015, August 18) for new school buildings. In the first 5 months of 2015, $13.6 million was reported to have been collected via this tax (Baca, 2015b, July 13). As of August 2015, 26 projects were funded across Colorado, and competition among schools for construction funding is said to be fierce (Kelley, 2015, August 31).

How drug education is handled is another important component of the Colorado legalization reform. Tax revenue is being allocated not only to upgrade schools generally, but also towards specific drug education and treatment programs. In Colorado Springs, for example, $2.28 million was allocated to three school districts in 2015 for behavioural health counselling and drug prevention education (Kelley, 2015, August 31). To date, the Colorado Department of Public Health and Environment (2015b) has released three public awareness campaigns, including one for the general public and the others aimed at youth education (see also Don't Be a Lab Rat, 2015; Protect What's Next, 2015). It has been noted that health industry workers such as nurses may require more training (Scriber, 2014), and a range stakeholders from law enforcement to accounting firms will be hoping for increased funding in future for additional training relating the marijuana industry.

Additional Issues

A number of other issues are relevant and require more research. Firstly, price is seen as a critical element and has been described in detail elsewhere If prices are too high, black-market activity may expand, while extremely low-cost marijuana is predicted to increase consumption rates among the most vulnerable (i.e. youth and dependent users) (Kleiman, 2015). Secondly, the relationship between medical and recreational markets is complex and evolving. Medical marijuana has long been viewed as a "Trojan horse" for full recreational markets (Hall & Weier, 2015; PBS Frontline, 1997-1998). However, powerful narratives used by advocates such as Gupta (2013, August 9) contribute significantly to the discussion, and the issue remains vigorously contested with emotion and anecdotes often substituting for lack of evidence. While an increasing amount of research into medical benefits of marijuana is being funded (e.g. D'Souza & Ranganathan, 2015), there remain significant hurdles to this research largely due to federal prohibition as outlined above.

Further issues include but are not limited to: "cannabis migration" by high frequency recreational users (e.g. CannabisRehab.org, 2015) and parents accessing marijuana as a medicine for their children (Pickert, 2015, July 30); environmental concerns relating to large scale cultivation (Warren, 2014); tourism, in particular revenue spikes in the Colorado high seasons (Baca, 2015a, August 13); how the public consumption of marijuana is regulated (e.g. Baca, 2015d, June 17; Murray, 2015, August 10); and gender in terms of both equal representation in the industry (Mitchell, 2015, March 3; The Cannabist, 2015e, June 9) and consumption patterns (Ingold, 2011, March 13). Furthermore, unexpected consequences such as increases in Colorado house prices require further research attention (CNN Money, 2015c, June 4).

Conclusions

Colorado implemented legislation that legalises marijuana for recreational purposes for those over the age of 21 almost two years ago. It would seem an appropriate time to attempt to describe some of the issues that have emerged during its operation. From the perspectives of both regulators and public health representatives, the legislation is intended to create an environment that minimises harm relating to consumption of marijuana. At this early stage, the model appears functional and seems to be evolving slowly in response to issues that have arisen. The regulatory process is reasonably transparent, has the ability to respond to issues as they arise, and there is equal access for a range of stakeholders including industry representatives and public health professionals to contribute to the final make up of regulations. Whether profit motivated companies should be granted full accessibility to the regulatory process before laws are even passed remains contentious. As yet, no drastic increases in harm have been noted as a consequence of the scheme. A funding mechanism has been implemented that provides funds for school construction projects, drug education and treatment programs and the creation and development of product testing infrastructure.

However, the scheme faces major challenges, of which the most notable appear to be federal prohibition which limits access to relevant national infrastructure, the growing influence of the cannabis industry that may seek to exploit loopholes in advertising restrictions, and immature testing regimes which can not yet cope with demand, thereby limiting the effectiveness of the regulation to provide a safe product for consumers.

One of the core principles guiding the new legislation was the protection of youth. This has been attempted with regulations that impose restrictions on the age of consumption and advertising of products. Further emphasis has been placed on youth education programs. To date, two public education programs aimed at teens, "Don't be a lab rat" and "Protect the future", have been released by the state. However, the uncertainty surrounding advertising loopholes that may permit youth targeting continues to be a cause for significant concern. How successful the regulations will be in terms of limiting user uptake in this important group remains unknown.

Beyond protecting youth, the harm-reduction approach of ensuring product is safe for human consumption is hindered by federal prohibition that prevents access to national testing infrastructure such as the FDA and EPA. This, in turn, has an impact on the stated aim of being able to respond to consumer needs in a timely fashion. The purity of Colorado marijuana has yet to reach levels promoted in the legislation, with a number of reports detailing unsafe levels of moulds, non-approved pesticides and other contaminants in products. While regulations have been passed that outline compliance requirements for testing of potency and purity, it has taken more than a year to start seeing some levels of enforcement to support that implementation. It is notable that testing facilities appear unable to cope with demand, creating significant delays. However, progress is being made in this area, despite only one lab currently being certified to test for pesticide residues in marijuana products.

A further aim of the regulations was legislation that was not unduly burdensome. The achievement of this appears questionable at this early stage. Furthermore the speed of regulatory evolution in response to changing consumer patterns such as dabbing appears to be hindered by lack of agreement between numerous stakeholders, although some progress has been made as the edibles legislation shows. How this regulation deals with a landscape that is changing the dynamic of the black-market will be fascinating to see.

To ensure product safety from the outset, policy makers need to be mindful of limitations of infrastructure before implementing policy that legalises marijuana. Furthermore, the proliferation and popularity of edibles may be an unintended consequence on bans of public consumption in the Colorado model. Finally, the model would look quite different without federal prohibition and this component remains problematic in assessing the Colorado model. Federal alignment does not appear to be a priority to 2016 Presidential candidates.

Chapter 6: Into the void: regulating pesticide use in Colorado's commercial cannabis markets

Subritzky, T., Pettigrew, S., & Lenton, S. (2017). Into the void: Regulating pesticide use in Colorado's commercial cannabis markets. International Journal of Drug Policy, 42(4), 86-96.

Introduction and background

In 2014, Colorado became the first jurisdiction internationally to legalise non-medical (recreational) cannabis for adults from "seed to sale". Standards for regulating cannabis plant cultivation appear not to have been addressed in the medicinal markets emerging in the US before 2010 (see e.g. Law Atlas, 2016). This can be linked to the memo of former Deputy Attorney General David Ogden (Ogden, 2009), that clarified the prosecuting of patients with serious illnesses or their caregivers in compliance with state laws on medical marijuana, will not be a priority for federal resources (Stout & Moore, 2009, October 19). As such, the Colorado State Government was among the first authorities to tackle the issue. The initial 2013 Task Force Report on the Implementation of Amendment 64 (A64) raised concerns about pesticide contamination noting there existed "no standards of practice for ensuring product safety in the marijuana industry" (Amendment 64 Task Force, 2013, p.66). A key objective of regulating cannabis is ensuring retail products are as safe as possible for consumption (Pacula et al., 2014). In the pre-legalisation black-market there were no applicable standards in place to test product quality and there have been numerous claims of nefarious cultivating practices (see e.g. DeAngelo, 2015; McLaren et al., 2008; Voelker & Holmes, 2015) to combat the threat of pest infestation (Cervantes, 2006). Danko (2010, p.49) has contended "... growers sometimes find themselves quite overwhelmed by pest issues [and] many more resort to nuclear tactics than are willing to admit it".

Reflecting this lack of legislative framework, the literature on policy regulation templates for pesticide use on cannabis is thin, although recently Feldman (2014-15) has provided an overview of pesticide laws in states with legalised cannabis production as at 2014. Furthermore, the US federal prohibition on cannabis has meant that guidance from the US Food and Drug Administration (FDA) and the Environmental Protection Association (EPA) is legally unavailable. (US Environmental Protection Agency, 2016b; US Food and Drug Administration, 2016). Indeed, no pesticide is currently registered in the US specifically for cannabis (Stone, 2014; Thomas & ElSohly, 2016). To begin to address this void, Kilmer (2014) noted that regulators need to consider purity as it relates to residual levels of solvents used for extracting tetrahydrocannabinol (THC) from plant matter, pesticides, and the presence of other contaminants such as fungi, bacteria, and mould. It would also seem logical to draw lessons from the regulation of tobacco, which, like cannabis, can be smoked or vapourised and is susceptible to pest infiltration (Barry & Glantz, 2016a; Daley et al., 2013; McDaniel, Solomon, & Malone, 2005). However, it is not apparent that Colorado regulators have examined this potential resource in relation to cultivation standards. The specific issue of pesticide use (and abuse) on cannabis crops has received significant coverage in local media reports in Colorado as the State Government attempts to create workable policy that reconciles the delicate relationship between public safety and crop protection. The potential public health threat of pesticide usage on these crops was explicitly recognised by Governor Hickenlooper's executive order in November, 2015 that required state agencies to address the issue of contaminated cannabis (Colorado Department of Revenue, 2015a).

This paper has the broad aim of examining multiple data sets to provide a thick descriptive account into the issues and complexities Colorado's pioneering and evolving attempt to regulate the use of pesticides on commercial cannabis plantations. First, drawing on existing literature, an outline is provided of what is currently known regarding the regulation of pesticide usage on cannabis cultivation with specific focus on: (i) stipulating a clear definition of pesticide and related issues; (ii) the potential public health threat of pesticide use; (iii) basic methodologies of testing for pesticides; and (iv) outlining concepts related to developing quality assurance guidelines for cultivators. Second, relevant Colorado Government documents and the Retail Marijuana Code (RMC) are reviewed to explore the current regulatory status of pesticide use in Colorado. Third, samples of relevant articles from the Denver Post and cannabis industry niche media together with interviews with key stakeholders and field notes from relevant conferences and facility tours in Denver, October 2016, are bought together to explore issues relating to pesticide use that have unfolded since the introduction of the recreational cannabis market.

Defining pesticide and issues relating to cannabis crops

The use of pesticides on cannabis crops is a complex and confusing issue for a range of stakeholders including cultivators, regulators, retailers, testers, consumers, and public health researchers. While cannabis growers are interested in pest management to defend crops (referring to pest in the widest sense as invertebrates, weeds, pathogens, and insects), regulators are concerned with pesticide management and reducing the potential for risk to public health, in particular to consumers and workers (Ehler, 2006). In Colorado, some products, such as federally banned plant growth regulator (PGR) daminozide (described below), have been classified simultaneously as "pesticides" (Buffington & McDonald, 2006) and "harmful chemicals". The distinction appears to be in line with EPA labelling guidelines (US Environmental Protection Agency, 2014) and is important because, to complicate things further, the Colorado State government offers separate license types for cannabis testing labs tasked with analysing plant matter for these different kinds of contamination. To incorporate all relevant issues, this paper defines pesticides in the broadest sense following the British Pharmacopoeia (2016) as it relates to herbal drugs:

> A pesticide is any substance or mixture of substances intended for preventing, destroying or controlling any pest, unwanted species of plants or animals causing harm during or otherwise interfering with the production, processing, storage, transport or marketing of herbal drugs. The item includes substances intended for use as growth-regulators, defoliants or desiccants and any substance applied to crops, either before or after harvest, to protect the commodity from deterioration during storage and

Potential public health threat

Cannabis can be consumed in a variety of ways. Smoking is thought to be the most toxic mode of delivery (Hall & Fischer, 2010), and remains the predominant method of consumption for recreational consumers (Pacula et al., 2015). In a study testing toxicity from three common pesticides, Sullivan, Elzinga, and Raber (2013) demonstrated that chemical residues will transfer into mainstream smoke, and therefore the end-user, at levels ranging from 1- 10% for filtered water pipes up to 60-70% for unfiltered glass pipes. Although it remains unknown precisely how damaging these chemicals are to humans, the fact they are present in smoke at such high levels should be concerning. A study of pesticide use on cannabis crops in Oregon found a wide range of pesticide types and high levels of residual chemicals in harvested cannabis (Voelker & Holmes, 2015). The study also found support for the hypobook that cannabinoid extraction processes for creating high THC products (such as oils and waxes some of which are also used in cannabis confectionaries or 'edibles') intensify the levels of pesticides in those concentrates. Cannabis concentrates are generally manufactured by extracting THC from 'trim' or left over leaves of the plant, which are otherwise a waste-product of the cannabis cultivation process that aims to produce flowering heads (The Marijuana Policy Group, 2014). Voelker and Holmes (2015) found that pesticide levels were approximately 10 x higher in concentrated cannabis products than the flower heads. This is concerning because concentrates are growing in popularity in Colorado and are often "dabbed", a process of smoke or vapour inhalation of "dabbed concentrate" involving a specialised glass or ceramic pipe (for details see Kleiman, 2015; Stogner & Miller, 2015; Subritzky et al., 2016b).

Plant growth regulators (PGR).

Included in the definition of pesticide above are "growth regulators". Well known industry publication *High Times* described the PGR class of products essentially as chemicals used to produce shorter, more uniform plants with a higher density (and therefore yield) of buds/flowers per plant (Sirius, 2016, January 26). They have been shown to increase the effectiveness of growing from cuttings or 'cloning', a long-used practice in cannabis cultivation (Lata, Chandra, Khan, &

ElSohly, 2010; Slusarkiewicz-Jarzina, Ponitka, & Kaczmarek, 2005). These chemicals, while apparently widely used in growing commercial and personal cannabis crops, are also of interest to those seeking to produce pharmaceutical grade (standardised) cannabis (Logroño, 2014). However, it is claimed they present public health threats including infertility, liver damage, and cancer (Cervantes, 2015; Huang & Stone, 2003; Sirius, 2016, January 26). Two of these chemicals, paclobutrazol and daminozide, are of particular concern in the cannabis cultivation arena as they have been found unlisted in a number of cannabis growing fertilizers which have been sold around the world in hydroponic stores and other retail outlets (Hermes, 2011). According to Cervantes (2015, p.406): "No growth regulator is labelled for human consumption. All growth retardants leave residues in the plant and some, like paclobutrazol (reportedly contained in products with brand names of Bonzai or Bushmaster) remain in the plant for years and will show up in the buds and other foliage". The extent to which these products are addressed by regulators in Colorado is examined below.

The process of testing cannabis for pesticides

Testing cannabis is complicated, requiring compliance with stringent analytical processes. Standardisation of cannabis testing protocols is a major challenge given variation in federal and states laws, the issue of intellectual property of testing laboratories, and the complexity of chemical constituents within the plant. This section aims to give a brief and general overview to illustrate the difficulty of the issue facing Colorado regulators with regards to this emerging area of regulation.

Basic guidance documents on good laboratory practices, health and safety, and method validation were available to Colorado regulators as they began developing policy (see e.g. National Pesticide Information Center, 2016; Thomas & ElSohly, 2016; United Nations Office on Drugs and Crime, 2009; Voelker & Holmes, 2015). Identification of chemicals in pesticides that are potentially hazardous is an important starting point and several resources are available. The Pesticide Action Network (2016) lists information relating to over 6000 pesticide active ingredients on its database. However, attempting to identify this number of compounds in cannabis products is not feasible due to cost, yet Voelker and Holmes (2015, p.18) outlined criteria to reduce this to a manageable number of active compounds (approximately 120) while following the broad definition above to include "...insecticide, fungicide [and] PGR...". Furthermore, D'Amato (2015) and Beyond Pesticides (2015) have recommended that section 25 (b) of the Federal Insecticide, Fungicide, and Rodenticide Act (FIFRA) that outlines minimum risk pesticides exempt from registration (US Environmental Protection Agency, 2016a) be followed until research on tolerance levels has been undertaken. Additionally, a list of pesticides likely used in cannabis cultivation is available at American Herbal Pharmacopeia (2013).

The next step involves testing harvested cannabis for residues of those pesticides identified. This generally involves collection of a representative sample, extraction with suitable solvents, clean-up of solvents to remove interferences, separation of components (chromatography), and detection of targets (Daley et al., 2013). It has been stated that this method should be able to detect extremely low concentrations of residues in a high number of compounds (Daley et al., 2013). Voelker and Holmes (2015, p.7) outline a testing methodology developed by an Oregon lab (one of the authors is the lab director) based on the "universally accepted AOAC 2007.01 multi-residue method, generally known as QuEChERS" (Quick, Easy, Cheap, Effective, Rugged and Safe). This method is claimed to vastly simplify the analytical process (Anastassiades, Lehotay, Štajnbaher, & Schenck, 2003; CVUA Stuttgart, 2016; Payá et al., 2007). A complicating factor is the hundreds of compounds and approximately 100 cannabinoids that have been identified in the cannabis plant to date (Leaf Science, 2015; Thomas & ElSohly, 2016), which creates a major technical challenge (Voelker & Holmes, 2015). As such, Voelker and Holmes (2015, p.7) enhanced the methodology with "specific adaptations for Cannabis and Cannabis extracts" that combine the particle separation techniques and instrumentation of gas and liquid chromatography (for an evaluation of the suitability of three QuEChERS methods for pesticide determination in cannabis see Pérez-Parada et al. (2016) and for a simple overview of instrumentation see Celine (2011), Clark (2007), and Gen Tech Scientific (2015)).

Concerns relating to variation of test results within samples and individual plants have been observed in a number of reports regarding cannabis testing generally (e.g. Gieringer & Hazekamp, 2011; Thomas & ElSohly, 2016; Unger et al., 2014; United Nations Office on Drugs and Crime, 2009). To address this and other concerns, particularly in relation to validation of test results, Unger et al. (2014) made the following recommendations: (i) labs should be certified to the ISO 17025 standard; (ii) accreditation by an independent third party should be encouraged; (iii) all methods with public health implications should be included in the accreditation; (iv) all labs must pass regular proficiency testing programs; and (v) lab directors must hold a doctorate in a relevant field or several years of relevant experience (a similar rule is incorporated in the Colorado regulations). As explained below, the development of proficiency standards and a reference library for methodologies remains a work in progress in Colorado.

Developing cultivation standards for quality control

While the above resources provide a starting point for regulations pertaining to testing cannabis for pesticide residues, they do little to assist cannabis growers to decide between available pest control options. Crops damaged by pests do not appear to be covered by industry insurance (e.g. Cannasure, 2016), making it important for cultivators to have access to guidelines that can reduce their risk of loss. Good agricultural and collection practices (GACP) is a broad approach that applies to medicinal plants and outlines standards for each stage from seed selection, through cultivation, harvest, drying, and storage (World Health Organization, 2003). Integrated pest management (IPM) is an element of GACP that describes practices to reduce the use of pesticides on plants (Cervantes, 2015; Ehler, 2006; Grow HD, 2011; Rosenthal & Imbriani, 2012; Spencer, 2016; Thomas & ElSohly, 2016; World Health Organization, 2003). IPM involves prevention and monitoring before resorting to control (Solomon, 2015). IPM can be considered as a set of cultural practices that fall into four groups as described by MJ News Network (2016): (i) environmental, which refers to creating a low risk growing set up; (ii) monitoring, to identify any issues early; (iii) indirect controls, such as making adjustments to lighting, soil, and temperature (companies such as Surna for example, offer air sanitation products they claim provide safe alternatives to pesticides and other contagions (Surna, 2016)); and (iv) direct control, which may include chemical or biological interventions and should be kept at a minimum and used only as directed on labels by qualified staff (World Health Organization, 2003). The final point is particularly relevant as it specifically excludes a systematic regimen of pesticide sprays. It should be noted that techniques will vary according to whether the plant is grown indoors or outdoors (due in part to regulations in Colorado, the majority of cannabis is indoor grown). It has been stated that indoor hydroponic cannabis is a bigger threat to public health due to the perception that use of chemical fertilisers is more prevalent with this technique (McLaren et al., 2008).

Results

Review of Colorado State Government documents

Although local government agencies in Colorado can also develop legislation regarding cannabis (see e.g. City and County of Denver, 2016; Denver Public Health Inspections Division, 2015), this section focuses on documents from Colorado State. As stated above, the Colorado Government faces a major challenge in regulating a highly complex issue with no historical precedent upon which to draw. To address this, the state settled on a collaborative regulatory model that relies on multiple stakeholders to "...deliberate and provide direction and guidance for the proposed language with which to begin its formal rulemaking process" (Colorado Department of Revenue, 2016b; see also Hickenlooper, 2014). While this model achieves the objective of accessing the expertise of a range of partners, including representatives from the cannabis industry, public health, academia, and regulators, concern has also been noted at the potential conflict of interest between industry profit seeking and public health concerns (Lenton, 2014b; Subritzky et al., 2016a). This point is discussed in more detail below.

As a pioneering jurisdiction in cannabis regulation and in the name of public interest, the State has taken the admirable step of establishing an accessible and transparent online portal that archives documents from a range of divisions, many of which are relevant to this study. The scale of the market is described in the documents. As of June 1, 2016, licenses had been issued for 788 medical and 554 recreational cannabis cultivation facilities (Colorado Department of Revenue, 2016a). Furthermore, total plants cultivated across both sectors averaged over 600,000 per month in the state's latest figures (from 3rd quarter in 2015), resulting in the monthly sale of approximately 25,000 pounds (11,340 Kgs) of flower, 700,000 infused edible units, and 80,000 non-edible infused products (Brohl, Kammerzell, & Koski, 2015a). At time of writing, 14 facilities were licensed by the state to test the quality of recreational cannabis (Colorado Department of Revenue, 2016a). The majority of these labs have received certification for three of the seven certifiable testing categories outlined in the RMC including potency/ homogeneity, microbial contaminants, and residual solvents contamination (full details available at Colorado Department of Revenue, 2016a). As discussed in more detail below, it is notable that no facility has yet been certified to test specifically for pesticides or harmful chemicals[3].

From the documents examined, three issues regarding pesticides in cannabis in the Colorado legal market remain unclear. First, of the 80,000 non-edible infused products sold each month, it is unknown what proportion of these are concentrates that are smoked or other product types such as salves that are applied topically to the skin where they are absorbed. Second, the volume of wholesale transactions regarding trim material, while alluded to (The Marijuana Policy Group, 2014), remains unknown and appears not to be reported in publicly available Government documents. Finally, these documents do not stipulate whether the testing facilities use validated testing methodologies.

The documents prepared and collated by the Colorado State Government are insightful in addressing criteria relating to pesticide use, and summaries of work group meetings of stakeholders for the development of pesticide regulations. These are examined in turn below.

After initial confusion as to which department had authority to develop and disseminate criteria for pesticide identification, Senate Bill 16-015 (2016) allowed the Governor to designate an agency for this task. Following the Pesticide Applicator's Act (PAA) (Colorado Department of Agriculture, 2015d) that requires use to be consistent with product labels, the Colorado Department of Agriculture (2015a) compiled a list of acceptable pesticides to be used in cannabis cultivation (Colorado Department of Agriculture, 2016b). The list is entirely dependent on language on the labelling, which, while appearing to be in line with guidelines noted above (US Environmental Protection Agency, 2014; World Health Organization, 2003), is not guided by any empirical

---

[3] As noted in Chapter 10, this position took until five years after implementation to evolve

evidence that demonstrates the product is safe for consumption when consumed because relevant research has not yet been conducted. Some specific aspects include whether the pesticide label specifies if the product is suitable for applications such as food crops, indoor or outdoor farms, and commercial or private grow sites (Colorado Department of Agriculture, 2015a). The acceptable pesticides list is constantly evolving and new products are added and removed regularly (Colorado Department of Agriculture, 2016b, 2016c). In June, 2016, approximately 200 products including insecticides, fungicides, and PGRs were present on the allowed pesticide list (Colorado Department of Agriculture, 2016b). Some selected examples of pesticides that cannot be used have also been listed (Colorado Department of Agriculture, 2015e), with notable omissions from this exclusion list including paclobutrazol and daminozide, which, as noted above, are prominent in PGRs. The CDA also outlines criteria for applying to use a federally registered pesticide product via a Special Local Needs (SLN) registration (see e.g. Colorado Department of Agriculture, 2015b, 2015c; Housenger, 2015), although to date no such exemption has been awarded to producers of Colorado cannabis.

A final cluster of relevant state government documents consists of agendas and minutes of work group meetings relating to this issue. In compliance with the PAA mentioned above, the Pesticide Advisory Committee (PAC) was established in 2013 (Colorado Department of Agriculture, 2016a). Several meetings have taken place from 2013 to date, with cannabis first appearing on the agenda in 2015 (Pesticide Advisory Committee, 2015, 2016). In addition to this broader Committee, specific cannabis-focused pesticide work group meetings commenced in early 2016. The overall purpose of these meetings is, "To work with impacted stakeholders to determine a path forward for testing marijuana/marijuana products for pesticide residues and for marijuana testing facility pesticide analysis certification" (Colorado Department of Public Health and Environment, 2016f). During these meetings, various sub-committees were created to examine discussion items such as Method Detection Limits (MDL), products to be tested, and sampling protocols (see e.g. Colorado Department of Public Health and Environment, 2016a, 2016b, 2016c, 2016d). A notable omission in these documents is the specific listing of meeting attendees (described simply as "impacted stakeholders"), however it is assumed attendees are similar to those listed in HB 15-1283 Working Group (2015), which lists representatives predominantly from testing labs and CDPHE. It is unclear whether cultivators, cannabis consumer groups, manufacturers, or retail outlets were invited to participate in the meetings. It has been noted elsewhere that the work group model in Colorado can and has led to 'regulatory paralysis' on other issues (Subritzky et al., 2016b). While it is unclear whether this has been a factor in creating regulations for pesticide use, an alternative model would be to include independent cultivation consultants and lab technicians with no attachment to the specific industry but with documented expertise in producing industrial-sized crops free of pesticides to develop initial language for the regulations.

Review of Retail Marijuana Code (RMC)(1 CCR 212-2, updated November 30, 2015)

Overview and definition.

A significant development in the pesticide regulations was House Bill 15-1283 (2015) that required the CDPHE to create and maintain a reference library for cannabis testing proficiency standards. Although pesticide testing methodologies are not explicitly listed in the Bill requirements, the associated document that was created as a result of the Bill does now contain a section with this focus. The document includes a reference to a QuEChERS procedure and various methods of liquid and gas chromatography (Colorado Department of Public Health and Environment, 2016g). Meetings related to this Bill are ongoing (Colorado Department of Public Health and Environment, 2015a). Other legislation of interest includes Senate Bill 15-260 (2015) that brought the testing of medical products in line with requirements for recreational cannabis, and House Bill 16-1079 (2016) that attempted (and narrowly failed) to provide provision for a certification program for cannabis that is 'pesticide free'.

The official definition of pesticide in the regulations as stated in the RMC is:

> *"Pesticide" means any substance or mixture of substances intended for preventing, destroying, repelling or mitigating any pest or any substance or mixture of substances intended for use as a plant regulator [PGR], defoliant or desiccant; except that the term "pesticide" shall not include any article that is a*

"new animal drug" as designated by the United States Food and Drug Administration." P.6

This definition seems a positive attempt from a public health perspective to limit the potential for harm, as it includes potentially risky products such as growth regulators. However, it appears to be limited to the actual cultivation and drying phases, and is not the all-inclusive definition proposed above (British Pharmacopoeia 2016) that broadly includes any substances used to protect material before or after harvest. In addition, the pesticide regulations in general remain undeveloped. For example, the RMC lists banned substances for other contamination such as microbials, residual solvents, and metals, but not pesticides (accepted pesticides for cannabis cultivation are outlined at the CDA website as noted above). Additionally, no accepted maximum residue levels (MRL) have been specified for pesticides as they have for other sources of contamination.

Certification types.

In relation to testing, the following certification types are stipulated: (i) residual solvents; (ii) poisons or toxins; (iii) harmful chemicals; (iv) dangerous moulds, mildew, or filth; (v) harmful microbials, such as Salmonella; (vi) pesticides; and (vii) THC and other cannabinoid potency. This has led to some confusion regarding, for example, Daminozide. This PGR appears in the RMC under the separate category of "harmful chemical", yet is not listed on the list of explicitly banned pesticides. Reference to Paclobutrazol was not found in any of the data sets. Given the breadth of the definitions of pesticides provided, it would appear logical, from a licensing perspective, to merge the majority of these categories to streamline processes. For example, if certification for pesticides included testing for harmful chemicals and microbials, resources could be focused on what substances and residue levels are permitted.

Instrumentation.

Another issue concerns the specification of the instrumentation and analytical approaches that are required to measure contamination. The following analytical instrumentation is listed in the regulations: Gas Chromatography (GC); Gas Chromatography Mass Spectrometry (GC/MS); Thin Layer Chromatography (TLC); High Performance Liquid Chromatography (HPLC); and Liquid Chromatography Mass

Spectroscopy (LC/MS) (see Reichard (2013) for an overview of the use of this equipment). Generally, the regulations relate simply to record keeping and adhering to the operation manual of the equipment. It should be noted, however, that machines come in a variety of different models that can be set up in multiple configurations, within which calibration tolerances can be specified, and it is not apparent that this important detail is addressed by the regulations.

Rich description: media articles, interviews, and field notes

The following section brings together material from mass and niche media reports, stakeholder interviews, and field notes relating to the use of pesticides in the cultivation of cannabis. The results are presented in the context of the two major issues that were evident across the data sets: public health and the need for further work to close substantial knowledge gaps.

Threat to public health.

In an interview, cannabis cultivation expert Jorges Cervantes alluded to the extent of problems associated with using pesticides in black-market cannabis cultivation:

> *"Until testing started everyone had problems with it. They would cheat and they'd feel good about it. And they'd have Eagle 20 [see below] or systemic fungicides and pesticides on there".*

As noted above, from a public health perspective most concern should focus on the manufacturing of edibles and concentrates as the extraction process can intensify not only selected cannabinoids such as THC, but also levels of toxicity from residual pesticides. The issue was clarified in an interview with Seth Wong, President of TEQ Laboratories in Denver:

> *"You may get a non-detect in a plant and that doesn't mean that you didn't find it …, it just means it is below your limit of detection or it was non-detectable by us. And you can have a very low limit down into picograms. If you take that plant product and concentrate it down into an edible or a dab, you may not just have concentrated your cannabinoids, you may have also*

concentrated your pesticide. We have seen people concentrating a thousand times down on what they had ..."

One compound, Myclobutanil (Mergel, 2011), the active ingredient of branded pesticide Eagle 20 has come under extensive scrutiny as it appears to be commonly used and is representative of potential public health risks. According to Seth Wong, the method of consumption is an important consideration relating to this and other chemicals, particularly due to lack of research.

> *"We don't know the difference of what that pesticide does to you if it is just ingested or if it is smoked. Some of them have applicable uses and that's a direct application to a plant, but that plant is not necessarily smoked. So if you smoke it, and that's the case with myclobutanil that converts to cyanide once it gets treated with a flame, you've got myclobutanil on your cannabis bud and someone goes to smoke it you have potentially converted that to cyanide and potentially inhaled it".*

Considering the potential risk to public health, it is appropriate to consider why Eagle 20 is apparently commonly in use in a regulated market that aims to reduce the potential for harm to consumers. Based on his experience, Seth Wong provided some perspective:

> *"Because it is a really effective pesticide for controlling your marijuana crop and ... growers, I believe, think they can remediate or purge the plant of any potential myclobutanil that they have used. So you can treat your plant with pesticides and then send it through essentially a cleaning cycle [known as flushing] where you have 2 weeks off and then you send it pure clean water and growers believe that will purge it out. But that hasn't been studied yet, so we don't know. We have a lot of anecdotal evidence, but we don't have scientific data to back it up".*

This lack of research regarding cultivation techniques is significant given observed instances of farmers at the Cannagrow Expo describing an apparent adversity to risk. With millions of dollars invested and a very real risk of pest infestation, growers appeared hesitant to change anything in the cultivation process unless concrete proof of the success of alternative methods is provided. Furthermore, Seth Wong's explanation appears to demonstrate a potential vulnerability in the system. Cannabis products are required to be tested before they arrive at a manufacturer. If the use of "flushing" techniques during the final weeks of cultivation reduces residual levels of chemicals to non-detect status, then manufacturers may assume they have received pesticide-free product. However, when the newly manufactured edible or concentrate is retested, that pesticide may become detectable due to intensified toxicity. Such an occurrence can lead to a loss of consumer confidence and a breakdown of trust between segments of the cannabis industry, particularly cultivators, manufacturers, and testing laboratories. This in turn can impact of ability of manufacturers to produce pesticide free products. Numerous examples have been reported in The Cannabist of this lack of trust - the following are representative. After having thousands of edible products recalled, a spokesman for a large infused product manufacturing firm reportedly blamed both cultivators and the methods used by a cannabis testing lab contracted by the City of Denver:

> "The cultivators weren't being upfront with us," Pot recall: EdiPure pulls 7,770 edibles over pesticides, December 1, 2015

> "The methods employed by this particular lab are dubious at best, relying more on voodoo math and junk science than certified and standard scientific testing methods," Amid EdiPure's third pesticide recall, edibles biz calls city's testing 'dubious', December 8, 2015

This accusation was vigorously denied by the lab in question that claimed to use industry-leading instrumentation and analytical methodologies. Furthermore, in a separate case, an example of deceitfulness by a branded pesticide was reported by The Cannabist with specific regard to accurate labelling:

> The product, Guardian, had been marketed as a 100 percent natural pest control, but has been pulled from shelves after it was found to contain abamectin, a widely used insecticide, Oregon, other states stop sales

of pot pesticide because of labelling problem, February 9, 2016

The second major public health concern relates to the use of PGRs. Cervantes was unequivocal about how to solve this problem:

> *"Stay away from all of those, I don't like them at all, there's no reason to regulate the growth. Regulating growth, they do that for consistency or if they want to do less intermodal space, that's the biggest thing. If I was a regulator, I would just ban them."*

Knowledge gap and need for collective learning.

The multiple data sets included in the analysis indicated that the key challenges Colorado faces as a pioneering jurisdiction for the legal cultivation of cannabis are the lack of knowledge available for regulators and lack of cultivations standards available to growers. Federal prohibition was consistently named as a causal factor for the knowledge gap. For example, The Cannabist reported Whitney Cranshaw, a Colorado State University entomologist and pesticide expert, as saying:

> *"There is no federal agency that will recognize this as a legitimate crop. ... Pest-management information regarding this crop devolves to Internet chats and hearsay", Unknowns abound in pesticide use for growing pot, July 20, 2015*

Considering the cultivation of medicinal cannabis has been legal in Colorado since 2000 (and 1996 in California), the question arises as to why the issue had not been dealt with previously. Industry pioneer Ean Seeb explained that federal prohibition had been problematic in the early establishment of testing labs:

> *"The whole license type of a laboratory only came about after recreational started. There were test labs set up, and it created quite the conundrum because cannabis is still federally illegal. So when the first testing labs in Colorado set up and applied for DEA approval to be able to test things and receive samples, when the DEA came and saw that there was cannabis there they raided the lab and shut it down. A lot of*

people were very scared to start test labs because they had a fear that they were going to be shut down by the DEA. So what is the point of investing millions of dollars and creating all this lab equipment and setting up standards and procedures if the government is going to come in and shut it down? In A64, part of the regulations that were enacted spoke to testing, so it created really a new part of the industry or a fourth license type which was a laboratory".

As stated above, Colorado embraced what is often described as a "collaborative process" to enhance the collective learning of stakeholders. Interviews with senior regulators clarified those strong partnerships exist predominantly between key internal stakeholders including the DOR, CDPHE, CDA, and the Office of Marijuana Coordination in relation to cannabis regulations. In regard to external stakeholders, such as segments of the cannabis industry, opportunities are afforded for them to present their perspectives and experience, however they are not equal partners in the process. Director of Marijuana Coordination Andrew Freedman was clear about their involvement:

"The tone of collaboration started with the A64 taskforce. We are not going to sit inside and make regulations in a bubble, we are going to hear from anybody who has an opinion on this. The A64 taskforce was a huge operation to put together and those are the groups we reach back into when we see a place that needs substantial change. I think it makes for better policy, we do end up thinking about things we don't normally think about.

Pesticide use was one of the harder ones because outside of the world of regulation people were using a lot of pesticides that they wanted to continue to use. And it was less of a give-and-take moment because, you know, there are federal standards about which pesticides should be used and we can basically apply those standards to marijuana. And we did, and a lot of the pesticides they were using do not fall within those standards".

Understanding the level of industry involvement in developing regulations is important from a public health perspective. Field notes from the cannabis growers expo and informal discussions with cultivators indicated that segments of industry have unique perspectives that are relevant to the process. For example, production managers spoke of sustainable and organic cultivation strategies that have arisen from the industry and could potentially be included in regulations. Several reports in The Cannabist, however, indicated that the industry had slowed or attempted to weaken the regulatory process as it related to pesticides:

> *"Three years of e-mails and records obtained by The Denver Post and dozens of interviews show state regulators struggled with the issue while the cannabis industry protested that proposed limits on pesticides would leave their valuable crops vulnerable to devastating disease. As the state was preparing a list of allowable substances that would have restricted pesticides on marijuana to the least toxic chemicals, CDA officials stopped the process under pressure from the industry" Deep dive: Why Colorado has struggled to regulate pot pesticides, October 4, 2015*

Former Colorado agriculture commissioner John Salazar was reported in The Cannabist stating that the marijuana industry:

> *"Was the biggest obstacle … anything we wanted to allow simply was not enough for that industry", Colorado yields to marijuana industry pressure on pesticides, October 5, 2015*

Ultimately, however, the State appears to have displayed leadership on the matter by creating a list of approved pesticides and taking steps to enforce these. Freedman stated in an interview:

> *I think we have stayed away from regulatory capture for the most part because … we will say to industry we would love to help find a way forward on this, but here are our principles that we decided as a group that we can't move away from. We had to put a lot of millions of dollars of marijuana on hold and I think that upset a lot of people quite a bit.*

In regard to the criticism directed at the state over the time taken to develop regulations, Freedman offered valuable context.

> *"Part of the problem again is some of that is the expertise of the CDA, some is the CDPHE and all of that runs through the DOR's regulatory system. On pesticides we reached the determination that the CDA decides what sort of pesticides can be used and if there is a violation the DOR is then in charge of destruction. Working out exactly when it passes from the CDA to the DOR took a bit of time".*

Again, an article in The Cannabist was insightful. Mitch Yergert of the CDA reportedly pointed out that:

> *"CDA felt there was a need to further explore all possibilities of how best to regulate and identify what pesticides could be legally used on marijuana. During this process, we believe we have identified a better way forward than what we originally proposed in April of 2014". Colorado yields to marijuana industry pressure on pesticides, October 3, 2015*

From this analysis it is unclear precisely what role the industry played in developing or inhibiting the regulations pertaining to pesticides. The Executive Director of the DOR, Barbara Brohl, who has years of experience overseeing other highly regulated industries in Colorado including alcohol and gaming explained when interviewed that the process is possibly more accurately described as "negotiated rulemaking", and while there is room for industry input it must be remembered that they:

> *"... are still for profit companies so they have an incentive to increase the services they are providing".*

The issue of the role industry should play in the developing regulations and setting standards is crystallised by the entrance into the cannabis market of large agri-businesses with extensive resources. In a Marijuana Business Daily article, Jim Hagedorn, CEO of Scotts Miracle-Gro, reportedly stated the intention of his company to:

"... invest, like, half a billion dollars." Scotts Miracle-Gro's Big Marijuana Plunge Exposes Industry Fault Lines, July 2016

From a public health perspective, there is a risk and reward component to involving industry in the process of developing regulations. On the one hand, they have the potential to add significantly to the collective learning by bringing vast experience to the creation of standards surrounding the pesticide issue. James Lowe, president of cultivation at MJardin, a Denver consultancy specializing in cannabis cultivation, reportedly stated in the Marijuana Business Daily:

> *"That's been a problem in the cannabis industry. You get unlabeled or mislabeled fertilizers. You get people that are making false claims and claims that can't be verified. When the Miracle-Gros of the world come into the industry, they stay away from the snake oil. They will help set standards for the industry." Scotts Miracle-Gro's Big Marijuana Plunge Exposes Industry Fault Lines, July 2016*

Conversely, companies exist to create profit rather than improve public health outcomes, so any standards developed with corporate influence should be viewed with caution. As has already been noted, no pesticide is currently registered federally in the US for the use on cannabis. According to Seth Wong, registering a pesticide federally is resource intensive.

> *"To take a pesticide through a trial in order to certify it for cannabis use can take three years that involves a huge number of studies and 10 – 20 million dollars and then some. So this process of actually certifying a pesticide for cannabis especially in the place where the market place is right now, nobody seems too aggressive to pursue that avenue just yet".*

The tipping point, however, may arrive sooner rather than later. It was reported that Scotts Miracle Gro has begun discussions with the EPA regarding the matter. The following statement by CEO Hagedorn was reproduced in The Cannabist from an earnings transcript:

> *"We are continuing to work with both individual states and the EPA for special — for the first time ever —*

registrations that allow pesticidal products to be used on — and we'll be the only one offering pesticidal products that can be used on cannabis. So I think that's an opportunity for us". Scotts Miracle-Gro in talks with EPA about marijuana pesticides, November 4, 2016

In short, it appears the company is positioning itself to hold a monopoly on pesticides that are federally approved for use on cannabis crops. When asked for his thoughts regarding the role of Scotts Miracle Gro in setting standards in the industry, Cervantes commented that:

"Yeah with those big guys, see they've got distribution, they run it like a business rather than like a summer club. They will do whatever they are forced to do, it's a business. We should definitely be suspicious".

Discussion

The US election in November 2016, was potentially a watershed moment in the legalisation of cannabis for recreational purposes with voters in Arizona, Maine, Massachusetts, Nevada, and most significantly, California approving ballot measures. This means one in five US citizens will soon have access to legal cannabis for recreational purposes and over half for some form of medicinal cannabis treatments. Cannabis policy is also under going significant change internationally.

At the time of writing, four years have passed since the recreational cannabis market in Colorado was legalised. The regulations relating to pesticides are yet to be finalised, and continue to evolve. This reflects the complexity of the issue and should not be unexpected given the Colorado scheme is breaking new ground. Furthermore, reports from Oregon and Washington State indicate other jurisdictions with legalised cannabis in the US face challenges (Harbarger, 2016, November 3; Johnson, 2016, September 16). In addition, Steep Hill Labs recently found that 84% of samples in California tested positive for pesticide residues and 65% of all samples contained Myclobutanil (Steep Hill, 2016, October 19).

It should be noted that Colorado has made significant progress in developing regulations for pesticide use in cannabis cultivation although major challenges remain. It is important that other jurisdictions are aware that establishing enforceable regulations and creating cultivation standards is both time and resource intensive. Little research has been conducted on public health risks associated with the use of pesticides on cannabis cultivation. While much remains unknown, incorporating lessons from the Colorado model can assist regulators in other jurisdictions considering a legal cannabis policy to develop regulations for pesticide use on cannabis crops.

As jurisdictions grapple with this issue, they will need to develop collective learning. An essential question is to what extent industry should be involved to set standards and develop regulations to fill the gap. Segments of the cannabis industry have highly specialised expertise and may provide a useful resource for the development of both regulations and standards. However, as noted by some of the interviewees, caution is necessary. Left to its own devices, industry may look to exploit the lack of standards or employ less-than-scientific cultivation models based on hearsay. The Colorado approach attempts to balance this by encouraging industry input while staying true to principles outlined by the A64 taskforce that focus on enforceability and public health. While there have been reports of "regulatory paralysis", overall, regulatory capture by the industry appears to have been avoided.

Chapter 7: Cannabis and youth protection in Colorado's commercial adult-use market: a qualitative investigation.

Subritzky, T., Lenton, S., & Pettigrew, S. (2019). Cannabis and youth protection in Colorado's pioneering commercial adult-use market: a qualitative investigation. International Journal of Drug Policy, 74, 116-126. https://doi.org/10.1016/j.drugpo.2019.09.007

Introduction

Arguments both for and against the legalisation of cannabis often mention the issue of youth protection. Those who view the prohibition of cannabis as the best way to protect youth from risks associated with the early initiation of consumption tend to argue that legalisation of the drug will result in wider availability and greater risk of exposure for adolescents, ultimately increasing usage in this important cohort (Caulkins et al., 2015). By comparison, advocates for regulated cannabis models generally contend that youth are already widely exposed to the drug and are best protected by regulating the availability of cannabis products, and also argue that part of tax revenue generated can be directed toward funding targeted youth prevention and education programs (Drug Policy Alliance, 2019a).

An oft-stated perceived advantage of commercial models of cannabis regulation is that they are the most likely to maximise revenue generation for the State, which can then be appropriated to public health initiatives such as youth prevention education campaigns (Caulkins et al., 2016; Caulkins et al., 2015; Rolles & Murkin, 2016). Indeed Caulkins et al. (2015) argued that departments of revenue may even prioritise revenue generation over public health goals. Conversely, the risks of youth exposure are thought to be amplified in commercial markets where prices were expected to (and did) decline (Marijuana Policy Group, 2018; Subritzky et al., forthcoming; Subritzky et al., 2016b). According to Gravelle and Lowry (2014), the elasticity of demand among youth is greater than for adult cannabis consumers generally, which implies that price is an important element in youth consumption decisions. In addition, according to Pacula et al. (2014, p.1022), "hundreds of studies on alcohol and tobacco show that raising prices reduces consumption and a long list of related health and social harms".

Five years after the State became the first jurisdiction worldwide to implement a fully regulated seed-to-sale recreational cannabis market in 2014, important practical lessons can be learned from the Coloradan experience. It is important to note that even with the introduction of the CRCM, cannabis remained prohibited for recreational use for those under the age of 21 and 18 for medical cannabis. In this sense, at least legally, prohibition laws have not changed for young people in the State.

The paper focuses on the theme of youth protection in the context of a legal, commercial distribution model of cannabis in Colorado. It reports the outcomes of an analysis of a sample of government documents from the pre-implementation phase of the CRCM (November 2012 - December 2013) and semi-structured interviews were conducted in 2016 and 2017 with 32 key stakeholders intimately involved in the initial development of the Retail Marijuana Code (RMC) in Colorado.

The following subsections of this Introduction address: (i) risks associated with early initiation of cannabis consumption; (ii) age restrictions and a range of prevention messaging approaches; (iii) the evolution of Coloradan prevention campaigns; and (iv) latest youth consumption statistics from national, state, and local surveys.

The Results section includes two main sections that report on the analysis of both the government documents and interviews data sets. In the government documents data set, the themes of retail advertising restrictions and education emerged from the analysis. Three themes emerged from the interviews data set: when funds should be appropriated; impact assessment (including the issues of changes to school data and methodological considerations); and evolving messages in prevention education campaigns. The Discussion includes a comparison of the two data sets and lessons and recommendations for other jurisdictions considering cannabis policy reform.

Higher risks associated with early initiation

According to Szabo (2014, p.700), "the epidemiological evidence on cannabis dependence and adverse effects on cognitive performance and poorer educational outcomes provide good reasons for reducing cannabis-related harm among adolescents". Additionally, Fischer et al. (2017) did a systematic review that searched for harmful cannabis consumption, identified a multitude of studies highlighting elevated risks associated with early initiation of consumption (i.e. under the age of 21 unless otherwise stated). For example, evidence suggests that the initiation of cannabis consumption under 18 increases the risk of dependence to 1 in 6 (approximately 16.5%) (Anthony, 2006; Szabo, 2014), which compares to dependence rates of 9% for people who have ever consumed cannabis and around 2% of the general population (Room et al., 2010).

As has been noted by several scholars, the brain is still developing until at least the age of 21 (e.g. Gogtay et al., 2004), and potentially up to 25 (Szabo, 2014). Thus, prenatal and adolescent exposure to "environmental insults" such as THC are particularly concerning (Volkow et al., 2014, p.2220). Further, regular consumption of cannabis in adolescence has been associated with impaired neural connectivity in regions of the brain involved with alertness, memory, and learning, compared with control groups (Batalla et al., 2013; Filbey & Yezhuvath, 2013; Zalesky et al., 2012). These risks are thought to be magnified by an adolescent's high number of days of use and high amounts used per day (Caulkins et al., 2015; James, James, & Thwaites, 2013; Lisdahl, 2013).

Age restrictions and prevention messaging.

Age restrictions are seen as an important control on limiting youth access to cannabis (Rolles & Murkin, 2016). However, finding the right balance is critical – if the age is too high then a black market may be incentivised, while if it is too low there may be increased risk of higher consumption rates (Rolles & Murkin, 2016). In addition, age restriction effectiveness depends on enforcement levels (Rolles & Murkin, 2016). Media coverage of industry compliance based on mandatory state government annual reports indicated that recreational cannabis stores in Colorado prevented 95% of underage purchases, similar to alcohol (89%) and tobacco stores (94%) (CBS Denver, 2018, May 25; Colorado Department of Revenue Marijuana Enforcement Division, 2017).

Rolles and Murkin (2016) pointed out the need for age restrictions to be supported with prevention education and evidenced-based harm reduction programs. How cannabis prevention messages are framed is an important public health consideration. A legalised cannabis market may, by its existence, send confused messages with youth potentially assuming cannabis to be safe if it is available for sale, particularly if it is also a legal medicine, and prevention programs and messages might have to change in legal cannabis contexts (Caulkins et al., 2015). Kilmer (2014, p.2) has argued that "even the best [drug] prevention programs are not particularly effective", however real-world evidence on the effectiveness of youth prevention and harm reduction education campaigns in legal commercial cannabis markets is thin. Investigating the Coloradan experience can begin to address this evidence deficit.

Several stakeholders proposed that with the right information, youth will make good choices around cannabis consumption. For example, in discussing an education campaign in the City of Denver, Mayor Hancock reportedly stated: "Teens want facts and they want to be able to make their own decisions. When we give teens the facts and equip them with knowledge, they make smarter choices about using marijuana" (Marijuana Moments, 2019, Mar. 19). The same contention was made by the National Institue on Drug Abuse (2019). Where they seem to differ is on what the facts are and how they should be presented. Traditionally, prevention messaging has tended to focus on abstinence-only programs such as the 'just say no' campaigns of the 1980s and Drug Abuse Resistance Education (2019), while more recently there has been an increase in harm reduction focussed messaging (e.g. Drug Policy Alliance, 2019c).

Evolution of Colorado's prevention education messaging

The retail marijuana education program logic model developed by the Colorado Department of Public Health and Environment (2014) provided a high-level overview of the strategy undertaken by the State. According to Ghosh et al. (2016), central aims of the model included the protection of vulnerable populations such as youth and data collection for impact assessment. Both the Colorado Department of Public Health and Environment (2019a) and the Colorado Office of Behavioral Health (2019) have developed comprehensive cannabis prevention messaging resources for communities, together with detailed annual reports (e.g. Colorado Department of Public Health and Environment, 2017c).

At time of writing, Marijuana Tax Fund appropriations to prevention education had increased significantly since initial implementation of the CRCM (Colorado Office of State Planning & Budgeting, 2017). In Colorado there have been at least three state-run prevention campaigns since 2014 including: (i) 'Don't be a lab rat'; (ii) 'protect what's next'; and (iii) 'responsibility grows here' (Colorado Department of Public Health and Environment, 2017c, 2019b, 2019c). In addition, local jurisdictions such as City of Denver (2019b) have implemented their own prevention education programs.

National, state, and local data indicate no increase in consumption among youth

It was widely predicted that the implementation of a commercial adult-use cannabis market in Colorado would lead to higher rates of consumption among youth (e.g. Caulkins et al., 2015), however early evidence has not supported this contention, with recent data reporting 'encouraging trends' (Colorado Department of Public Health and Environment, 2018d). For example, five years after the implementation of the CRCM, latest data indicate no statistically significant increase in youth consumption patterns with multiple data sets finding that, while perception of cannabis harmfulness has markedly decreased among adolescents in Colorado, an associated effect of increased consumption has not been identified, with similar usage rates to pre-legalisation (Brooks-Russell et al., 2019; Brooks-Russell et al., 2018; Colorado Department of Public Safety Division of Criminal Justice, 2018b). These data are similar to survey findings from previous studies that first began to accrue in late 2015 in the form of national survey results such as Substance Abuse and Mental Health Services Administration (SAMHSA) (Hughes, Lipari, & Williams, 2015) and Monitoring The Future (MTF) (Johnston, O'Malley, Miech, Bachman, & Schulenberg, 2015).

In the City of Denver, there is evidence from a small survey of 500 participants that consumption rates among youth had dropped to below the national average for the first time in decades (City of Denver, 2019a). These results reportedly led Denver Mayor Hancock to declare that prevention education programs in the jurisdiction have been "a success" (Marijuana Moments, 2019, Mar. 19).

Critique of data collection methodologies

It has been argued that in the US generally, data systems for measurement of the quantity of cannabis consumed, as opposed to prevalence of use, are insufficient (Caulkins et al., 2016; Kilmer, 2015b, November 25). The potential for bias in self-report surveys, confounding due to some people being? excluded from the sampling frame, and shortcomings of existing survey instruments were also noted (Ghosh et al., 2015; Kilmer, 2015b, November 25). Thus it may be years or decades before the consequences of newly legalised commercial marijuana markets, such as that in Colorado, are revealed (Pacula & Sevigny, 2014). In specific regard to Colorado data collection instruments, Ghosh et al. (2015) provided a timely overview of measures implemented to monitor prevalence of use, public health effects, and challenges associated with assessment. They noted that a problem with using the existing population-based surveys was that they did not include validated questions addressing issues such as variation in methods of marijuana consumption, home storage, cultivation, and intoxication.

Results

Data set 1: government documents – pre-implementation phase November 2012 – December 2013

Youth protection

A key objective stated in most government documents (n=11) under investigation was the protection of youth and this issue emerged in the sample across multiple stages of the pre-implementation phase of the CRCM. In general, the documents highlighted the importance of youth protection and designated specific responsibilities in this regard to the Colorado Departments of Public Health and Environment and Human Services. For example, text in A64 was explicit about youth protection and continued prohibition for those under 21 years of age:

> *"Marijuana should be legal for persons twenty-one of age or over ...*
>
> *Nothing in this section is intended to ... allow a person under the age of twenty-one to purchase, possess, use, transport, grow or consume marijuana*
>
> *Individuals will have to show proof of age before purchasing marijuana" (A64, P.1)*

While this text clearly articulated rules intended for the CRCM, it did not differentiate it from the existing medical market. Thus, an immediate complication related to the 18-year age limit for medical cannabis, which is problematic for assessing the impact of the retail scheme, as well as confusion around how "youth" is defined. Those between the ages of 18 and 21 would be required to join the patient registry by obtaining a doctor's certificate and applying for a red card, should they wish to legally consume cannabis. Failure to do so could result in a minor in possession charge, counselling, and community service as was stipulated in SB13-283, which highlighted the continued prohibition of recreational cannabis for those under 21.

The A64 Task Force listed several recommendations in their report regarding the matter. Notably, the report suggested on-going training for youth-focused professionals relating to cannabis impairment, paraphernalia, risks, and ongoing development of materials aimed at preventing youth from consuming cannabis. For example:

> *K – 12 educators/ counsellors; Colorado Education Association and Colorado Department of Education; prevention specialists; university staff, Colorado Commission on Higher Education; Child Welfare Services, Colorado Department of Human Services.*
>
> *...*
>
> *Marijuana use prevention for those under age 21... Target markets include parents, students, and educators... Materials can include websites, brochures, billboards, public service announcements, etc. A64 Task Force Report, P.153 – 154.*

Retail advertising restrictions

A major public health concern regarding commercial cannabis markets is that advertising and promotion may disproportionately impact vulnerable segments of the population such as youth and people with problematic cannabis use. The issue of retail advertising restrictions emerged from six documents within the context of youth protection including A64, A64 Task Force Report, HB 13-1317, RMC 2013 (Temp), RMC 2013 (Perm), and MMC 2013 (Perm), all of which indicated that the protection of youth was a high priority. The following justification for advertising restrictions is representative:

> *Amendment 64 allows for legal access to and use of marijuana only for adults over 21 years of age. As such, and to protect the health, safety, and well-being of youth, marketing and advertising of marijuana products and accessories should be carefully regulated to avoid reaching persons under 21 years of age. A64 Task Force Report, p.53-54*

The extent to which advertising restrictions should be applied was apparently open to some debate. In the end, a rule stipulating 30% likelihood of being seen by minors as the acceptable standard in line with restrictions on the promotion of alcohol in the State was incorporated, which was itself rather arbitrary and difficult to define. The following text provides both an indication of the process of how the advertising rules were consolidated at the final stage of the rulemaking process and justification for the decisions made by the Colorado Department of Revenue (CDOR):

> *The [CDOR] received extensive comments reflecting the strong influence advertising has on minors' decision-making with regard to substance use and abuse.*

> *Nearly all live testimony at the rulemaking hearing requested less restrictive advertising rules, but written commentary included multiple perspectives. The written and oral testimony and commentary included a variety of recommended standards for determining when advertising has a high likelihood of reaching minors.*

> *Voluntary standards adopted by the alcohol industry direct the industry to refrain from advertising where more than approximately 30 percent of the audience is reasonably expected to be under the age of 21. After reviewing the rulemaking record, the [CDOR] has determined ... it is appropriate to model the retail marijuana advertising restrictions on this voluntary standard used by the alcohol industry.*
>
> *This standard is consistent with the directive in the state constitution [A64] to regulate marijuana in a manner that is similar to alcohol, while also recognizing that the legal status of the marijuana industry and the legal status of the liquor industry are not the same.*
>
> *The [CDOR] will continue to evaluate the best way to ... establish appropriate advertising restrictions for this emerging industry, and will in particular continue to monitor and evaluate advertising, marketing and signage to protect the interests of those under the age of 21 and to prevent underage use of marijuana. RMC 2013 (Perm), P.107 - 108)*

The above text offers insights into the advertising rules stipulated in the RMC 2013 (Perm). Restrictions are clearly focused on shielding youth, which is a consistent thread in all relevant documents for this section. Furthermore, restrictions placed on regulators by A64 (highlighted in the text) prevent some public health best practice from being deployed (e.g. zero advertising). This aspect highlights the point that from a public health perspective, it may be better for cannabis reform to be driven by regulators as opposed to direct democracy initiatives, particularly if those initiatives are constitutionally enshrined as is the case (uniquely) in Colorado.

The statement that the CDOR will continue to evaluate advertising restrictions seems to be an indication that the recreational rules were not finalised in the pre-implementation phase, but rather they constituted an initial framework that could be modified within the Coloradan rulemaking process as and when issues and unintended consequences arise. Table 8 below lists the different sections of the advertising regulations in the RMC 2013. While not reaching optimal levels of public health best practice regarding cannabis advertising, the initial restrictions in the CRCM were reasonably comprehensive.

Table 8: Overview of advertising restrictions in the RMC 2013

Series ID	Series name
R 1102	No false or misleading statements
R 1104	TV (30% rule)
R 1105	Radio (30% rule)
R 1106	Print media (30% rule)
R 1107	Internet (30% rule)
R 1108	Targeting out of state people prohibited
R 1109	Signage and advertising
R 1111	Signage and outdoor (local ordinances) + generally prohibited
R 1112	Not target minors
R 1113	Mobile devices
R 1114	Pop up advertising
R 1115	Event sponsorship – ok, event advertising (30% rule)

RMC 2013 (Perm) P.107 - 117

Education

In the Introduction it was pointed out that cannabis prevention education is an important public health intervention. Content relating to education was identified in five of the documents, including both Governor executive orders, the A64 Task Force Report, the GA Report, and SB 13-13283 (which related to issues that received consensus approval from the A64 Task Force Report). In general, the references indicate an intention to implement programs as opposed to actual implementation. The following extracts are representative:

> *The Office of the Governor, in consultation with the CDHS, the CDPHE, the CDPS and other state agencies deemed appropriate ... shall establish a marijuana*

*educational oversight committee composed of
members with relevant experience in marijuana issues.
This marijuana oversight committee shall develop and
implement recommendations for the education of all
necessary stakeholders on issues related to marijuana
use, cultivation, and other relevant issues. Further, if
this committee finds it appropriate, it shall encourage
professions to encourage marijuana education as part
of continuing education programs.*

*The Office of the Governor, in consultation with the
CDHS, the CDPHE, the CDPS and other state agencies
as deemed necessary shall develop and deploy
education materials regarding appropriate retail
marijuana use, the prevention of marijuana use by
those under twenty-one years of age, and materials to
discourage driving while under the influence of
marijuana. The Office of the Governor will utilise
established best practices, existing federal and state
resources and innovative tools in developing and
deploying these educational materials. EO D2013-007,
June 11 2013, p.2*

*The division is not required to perform the duties
required by this section until the Marijuana Cash Fund
… has received sufficient revenue to fully fund the
appropriations made to the CDOR, and the General
Assembly has appropriated sufficient moneys for the
fund for such duties. SB 13-283, May 28, 2013, p.8*

These extracts appear to highlight the importance of youth prevention
initiatives that were to be implemented alongside cannabis
legalisation. For example, it is apparent that government agencies
such as CDHS, CDPHE, and CDPS that have skills and experience
relevant to protecting youth from cannabis were tasked with
developing youth prevention education programs. Crucially, however,
the text also identifies a lag of at least two years before implementation
of the prevention programs, as they were not to be undertaken until
sufficient revenue had been appropriated from the Marijuana Tax
Fund. This timing around when funds were appropriated for youth

prevention campaigns is discussed in more detail in the analysis of the interview data below.

Data set 2: interviews – post-implementation
Appropriation of funds: not if but when

While there were examples in the interviews of the CDOR strategizing to increase revenues (in line a key objective stipulated in multiple pre-implementation documents to 'establish a reliable funding mechanism'), there was no indication that public health objectives were compromised as a result. Rather, multiple interviewees (n=5) indicated that the major challenge associated with funding in the CRCM related not to how or who is funded, but when. In general, interviewees discussing this perspective contended that a lack of prefunding hindered the initial implementation of public health objectives stipulated in the A64 Taskforce Report (including data collection for impact assessment) and prevention education campaigns for youth.

The statement below by the Executive Director of the CDOR is representative of interviewee responses on the issue. She noted that an initial decision was made that cannabis-related expenses would be self-funded through tax revenues generated from sales. The logic behind this was reportedly that it was not appropriate for cannabis-related policy funds to be drawn from the State's general account.

> "It was decided that the regulation of recreational marijuana should be self-funded – that just seemed like the appropriate position to take from the outset. The Marijuana Enforcement Division (MED) gets first bite at the apple and so does the tax division. We get what's called same year appropriation. So the same year that this comes in we get to spend it. And then after that the next year it really goes to things like youth prevention, substance abuse prevention, treatment, and impact assessment". Group Interview: _Barbara Brohl - Executive Director CDOR (speaker)_, Ron Kammerzell - Senior Director of Marijuana Enforcement Division, Mathew Scott - Senior Director of Taxation, Heidi Humphreys - Deputy Director CDOR, May 2017, Denver.

This extract highlights an important lesson that may need consideration by regulators in jurisdictions legalising cannabis, namely *when* revenue is appropriated. This issue is revisited in the discussion below.

Impact assessment

In interviews where impact assessment was discussed in the context of youth consumption (n=4), the following topics were discussed: (i) no increase in youth consumption, although it remained too early to make definitive judgements (as this issue is largely reflected in the consumption statistics presented above, it is not discussed further in this section); (ii) changes to school data collection; and (iii) methodological considerations.

Changes to how school data are recorded

One element of the issue of impact assessment that emerged from the interviews related to the necessity of changing how cannabis-related drug expulsion data were recorded, and that such change reportedly needed to be considered in the context of broader changes to education policy in the state. According to the State's senior cannabis impact statistician:

> *Prior to the last school year the 2015/2016 school year, when they were collecting information on school discipline so suspensions, expulsions, law enforcement they had the category of drugs. We trended on that for a decade but it's only drugs. And anecdotally they would say yeah it's mostly marijuana but they couldn't actually tell you it's 20%, it's 80% its 90%. In the last school year they actually broke marijuana out separately and so we were able to get a sense of okay 60% of expulsions for drugs are for marijuana 80% percent of suspensions that are for drugs are for marijuana.*

> *The other issue that occurred right around the time where we voted on legalization was the Department of Education really started pushing schools to use other types of discipline rather than suspension or expulsion because suspensions and expulsions have long term impacts on kids' outcomes. So graduation, good*

college, getting a decent job all those things are impacted by getting expelled when you are in 8th grade it can be a persistent effect.

And so they really worked with the schools and there was a lot of paths that really tried to minimize suspensions and expulsions. So what you find with drug expulsion, drug expulsions have gone down. They went down because of a change in policy. There was a state-wide change of policy. So that's one of those things where there's various variables ... that has nothing to do with drug legalization or marijuana legalization. It has everything to do with policy surrounding suspension and expulsions. Jack Reed, Statistical Analyst, CDPS, May 2017

From this extract it is apparent that how drug consumption data were recorded in schools was changed to include cannabis specific data. The multi-faceted nature of cannabis policy and how at times impact data may be influenced by broader policy changes were also highlighted.

Methodological considerations

In the Introduction section, critiques of cannabis data collection instruments in the US generally were presented, and these were addressed in an interview with the Director of the Healthy Kids Colorado Survey. First, the gap pertaining to prevalence data (as opposed to frequency data) was discussed:

"Yes, what we commonly report is the proportion of students who say they've used at all in the last 30 days. So what's getting masked there is the distribution of the frequency of use within the 30 days. So, how many daily users. We know that too. We just don't use that as an indicator. What we see is this kind of bimodal thing where we got a chunk of kids who are using once or twice in a month in our snapshot and then a chunk of kids who are using 20 times or more in a month and not that many in the middle. So we have kind of heavy users and not heavy users and we don't know what they're using or all the times the user uses in a day we

don't know. Is it one joint or is it 5 joints?" Ashley Brooks-Russell, PHD - Professor UC Denver. Project Director Healthy Kids Colorado Survey, Denver, May 2017

From a public health and/or harm reduction perspective, this nuanced approach to identifying the highest risk consumption patterns is desirable. As more datapoints accrue it is likely this gap will be filled in coming years. In addition to these limitations, there was also a methodological critique of self-report data collection, namely that the HKC data may lack reliability due to the reliance on self-report. In response to this criticism that self-report data was potentially open to false reporting, the HKC survey project leader provided a robust defence of the methodology noting that this was merely one datapoint and needed to be considered together with other data from different surveys with different methodologies.

> *"We have been struggling with that critique and other kind of methodological critiques of our survey effort coming out of advocate organizations out of Florida, Project Sam and it's very frustrating to me. What I would say is a couple of things. First of all, I don't think self-reported data is the only data point that's worth looking at. School discipline data, principals' anecdotal observations. I think we need to triangulate these. So go ahead and look at juvenile justice data or school reports of disciplinary action or confiscated drug materials on campus; sure and those are all valid data points and they speak to different things because I think that indicates use on school property which is different than youth use overall because our survey doesn't ask about where they use. So the fact that they're bringing more things to school or using more openly might be a different issue perhaps than frequency of use, which is what our survey looks at.*
>
> *There is very likely some underreporting. There is some evidence of some overreporting on some youth surveys. It depends on how much students feel that their responses are confidential and we do paper based and that's kind of mandated by the [Centres for Disease Control and Prevention] CDC and the idea is that youth*

can feel a high degree of confidence because they can cover their answers and they protect it and as we move to maybe tablets you maybe have that privacy but with big computer screens they just don't, right?

However, Monitoring the Future and the [Youth Risk Behaviour Survey] YRBS both use school-based sampling. Very different efforts and they've both been going on for a long time and nationally and in these states we're seeing the exact same patterns. So, we're not an anomaly in Colorado. The national estimates of marijuana are flat. So the secular trends were consistent with that. So there is something larger than just our laws and our sample is just massive. I mean, 20,000 students. It's very robust. Then, national survey drug use and health which use very different sampling methods. They do in person interviews whereas we do paper based.

Our survey, we have 100 questions on there." Ashley Brooks-Russell, PHD - Professor UC Denver. Project Director Healthy Kids Colorado Survey, Denver, May 2017

The above-detailed outline of the HKC survey is persuasive and highlights how data collection is evolving generally with the advent of technology and also in regard to cannabis data collection specifically - most notably with the addition of new questions. Despite the critique of self-report data, there is no evidence in the case of the HKC survey at least that reported rates of consumption should be called into question, particularly as they mirror trends identified in other state and national surveys.

Despite these data indicating 'positive trends', there was near consensus in related interviews that it was too early make definitive judgements on policy outcomes. The impact data presented above can be considered initial indications that will likely evolve over decades. The following example is representative:

I think it's too early to know ... we caveat it by saying in the first three years we haven't seen an increase in

The above extract emphasises how it will likely take years of accruing a variety of data points to formulate an accurate picture of consumption patterns in what is an ever-evolving landscape both in terms of policy and consumption patterns. Nonetheless, the above perspectives are among the first to document the first years of experience in a 'real-world' legal commercial cannabis market and provide a starting point around which further evidence can accrue.

The evolving message in prevention education: what are facts and how should they be framed in legalised contexts?

Notwithstanding that the appropriation of funds from CRCM revenue for youth prevention education programs was delayed as noted above, from the interviews it was apparent there were varying perspectives associated with how prevention education should be approached in a jurisdiction where a formerly illegal substance became legal. Interview participants differed in their perceptions of what 'public health messages' should be promoted, with options ranging from any consumption under the age of 25 having potentially catastrophic outcomes through to arguments that adolescents don't respond to brain damage messaging and thus the focus should be on engagement. An example of this challenge was described in an interview:

> *So that was an initial struggle I think for us as a local public health entity trying to be able to describe here's what the health impacts are ... among youth that are going to be using marijuana before they reach the age of 25. So that was maybe the first piece - just trying to have a conversation and talking about some of the benefits while also talking about some of the downsides or some of the risks associated with it. Heath Harmon, Director of Health Division for Boulder County Public Health, August 2017, Skype.*

An advocate for very strong messaging explained her perspective:

"I met … an adolescent psychiatrist at Columbia, [he told me] that adolescents who started smoking pot at 13, when they walk in at 18, he has found that there's been permanent brain damage for the most part where their motivation has been lowered and their I.Q.

I live in a state that legalized marijuana and I would like to think that they're responsible enough to educate young people to stay away from this and not try it until they're much older if they want to try it, like 25 when your brain is fully developed". Lexie Potamkin, Founder Principals for Principles, May 2017, Aspen

As noted above, 13 years of age is considered a high-risk demographic for the initiation of a cannabis consumer career. While the argument has already been presented that early onset of cannabis consumption increases risks associated with cannabis (such as cannabis use disorder), the recommended age of a minimum of 25 in this extract is at the most cautious end of the spectrum (in line with NIDA guidelines previously described).

In Colorado where legal ages of consumption are set at 18 and 21 for medical and recreational respectively, preventing consumption until 25 may not be a realistic goal for public health officials or regulators. The demographic of 18-20-year-olds who may consume cannabis legally if they have obtained a medical card further complicates matters. Questions can be raised about the difficulties of enforcing this recreational age limit at places such as universities where thousands of accounts of cannabis consumption have been documented in the grey literature (e.g. Perry, 2005), and it would seem reasonably self-evident that university students may be exposed to cannabis in a legal environment, and are a likely target for diversion.

How cannabis prevention messages should be framed, particularly for those under 18, is an important consideration. While the above extract emphasises brain damage to those under 25 as central to the potential message, alternative views on prevention education were also presented in the interviews. For example, Dr Wolk, Executive Director of the CDPHE claimed that his department had learned lessons around that style of messaging and moved away from emphasising brain damage as central to education campaigns. The extract below highlights contrasting approaches to messaging.

"I think we learned a lesson because we adopted a program shortly after I got here from the Governor's office which took this biased approach [Don't be a lab rat]. You know, [the campaign had] life-sized cages and of course the advocates became unglued, [they] were trying to set up images of jails and criminalization and of course people would go into these cages and take selfies of getting high.

And public health means you have to engage the people who are most likely to use ... So, we have to engage and educate ... we completely changed the tone of the campaign. So, now it's lighter. It's got more of an engagement strategy.

The other thing that we really learned as it related to kids is they don't want to hear about how it's bad for their developing brain or causing brain damage.

They were more likely to be impacted by messages around how marijuana could get in the way of what's next, so we targeted towards you might not be able to graduate. You might not be able to drive a car. You might not be able to get a job. You know all of these things are affected by using marijuana when you're still in your youth.

...

[One] component is the trusted adult campaign, which as our research and our survey data shows, that if kids have a trusted adult, they're less likely to engage in all kinds of behaviours; marijuana use, other drug use, alcohol, sex, whatever it is. Those who are teachers, doctors, coaches. You know aunts, uncles, whoever, to say you're the key to what's going to keep kids from using marijuana, not the public health department or doctors even". Larry Wolk, MD - Executive Director CDPHE, May 2017, Denver

The above text provides an example of prevention messages in legalised contexts reportedly evolving after originally taking a more penal focussed approach, with an emphasis on engagement. There are challenges to finding the right balance between scaremongering, which could potentially lack authenticity and isolate adolescents, or playing down potential harms associated with early initiation of cannabis use. A second point relates not to the message itself, but who is presenting it. The contention that youth pay more attention to trusted adults than public health officials is important with the apparent implication that education campaigns also need to provide parents with factual information.

An additional point is that this prevention education campaign strategy appears to focus solely on the harms associated with the enforcement of prohibition for those underage as opposed to any harms resulting from consumption of the drug *per se*. It is unclear whether this was a deliberate strategy as this was not addressed in interviews. Finally, the controversial nature of this engagement strategy was highlighted by a senior regulator in an interview:

> *"I think other people argue, "No that's a place where you're letting the industry soften your message". But hard messages haven't worked and so we try to stick with messaging that we know that works". Andrew Freedman, Director Office of Marijuana Coordination (Governor's Office), November 2016, Denver.*

Discussion - Comparing the data sets

Analysis of data set 1 (government documents) established that youth protection was stipulated as a priority objective by regulators, with the main focus being on advertising restrictions and the importance of education programs to reduce risks. In data set 2 (key stakeholder interviews), identified issues included the delayed appropriation of related funding, challenges relating to impact assessment, and evolving messages in prevention campaigns. Thus, in comparing the two data sets, tentative associations can be proposed between stated policy objectives and outcomes.

Despite real-world challenges and limitations to public health best practice that were identified (e.g., delays to initial funding for related youth prevention campaigns and challenges to data collection for impact assessment purposes), multiple interviewees commented on data reporting no statistically significant increase in observed youth consumption patterns in the initial years of the CRCM implementation. These comments can be linked to the latest consumption data from 2019 noted in the Introduction that indicate a continuation of that trend.

The evolution of prevention messaging campaigns to more of an engagement strategy by the CDPHE was established according to an account by the executive director of the CDPHE. Beyond indicating 'encouraging trends', the relationship between prevention education strategies and youth consumption rates is still emerging and more research is needed to further examine the effectiveness of prevention campaigns. However, the current study makes a novel contribution to the cannabis policy literature by highlighting these initial associations.

Chapter 8: Weighing the risks and benefits of a collaborative governance approach to implementing marijuana policy in the US: Evidence from the field in Colorado

Introduction

An intense or 'wicked' public policy problem is one that is difficult to solve due to, for example, lack of consensus around defining the problem, incomplete or contradictory knowledge, insufficient funding, and interconnectivity of the problem across a range of stakeholders (Rittel & Webber, 1973; Weible & Sabatier, 2006). This definition is applicable to the implementation of recreational cannabis policy, which is complex and impacts multiple stakeholders including numerous government departments (such as the departments of Agriculture, Revenue, Public Health and Environment, Public Safety, Transport, Education, and Human Services), public health representatives, families, communities, the cannabis industry, law enforcement, and consumers among others (e.g. City of Denver, 2015, 2018). Variations in cannabis policy in the US are also implemented at local, state, and federal levels, and contradictions between these variations are inherent. In Colorado, for example, the legal adult-use cannabis market exists despite federal prohibition of the drug, which has hindered state regulators' access to relevant federal resources such as the Food and Drug Administration (FDA) (Subritzky et al., 2017). To further confound matters, Colorado was the first jurisdiction world-wide to implement a fully seed-to-sale recreational cannabis market, which meant there was an extensive knowledge vacuum for regulators to devise rules around a previously prohibited substance (Subritzky et al., 2016b). This pioneering nature of the scheme created obvious challenges (no template or experience to draw on) and led former Director of the Office of Marijuana Coordination in the Governor's

Office Andrew Freedman to reportedly note that the State was "building the plane as we fly it" (Westword, 2017, June 28).

Colorado used a collaborative governance (CG) approach to allow implementation of the policy in Jan. 2014, just 13 months after it was legalized (Kamin, 2015). The CG process has been described as critical to enabling regulators in Colorado to devise comprehensive cannabis regulations within the tight deadlines stipulated in A64, the constitutional amendment that legalized cannabis in the State (Hickenlooper, 2014; Hudak, 2015b). Indeed, "in a mere three months, the A64 Task Force developed a comprehensive framework for the legislation and regulations needed to implement A64" (Blake & Finlaw, 2014, p.366).

This chapter examines three data sets ranging from late 2012 to mid-2017 relating to the CG approach to implement the CRCM. These data sets include hundreds of pages of government documents, over 1000 mass and niche media articles, and face-to-face interviews with 32 key stakeholders involved in the CG process such as senior regulators and executive level cannabis industry representatives. The Ansell and Gash (2008) contingency theory of CG is used as a framework to examine these data sets for examples of benefits and risks associated with CG in the implementation of the CRCM policy. Thus, in this paper a theoretical framework is applied to real-world qualitative data to grow the evidence base on both CG and cannabis policy implementation.

As cannabis reform continues in the US and internationally, CG has arguably become the default model for jurisdictions implementing legal cannabis policy, with prominent examples in California and Canada. However, the literature on the effectiveness of CG for implementing cannabis policy that aligns with regulatory objectives such as harm reduction is thin. As the first jurisdiction to embrace this approach, the Coloradan experience provides an important example for scholars of drug policy specifically and policy analysis more broadly in relation to the implementation of complex or wicked policies.

In this section of the paper: (i) the theoretical foundations and benefits of CG are introduced; (ii) a critique of CG is presented from a public health perspective with examples from the alcohol and tobacco industries; and (iii) the Ansell and Gash (2008) contingency theory of CG is summarised as the foundation and framework for subsequent analysis of the data sets examined in the paper.

Theoretical Foundations of Collaborative Governance

The collaborative approach to policy making has a fairly long academic pedigree, with roots "back to the birth of American federalism itself" (Emerson, Nabatchi, & Balogh, 2012, p.3). CG evolved in response to ineffective downstream policy implementation, as an alternative to interest group adversarialism, and generally as a response to solving 'wicked' problems (Ansell & Gash, 2008; Innes & Booher, 2010). CG offers the potential to expand democratic participation, and develop "sophisticated forms of collective learning and problem solving" (Ansell & Gash, 2008, p.561). Conceptual frameworks for collaborative policy-making include: collaborative governance (Ansell & Gash, 2008); collaborative public management (McGuire, 2006); cross sector collaboration (Bryson, Crosby, & Stone, 2006); and collaborative planning (Healey, 1996, 2003; Innes & Booher, 1999, 2010). As discussed below, the Ansell and Gash model of CG was selected as the most relevant to the Coloradan model.

Theoretical foundations of CG emerged from the Habermasian Theory of Communicative Action, in which language and undistorted communication are seen as central to achieving consensus and action (Habermas, 1981/2015; Tewdwr-Jones & Allmendinger, 1998). As noted by Innes and Booher (2010), the Habermas theory considers dialogue rational (and therefore, it is argued, a solid foundation for knowledge creation), if it meets certain speech conditions. These conditions include: (i) dialogue between differing interests must be face-to-face; (ii) communication must be sincere, without coercion, with all participants having equal access to information; and (iii) participants should not be influenced by power or peer pressure. In addition to these speech conditions, Innes and Booher (2010) add the elements of diversity and interdependence among stakeholders as essential for successful collaboration. This is in line with Gray (1989, p.6), who noted that successful collaboration is possible only when stakeholders acknowledge that "each needs the other to advance individual interest". Under these conditions, Innes and Booher (2010, p.36) argue "the dialogue can produce innovations that lead to an adaptive policy system in a context of complexity and uncertainty".

These theoretical elements are generally considered in the literature around varying perspectives of consensus building, which can be examined through the lens of mediated negotiation. For example Fisher and Ury (1981), in developing a ground-breaking framework for alternative dispute resolution, delineated several principles as central to collaborative negotiation. These stipulated: (i) the separation of the problem from people involved in the CG process to avoid emotional and ideological responses; (ii) focussing on the detailed interest as opposed to broad position; (iii) multiple options and perspectives should be considered before agreement is reached; (iv) objective criteria are used to reach agreement; and (v) stakeholders need to consider a best alternative if their favoured outcome cannot be achieved. Susskind and Cruikshank (1987) discussed the concept of negotiated approaches to consensus building that could potentially break impasses and allow stakeholders to move from zero-sum, adversarial conflict to win-win situations. In general, the argument for moving from adversarial to collaborative approaches to policy making is based on the possibility of conflict mitigation and integrating science through multi-party research and information sharing (Weible & Sabatier, 2009).

Critique of Collaborative Governance

Unsurprisingly, the collaborative approach to regulatory development has challenges around its structural complexity, which may have implications for its practicality (Huxham, Vangen, Huxham, & Eden, 2000). Furthermore, the model is associated with risk, most notably capture by industry and paralysis in the regulatory process due to failure to reach consensus. According to Stigler (1971, p.3), regulatory capture occurs when "regulation is acquired by the industry and is designed and operated primarily for its benefit". While Stigler was interested in the petrochemical industry, examples of capture have been observed in many other industries including alcohol, tobacco, agriculture, food, and pharmaceuticals, in each instance with severe consequences for public health. Moodie et al. (2013) noted how industries can impact public regulations with both soft and hard power. Soft power relates to the influence of culture and ideas, while hard power may involve developing institutional and financial relationships. Strategies employed across these industries include: funding 'think tanks' to bias research findings; the employment of health professionals and policy makers; lobbying public officials to minimise and oppose regulations; and encouraging voters to resist public health regulations. An example of the latter strategy includes tobacco campaigns that argue use of tobacco is a personal choice that should not be controlled by 'nanny states' (Moodie et al., 2013).

Furthermore, Rosenbloom and Gong (2013, p.546) contended that CG models "can seriously blur the boundaries between state and society, the public and private sectors, and government and business". More specifically, they argued that CG models are exposed to two levels of corruption risk. First, as collaboration expands beyond individuals and agencies, corruption may expand as more opportunities arise "in the guise of coordination and cooperation, for government officials to collude and trade with … nongovernmental actors in pursuit of private gains" (Rosenbloom & Gong, 2013, p.548). They contend this may happen not simply as a result of increased interaction, but also because of the interdependence on which CG models rely. Second, according to Rosenbloom and Gong (2013), the cost of monitoring may increase, resulting in decreased ability to hold stakeholders accountable. This creates a need for more nuanced integrity mechanisms. Additional risks include manipulation of the process by powerful stakeholders, lack of commitment, and distrust. At the most cynical extreme it has been stated that while "policies and initiatives are usually born in hope and optimism, [they] eventually decline in sadness and disappointment" (Baldwin, Cave, & Lodge, 2012, p.68; Kaufman, 1971).

A major reason for this scepticism is based on lessons from alcohol and tobacco where industry groups seek to maximise profit above all. For this reason, multiple scholars have argued to keep the alcohol industry out of the policy process generally speaking (e.g. Cowlishaw & Thomas, 2018; Miller & Harkins, 2010). Representative of this view, McCambridge, Kypri, Miller, Hawkins, and Hastings (2014, p.1) concluded that: "… working with, and for, industry bodies … helps disguise fundamental conflicts of interest and serves only to legitimize corporate efforts to promote partnership as a means of averting evidence-based alcohol policies". In addition, Miller and Harkins (2010) argued that the alcohol industry among others engages a broad range of strategies and tactics to both promote and defend profit-making operations. The authors examined four areas including science, civil society, the media, and policy and concluded that lobbying is the primary tactic of wide-ranging strategies to capture various arenas of decision making (regulatory capture).

Despite these concerns, several authors have contended that the CG process in Colorado was largely successful in allowing for the creation of a complex set of regulations, with no template and within tight deadlines, and at least in terms of policy implementation as distinct from policy outcomes (Hudak, 2015b; Kamin, 2015). In this paper we investigate CG approach in the CRCM, and to this end clarifying a theoretical framework is helpful.

The Ansell and Gash Contingency Theory of Collaborative Governance as an Interpretive Framework

According to Ansell and Gash (2008), CG has the potential to increase collective learning, particularly specialised knowledge that draws from a range of institutions. However, as noted above it also comes with risks such as regulatory paralysis and capture by industry (Ansell & Gash, 2008). Ansell and Gash (2008, p.544) contend that many conceptualisations of CG are "focussed on the species rather than the genus", in the sense of being derived from individual case examples as opposed to a common method of developing policy. They addressed these issues when reviewing 137 cases of CG across a range of policy areas with the aim of developing a contingency theory of CG that can potentially mitigate risks in real-world settings. They provide a more restrictive definition of CG than is commonly found in the literature:

> A governing arrangement where one or more public agencies directly engage non-state stakeholders [both individual citizens and organisations] in a collective decision-making process that is formal, consensus-oriented, and deliberative and that aims to make or implement public policy or manage public programs or assets (Ansell & Gash, 2008, p.544).

Ansell and Gash (2008) articulated six necessary criteria for collaborative governance: (i) public agencies are responsible for instigating public meetings; (ii) participants must include non-state representatives; (iii) all stakeholders are expected to contribute to and engage in decision making, as opposed to state agencies consulting them; (iv) public forums are formally organised; (v) the goal of public meetings is always to reach consensus, even if it is not achieved in practise; and (vi) the collaboration is focused on policy that impacts the general public.

As will be discussed in more detail in the results section, each of these criteria appears to have been met in the Coloradan CG model, suggesting that the Ansell and Gash (2008) model is appropriate for examining the implementation and evolution of the CRCM regulatory process.

The Ansell and Gash CG model consists of four core components that constitute high risk areas and risk mitigation strategies including: (i) starting conditions; (ii) facilitative leadership; (iii) institutional design; and (iv) the collaborative process. These are now briefly described.

First, starting conditions of collaborations may discourage or facilitate cooperation between various stakeholders. This component is divided into three sub-elements, namely:

(i) Risk: Regulatory capture and power imbalance. Scepticism around CG tends to be concentrated in the notion that the process may be prone to manipulation, particularly if industry groups are over-represented or perceived as advantageously placed throughout negotiations (McCloskey, 1999).
Risk Mitigation: If an imbalance is identified, it is essential that strategies to empower weaker groups are incorporated into the process (e.g. Fawcett et al., 1995; Larkin, Cierpial, Stack, Morrison, & Griffith, 2008; Mitchell, 2005). A framework for assessing power imbalances in CG models has been delineated by Purdy (2012).

(ii) Incentives to participate. Ongoing participation is linked to: available resources (given most participation is voluntary and unpaid); levels of interdependence among diverse stakeholders; the availability of alternative channels of mediation, such as the court system; and managing inclusivity of stakeholders within the process (Johnston, Hicks, Nan, & Auer, 2010).

(iii) Prehistory of antagonism or cooperation. If there is a history of antagonism among stakeholders, additional time investment to build trust may be required (given the history of prohibition, this was potentially of relevance in the Coloradan context).

Second, facilitative leadership that brings stakeholders together in a collaborative spirit is crucial. Ensuring integrity and legitimacy in the consensus-building process by setting clear ground rules and exploring mutual gains are core objectives at the facilitative level of leadership (as opposed to the levels of mediation and intervention). According to Ryan (2001), collaborative leadership is effective when it includes sufficient management of the process, technical credibility, and wide acceptance of decisions. Under the Ansell and Gash model, when starting conditions are sub-optimal (e.g., where there is a perceived power imbalance or history of antagonism), strong leadership is seen as essential for positive outcomes. In specific regard to the CRCM, Hudak (2015b) contended the tone of this leadership was set at the gubernatorial level by Hickenlooper (discussed in more detail below).

Third, institutional design is an important variable within the Ansell and Gash approach. It relates to the fundamental protocols and rules of the collaboration and is central to its perceived legitimacy. Important design considerations include:

I.   Broad inclusion of impacted stakeholders in the process.
II.   That the transparency of the process is imperative, and closely linked to building trust and the legitimacy of process. Transparency may build trust by demonstrating to stakeholders the process is not simply "... a cover for backroom private deals" (Ansell & Gash, 2008, p.557).
III.   The notion of consensus-building is also an important design element, and more specifically whether (or not) reaching consensus is a formal goal of the collaboration. On the one hand, demanding consensus may lead to decision stalemates (regulatory paralysis) and/or lowest common denominator outcomes, while on the other hand it can assist with promoting cooperation.
IV.   A final design consideration relates to implementing deadlines, which may put limitations on the scope of discussions but also reign in meetings that continue in perpetuity.

Fourth, under the Ansell and Gash model, the collaborative process consists of multiple elements including:

I.   Face-to-face dialogue is noted as necessary but not sufficient because there is the possibility of increasing antagonism by reinforcing stereotypes, as well as potentially breaking down barriers.

II. Trust building is an essential component, and depending on starting conditions may require a substantial investment of time over a long period.

III. Commitment to the collaborative process is linked to incentives to participate outlined above and may require supporting decisions contrary to stakeholders' initial objectives. Additionally, if industry stakeholders' incentives are simply profit-related, then steps to limit capture must be incorporated. Within this element, stakeholders may take 'ownership' of the process, whereby instead of trying to lobby and influence policy makers from the outside, as in traditional adversarial and managerial approaches, stakeholders actively participate in collaborative decision making. In this sense stakeholders share responsibility with their opponents. Once again, trust and interdependence are essential to enhance commitment.

IV. Shared understanding builds on the notion of ownership whereby stakeholders embark on a common mission or objective.

V. Intermediate outcomes, such as joint fact-finding missions (collective learning), are included as important in the collaborative process. In this sense, small, tangible wins are accrued and contribute to momentum building.

According to Innes and Booher (2010, p.24), "for practise and experience [of CG] to amount to knowledge, it must be intertwined with theorising". This "praxis" can provide a link to deeper understanding that cannot be fully articulated by theory alone (Innes & Booher, 2010, p.23). Thus, applying a CG theoretical framework to data that represent elements of the practical, real-world Coloradan experience of cannabis policy implementation, offers the possibility of generating new insights.

Results

Coverage of Collaborative Governance Across the Corpus

The data corpus was coded deductively for examples of CG, returning a wealth of data for analysis. The overarching CG theme was identified in all 13 government documents, 203 of the media articles, and 18 of the interview transcripts.

The government documents tended to include elements relating to the institutional design of CG such as facilitative leadership, collective learning, and logistics around formal work group meetings that were stipulated as a core component of the Coloradan CG model.

The media sample provided reasonably extensive coverage of aspects of CG in 2014, although this decreased in the sample over the three years examined. As the largest data set, the media sample is presented in Table 9 below for additional clarity. As can be noted, 93 mass media articles contained text coded under the broad rubric of CG in 2014 (roughly evenly split between the Post and Gazette, decreasing to 44 in 2015 and 15 in 2016). Niche media coverage of CG included 49 related articles in 2015 and just 2 in 2016.

Table 9: Coverage of collaborative governance in mass and niche media articles 2014 – 2016

Article Type and Year	Number of articles
Post 2014	53
Gazette 2014	40
Total Mass Media Articles 2014	93
Post 2015	24
Gazette 2015	20
Total Mass Media Articles 2015	44
Post 2016	8
Gazette 2016	7
Total Mass Media Articles 2016	15

Total Niche Media Articles 2015	49
Total Niche Media Articles 2016	2
Grand Total	203

Data set 3 included discussion of CG by 18 interviewees representing regulators, public health officials, and the cannabis industry. Interview participants discussed the following sub-elements of CG most prominently: collective learning and addressing the knowledge gap as a pioneering jurisdiction; policy implementation and enforcement; regulatory capture, regulatory paralysis, transparency and trust, and work groups.

Having summarised the extent of CG coverage across the corpus, the A & G model is now applied to these data from two perspectives of the CG process, namely policy implementation and policy evolution. First, following the A & G model, conditions for policy implementation are assessed relating to starting conditions, facilitative leadership, institutional design, and the CG process.

Starting Conditions

Perhaps surprisingly given the controversial nature of cannabis legalization, there are indications from across the corpus that starting conditions were favourable for the CG process to develop the world's first Retail Marijuana Code (RMC). The A & G framework stipulated three important sub-elements of starting conditions that may limit or enhance the effectiveness of CG, namely regulatory capture and power imbalance, incentives to participate, and prehistory of antagonism. These are explored below.

Regulatory Capture and Power Imbalance

Given that no regulations existed for the newly legalized adult-use cannabis market at the start of the CG process, it is difficult to assess regulatory capture in this initial phase. For this reason and its relevance to study objectives, regulatory capture is explored as a standalone theme below. Thus, the most obvious risk of power imbalance within the starting conditions would seem to be if an authoritarian approach to rulemaking was undertaken by regulators. However, no examples were identified in the corpus of external stakeholders expressing concerns in this regard. On the contrary, several interviewees indicated that the state deliberately took steps to reduce the risk of power imbalance. The following is representative:

> [We found] that when people come to the table and they believe that they are being heard and their concerns are being heard and they are being heard and carefully considered, they are more willing to voluntarily contribute because they have a vested interest in the solution. So what we have found is that we get really a lot better results and people work together to improve outcomes when they know their point of view is being taken seriously. *Group Interview: <u>Barbara Brohl - Executive Director CDOR (speaker)</u>, Ron Kammerzell - Senior Director of Marijuana Enforcement Division, Mathew Scott - Senior Director of Taxation, Heidi Humphreys - Deputy Director CDOR, May 2017, Denver.*

In addition to this view presented by state regulators (who hold the bureaucratic power), non-state stakeholders expressed similar views as illustrated below in relevant sections. Thus, according the data examined in this paper, risks associated with power imbalance do not appear to have adversely impacted starting conditions of the CG process in the CRCM.

Incentives to Participate

As noted, the A & G model outlines multiple factors that may influence the ongoing participation of stakeholders. From both the government documents and media samples it is apparent that incentives to participate included self-interest and a 'sense of being part of history'. Self-interest is a key incentive to participate in the CG process, and this aspect was also recognised in government documents, for example:

> All stakeholders share an interest in creating efficient and effective regulations that provide for the responsible development of the new marijuana laws. *Government Document: Governor's Executive Order (B2012-004): Creating a Task Force on the implementation of A64, Dec. 10 2012, P.1*

The ground-breaking nature of the policy was also described in government documents and media articles, particularly around the time of implementation in January, 2014. The following extracts are representative:

> Members of the Task Force concluded their work with the understanding that, for good or ill, they had played an historic role in the evolution of marijuana policy in the United States. Government Document: A64 Implementation Task Force Report, P.5

> A64 presents issues of first impression in Colorado and the US as no state previously has legalized marijuana for recreational use in the face of federal legal restrictions. Government Document: Governor's Executive Order (B2012-004): Creating a Task Force on the implementation of A64, Dec. 10 2012, P.1

In addition to these official statements, there was significant media attention focused on the policy implementation. The following extract is an example of how that coverage was framed as an historic event:

> Lucas DaSilva of Georgia drove through the night and slept in his car with his dog Marley before settling at the front door of the Telluride Green Room around dawn Wednesday. A few hours later, he emerged from the store $180 lighter but holding six grams of African Queen, Acapulco Gold, Bubble Gum herb, and several edibles.

> "I'm at a loss for words. Happy New Year!" he yelled, arms outstretched amidst cheers from the line. "This is history I just made. I can't believe it. Such a blessing." Mass media article: The Post - Scenes from Day 1 of Colorado's recreational marijuana sales, Jan. 1 2014

From these extracts it seems reasonably self-evident that the new policy was novel and historic in nature, and it seems reasonable to conclude this may have been a motivating factor in terms of participating in the CG process in the early years. In the context of starting conditions, it seems that there was sufficient incentive to participate in the CG process for stakeholders selected. Nonetheless, it is important to note the data corpus ranges from 2012 to 2017, and since then much larger jurisdictions (e.g., California and Canada) have legalized cannabis for adult-use, and as such the novelty factor initially apparent in Colorado may be less a compelling reason for participation in future. The conditions were unique for a pioneering jurisdiction that by definition cannot be replicated.

Prehistory of Antagonism or Cooperation

Given the previously prohibited status of cannabis and a clear history of antagonism between the state, cannabis cultivators, and cannabis consumers (Bonnie & Whitebread, 1974), this sub-element of the starting conditions theme seems at face value to constitute significant risk to the CG process. However, there is no evidence in the corpus that this risk impacted the CG process initially. Rather, a pattern of cooperation was identified among the A64 Implementation Task Force in particular. This pattern was most clearly articulated in interviews with stakeholders intimately involved in the CG process at the pre-implementation phase. The following extracts from interviewees retrospectively discussing their experience working as members of the A64 Implementation Task Force are illustrative. First:

> *The thing I enjoyed about it [the Task Force work] was that people from two ends of the spectrum on a debate were able to come together and agree upon certain things. Interview: DR Kenneth Finn, pain physician at Springs Rehabilitation, member public health work group and scientific advisory committee, August 13, 2017*

In the interview with Dr Finn it stated that as a pain physician he had strong reservations about legal recreational cannabis in Colorado, so it was perhaps surprising that an opponent of the CRCM was nonetheless supportive of the CG process undertaken in Colorado. A second perspective was provided in an interview with a constitutional scholar who was also an A64 Implementation Task Force Member:

> *There have been a number of issues where the regulated, that is the industry, and the regulators have been in total agreement. Public education has been one of those. Banking has been an important one of those. Outdoor advertising seems like it's one of those, where you might expect antagonism between industry*

and regulators you see in fact cooperation and not in a way gives worries about capture or rather regulatory breakdowns, but simply a natural alignment of interest. Interview: Sam Kamin, Professor of Marijuana Law and Policy, University of Denver, May 2017

According to the A & G model, when a prehistory of antagonism is identified a time investment to build trust or strong facilitative leadership may mitigate risks to the CG process. The aspect of facilitative leadership is considered further in the following section, however there are clear indications in the above illustrative extracts that starting conditions for the CG process in Colorado were not unduly impacted by potential risks outlined in the A & G model.

Facilitative Leadership

According to the A & G model, facilitative leadership includes exploring mutual gains by bringing stakeholders together in a collaborative spirit; setting core objectives and clear ground rules to ensure both the legitimacy and integrity of the consensus building process, in a manner that brings credibility and wide acceptance of decisions. Indications of strong facilitative leadership exhibiting these criteria were identified in a gubernatorial Executive Order and interviews with Barbara Brohl, the (at time of interview) Executive Director of the Colorado Department of Revenue (CDOR) (the state licensing Authority for medical and recreational cannabis in the State).

First, in line with Hudak's observations noted in the introduction of this paper, an example of strong facilitative leadership by State Governor Hickenlooper was most apparent in a gubernatorial Executive Order for establishing a Task Force to implement the legalization of cannabis as stipulated in A64. The document related to the initial 3-month CG process incorporated by the A64 Implementation Task Force (Dec. 2012 – Feb. 2013) and included comprehensive descriptions of the mission and scope, required membership, transparency, and timeline for the project. For example, the mission and scope clearly outlined the expected spirit of collaboration:

Task Force members are charged with finding practical and pragmatic solutions to challenges of implementing A64 while at all times respecting the diverse perspectives that each member will bring to the work of the task force. The Task Force shall respect the will of the voters of Colorado and shall not engage in a debate of the merits of marijuana legalization or A64. Government Document: Governor's Executive Order (B2012-004): Creating a Task Force on the implementation of A64, Dec. 10, 2012, P.1

This document also outlined a framework for Task Force objectives, membership, public meetings, and timelines, which was fleshed out in the resulting report of the A64 Implementation Task Force and is further considered within the context of the institutional design below. As a small aside, this Executive Order also clearly articulated the six A & G criteria necessary criteria for CG described above including the state instigating public meetings, the inclusion of non-state representatives, formally organized public forums, a goal of reaching consensus, and a public policy focus.

The A & G model also identified failure to reach consensus as a potential cause for delay when multiple stakeholders are participating in the process. To mitigate this risk, A & G argued that a facilitative leadership strategy is essential. As noted above, Barbara Brohl was the executive director of CDOR, which was mandated SLA in A64 to oversee the development, implementation, and enforcement of regulations for the adult-use cannabis market. It is under her leadership that the collaboration took place so her view clearly offers authoritative insight. In an interview in 2017 she provided her perspective on reaching consensus in a highly controversial and emotional policy area:

> *Participants are not equal partners and I don't want to go so far as to say it's consulting, but I think they come in as an active participant. In the end, I'm the state licensing authority and the state licensing authority has been given great authority here in the state to implement the rules that are required to effectuate the implementation of this [new marijuana policy]. I wouldn't say that everyone around the table is equal, but I will tell you that I carefully consider everybody around the table's inputs, concerns, and issues.*
>
> *In the end, I have been given the authority to actually make those decisions. So, if I can get them to consensus*

and if I can get them to collaborate and I can get them to the right result, that is the goal. But if not, I will make a decision based on what is best for the state of Colorado, best for this industry, and best for the individuals that I have a public safety responsibility for. Group Interview: Barbara Brohl - Executive Director CDOR (speaker), Ron Kammerzell - Senior Director of Marijuana Enforcement Division, Mathew Scott - Senior Director of Taxation, Heidi Humphreys - Deputy Director CDOR, May 2017, Denver.

From over three hours of interviews with Executive Director Brohl (in two separate group interviews), it was apparent that she was focused on implementing the will of the people as stipulated by the requirements of A64, in a manner that was reasonable, responsible, and, most importantly, effective. This appears to have been a crucial factor in the ability of the A64 Task Force to achieve very tight deadlines. Thus, while Hudak (2015b) contended the tone of this leadership was set at the gubernatorial level by Hickenlooper, who clearly played a role, it is similarly likely that Brohl's leadership made an important contribution in preventing regulatory paralysis in practice, at least in the context of the pre-implementation phase that was described in the interview.

Institutional Design

According to the A & G model, basic ground rules and protocols create the procedural legitimacy essential to the process of collaboration. In particular, the authors highlighted four important design considerations including broad inclusion of impacted stakeholders, transparency, an aim to reach consensus, and implementing deadlines. As noted above, these can be found in the Governor's Executive Order (B2012-004), which specified the following aspects of the CG process: (i) background and purpose; (ii) mission and scope; (iii) membership; (iv) open meetings; and (v) duration. Building on the Executive Order, the A64 Implementation Task Force Report described comprehensive guidelines around these matters. For example:

The Task Force, created by the Governor on December 10, 2012, in Executive Order B2012-004, was asked to identify the legal, policy and procedural issues that need to be resolved, and to offer suggestions and proposals for legislative, regulatory and executive actions that need to be taken, for the effective and efficient implementation of Amendment 64 - the constitutional amendment authorizing the use and regulation of marijuana in the State of Colorado. The Executive Order directed the Task Force to complete its work by February 28, 2013, and to then report its recommendations and findings.

...

The Task Force included members of the Colorado General Assembly and representatives of the Attorney General's office, state agencies, law enforcement, the defense bar, district attorneys, the medical profession, the marijuana industry, the Amendment 64 campaign, marijuana consumers, academia, local governments, and Colorado's employers and employees. Five working groups, comprised of task force members and additional subject matter experts from around the state, met weekly during January and February. The working groups heard testimony from stakeholders and members of the public and then developed and drafted implementation recommendations, which were further vetted, revised, adopted or rejected in the meetings of the Task Force. All meetings of the Task Force and its working groups were open to the public, and there was time set aside at each of the meetings for public input and comment.

Although the Task Force included many diverse perspectives, each member remained faithful to the Governor's charge to respect the will of the voters of Colorado and not to engage in a debate of the merits of marijuana legalization or Amendment 64. All of the recommendations in this report were approved by at least a majority vote and many represent a consensus view. Government Document: A64 Implementation Task Force Final Report, P.5

This extract articulates details relating to the four design elements stipulated in the A & G model. For example, the wide range of stakeholders listed above appears to align with the sub-element of broad inclusion with a range of non-state participants representing the cannabis industry, public health, consumers, and law enforcement among others. Furthermore, the transparency of the process was described by public meetings with opportunities for public input. This aspect can also be considered with a wider lens encompassing the entire rulemaking process in Colorado, which also includes public hearings as an integral component. The aims of consensus-building and time limitations are also outlined in the extract. Considering these sub-elements together, from the corpus under investigation it appears that the institutional design of the scheme in Colorado created conditions conducive to a potentially effective CG process.

Beyond this technical description of the design, some perspective of what the A64 Implementation Task Force was broadly trying to achieve was provided in an interview, which was illustrative of a general tone identified in multiple interviews:

> *The tone of collaboration started with the A64 Task Force where it was decided we're not going to sit inside and make regulations in a bubble. We are going to hear from everybody who has an opinion on this. And the A64 Task Force was a huge operation to put together. I think it makes for better policy. But also, I think it makes the industry, public health, the concerned groups buy into the process a little bit more. Interview: Andrew Freedman, Director of the Office of Marijuana Coordination October 2016*

This extract provides an illustration of the value the State placed on the collaborative process to capture the broadest possible range of knowledge around the issue. It encapsulates the fundamental purpose of collaboration in creating policy and should be considered in the context of no existing template and a knowledge vacuum in terms of how cannabis should be regulated.

The final sub-element for considering the conditions for CG according to the A & G model is the CG process itself. As noted, important elements include face-to-face communication, trust-building, and commitment to the process. By implementing measures in line with CG best practice (e.g., a clear definition of purpose, strong guidelines, explicit target deadlines and broad inclusiveness of stakeholders), it is apparent that Coloradan regulators avoided many pitfalls associated with the approach. As these aspects have been addressed to some extent above, they are not considered further here.

Having identified multiple instances in the corpus relating to starting conditions, facilitative leadership, institutional design, and the CG process in Colorado, it is possible to conclude that fundamental elements outlined in the A & G model as important for successful collaboration in policy-making appeared to be largely in place (at least from the perspective of initial policy implementation and developing the initial RMC as opposed to policy evolution and outcomes).

Nonetheless, there appeared to remain extensive risks for regulators given the diversity of issues that needed to be resolved. Rich examples of the more pressing issues that required new regulations were prominently evident in the interviews data set. These included developing cultivation and quality testing standards; age limits; driving rules such as detecting impairment; public health, safety and environment rules; education; impact assessment, and much more.

The corpus is now examined to identify instances of benefits and risks associated with CG as the policy evolved. These included collective learning, regulatory paralysis, and regulatory capture.

Collective Learning and Addressing the Knowledge Vacuum

As noted above, one of the most important potential benefits of the CG approach is the opportunity for collective learning by bringing together multiple stakeholders who in combination have a broad range of expertise. In all three data sets the most common examples of collective learning were framed within the knowledge void - both for regulators with no previous experience and cultivators who, while presumably in possession of cannabis cultivation expertise, were likely unfamiliar with the new bureaucracy and costs associated with growing cannabis compliantly.

Knowledge gap

Given the pioneering nature of the Coloradan scheme, the knowledge gap was described across all three data sets as being more pronounced than in more traditional policy realms. The knowledge gap related to three primary issues: (i) historical federal prohibition (and therefore no regulatory template); (ii) the State's lack of access to federal resources (due to continued prohibition at the federal level); and (iii) a continued inability to research the impacts and benefits of consumption due to ongoing federal restrictions. These issues are examined below.

First, data from the media and interview data sets indicated that prohibition created a large knowledge gap because records of cultivation and consumption activity would provide evidence of an illegal activity, which likely led to secretive record keeping.

> *This industry came up in stealth, born in basements and crawl spaces. Mass media article: The Post - Pot growers cultivating in the shadows seek US patent protection, December 26, 2014*

> *The industry needs a lot of education ... I believe most of the people want to comply but a couple of things they don't understand are pesticide regulation, which is fairly complex, and the other thing is they've kind of done all this underground and so they're used to doing it a certain way. So they're kind of re-learning how to do all that. But it's a lot of education and a lot of learning and a lot of people. It's just a massive industry that all of a sudden showed up, and moving that curve is hard. So that's a big issue, I think, and that's one of the things that doesn't change overnight.*

> *...*

> *initially when we were doing complaint investigations -- I don't have the exact number off the top of my head but we were finding 50 or 60 percent of the samples were contaminated after a year or two we are down to about 15%. So we believe it's getting better. If it was a regular Agriculture commodity we would see it as less than one percent typically. We are going towards that and we are getting closer.*

> *Interview: Mitch Yergert, Director for the Division of Plant Industry, Colorado Department of Agriculture, Denver, May 2017*

Furthermore, the historical prohibition in the State also clearly impacted regulators as, by definition, black-markets are not regulated. As such, there was no template or best practice guidelines for regulators to follow.

Second, from the media and interview data sets it was apparent that continued federal prohibition limited the ability of regulators to access relevant federal resources. For example:

> *Marijuana remaining illegal on the federal level does present some interesting wrinkles for regulators. Rules that typically would land under the US Food and Drug Administration fall in-house for state regulators, ... topics such as potency, refrigeration, and safety of edibles. Mass media article: The Post - Five immediate concerns for states with new marijuana laws, November 11, 2016*

A further indication was provided in an interview with a senior agriculture official:

> *You just have to get your mind around this is a different paradigm ... and you have to do stuff that the federal government typically would do. Interview: Mitch Yergert, director for the Division of Plant Industry, Colorado Department of Agriculture, Denver, May 2017*

Third, there were multiple examples of the knowledge gap in the context of restrictions on research into the impacts and benefits of cannabis consumption. The following examples from senior public health officials in the state are representative:

> *The fact that on a federal level it's still considered illegal makes it challenging to conduct research. It makes it challenging to obtain product to research that mimics the product that people are consuming rather than what is scientifically grown and allowed from the University of Mississippi. Interview: Dr. Larry Wolk, Executive Director of the Colorado Department of Public Health and Environment (CDPHE), Denver, May 2017*

I think another piece is that there's not a whole lot of research available to help describe what legalized marijuana on a commercial sort of market is and what the impacts are going to then be on that local community. Interview: Heath Harmon, Director of Health Division for Boulder County Public Health, August 2017

From the examples presented above, there is a strong indication that regulators in Colorado were faced with challenging circumstances in terms of a knowledge gap. When considered in light of the A & G model, these challenges would seem to increase the appeal of taking a CG approach to implementing the nascent policy.

Collective Learning

The government documents data set provided demonstrable collective learning outputs, most notably in the A64 Implementation Task Force Report and the RMC itself (in terms of both its initial form and the extent it evolved as a dynamic document over the five years under investigation in this paper). These two documents are now examined in turn.

First, the Task Force Report stipulated guiding principles and provided an overview of recommendations for ...:

All of the Task Force recommendations stem from one or more of these Guiding Principles:

- *Promote the health, safety, and well-being of Colorado's youth*
- *Be responsive to consumer needs and issues*
- *Propose efficient and effective regulation that is clear and reasonable and not unduly burdensome*
- *Create sufficient and predictable funding mechanisms to support the regulatory and enforcement scheme*
- *Create a balanced regulatory scheme that is complementary, not duplicative, and clearly defined between state and local licensing authorities*

- *Establish tools that are clear and practical, so that interactions between law enforcement, consumers, and licensees are predictable and understandable*
- *Ensure that our streets, schools, and communities remain safe.*
- *Develop clear and transparent rules and guidance for certain relationships, such as between employers and employees, landlords and tenants, and students and educational institutions*
- *Take action that is faithful to the text of Amendment 64*

...

Summary of the Recommendations

The Task Force considered nearly 100 individual recommendations developed by its five Working Groups. It approved 73 of these, which have been consolidated into the 58 recommendations.

...

The 58 recommendations are presented in 17 categories, for the ease of lawmakers and agency officials in locating recommendations related to different issue areas surrounding the use and regulation of marijuana. Recommendations are offered for the following activities:

- *Creating and financing the new regulatory structure*
- *Taxation of marijuana through both excise and sales taxes, to support regulatory and enforcement costs, as well as other state programs including several suggested by this Task Force related to marijuana education and studies*
- *Transitioning to a system that regulates and enforces both medical and adult-use marijuana*
- *Specifying requirements for licensees, operations, and interactions with consumers*
- *Consumer safety issues such as signage, marketing, advertising, packaging, labeling, restricting THC content in infused products, restricting additives and adulterants in marijuana products, and encouraging good cultivation and laboratory practices in the industry*

- *Educating citizens about the effects and risks involved in marijuana use and conducting studies on the effects of marijuana use on public health and safety*
- *Amending statutes to reflect the legal status of limited, adult-use marijuana in Colorado and to indicate penalties for certain marijuana offenses, including the treatment of juveniles in the possession and the transfer of marijuana to persons under 21 years of age*
- *Specifying rules for home cultivation of marijuana*
- *Requesting resolution of federal restrictions on banking and allowable tax deductions for legal marijuana businesses in Colorado*
- *General guidance for employers and employees, property owners, the enforcement of contracts, and the legalization of industrial hemp in Colorado*
- *Forming a follow-up task force in three years, to review the recommendations of this Task Force in light of the actual implementation of Amendment 64.* Government Document: A64 Implementation Task Force Report, P. 12 – 15

The above extracts provide context and concrete examples of learnings developed throughout the initial CG process of policy implementation. Both the competing objectives and the range of issues that the A64 Implementation Task Force addressed highlight the complex (wicked) nature of implementing cannabis policy and should be further considered in light of the State's pioneering status and the tight deadlines required for implementation. A number of recommendations were made by the various work groups, of which approximately three quarters were accepted by the Task Force (and ultimately passed into law). The breadth and depth of these recommendations would seem to be an important benefit of the CG process (once again within the context of policy *implementation* as distinct from *evolution*).

However as noted above, according to the A & G model, short timelines may impact on the quality of policy outcomes reached during the CG process. For a deeper analysis of this point, an examination of the evolution of the RMC was undertaken to provide an indication of how collective learning occurred over the five years since the CRCM was implemented.

By mid-2018, the RMC was in its 10th iteration and consisted of 262 pages covering 18 rule categories such as licensing, retail marijuana cultivation, manufacturing, and testing for quality control. This compares with 124 pages in the first iteration in 2013 and provides an illustration of increased regulatory complexity as the CRCM has matured.

The following examples of the reported pace of regulatory change were sourced from across the data sets:

> *"The rulemaking within the CDOR is sort of a continual process ... [that] sort of repeated the initial process that we did with the [A64 Implementation] Task Force, which tried to get as many of the stakeholders around the table as possible, take public comment and try to draft rules by consensus.*
>
> *...*
>
> *There are probably 30 to 50 bills a year having to do with cannabis still. Now five years into regulation that's still - the legislative piece is still an important one."*
> *Interview: Sam Kamin, Professor of Marijuana Law and Policy, University of Denver, May 2017*

From this text, it is unclear whether the pace of evolutionary change is a reflection of the complexity of the policy being implemented or that the quality of the initial regulations perhaps suffered as a result of too short a timeline for the initial development of regulations (or other potential risks associated with CG process). On the one hand, the short timeline was stipulated in A64 so regulators had no option to extend the pre-implementation phase when the first iteration of the RMC was crafted. Within this context, the recommendations listed above appear comprehensive and wide-ranging frameworks to be built on. On the other hand, regulating cannabis is clearly a complex matter and this has implications relating to how long the critical pre-implantation phase should be. While having sufficient time to develop effective rules would seem preferable, finding perfect policy could be an exercise in perpetuity so it is essential to find a balance. Additionally, it is to be expected that cannabis policy will evolve as markets mature and having a robust rulemaking process such as that in Colorado to deal with change is fundamental to adapting policy effectively. On balance, tight deadlines appear to have focused as opposed to hindered the CG process (at least in the context of the pre-implementation phase).

Regulatory Paralysis

Given the pace of regulatory change noted above, on the face of it, regulatory paralysis does not appear to have been overly problematic in the pre-implementation phase of the CRCM, particularly as there seems to have been strong facilitative leadership that addressed this potential issue. According to Brohl in an interview in 2016:

> It was a very, very quick turnaround with a very aggressive schedule. Group Interview: <u>Barbara Brohl - Executive Director CDOR (speaker)</u>, Jim Burrack Director Marijuana Enforcement Division, Denver, Nov. 2016

However, pockets of paralysis were identified primarily in the media articles data set (n=7) in issue-specific contexts as the policy evolved post-implementation, most notably related to the State's initial grappling with how edible cannabis products should be labelled. The following extracts are representative:

> A months-long panel of doctors, pot regulators, and edible-marijuana makers failed to agree last year on how to make those foods "clearly identifiable" when out of the wrapper. A stamp or marking may work for chocolates or candies, but not marijuana-infused liquids, sauces or bulk foods such as loose granola. Mass media article: The Post - New Colorado bill scraps plans for changing look of pot edibles, Mar. 24, 2015

> After a state-wide task force failed to come up with recommendations last year, lawmakers have been handed the issue of edibles and how to regulate them. Mass media article: The Gazette - Study shows pot arrests in Colorado have dropped 84% since 2010, Jan. 7 2015

> Colorado's marijuana industry initially was hesitant about the change, pointing out in regulatory meetings that alcohol makers aren't required to dye their drinks funny colors to make sure parents don't let kids get

hold of the booze. Some of the industry expectation was, 'Let's keep it on the parents and the users in keeping it away from children or people who shouldn't use it'. Mass media article: The Gazette - New look of marijuana edibles designed to avoid uncertainty, Oct. 1, 2016

These extracts provide an example of risks associated with the CG process as experienced in the 'real world' context of the CRCM. From these extracts two aspects are apparent. First, when multiple stakeholders from a wide range of backgrounds gathered to address complex policy issues relating to cannabis policy implementation, there were instances when consensus could not be reached. On the one hand, from the above text it appears that industry was responsible for delays by trying to weaken restrictions, however the point that compares the regulation of alcohol to that of cannabis highlights text in the constitutional amendment A64 stipulating that cannabis should be regulated similar to alcohol. From this perspective, the cannabis industry appeared to be clarifying that legal requirement, and this is an indication of the complexity of the new policy that was framed around multiple guiding principles as described above.

On the other hand, there is an indication that the mature rulemaking process in Colorado enabled progress on the issue at the legislative level. In this sense, it is apparent that when the CG process in Colorado stalled, a mechanism was in place that ultimately allowed the new policy to be implemented via the legislature. So while facilitative leadership was highlighted above as one factor that may mitigate risks of regulatory paralysis associated with the CG process, the ability of lawmakers to step in when necessary and override the process provides another.

Regulatory Capture

Discussion of regulatory capture related generally to either the implementation of the CRCM (i.e. largely relating to the pre-implementation phase when the initial RMC was crafted) or as the policy evolved post-implementation. It was identified most predominantly in the interviews and government documents data sets. In the case of implementation, most of the material seemed to indicate that regulatory capture had largely been avoided in the initial stages and that collaboration between industry and regulators had largely been mutually beneficial (although examples of regulations that appeared to favor industry over public health were also identified). Conversely, most regulatory capture related text identified in the corpus in the post-implementation context seemed to highlight continued, and perhaps increasing, risk of regulatory capture as the market evolved, particularly at the coal face of lobbying. Examples of these two perspectives are now provided:

First, when discussing the potential for capture in the context of the A64 Implementation Task Force, a senior regulator stated:

> *I think we stayed away from regulatory capture for the most part because we have to define in this group what are our standards and you know we'll say to industry, we would love to help find a way forward on this. Here are the things that we have decided as a group. Here are our principles that we decided as a group that we can't move away from. Interview: Andrew Freedman, Director Office of Marijuana Coordination (Governor's Office), Denver, Nov. 2016*

This text seems to support the material presented above that indicated risks to the CG process in the pre-implementation phase had been mitigated to a certain extent. For example, as noted, the A64 Implementation Task Force consisted of widespread participation by individuals with a broad range of backgrounds, with the cannabis industry representing a very small component of the overall group.

While there was little evidence of the industry 'capturing' the regulations during the CG process in the pre-implementation phase, some examples of regulations that appear to favor industry over public health objectives were identified. Notable examples related to advertising restrictions and the allowance of branded products:

> *Allow branding on product packaging and consumption accessories.*

> *Allow opt-in marketing on the web and location-based devices (mobile).*

> *Allow [marijuana retailers] to host their own websites. Government Document: A64 Implementation Task Force Report, p.53-54*

From a public health perspective, the ability for companies to use branded packaging is perhaps the most concerning of the above recommendations. The default public health position is a complete ban on advertising cannabis products in legal markets (based on alcohol and tobacco consumption) as described above.

Thus, notwithstanding some 'wins' for the industry in the initial regulations at the expense of public health, in general the first iteration of RMC did not appear to have been 'captured' by industry. Nonetheless, that is not to say the risk of capture has been averted, and the following subsection examines the concept from the perspective of policy evolution in the post-implementation phase.

Lobbying

The issue of lobbying was discussed in three interviews with cannabis industry executives in Colorado and tended to be described as a natural activity in the US context; a shift towards lobbying local jurisdictions (as opposed to the State), or as educating regulators. These angles are now examined.

First, an example of the perspective that lobbying is a natural activity in corporate America was provided by a cannabis industry entrepreneur and former chair of the National Cannabis Industry Association (NCIA), the first and largest organization representing interests of the cannabis industry in the US:

> I think it's very natural in a capitalistic society that people who are invested in something can permit their industry or their business to grow in a way that they see fit. I don't think it's unnatural to have lobbying. Every industry in America, for the most part, is involved in lobbying at some level because that is how you get bills past and that is how you make change.

> The fear of big pot and it being big tobacco and big alcohol I think is not something that we ever thought would come to fruition, being freedom fighters and being those who wanted to just seek change. As the business is starting to get larger there are more and more people that recognize the financial benefits to being involved in the industry, and so I think there are people out there that couldn't care less about the

plant, but recognize a financial opportunity. Some of them are starting to get involved in this industry and some of them have a lot of dollars and some of them are going to start to lobby for what they feel is best for their division, if you will, within the industry. I don't think it's unnatural or different from anything else in the country. ... in an open society where people have the freedom to do things as we do here in America, there is going to be lobbying dollars that go towards it. Is it ever going to be big tobacco, big alcohol, and big pot? I don't know, conceivably yes. This is the fastest growing industry right now in America. I think it's natural that a lot of people are going to want to have an opinion as to how this industry is shaped. Interview: Ean Seeb, Industry Pioneer and Lobbyist, Denver, Nov. 2016

The above extract highlights structural conditions in advanced western capitalist societies that encourage lobbying. It further illustrates the fact that regardless of whether the policy is implemented via CG processes or in more traditional adversarial approaches, there is an inherent risk that policy will be captured within the process. As noted above, concerns with the CG process include that it has the possibility to nurture these conditions by allowing industry a place inside the rulemaking tent.

What is missing from this text is an acknowledgment that, as a psychoactive drug with the potential to cause harm, cannabis is not a typical product. In this regard, the comparison with alcohol and tobacco is insightful as it crystalizes the public health concerns noted above.

Second, an interview with an industry CEO provided an example of an apparent shift in strategy towards lobbying at the level of local jurisdictions together with an example of how his firm decided it was necessary to educate local regulators:

Interviewer question: *You mentioned a potential area of growth is that the majority of local jurisdictions in Colorado haven't yet approved recreational cannabis in their area. I believe it was only about a third (approximately 80 out of 250 jurisdictions) that* *initially implemented A64. So that is a big area of interest I would assume?*

Interviewee: *"Yeah, very much so. ... I have an internal staff that does part of that work in conjunction with external lobbyists that we hire. So it's a combined effort and you know it's a lot of educating local governments about the ins and outs of the marijuana industry. Where and how they should focus their regulation efforts and trying to guide them into learning from those that have gone before. Like, this and that was tried in this jurisdiction, and it seems to be the consensus that this is not so useful, and these are the areas of concern that should be addressed. We also cautioning them to really try to find some continuity between what they craft and what the state regulations are.*

...

Generally, what we advise them to do is know what the state regs are, don't duplicate what's already there, but essentially defer to those and regulate time, manner, and place in terms of the local regulations [as was stipulated in A64]. Like where would you like to allow these dispensaries to be in your town [if you allow them]? What are the operating hours that you're comfortable with? And yeah, a few other particularities that relate to the local impact of that business.

And it's difficult too because the state regulations are pretty vast and complex. So to understand them, and then they're constantly changing and being revised, and that's one of the points that we make to local governments: look, even if you did a great job of mirroring what the state is doing, it's going to change and then you're committing yourself to have to keep pace of those changes and updating your code continuously so that it stays in sync with state. That's not an endeavor I think you [the local jurisdiction] want to take."

Interviewer question: *So does your firm do that lobbying in conjunction with other companies? Are you working with other companies or are you sort of taking it on yourself?*

Interviewee: *"Mainly just ourselves, although, you know a lot of the larger companies actually have in-house public affairs directors that are doing that so it's not uncommon for us to find ourselves in the same room as those folks.*

It's somewhat of an odd dynamic. We're competitors and we're vying for a spot which could be very limited either because the municipality has decided there are only going to be a few of these licenses allowed or they've made the zoning restrictions such that there is only going to be a few allowed by virtue of those zoning restrictions. So, we're kind of going for the same thing in terms of government getting the restrictions right and what works for us and what protects the community, but you know we're still competitors vying for limited space."

From this extract several aspects are notable. First, this example appears to demonstrate that lobbying is not confined to regulations at the state level and local jurisdictions are a clear target. Second, the aspect of knowledge gap analyzed above appears to remain an issue for new jurisdictions, even in a state where cannabis has been legalized for several years. Third, while this type of lobbying remains a concern from a public health perspective, there are indications from the above extract that companies are acting in their own self-interest as opposed to industry-wide coordination that is currently apparent in alcohol and other industries. Fourth, and perhaps most importantly, the extract provides a rich illustration that risks associated with regulatory capture may be increasing in the Coloradan context as the policy evolves and the market matures.

Summary of Results: Implementation Effectiveness, Policy Evolution, and Future Risk.

From the extracts presented above it is apparent that in the context of the CRCM, the CG process appears to have been largely effective in facilitating initial policy implementation in an environment where the biggest challenge facing regulators appeared to be an extensive knowledge vacuum for regulating a previously prohibited substance. Examples from across the corpus indicated that starting conditions combined with strong facilitative leadership and comprehensive institutional design were conducive to the CG process producing effective policy, at least in the pre-implementation phase. Furthermore, in the Coloradan context, there is evidence in the corpus of both an extensive knowledge gap and clear benefits associated with collective learning.

Conversely, the above analysis also provides an indication that as the recreational cannabis policy evolved in Colorado, so too, apparently, did risks associated with the CG process such as regulatory paralysis and regulatory capture. For example, the issue of labelling edible cannabis products illustrated difficulties in reaching consensus on some policy areas. As noted above, in this case it seemed that the legislative mechanism mitigated the risk to a certain extent by implementing a top-down policy to resolve the impasse. Overall, however, repeated references to the speed of policy evolution seem to support the contention that paralysis was not an enormous problem in the context of the pre-implementation phase. In this regard it is unclear from the data sets examined whether this policy evolution was an illustration of the complexity regulating cannabis or poor-quality recommendations due to exceedingly tight deadlines imposed by the constitutional amendment, A64. On balance it would seem likely both factors played a role. It should also be noted that while constant changing of regulations may not typically be considered ideal for industry, it could be interpreted as advantageous to well-resourced firms, potentially leading to reduced competition and the fertilization of monopolistic behaviour.

In addition, while there do not appear to have been instances of full regulatory capture in the corpus, examples of industry lobbying were provided, particularly lobbying focused at the local level. While it was also noted that these lobbying efforts tended to be individual company strategy as opposed to a unified industry-wide effort to influence regulations, risks remain. Finally, the risk of regulatory capture appears mitigated to some extent in the pre-implementation phase by the lack of an identified power imbalance in the starting conditions and a wide range of stakeholders, which ensured that industry stakeholders represented only 1 out 20 (5%) of participants selected to take part in the process.

Discussion

To the best of the authors' knowledge, the present study is the first to examine the implementation of the world's first fully legalized recreational cannabis market by applying a CG framework to the data corpus. The results of the analysis presented above have implications both in the field of cannabis policy and more broadly for policy analysis as a real-world example of CG policy implementation.

First, several other jurisdictions that have since implemented legal recreational cannabis models including California and Canada have followed a similar collaborative approach to that employed in Colorado, so it is important to consider the basic mechanics of the model. From the evidence presented in this paper, it is apparent that the CG process was helpful to address the knowledge vacuum and build collective learning in a complex and novel policy arena in the context of policy implementation. In this sense, regulators in other jurisdictions considering reform of cannabis policy may find the CG model helpful to address their own knowledge deficiencies given the global history of prohibition.

However, questions remain as to whether the CG approach holds sway in the context of policy evolution several years after initial implementation. For example, it would seem reasonable to conclude that after five years of experience regulating cannabis, policymakers likely have access to substantially more relevant knowledge than previously. As such it is legitimate to ask whether there is the same need to continue consulting the cannabis industry in the same way.

Recent legislative changes to restrictions on out- of- state investment in the CRCM may also accentuate risks associated with the CG process as larger businesses enter the fray, potentially creating conditions more fertile for increased investment (and presumably influence) in the cannabis industry in Colorado (e.g. Subritzky et al., forthcoming). Thus, an annual or biannual review of the CG process may mitigate these risks.

Second, the paper has implications for policy analysis more broadly as a real-world example of CG for implementation of wicked policy. Specifically, it provides an indication that risk mitigation strategies stipulated in the A & G model were apparently implemented in the Coloradan approach, and further that the policy was largely implemented effectively within tight deadlines. In addition, by highlighting continued risks associated with the CG model as the policy evolves, the paper makes a distinction between policy implementation and evolution, which may have implications for regulators considering the CG approach in other complex policy areas.

Chapter 9: Additional issues from media analysis

Political uncertainty

The conflict between federal prohibition and state legalisation was identified throughout the book, particularly in the context of changing administrations both federally and at the gubernatorial level in Colorado. In addition, concerns related to disparity between local and state laws were introduced in chapters 4. While based on government documents, media, and interviews political uncertainty was at the heart of many cannabis regulatory decisions in Colorado, it was deemed to be outside the immediate scope of the study objectives. Nonetheless, an analysis of the media data set relating to this theme is presented in here for consideration.

As previously noted, cannabis was legalised at the state level in Colorado despite remaining prohibited as a Schedule 1 substance federally. At the same time, the majority of local jurisdictions in the state opted to retain prohibition (Colorado Department of Revenue Marijuana Enforcement Division, 2014, 2017). Furthermore, as discussed in the documentary analysis, regulators were constrained by A64, which limited the implementation of public health best practice on a range of issues. The debate whether Colorado is in contravention of international treaties as described in the literature review received minimal coverage in the media sample and as such is not addressed in this chapter.

Legal and political uncertainty was one of the most prominently reported issues in the media sample (n= 438: 297 mass/ 141 niche). The analysis of the articles provided an indication of how the contradictory legal frameworks posed challenges for regulators and other stakeholders. Speculation around the changing political landscape was also prominently reported in the media sample. For example there was a spike in mass media coverage of the issue in Q4 2016, the period that saw Trump elected President. Two major facets of the 'legal and political uncertainty' issue emerged from the media sample including federal prohibition and local jurisdictions.

Federal prohibition

Articles with a focus on federal prohibition were prominent in media sample (n=215: 127 mass/ 88 niche) and broadly consisted of four sub-facets: (i) consequences of federal prohibition; (ii) coverage of US Department of Justice (DOJ) guidance; (iii) DEA scheduling; and (iv) politics.

Consequences of federal prohibition

The fact that cannabis remained federally prohibited in the US during the period under investigation is well known, while the consequences for regulators and other stakeholders have not been well articulated in the existing literature. The media sample included articles reporting on this sub-facet (n=66: 37 mass/ 29 niche). Two angles were covered prodigiously in the sample, namely, a lack of access to banking services for industry and lack of access to federal resources for regulators.

First, in a multibillion-dollar industry having access to bank services is clearly important. Articles highlighting the lack of access to banking services, which are federally regulated, tended to describe impact on aspects such as commercial operations, public safety, and transitioning from the black market that has traditionally conducted business in cash. Furthermore, according to report in the media sample, limitations to banking services expanded beyond the primary industry (cultivation, manufacture, sales) to those merely associated with it. Examples of this reporting include:

> By not having legitimate banking, that's just one more tool that state regulators cannot rely on in tracking and tracing aspects of the industry [former head of the Office of Marijuana Coordination] Andrew freedman said[4]. Denver Post: Five immediate concerns for states with new marijuana laws, November 11, 2016

> A lack of banking — from deposits to the simple act of writing a check to pay an employee — was the biggest challenge for every pot business.

> "It was apparent that a cash-heavy marijuana industry would be an invitation to corruption and criminal

[4] Andrew freedman was an interviewee for this study

214

*activity, so one of our priorities in implementing A64
was securing traditional banking and financial services
for legitimate marijuana businesses," Gov. John
Hickenlooper said.*

*..."While there has been a slew of issues, problems and
purported solutions to the challenge of providing
banking services to marijuana businesses in Colorado,
little has changed," the Colorado Bankers Association
said. "Dealing with the proceeds from the sale of
marijuana remains federally illegal."*

*...Problems acquiring bank accounts soon spread to
those merely associated to the industry. [For example]
landowners who leased property to marijuana
businesses had mortgages cancelled. Denver Post:
"Marijuana business owners have no dock to bank
cash", December 26, 2014*

*A large number of professionals have been unable to
access the financial system because they are doing
business with marijuana growers and dispensaries.
This group includes lawyers, security companies,
landlords, electricians, plumbers and even chemists
and researchers, who might be working with growers
and dispensaries. ... This business environment is an
invitation to tax fraud, robberies, money laundering
and organized crime. High Times: Bernie Sanders urges
federal regulators to ease up on pot banking policies,
December 15, 2016*

The above text highlights the intersectionality of the problem from
industry through to public safety and indicates that it was a priority
policy area for regulators. For example, the reported Hickenlooper
quote reflects the guideline set out in the Cole Memo to prevent
diversion of revenue to criminal enterprises as discussed in the
document analysis in the previous chapter. In this sense, state
regulators appear to have been caught in a catch 22 situation whereby
they are prevented by federal law from implementing policy that
would allow federal guidelines to be followed. The inability to access
banking services also impacted how tax revenues were collected by

the CDOR and is discussed in more detail in the following chapter that examines interviews with senior regulators.

Multiple articles indicated that attempts to resolve the issue hinged predominantly on the establishment of local cooperative banking institutions – efforts which reportedly failed due to the requirement of federal approval. As such the banking problem remained unresolved throughout the period under investigation.

A major argument for legalising cannabis is the purported benefits of creating a financial system where transactions can be tracked in a way that the illegal market could not, thereby removing criminal elements long associated with cannabis trade. The above text provides evidence that federal oversight of the banking system combined with the federal prohibition on cannabis prevented effective tracking of bank transactions even at state level.

Second, an additional consequence of federal prohibition identified in the articles concerned restricted access to resources from established federal departments such as the Environmental Protection Association (EPA), the US Department of Agriculture, and the Food and Drug Administration (FDA). An example includes:

> *Rules that typically would land under the US FDA fall in-house for state regulators, [former head of the Office of Marijuana Coordination] Freedman said, noting topics such as potency, refrigeration and safety of edibles. Denver Post: "Five immediate concerns for states with new marijuana laws", November 11, 2016*

The above text relates to the knowledge gap faced by regulators as a pioneering jurisdiction with no template. It indicates that, in addition to an already steep learning curve, due to the being the first jurisdiction to regulate recreational cannabis, exclusion of federal regulatory bodies (EPA, FDA, and Department of Agriculture) with considerable relevant expertise, processes and experience in related areas state was problematic. Lack of access to EPA resources was most prominently reported around the issue of pesticides and is examined in more detail later in the chapter (see issue 4: consumer safety).

US Department of Justice (DOJ)

Articles reporting on the role of the US Justice Department within the context of the CRCM (n=39: 14 mass/ 25 niche) tended to speculate on the impact of Jeff Sessions' appointment as attorney general, and interpretations of the Cole and Ogden Memos, which were outlined in the pre-implementation and introduction chapters respectively. An example includes:

> Jeff Sessions' selection as attorney general ... could be a setback to marijuana [legalization]. Sessions, who declared at an April Senate hearing that "good people don't smoke marijuana," is one of Congress's staunchest legalization opponents.
>
> ...
>
> Both the House and Senate have voted since 2014 to prohibit Justice from using federal money to prosecute medical marijuana businesses in states where it is legal. That prohibition, an amendment to an appropriations bill, must be re-approved every Congress.
>
> The attorney general's office could file lawsuits against states that are setting up regulatory systems. It could also repeal a landmark 2013 Obama administration policy [the Cole Memo] that stated the Department of Justice would largely defer to states to enforce marijuana laws. Colorado Gazette: "Legalisation up in smoke? Sessions could deal blow to marijuana movement", November 18, 2016

From the above text two underlying factors are apparent. First, the conflict between federal and state laws is highlighted. The reported threat of legal action by the federal government against states crystallises uncertainty around the legal status of cannabis in Colorado and is central to the issue. Second, Sessions' reported judgement of cannabis consumers illustrates a moral component in the legalisation debate that has surrounded the issue for almost a century as previously noted in the book. In contrast, experience from Colorado and other jurisdictions with legal cannabis schemes begin the process of potentially building objective evidence, which may better inform decisions about cannabis policy.

DEA scheduling

The apparent contradiction of DEA scheduling of cannabis in the most dangerous drug category with no accepted medical applications, despite almost 30 states offering legal access to some form of medical cannabis, was the focus of multiple articles within the context of federal prohibition (n=50: 13 mass/ 37 niche). Arguments that schedule 1 classification prevents research and reports of the threat of DEA enforcement, despite a lack of federal resources, were also prominent in the sample. Examples of reporting on these sub-facets include:

> *Newly appointed head of the DEA, Chuck Rosenberg, says that marijuana is "probably" not as dangerous as heroin.*

> *Rosenberg's comments ... are seemingly in conflict with marijuana's Schedule I classification under federal law, which places it in the same category as heroin and [more dangerous] than cocaine. NORML: "New DEA leader suspects marijuana is not as bad as heroin", July 30, 2015*

> *Federal restrictions on pot research have been a source of tension for years. Researchers, marijuana advocates and some members of Congress have accused the National Institute on Drug Abuse of hoarding the nation's only sanctioned research pot for studies aimed at highlighting the drug's ill effects. Colorado Gazette: "Pot research approved", March 14, 2014*

> *The DEA retains the legal ability to shut down anyone selling or growing pot, but there has been no coordinated federal attempt to close pot producers in multiple states. The agency has said repeatedly that it does not have the resources to pursue ordinary pot [consumers]. Denver Post: "Chugging along: The weed legalization train could get derailed, here's how", November 28, 2016*

From the above text, the ambiguity which surrounds the schedule 1 classification of cannabis is highlighted. Indeed, from the NORML extract, an organisation devoted to the legalisation of cannabis and representative of consumer perspectives, the quotation marks around "probably" seem to mock what they consider the absurdity of the current classification. Furthermore, the reference to both historical tension and the reported inference that research is limited to studies aimed at identifying harmful impacts of cannabis suggest that barriers exist to investigating medical efficacy.

Conversely, a small minority of articles in the sample reported an alternate view and provided justification for the schedule 1 classification. The following is an example:

> *Marijuana is a schedule I controlled substance — a dangerous substance with no recognized medical use — for a reason. It has not completed the course of proof required of all legal medicines sold in the United States. Until rigorous clinical trials can demonstrate therapeutic efficacy sufficient to outweigh its risks, marijuana will remain such, as the FDA reiterated in 2006. Let the research go forward, but not by abandoning standards. Colorado Gazette: "There's no proven clinical value for medical marijuana" June 12, 2014*

The above text illustrates an argument that is common in legalisation debates and is not easily dismissed by advocates of cannabis legalisation. It raises questions that have long been discussed in regards to medical cannabis including: (i) to what extent should anecdotal evidence be included in regards to quantifying efficacy of cannabis as a medicine?; (ii) should medical cannabis be confined to individual cannabinoids such as CBD or THC, which can be more easily be researched in the context of randomised controlled trials (RCTs)?; (iii) to what extent should cannabis be administered as 'whole plant medicine', which is more difficult to research in a clinical setting given the large pharmacological variability in the plant, despite having numerous reported benefits due to the so-called entourage effect, whereby cannabinoids combine in ways not easily researched to deliver therapeutic outcomes?; and (iv) how should acceptable risk be defined?

Politics

As described in the literature review cannabis policy has long been politically charged. Coverage of this sub-facet was widespread in the dataset (n=130: 67 mass/ 63 niche) and broadly reported two angles including the debate concerning states' rights versus the US Constitution and the presidential election in 2016.

Regarding the states' rights debate, most articles noted that ultimately the states are in tenuous position and legal businesses could be prosecuted at the federal level. An example of reporting on this sub-facet includes:

> Federal policy can be changed with the stroke of a pen. The new president can say to his or her attorney general: 'We should enforce the marijuana laws in all of the states.' That would be perfectly legal under the existing paradigm of federal law trumping state law, even in states like Colorado and others. Denver Post: After pot legalization, focusing on a new kind of black market, December 30, 2014

Given this uncertainty, it is not surprising that the build-up and aftermath of the 2016 presidential election was widely reported in cannabis related articles. Reports indicated both Trump and Clinton supported medical cannabis and took the position that states had the right to implement their own policy on recreational cannabis, regardless of what the federal law states. An example of this reporting includes:

> On the campaign trail, Trump promised to take a federalist approach to marijuana stating:
>
> "In terms of marijuana and legalization, I think that should be a state issue, state-by-state... Marijuana is such a big thing. I think medical should happen — right? Don't we agree? I think so. And then I really believe we should leave it up to the states." NORML: President-Elect Trump: Will You Support State Marijuana Laws?, December 9, 2016

This text reiterates the uncertainty of the legal status of CRCM and indicates that political aspects may play a role in policy outcomes.

While on the face of it Trump's reported stance on cannabis seems clear, the position statements of politicians before elections have been known to shift post-election. Furthermore, as noted above, the appointment of Jeff Sessions as US attorney general appeared to send a mixed signal given his reported preference to enforce federal law.

Local Jurisdictions

As noted in the previous chapter, A64 stipulated an additional level of regulatory autonomy for local jurisdictions, particularly over 'time, manner, place, and number' of licensed cannabis operations. The facet of local jurisdictions was widely reported in the media sample (n=171: 153 mass/ 18 niche), with the lion's share of articles focussed on City of Denver, Colorado Springs, and Pueblo County (the contrasting demographics of these areas were described in Chapter 1 of the book). An additional cluster of articles included reports on aspects of cannabis policy for over 40 Coloradan jurisdictions, providing an indication of the regulatory diversity in the State.

The cannabis regulatory apparatus in the City of Denver is well established and similar (though separate) in many aspects to the Marijuana Enforcement Division (MED) that oversees state level regulation. Indeed, since 2015 Denver has hosted an educational annual symposium to assist other jurisdictions with implementing a legal cannabis market. A wide variety of issues were reported in the media sample within the specific context Denver including: changes to home cultivation plant limits and unregulated medical cannabis collectives; ordinances to combat the smell of cultivation facilities; public consumption (see issue 6 below); enforcement of pesticides regulations (see issue 4 below); the disproportionate allocation of cannabis business licenses in communities of colour and low income; debate concerning restrictions placed on barriers to entry for new businesses; increased tax revenue; the high rate of support for A64 in Denver; and the international attention during implementation as a pioneering jurisdiction. An example of this reporting includes:

> Colorado's capital and largest city attracted international attention when its recreational pot shops opened Jan. 1 [2014] with long lines out the door. It hasn't let up.

*"We just met with France and Germany last week,"
Ashley Kilroy, the city's executive director on marijuana
policy, said in November about the many requests for
briefings she's gotten from government officials.*

...

*And it's reaped ... new local sales tax revenue — $7.6
million through September [2014], about half of that
from a special 3.5 percent tax approved by voters. It's
also gotten a share of a state marijuana tax.*

*The city in June tapped $3.4 million of the expected
proceeds to beef up its inspection and regulatory staffs,
expand public safety efforts and pay for a public
education campaign.*

...

*Given A64's nearly 10-point margin among Denver
voters, "we wanted to ensure that we adopted and
implemented the will of the voters," Kilroy said, "while,
at the same time, balancing that with public health
and safety and enforcing the regulations around it."
Denver Post: Colorado cities and towns take diverging
paths on recreational pot, December 27, 2014*

The above text highlights the novel and pioneering nature of the CRCM
roll out at the level of local jurisdictions. Furthermore, there is an
indication that the Denver regulatory body is focussed on public health
outcomes while also recognising that a substantial majority of the
population voted in favour of cannabis legalisation. Additionally, the
extract draws attention to the notion that while revenues were
increased, so too were operating costs associated with regulating the
market. Local autonomy of cannabis policy can broadly be considered
from two perspectives. On the one hand it could be viewed as
needlessly duplicitous, with businesses required to obtain licenses
from both state and local regulatory bodies. On the other hand, local
rules may add an additional layer of protection to fill gaps in state
regulations with potentially faster enforcement on non-compliant
businesses.

Articles in the media sample reporting on Colorado Springs and Pueblo County differed in their focus. For example, Colorado Springs, the second largest city in the state, is a jurisdiction that opted to continue prohibition of recreational cannabis (medical cannabis is legal), and there were reports of an extensive black market for recreational cannabis. In addition, given the large military base present in the area as described in Chapter 1, it is perhaps unsurprising that several Colorado Springs focussed articles highlighted how military veterans were denied access to medical cannabis due to pensions being administered federally. Regarding Pueblo County, the articles in general reported two angles. First, the cannabis market was described as an economic driver and an opportunity to increase jobs and raise revenue in the region, which has a low socio-economic demographic. Second, reports indicated Pueblo was the source of vast illegal outdoor cultivations that feed the out-of-state black-market, in large part due to favourable growing conditions in southern regions of Colorado. An example of reporting on these jurisdictions includes:

> Unlike Denver and several other cities, Colorado Springs did not approve recreational sales of marijuana. Yet our research found a flourishing black market of recreational pot procured as medicine and resold on the street. One teenager spoke in detail about clearing more than $1,000 a day by selling medical marijuana at local high schools. Colorado Gazette: Analyzing Colorado's grand experiment (editorial), March 22, 2015

This text highlights the complex nature of regulating cannabis across more than 200 jurisdictions in the State.

Political uncertainty discussion

Legal and political uncertainty was a fundamental consideration in the development of the RMC. A clear example is the issue of banking where public safety appears to have been impacted in the Colorado context due to external policy at the federal level. In addition, the exclusion of federal regulators such as the EPA, FDA, and Department of Agriculture is something that other jurisdictions should be aware of, as it has implications for budgets and allocation of tax revenues, whereby state level regulators may require additional funding to address issues such as cultivation standards. Furthermore, from the

Coloradan and more broadly the US experience, there is evidence the political aspect of cannabis policy does not magically disappear once the drug is legalised. This politicisation reflects similar findings on drug policy by Bruun, Pan, and Rexed (1975) and is consistent with the experience of Lenton and Allsop (2010).

From the above analysis it seems apparent that Coloradan regulators needed to consider whether federal prohibition would be enforced in the state, and devise regulations that may reduce this possibility. For regulators in other jurisdictions there is a lesson that creating some certainty around cannabis policy may be helpful both to streamline regulatory processes and align objectives between different levels of government be they federal, state, or local jurisdictions. In the US context, a degree of certainty was provided by the Cole Memo, which, as noted previously in the book, outlined federal guidance to states on the matter. However, this guidance was subsequently revoked by attorney general Jeff Sessions in January 2018, which further increased uncertainty. Consequently, the CDOR issued a guidance document stating the department would continue to follow the principles set forth in the Cole Memo (Colorado Department of Revenue, 2018). To further complicate matters Jeff Sessions was himself fired by President Trump in late 2018 on an unrelated matter. Thus, at the time of writing legal and political uncertainty around the CRCM remained a fundamental issue.

Public consumption

As noted in the pre-implementation chapter that drew on A64 and other documents, cannabis "consumption that is conducted openly and publicly or in a manner that endangers others" remained prohibited in the State after the implementation of the CRCM (A64,p.5). From media reports in the sample it appears that regulators interpreted this in the most restrictive manner, effectively banning the consumption of cannabis anywhere outside of private homes. Determining appropriate spaces to consume cannabis was listed as a key challenge for regulators in the literature review of the book (Pardo, 2014; Rolles & Murkin, 2016). Laws for public consumption of alcohol and tobacco, which include the licensing of establishments for consuming alcohol (bars), smoking bans in public indoor venues, and zoning restrictions, were described as potential starting points (Rolles & Murkin, 2016). Alternative approaches to this issue previously outlined in the book include the 'Dutch coffee shop model' (MacCoun & Reuter, 2001), and cannabis social clubs (CSCs) such as those in Belgium, Spain, and Uruguay that provide dedicated spaces for consumption (Belackova & Wilkins, 2018; Decorte et al., 2017).

The issue of public consumption was widely reported (n=61: 51 mass/10 niche). From the dataset it is apparent that the issue incorporates numerous in(ter)dependent factors such as youth protection, federal prohibition, and the autonomy of local jurisdictions. Six major facets of the public consumption issue emerged from the media sample: (i) arguments for and against public consumption; (ii) definitional challenges of 'open and public' consumption; (iii) who has jurisdiction?; (iv) cannabis social clubs and the private businesses model; (v) it's legal but where to consume?; and (vi) unintended consequences.

Arguments for and against public consumption

First, arguments ranged from opposition to any form of consuming in public through to support for consumption in designated areas of bars, restaurants, concerts, and other specially licensed venues similar to tobacco. Tobacco consumption laws are governed by the Colorado Clean Indoor Air Act that bans indoor smoking (Smoke Free Colorado, 2006).

Arguments supporting continued prohibition of public consumption tended to be couched within the idea of 'sending the wrong message to youth'. According to this view, consumption should take place only within private homes to prevent exposure among young people. An example of reporting on this facet includes:

> *"There's a big difference between adult marijuana use in the privacy of one's home and open and public consumption, which sends inappropriate and unhealthy messages to youth. [Colorado should] ensure that marijuana, if allowed at all, is for private adult use only and prohibit so-called "pot clubs" [CSCs] or any sort of public consumption in bars or restaurants". Smart Colorado: Lessons learned the hard way, September 28, 2016*

The notion that cannabis use in public places can 'send the wrong message' to youth reflects arguments described in the literature review against legalisation. However as will be discussed in more detail below, whether private member CSCs for example constitute a public space is open to debate.

An alternate view common in articles portraying the issue of public consumption encompassed the argument that in a state where cannabis is legal, there must be a provision allowing for it to be consumed in the company of others. Indeed, text in A64 that stipulates cannabis be 'regulated like alcohol' would seem to envision a scenario in which consenting adults are entitled to consume cannabis in social environments. Within this perspective two angles were reported, namely, whether cannabis should be allowed where alcohol can be consumed, or in 'separate but equal' marijuana establishments. An example of reporting on this facet includes:

> *People are torn as to whether marijuana use should be segregated in separate-but-equal cannabis establishments or integrated with other vices such as alcohol. Cannabis Business Times: Marijuana Legalization 2015: Proposed new law aims to allow cannabis in bars and clubs, but is that the best way to socially smoke pot?, July 27, 2015*

As noted in the literature review, there is an increased risk of harm associated with the combined use of cannabis and alcohol (Caulkins et al., 2015). From a public health perspective there is a preference that the two drugs are not consumed in unison, so separate establishments would be a preferred choice. The separation of cannabis and other drugs was also an explicitly stated objective in the Dutch coffee shop model (Grund & Breeksema, 2013). This distinction is expanded below in the context of local jurisdictions as it relates to a Denver ballot initiative for the social use of cannabis that subsequently passed and would have allowed cannabis to be consumed at bars, restaurants, and other venues. That integration was effectively vetoed at the State level however.

Definitional challenges

Second, multiple articles described definitional challenges associated with the issue of public consumption, the majority of which related to whether the term 'open and public' stated in A64 included or excluded private businesses. An example of reporting on this facet includes:

A ban on consumption in public has inspired public-versus-private debates [and] ... questions around state laws are contentious. Some in city government have said Colorado's pot-legalizing A64 prohibits the public consumption of marijuana, but Tvert and his colleagues (who wrote the amendment) disagree.

...

"As one of the people who conjured up A64 and was considered one of the two primary sponsors, I can attest to the fact that they're wrong," Tvert said. "A64 intentionally did not prohibit private businesses from allowing adults to responsibly consume marijuana on the premises. I don't know where they would get that. A64 said it would be illegal to consume openly and publicly, but it's not open or public if it's in a private business."

Denver marijuana czar Ashley Kilroy said the City doesn't regularly take a position on proposed ordinances but added that the issue of public consumption "has been on our agenda. All of that gets into a lot of legal analysis... there is that issue: If it is a private, commercial business that is open to the public, is it considered private?" Denver Post: New proposal: Allow more places for pot use in Denver, June 17, 2015

In addition to the question of whether the term 'public' includes private businesses, articles also described the conundrum of consumption on private property but within view of others for example in the back yard or on a porch. Furthermore, there were reports describing different interpretations of 'private homes' regarding whether residential property is leased or owner-occupied, as a lease may stipulate that cannabis consumption is forbidden. In this situation people who rent a home are effectively banned from consuming cannabis. From the articles on this facet it is apparent the definition of open and public consumption has been confusing and contested.

Who has jurisdiction: federal, state or local?

Third, in addition to arguments for and against, and definitional challenges associated with State laws that restrict cannabis consumption in public spaces, media stories in the sample described how rules vary across different jurisdictions within the State. For example, it was reported that possession and consumption of cannabis remained prohibited on federal land, which includes national parks, airports, and perhaps most notably for Colorado, ski slopes. This aspect received prominent coverage after a television news story highlighted several 'smoke shacks' at the well-known ski resort Vail. An example of reporting on this facet includes:

> "Despite Colorado law, marijuana remains illegal on federal lands period," said Scott Fitzwilliams, forest supervisor for the White River National Forest. "For the 22 ski areas in Colorado that operate on national forest system lands, marijuana is still prohibited. Let me remind everyone that you can be cited and fined for marijuana use and possession on national forests". Denver Post: Breck smoke shack razed by Vail, USFS after "Inside Edition" story, February 27, 2014

This distinction between federal and state laws highlights the conflict that was apparent in the wider context of the entire CRCM that functioned despite remaining prohibited as a Schedule 1 substance at the federal level. Articles in the sample also described attempts to resolve the public consumption issue at the level of local jurisdictions. In particular, the social use initiative in Denver noted above that passed by a citizen-initiated ballot measure was reported prominently in the sample. The range of articles describing this measure highlighted conflict between state and local laws. Examples of reporting on this facet include:

> Denver has approved a first-in-the-nation law allowing people to use marijuana in bars, restaurants and other public spaces, such as art galleries or yoga studios. Colorado Gazette: Denver passes social pot law, November 15, 2016

> State licensing officials delivered a blow Friday to Denver's voter-passed Initiative by announcing a new rule that will keep bars and many restaurants from applying for new social marijuana use permits. The new regulation starting Jan. 1 will make clear that liquor licensees cannot allow the consumption of

marijuana on their premises. It greatly expands the types of businesses that likely will be disqualified from applying for the new permits for on-site marijuana consumption. Denver Post: Bars just got nixed from seeking Denver social marijuana use permits, November 18, 2016

While the issue was not fully resolved during the time-period under investigation in this chapter, it seems evident that the State demonstrated leadership to reduce risk, while also allowing Denver to experiment with a potential solution at the local level. From the dataset, it seems that when Denver voters took this issue into their own hands by passing a ballot initiative (in a manner similar to A64 although at the local level), the State thought it was serious enough to effectively veto the possibility of consuming cannabis in bars, by stating that any establishment selling alcohol would lose its license should cannabis consumption be allowed. While this outcome seemed to limit the possibility of higher risk polydrug consumption, the conflict between jurisdictions is not ideal. It would seem better if the outcome was achieved with jurisdictions at various levels working in harmony towards public health objectives.

Cannabis social clubs and the private businesses model

Fourth, the debate surrounding CSCs in Colorado was prominent in media stories with public consumption related codes. According to several articles, CSCs have been posited as a potential solution to the public consumption issue. This reflects the literature that states these clubs can provide dedicated spaces for consumption (Decorte et al., 2017). However, there is an important distinction between the CSCs described in the literature review, which included the supply of cannabis (Belackova & Wilkins, 2018), and those reported in the media sample, namely, that in Colorado it is prohibited by State law to consume cannabis where it is sold. In this sense CSCs as described in the media sample relate to spaces only where cannabis is consumed, but not cultivated or traded (although there were a handful of reports of 'gifting' cannabis in exchange for a small donation as a way of subverting this restriction). Reporting on this aspect tended to be framed either in state-wide context or as primarily a matter for local jurisdictions. In both cases uncertainty around the legality of these clubs was a common theme in reports. An example of reporting on this facet includes:

The amendment that legalized marijuana doesn't give people the right to use it 'openly or publicly', ... but Colorado's constitution doesn't ban public use, either, leading to a confusing patchwork of local policies on weed clubs.

...

Denver[5] has existing pot clubs, but they operate somewhat underground with occasional police busts. Colorado Springs [where recreational cannabis remained prohibited at time of writing] has several clubs, but the City Council passed a ban in March stipulating that those operating before Sept. 23 have eight years to phase out their business. Nine clubs have filed suit seeking an injunction to stop the city from enforcing the ban. Colorado Gazette: Legal marijuana sparks debate on pot clubs, June 21, 2016

An additional facet identified in the media coverage of the social use of cannabis focused on small businesses whereby the consumption of cannabis is paired with an activity such as yoga, art classes, hiking, drinking coffee, or watching a movie. The matter received prominent coverage when actor Seth Rogan wanted to screen one his movies in a cannabis friendly cinema in Denver. An example of reporting on this facet includes:

Seth Rogen says he will screen his new film Monday night in a Denver movie theatre filled with marijuana smoke and hundreds of his fans.

...

"Seth has made millions of dollars on his movies promoting cannabis consumption, and now he has a national platform to address the public/private issues ... we face as the end of prohibition occurs," said Amy Dannemiller [an advocate of allowing some form of social consumption]. Denver Post: Seth Rogen in Denver: He wants to smoke weed in theater, but where?

---

[5] A CSC was visited on a field trip to Colorado in 2016.

The small business approach of the social use of cannabis is separate from CSC definitions outlined in the literature review that explicitly described not for profit regulatory options. However, from media reports in the sample it seems apparent that these types of businesses are central to the debate around the public consumption as potentially viable options within the context of a commercial model. An example of reporting on this sub-facet includes:

> *The 170-acre CannaCamp opening July 1 in Durango in southwest Colorado calls itself the nation's first cannabis-friendly ranch resort. Guests won't be given marijuana, because that violates state law. Instead, the resort allows guests to bring their own pot and use it while at the resort. In addition to horseshoes and hiking, guests are offered yoga sessions. Denver Post: Howdy, folks: Introducing a 420-friendly ranch resort, December 8, 2014*

Given the definitional challenges noted above it is open to debate as to whether this business model is legal in Colorado. This highlights once again an area of the rules that was not clearly defined during the initial period of implementation.

It's legal but where to consume?

Fifth, several reports broadly encapsulated the problem faced by tourists of having nowhere to consume cannabis publicly, and this includes both non-residents from out of state and residents visiting ski resorts. Examples of reporting on this facet include:

> *Visitors can buy the drug, but they can't use it in public. Or in a rental car. Or in most hotel rooms. Colorado Gazette: Legal marijuana sparks debate on pot clubs, June 21, 2016*

> *"The safety of our guests and our employees is our highest priority and we therefore take a zero-tolerance approach to skiing or riding under the influence. We do not permit the consumption of marijuana in or on any of our lifts, facilities or premises that we control". Denver Post: Breck smoke shack razed by Vail, USFS after "Inside Edition" story, February 27, 2014*

This text highlights the fundamental problem of there being almost nowhere to consume cannabis legally in Colorado. While the majority of coverage on this facet tended to describe the perspective of out of state tourists, the above example demonstrates this aspect is also applicable to Coloradan residents in a state that is well known for its resort economy and natural environment.

Unintended consequences

Sixth, several articles reported trends of increasing instances of public consumption (both as perceived by the general public and by number of citations issued for the offence) and linked these to restrictive laws. Examples of reporting on this facet include:

> The result is ... people toking up on sidewalks, in city parks and in alleys behind bars and restaurants — despite laws against doing so.
>
> ...
>
> From the capital city of Denver to mountain resorts like Aspen and Breckenridge, police wrote nearly 800 citations for the new crime of public consumption in 2014, the first-year recreational sales began. Colorado Gazette: Legal marijuana sparks debate on pot clubs, June 21, 2016

"I can tell you personally, I'm sure you have noticed this, too, but we smell it everywhere. Just everywhere". Colorado Gazette (editorial): Tough task for law enforcement, March 23, 2015

While reaction to strict public consumption laws may be one reason for increases in the offence, a causal link cannot be conclusively established between the two. In a state where recreational cannabis has been legalised it is perhaps unsurprising that an increased prevalence in public consumption has been reported. Furthermore, increased citations may be the result of increased enforcement on the issue as discussed below. Observations of public consumption may also reflect a broader cultural shift. An example of reporting on this facet includes:

> For me the difference is that people have become more brazen, smoking on patios at bars and things like that. Nobody's afraid of the cops anymore. Denver Post:

232

> *Cultural attitudes, images of marijuana users evolve in Colorado, Dec. 26, 2014*

Regardless of the extent increased public consumption is associated with restrictive laws, the argument that providing dedicated spaces to consume may reduce offences remains valid. It is from this perspective that increased public consumption is presented here as an unintended consequence of the rules.

Additional unintended consequences described in media reports include concerns of increased smoking in rental cars by tourists, increases in edible and vaporiser consumption (which are considered more discreet than traditional methods of consumption because they tend to be small and do not omit an odour), and increased enforcement costs. Examples of reporting on these sub-facets include:

> *Would pot-shop parking lots be full of overnight campers? Colorado Gazette: Marijuana sales set to roll, January 1, 2014*

> *Vaporizers and e-cigarette devices have made it difficult to police public use. Editorial: Colorado Gazette: Regulation still ineffective, March 22, 2015*

> *The Denver Police Department, however, is spending more money on marijuana enforcement in 2014 than before. But its additionally budgeted $410,005 is being used primarily for new hires (a sergeant, detective and crime lab scientist) and is funded by the 3.5 percent special sales tax on recreational pot — and not taxpayers as a whole, according to Kilroy's office, which also added that an additional $175,000 has been appropriated for 2015 to hire more park rangers to enforce public consumption laws. Denver Post: After pot legalization, focusing on a new kind of black market, December 26, 2014*

On the face of it, reports of increased public consumption appear to describe the polar opposite of the law's presumed objective, namely to reduce prevalence of this offence (in order to protect youth from exposure to this activity). While the issue needs to be considered in the context of wider legal and cultural changes in Colorado, it seems apparent that the desired outcome of discrete consumption has not been achieved.

Public consumption discussion

If the Dutch coffee model suffers from a 'back door problem' due to the non-regulation of cannabis cultivation, then perhaps the Colorado model has issues with the front door where there is no legislated place of consumption outside of private homes. From the analysis above it is apparent that there is a need to provide a clear definition of public consumption. In this sense the matter can be linked to the constitutional constraints of A64 examined in the pre-implementation chapter. It is also important to consider that definitions of social use may include CSCs and/or private profit-making businesses offering services such as yoga classes. From the media reports it seems there has been an increase in demand for these types of services.

Furthermore, in an ideal world, the rules within various jurisdictions should be clearly defined, while working in harmony towards shared requirements whenever possible. As noted above in the case of bars allowing the consumption of cannabis, when the goals do not align in the CRCM, the State can override local rules. Nonetheless, regulation at the local level seems to be the solution of choice in Colorado to move forward from the impasse, as demonstrated by the Denver ballot measure. While it seems logical that allowing some form of social consumption in dedicated spaces may reduce incidences of public consumption, during the time-period under investigation the issue remained unresolved and controversial.

The results of the analysis also highlight conflict with state laws and the debate around the separation of cannabis and alcohol. From a public health perspective, when considered against the literature, allowing cannabis consumption in bars carries higher risk than 'equal but separate' establishments. This point goes to the 'substitute or complement' debate outlined in the literature review, whereby it remains unclear whether the consumption of cannabis will substitute for alcohol (thereby reducing public health risk), or complement it (thereby increasing public health risk) (Caulkins et al., 2015).

From the articles examined it appeared that the only situation where consumption of cannabis was unambiguously legal for adults was behind closed doors in private, owner-occupied homes. While this situation is intended to shield children from observing cannabis consumption activity, whether it is ideal in cases where children live in the homes is open to debate.

Chapter 10: Practical lessons learned from the first years of the regulated recreational cannabis market in Colorado

Subritzky, T., Lenton, S., & Pettigrew, S. (2019). Practical lessons learned from the first years of the regulated recreational cannabis market in Colorado. In T. Decorte, S. Lenton & C. Wilkins (Eds.), Legalizing cannabis. Experiences, lessons and scenarios. London: Routledge.

Part 1 Introduction and background

Colorado has a long history of cannabis reform having first decriminalised possession in 1975, legalised medical cannabis in 2000, regulated and commercialised the medical market in 2009/10, and, to much fanfare, implemented the world's first seed-to-sale cannabis market for pleasure in 2014. The so-called adult use, or recreational cannabis market, was legalised via A64 (Colorado Amendment 64, 2012), a citizen-initiated constitutional amendment as opposed to government led legislative change. It took place against a backdrop of federal prohibition in which cannabis remained a schedule one drug under the Controlled Substances Act (Drug Enforcement Administration (DEA), 2018). The movement for legalisation was backed by the Campaign to Regulate Marijuana Like Alcohol (2012), which is reflected in the Coloradan approach that is often described as the standard commercial model based on for profit sales by licensed businesses, similar to alcohol bottle shops (Caulkins et al., 2015). The commercial model is concerning from a public health perspective as it incentivises the sale of cannabis with profit, whereas a public health approach would seek to reduce cannabis consumption and associated harms, particularly among vulnerable populations such as youth and people with problematic use (Subritzky, 2018).

While the Colorado recreational cannabis market (CRCM) can be considered from numerous perspectives, in this chapter we apply a public health lens and aim to document some of the practical issues associated with implementing the scheme. The chapter includes data reviewed and analysed as part of a PhD study by the first author that investigated the first four years of the scheme's conception, implementation, and evolution. Data sources included the Colorado Official State Web Portal and other government documents such as House and Senate Bills, Governor Executive Orders, state mandated impact and taskforce reports, Legislative Council records, industry notifications, and work group meeting minutes. Additionally, the following were examined: the Retail Marijuana Code (RMC); industry periodicals; emerging literature from noted cannabis scholars; media stories; interviews with senior regulators, industry executives and front-line public health officials; and field observations from tours of cultivation facilities, dispensaries, trade shows, and policy symposiums. The chapter is organised into three parts. Part 1 includes: (i) latest market insights around patterns of consumption in the State; (ii) a brief review of the emerging literature on the CRCM; (iii) the public health framework employed in Colorado; and (iv) a summary of the Retail Marijuana Code (RMC) and its evolution. In Part 2, tensions between public health and commercial profit are explored with a focus on: (i) constitutional constraints on public health best practice; (ii) marketing and advertising, most notably at the coal face of regulating controls by for-profit firms; (iii) budtenders, the sales people in retail stores; and (iv) the public health risks associated with the application of chemical pesticides for protection of commercial crops. Part 3 brings the material together to highlight important lessons learned from the CRCM for regulators in other jurisdictions considering the legalisation of cannabis for adult use.

Market insights

Up until the implementation of the CRCM (and other US state schemes that have subsequently been implemented), evidence on legal commercial cannabis markets comprised hypothetical modelling based on extrapolating from other legal substances and illegal cannabis markets. In the five years since the implementation of the CRCM, evidence has been accruing that indicates: (i) recreational sales and state revenues from taxes and fees have increased year on year; (ii) the market share of high potency products is increasing; (iii) prices have decreased per gram; (iv) a minority of people who use cannabis consume the majority of cannabis sold in the State; (v) there is no evidence that consumption has increased among youth or adult consumers, with latest data suggesting similar patterns to pre-legalisation; and (vi) increased driving fatalities associated with cannabis-impaired driving, although challenges remain around these data.

First, according to data from the Colorado Department of Revenue (2019b) total sales for both recreational and medical markets increased from approximately $US700 million in 2014 to over US$1.5 billion in 2017. In 2018, total sales since implementation passed US$5 billion. State revenue from related fees and taxes increased from almost US$70 million in 2014 to almost US$250 million in 2017 (Colorado Department of Revenue, 2019c). Over 85% of this revenue comes from the recreational market, which reflects disparities in tax rates in the two markets. The CRCM applies a 15% excise tax, a 10% special marijuana sales tax, and a 2.9% state sales tax (changed in 2017 as noted below), while the medical market is subject to just the 2.9% state sales tax.

Second, data collated by the Marijuana Policy Group (2018) that compared product type (flower, concentrates, edibles, non-edibles, shake/trim, and other cannabis products), showed that the market share of high potency concentrates increased from 11.6% in 2014 to 23.4% in 2017 in the recreational market. In the same period, flower sales reduced by an approximately corresponding amount from 66% in 2014 to 54% in 2017.

Third, retail prices for cannabis have been dropping in both markets for concentrates and flower but less so for edibles. For example in the recreational market the retail cost per gram of concentrates dropped from US$43 in March 2014 to US$21 in November 2017 and the price of flower dropped from almost $15 per gram to $5 per gram over the same period (Marijuana Policy Group, 2018). Other data from the same group show that prices per gram tend to be lower in metropolitan areas with higher outlet density.

Fourth, using Colorado data on consumption from multiple federal and state data sources, the Marijuana Policy Group (2018) confirmed that the majority of cannabis is used by a relatively small proportion of heavy consumers. They estimated that people who use cannabis 26-31 days a month comprise 22.5% of consumers, however this group is responsible for 71.1% of all cannabis consumed in the State (Marijuana Policy Group, 2018).

Fifth, multiple datasets have indicated that while perception of cannabis harmfulness has markedly decreased among adolescents in Colorado (for whom possession, purchase, consumption and cultivation of cannabis remains illegal),_an associated effect of increased consumption has not been identified, with rates of use similar to pre-legalisation in this important cohort (Brooks-Russell et al., 2018). Similarly, no significant increase in adult consumption was identified in the latest available data compared to pre-legalisation, although Colorado remained above the national average by 8% in 2016 (Colorado Department of Public Health and Environment, 2017a).

Sixth, there are reports of increased traffic fatalities in Colorado involving cannabis since the CRCM was implemented (Denver Post, 2017, Aug.25). However, this increase cannot yet be conclusively linked to the legal adult use market given challenges with data collection for this issue (Colorado Department of Public Safety Division of Criminal Justice, 2018a). For example, there are data indicating increased fatalities where the driver tested positive for cannabis from 55 in 2013 to 125 in 2016 (Rocky Mountain High Intensity Drug Trafficking Area, 2017) [6].. Indeed, data from the Fatality Analysis Reporting System (Fars) indicated that 20% of total road fatalities were cannabis related in Colorado in 2016 compared to 6% in 2006 (National Highway Traffic Safety Administration, 2018). However, these data are problematic due to changes in data collection and reporting. As noted by the Colorado Department of Transportation (2018, p.1), "only active forms of THC such as Delta 9 can cause impairment... [and] Delta 9 level information was not available prior to 2014". Furthermore, increased rates of testing means that higher fatalities linked to cannabis could be the result of improved data collection (Colorado Department of Transportation, 2018).

Additionally, there is evidence of a 30% increase in unintentional exposures to cannabis by children in Colorado from 2009 to 2015, which accounted for approximately 6 out of every 1000 accidental poisoning admissions (Wang et al., 2016). Notably, this increase has been linked

[6] Although data from the Rocky Mountain High Intensity Drug Trafficking Area (RMHIDTA) is official federal data and reportedly informed former US Attorney General Jeff Session's decision to revoke the Cole Memo that provided federal government guidelines for states with legal cannabis markets (Office of the Attorney General, 2017, 2018), some commentators and state Governors have raised issues about how the RMHIDTA interpret and present data (e.g. State of Alaska, 2017; State of Colorado, 2017; State of Oregon, 2017; State of Washington, 2017).

to the commercialisation of the medical market in 2009 and rates of increase since implementation of the recreational market are not statistically significant (Colorado Department of Public Health and Environment, 2016e). No fatalities linked to this issue have been recorded in the State, and symptoms appear limited to an uncomfortable few hours but no long-term damage (Kleiman, 2018). Latest data indicate that 6% of pregnant women in Colorado consume cannabis during pregnancy (Colorado Department of Public Health and Environment, 2017a).

Finally, data indicate that the 10 largest operators controlled approximately 25% of the market (Marijuana Policy Group, 2018). However, it remained highly competitive in comparison to other industries based on the Herfindahl-Hirschman Index, indicating that a "big cannabis" style market consolidation is yet to establish itself in the State (Marijuana Policy Group, 2018).

The emerging literature

Several scholars have begun to make important observations regarding potential implications for regulators *implementing* cannabis policy (as opposed to policy outcomes) based on the Colorado model, with many highlighting the complexity of creating a commodities market for the legal sale of cannabis. Blake and Finlaw (2014) described the massive undertaking and urged policymakers to be cautious in legalising distribution networks for the drug. Kleiman (2015) pointed out the multi-faceted nature of the scheme and difficulties with measuring impacts. For example, variation in cannabis potency testing, which reflects differences in sampling, equipment, and procedural methodologies, was recognised in Colorado House Bill 15-1283 (2015), which stipulated an allowable variance of plus or minus 15% in potency results for flower and concentrated products (Lenton & Subritzky, 2017). The Blue Ribbon Commission on Marijuana Policy (2015), a cannabis policy advisory body, noted cannabis legalisation is not a single event, but rather an evolving process that requires continuous attention over many years.

Subritzky et al. (2016b) identified approximately 20 issues with major challenges for regulators associated with the implementation of the CRCM, ranging from how to deal with public consumption of cannabis through to transitioning from a black to a regulated market, and concerns around environmental degradation and excessive energy consumption. Furthermore, Kleiman (2016) contended that voter driven cannabis legalisation initiatives hinder the ability of regulators to fully implement best practice public health policy. While it has been noted that creating a regulated market on an established medical cannabis model may expediate the process of implementation in recreational markets (Ghosh et al., 2015; Kamin, 2017b; Kilmer & MacCoun, 2017), it has also been pointed out that a medical cannabis foundation can facilitate grey markets, particularly in Colorado where designated patient caregivers can grow hundreds of cannabis plants legally, yet outside the scope of the retail or medical marijuana codes (Blake & Finlaw, 2014).

Based on the Coloradan experience, and perhaps counterintuitively, Kamin (2015) observed that the potential for increased tax revenue and cost savings associated with enforcement can be easily overstated, and may not provide a compelling argument for legalisation *per se*. Moreover, Subritzky et al. (2016a) documented a cannabis industry publication, which, like the tobacco industry before it, targeted commercial activities at people who consume cannabis on a daily basis because of their status as 'the backbone of the industry', thereby highlighting public health concerns of the commercial approach. Additionally, the increasing popularity and public health risks associated with edible cannabis products have been described, particularly in relation to slickly packaged products that resemble children's confectionaries, and difficulties associated with controlling or titrating the dose (MacCoun & Mello, 2015). Challenges to implementing and enforcing cultivation standards, predominantly around the application of pesticides, plant growth regulators, and other chemical additives have also been laid out (Subritzky et al., 2017), and are discussed in more detail below. Furthermore, complications relating to federal prohibition have been well documented, most notably around the associated lack of access to banking services that can create a public safety risk associated with hold-ups and related crime due to hundreds of millions of dollars in cash being transported and used to pay tax revenues and other business-related expenses (Blake & Finlaw, 2014; Subritzky et al., 2016b).

While observing that it was too early to judge the success of the policy itself, Hudak (2015b) contended that by and large regulators implemented the commercial framework successfully within tight deadlines stipulated by A64. The document specified that "Not later than July 1, 2013, the Department shall adopt regulations necessary for implementation [of the CRCM] ... [and] begin accepting and processing applications on October 1, 2013" (Colorado Amendment 64, 2012, p.6-9). Indeed, "in a mere three months, the A64 Task Force developed a comprehensive framework for the legislation and regulations needed to implement A64" (Blake & Finlaw, 2014, p.366). Based on the Coloradan experience, Carnevale, Kagan, Murphy, and Esrick (2017) offered recommendations in five areas: production and cultivation, governance, public health and safety, taxation, and possession and consumption. Most notably, they articulated the utilitarian value of unifying medical and recreational cannabis markets and recommended unification of the two markets to maximise regulatory efficiency and minimise associated costs (Carnevale et al., 2017). This recommendation is at the cutting edge of cannabis policy and remains controversial, with international controls stipulating the two markets should be kept completely separate (Mead, 2014), despite considerable ontological and regulatory similarities under the Marijuana Enforcement Division in Colorado (MED). Indeed, the 2018 Sunset review in Colorado recommended unification of the codes, which has a number of implications for regulators, industry, and academia alike (Colorado Department of Regulatory Agencies, 2018). This unified market plugs into therapeutic and/or wellness conceptions of cannabis consumption (e.g. Subritzky, 2018), and is described in Appendix 1 of this book.

Another issue is whether the cannabis industry should be 'inside or outside the tent' when regulations are being drafted and implemented. In Colorado, faced with a lack of knowledge about regulating recreational cannabis, the exclusion of Federal regulatory agencies because of the federal prohibition, and a tight timeline stipulated in A64, bureaucrats adopted a 'Collaborative Governance approach' (Ansell & Gash, 2008) based on 'pragmatism and mutual respect' (State of Colorado, 2012). Although other jurisdictions including California and Canada have adopted a similar approach, there is evidence that the industry has unsurprisingly lobbied hard for regulations that maximise profits and minimise 'unnecessarily burdensome' regulations (Subritzky et al., 2016a).

Colorado public health framework

Policymakers in Colorado have stated that the CRCM is public health driven (Hickenlooper, 2014). The Colorado Department of Public Health and Environment (CDPHE) stated their primary goal was to implement policy that protects vulnerable populations and collects data to measure the impact of the legal cannabis policy (Ghosh et al., 2016). Accordingly, they conceptualised a public health framework that draws on the expertise of "second-hand smoke prevention specialists, ... environmental health and food safety experts, acute and chronic disease epidemiologists, toxicologists, laboratorians, maternal–child health and health communications experts, and poisoning and injury prevention specialists" (Ghosh et al., 2016, p.21). The framework includes three main components: (i) assessment; (ii) policy development; and (iii) assurance (Ghosh et al., 2016). These are now briefly described.

First, the assessment aspect of the CDPHE framework relates to the monitoring of two issues, namely the prevalence of use and health effects. Regarding surveillance of prevalence, the addition of several cannabis-related questions to existing population-based surveys was undertaken. Issues of interest include cannabis preparation, dosage, frequency of use, and methods of consumption (Ghosh et al., 2016). Concerning the monitoring of health effects, changes to data collection were made in terms of how cannabis data are recorded at hospitals and emergency departments. The CDPHE is also attempting to develop better data sources around the issue of cannabis-impaired driving (Ghosh et al., 2016). A notable aspect of this is the lack of baseline data available pre-legalisation, which makes impact assessment difficult.

Second, according to Ghosh et al. (2016, p.24), policy recommendations were developed based "on the successes of the past 50 years of public health progress to reduce the prevalence of tobacco use ...". Specifically, the CDPHE included recommendations by the Community Preventive Services Task Force (2014) and Pacula et al. (2014), such as increased unit price via taxes, and smoke-free policies including Colorado's Clean Indoor Air Act. In addition, public health lessons from alcohol include limitations on opening hours and outlet density of retail stores (Babor, 2010; Livingston, 2008). These aspects are regulated in the CRCM by local jurisdictions who were empowered by A64 to oversee the "time, place, manner, and number of marijuana establishment operations" (Colorado Amendment 64, 2012, p.8-9).

Ghosh et al. (2016) further contended that rules established for labelling and packaging of recreational cannabis products are equal to, or exceed requirements for tobacco, although this has been contested by Barry and Glantz (2016b). By 2018 the RMC stipulated that labels should not: be designed to appeal to children; contain false or misleading statements; or make any health benefit claims (Colorado Secretary of State, 2019). In addition, the following text must be included on labels of retail cannabis products, "This product was produced without regulatory oversight for health, safety, or efficacy. ... There may be long term physical or mental health risks from use of marijuana including additional risks for women who are or may become pregnant or are breastfeeding. Use of marijuana may impair your ability to drive a car or operate machinery" (Colorado Secretary of State, 2019, p.194).

Education is specified within the policy development component of the Colorado public health framework. It is the responsibility of the CDPHE to implement mass-reach health communications that increase public awareness around cannabis laws and the responsible use of cannabis. While Barry and Glantz (2016b) contended that the resulting Coloradan public health messaging is youth focussed and does not extend to the adult population, this is open to debate. For example, the 'Good to Know Colorado' campaign aimed to "educate all Colorado residents and visitors about safe, legal, and responsible use of marijuana" (Ghosh et al., 2016, p.24). Additional campaigns and comprehensive information on the potential harms associated with cannabis consumption from risks to youth through to dependency by adults are listed on the Colorado Official State Web Portal (2018). Prevention messaging campaigns are an important intervention to reduce harms at the population level (Ghosh et al., 2016).

The third component relates to assurance and includes enforcement of regulations, ensuring a competent workforce, and evaluation. The task of ensuring compliance is generally overseen by MED, who operate directly under the Colorado Department of Revenue (CDOR). Regarding a competent workforce, the CDPHE had an initial focus to expand its network of public health professionals at the city and county levels, and hosted educational conferences for cannabis policy regulators (Ghosh et al., 2016). The final aspect of assurance considered under the CDPHE framework is the evaluation of data collection and surveillance efforts, education campaigns, and perceptions of risk associated with cannabis consumption (Ghosh et al., 2016).

In line with increasing revenues, appropriations from the Marijuana Tax Cash Fund have increased in a number of areas. For example, large increases in funding can be noted for the Department of Education, particularly with regard to the school health professionals grant program, and the Department of Human Services including US$12 million for increasing access to effective substance disorder services. Substance abuse is also addressed via the CDPHE with US$9 million allocated for grants in the 2017/18 financial year (Colorado Office of State Planning & Budgeting, 2017). Additionally, as stipulated in A64, the first US$40 million in excise tax revenue annually is deposited in the Building Excellent Schools Today (BEST) Fund that "prioritises funding based on issues such as asbestos removal, building code violations, overcrowding, and poor indoor air quality" (Colorado Legislative Council Staff, 2015, p.1).

Evolution of Retail Marijuana Code (RMC)

Many practical issues associated with the regulation of cannabis policy have previously been articulated (Caulkins et al., 2015; Rolles & Murkin, 2016; Room et al., 2010). Pardo (2014) summarised the first iteration of the Retail Marijuana Code (RMC) including taxation, production and distribution limits, labelling, and quality control requirements, and made comparisons with Washington and Uruguay regulations. Furthermore, in regard to overall production, it was clarified that in Colorado the quantity and numbers of licensees are determined by the free market mechanism as opposed to pre-set limits used in other states (Kamin, 2017b).

At the time of writing in mid-2018, the permanent version of the RMC was in its 10th iteration and consisted of 262 pages, which compares with 124 pages in the first iteration in 2013 (Colorado Secretary of State, 2019). This provides an indication of how the regulations have become more complex as the CRCM has matured. Indeed, the RMC can be considered a dynamic document that is continuously evolving (Blue Ribbon Commission on Marijuana Policy, 2015).

According to the RMC 2013:

> *"The rules accomplish the state of Colorado's guiding principle: to create a robust regulatory and enforcement environment that protects public safety and prevents diversion of Retail Marijuana to individuals under the age of 21 or to individuals outside the state of Colorado"* (Colorado Secretary of State, 2013, p.3).

The extent to which this has been achieved remains open to debate. An undoubted strength of the CRCM, however, is a well-established rulemaking process in the State that allows for swift implementation of new rules as required (Colorado Secretary of State, 2018b, 2018c). Since June 2013 there have been 15 emergency/temporary rule adoptions together with the 10 permanent rule iterations of the RMC (Colorado Secretary of State, 2019). In general, emergency rules may be introduced within the Administrative Procedure Act framework when "immediate adoption of the rule is imperatively necessary to comply with state or federal law or federal regulations or for the preservation of public health, safety, or welfare" (Colorado Secretary of State, 2018a, Section 24-4-103(6a)). Emergency rules allow for timely temporary adoption of regulations and add an important element of flexibility for cannabis regulators in Colorado, particularly given the potential for unexpected consequences of regulations in a pioneering jurisdiction. Emergency rules expire after a period of 120 days unless converted to permanent through the full regulatory process.

By 2018, the RMC consisted of 18 rule categories including: General applicability; Licensing; Licensed premises; Retail marijuana store; Retail marijuana cultivation facilities; Retail marijuana products manufacturing facilities; Retail marijuana testing facilities; Transportation and storage; Business records and reporting; Labelling, packaging, and products safety; Signage, marketing, and advertising; Enforcement; Discipline; Division, local jurisdiction, and law enforcement procedures; Retail Marijuana Testing Program; Retail Marijuana Transporters; Retail Marijuana Establishment Operators; and Retail Marijuana Transfers to Unlicensed Medical Research Facilities and Pesticide Manufacturers.

Broadly, key changes to the market since implementation include: (i) ending the requirement for vertical integration and the introduction of mandatory potency testing in 2014; (ii) removal of the statutory two year resident rule for (up to 15) investors in 2016 (SB 16-040, 2016) [7]; (iii) standardised edible serving amounts of 10 mg THC per portion introduced in 2016; (iv) the new tax structure in 2017 (whereby the State retail marijuana sales tax was increased from 10 % to 15% while the standard 2.9% State sales tax was exempted); and (v) mandatory testing for pesticides in flower and trim products in August 2018 (Marijuana Policy Group, 2018).

Part 2 Tension between commercialism and public health

Although regulators followed the public health framework described above, the commercial model of cannabis regulation remains a concern (Lenton, 2014a). Indeed, respected scholar Kleiman described the for-profit model as the second worse outcome behind prohibition. He reportedly stated, as seems apparent in the data presented above, that "marijuana companies' best customers are the problem users" (Lopez, 2014, December 17). The following section of the chapter explores the tension between public health and private profit within the context of a commercial cannabis market, with a focus on the issues of constitutional constraints, marketing and advertising, budtenders, and the application of pesticides for crop protection.

Constitutional constraints on public health best practice

According to Governor Hickenlooper (2014, p.1), "[Colorado is] working as a convener for all interested parties and experts to shape public policy that utilizes the decades of public health lessons gained from regulating alcohol and tobacco". However, the requirements of A64 hindered the ability of regulators to implement public health best practice on several fronts including: tight deadlines for market implementation; installing the CDOR as overseeing regulator (as opposed to, for example, public health or human services departments); outlining a commercial market structure based on the

---

[7] HB 18-1011 (2018) would have further increased flexibility for out-of-state investors in 2018 by allowing an unlimited number of investors and removing background checks. However, after it was passed through the General Assembly it was vetoed by Governor Hickenlooper due to concerns about federal restrictions (State of Colorado, 2018).

licensing of for-profit businesses; and lack of constraints over product diversity

In terms of product diversity, it is useful to highlight public health limitations identified in A64 that came about due to a generous definition of cannabis. The broad definition of cannabis stipulated in A64 follows:

> *"Marijuana or Marihuana [or cannabis] means all parts of the plant of the genus cannabis whether growing or not, the seeds thereof, the resin extracted from any part of the plant, and every compound, manufacture, salt, derivative, mixture, or preparation of the plant, its seeds, or its resin, including marihuana concentrate. Marijuana or Marihuana does not include industrial hemp, nor does it include fiber produced from the stalks, oil, or cake made from the seeds of the plant, sterilized seed of the plant which is incapable of germination, or the weight of any other ingredient combined with marijuana to prepare topical or oral administrations, food, drink, or other product" (Colorado Amendment 64, 2012, p.3).*

It has been argued that cannabis policy with a public health focus should include regulatory control over product diversity that encourages production of less harmful product variations such as those with lower THC potency or more balanced THC:CBD profiles in standard preparations of cannabis flower (Borland, 2003; Fischer et al., 2017; Rolles & Murkin, 2016). In contrast to these public health recommendations, the constitutionally defined cannabis allows for limitless product innovation, which in addition to higher public health risks, is also vastly more complicated to regulate effectively.

As a direct result of this A64 definition, dispensaries in Colorado offer a wide range of cannabis products including flower, concentrates, topicals, tinctures, and edibles. The lion's share of merchandise consists of three broad preparation types: flower, high potency concentrates, and THC infused edible confectionaries (Marijuana Policy Group, 2018).

Marketing and advertising

From a public health perspective, the recommended default position for advertising regulated cannabis products is a complete ban (Rolles & Murkin, 2016). In Colorado, regulators were restricted by A64, which stipulated that cannabis be regulated like alcohol (this issue is separated from the above section due to its importance). Advertising in the alcohol industry in Colorado is governed by a voluntary industry standard that *encourages* restraints on advertising when there is a greater than 30% likelihood of it reaching minors. As stated in the RMC 2013:

> *Voluntary standards adopted by the alcohol industry direct the industry to refrain from advertising where more than approximately 30% of the audience is reasonably expected to be under the age of 21. After reviewing the rulemaking record, the CDOR has determined ... it is appropriate to model the retail marijuana advertising restrictions on this voluntary standard used by the alcohol industry. This standard is consistent with the directive in the state constitution to regulate marijuana in a manner that is similar to alcohol (Colorado Secretary of State, 2019, p.107-108).*

Beyond the obvious issue that in Colorado the RMC appears to condone a 30% likelihood of children being exposed to cannabis advertising, on the face of it there does not appear to be any protection for adult populations, particularly those with heavy consumption patterns (and therefore higher risk). However, the process of devising advertising restrictions was considered at length, and included several phases and collaboration between multiple departments, most notably the CDPHE and the Colorado Department of Human Services. In general, the restrictions are focused on youth protection and lessons from tobacco. For example, RMC advertising restrictions are modelled on the Framework Convention on Tobacco Control (FCTC) and the Masters Settlement Agreement (MSA). From stakeholder interviews, it is apparent that experience from tobacco was a central focus. The following extract is indicative:

> *"We took a very hard look at the [MSA] and the requirements of that with respect to advertising tobacco products and many of the concepts that are*

While lessons from tobacco are certainly helpful for devising advertising restrictions on cannabis sales, it is important to note that cannabis is an intoxicant in a way that tobacco is not. In this sense, the public health risks differ in important ways, most obviously around the issue of driving. While the advertising restrictions in the RMC are reasonably comprehensive, notable gaps relate to: (i) strain reviews; (ii) social media; and (iii) celebrity branding. These are now discussed.

First, there are numerous websites that publish strain reviews under the guise of providing valuable consumer information (e.g. Leafly.com, 2018; The Cannabist, 2018). However, the utility of this information is increasingly contested, and it can be argued that the naming of cannabis strains by cultivators is driven more by strategic marketing than scientific evidence. A gap in the RMC relates to the genetic (in)consistency of cannabis varieties or strains (again this can be linked to how cannabis is defined in A64). Based on an exploratory study of samples from Coloradan dispensaries, Schwabe and McGlaughlin (2017) identified considerable genetic variation among strains with the same names. Indeed, Mowgli Holmes, a molecular and evolutionary biologist and CEO of an agricultural genomics company reportedly stated "No one has any idea what they're smoking. Everything is name draw, so consumers and patients don't know what they're getting" (Rolling Stone, 2018, Jun.12). Furthermore, the names of award winning strains are replicated by multiple dispensaries with diverse genetic lineage and cultivation techniques (observations from the field).

Second, social media is inundated with advertisements for cannabis products and stores, as can be found on any of the major platforms with a cursory search for hashtag phrases such as #cannabis or #marijuana. Studies examining the high prevalence of 'dab tweets' are insightful in this regard (Cavazos-Rehg et al., 2016; Daniulaityte et al., 2015). Furthermore, in a study of almost 1000 mass and niche media articles focused on the CRCM, several hundred contained text from which codes were derived for 'social media', and/or 'Twitter', 'Facebook', or 'YouTube'. Articles offering advice on the 'do's and don'ts' of social media marketing for cannabis stores were particularly notable (e.g. Ganjapreneur, 2016, Jul.12). These concerns relating to the proliferation of advertising cannabis products on social media were recognised in a stakeholder interview with a senior public health official in Colorado:

> *"It's definitely ... an area of concern. ... I think realistically when we're ... wanting to limit the amount of advertising that can be seen by youth, we have to look at ... wherever that's going to be available. So social media is always going to be something of concern".*
> *Interview: Heath Harmon, Director of Health Division for Boulder County Public Health, August 2017.*

Third, celebrity branding of cannabis products could be a consequence of the recommendation in the A64 Task Force Report to allow branded products to be sold in the State. This is despite public health recommendations that stipulate plain packaging (Rolles & Murkin, 2016). Since the CRCM was implemented, numerous celebrities have entered or stated intention to enter the industry as producers of branded cannabis products including Willie Nelson, Snoop Dog, Whoopi Goldberg, Melissa Etheridge, the family of Bob Marley, Tommy Chong, Gene Simmons (of the band KISS), and Mike Tyson (CNN Money, 2018, Apr.10). These celebrities have been afforded significant free coverage, both in consumer-focussed niche media and on mass market platforms. In Coloradan retail cannabis stores, these branded products tend to be prominently positioned with high visibility (observations from the field). Regulating plain packaging of products may reduce this glorification of cannabis products.

Budtenders and the retail experience: observations from the field

Budtenders are sales people employed to sell cannabis at both medical and recreational stores in Colorado. All employees of a retail cannabis store must hold an occupational license. There are two types of occupational license that relate to key and support employees, of which budtenders are considered the latter. The criteria for obtaining an occupational license include being at least 21 years of age, of good moral character, a resident of Colorado, and payment of the relevant fee (at the time of writing this was US$75 for support staff) (Colorado Department of Revenue Enforcement Division, 2018a).

While budtenders often receive training on issues of legal compliance, it is not a requirement. The regulations for both medical and adult use cannabis dispensaries in Colorado do not stipulate any specific training that budtenders must undertake – this is left entirely at the discretion of business owners and/or marketing strategists. Similarly, they are not required to have knowledge of the pharmacology of the plant (which has over 100 different cannabinoids), numerous methods of consumption, multiple product types, and the large variations in potencies and individual consumer tolerance. Informal discussions with budtenders indicated that larger chains tended to offer more comprehensive training in regards to product knowledge, compliance, and the sales process (observations from the field). Little mention of public health considerations were noted, with the exception of offering dosing advice for purchasers of edibles, particularly those from out of state (observations from the field).

Further insight is provided by a job advertisement for a budtender listed by Native Roots, one of the largest operators in the state with 19 outlets at the time of writing. From this text it appears that budtenders are expected both to have a high knowledge of products in advance, and to "care", however it is apparent that sales performance is the dominant key performance indicator (KPI).

> *A caring, considerate and enthusiastic attitude for the industry is a must. Working knowledge of cannabis products as well as all current rules regulating retail and medical marijuana are required.*
>
> *Budtenders will be challenged by sales goals set by management. We are looking for candidates that will creatively contribute to the success and expansion of our company. This position gives a self-driven and motivated candidate room for development and growth. Medical & recreational budtender – Denver, Co (Native Roots, 2018).*

An additional issue is in-store labelling as noted in field observations in 2017. In general, cannabis stores in Colorado offer pre-packaged goods such as edibles and concentrate cartridges, and fresh produce such as flower. The pre-packaged products are in branded packaging and include all product information on labels as required by the RMC. However, the label information for fresh produce such as flower placed in jars of displayed product is generally limited to strain name, THC percentage, and species type, that is sativa, indica, or hybrid (observations from the field). Budtenders, under consistent queue pressure, represent the only option for consumers to make enquiries regarding additives used during the cultivation process before purchase, and furthermore it is unrealistic that their training will extend to knowing what additives were applied during cultivation. This observation relates to the RMC 2018 rule 1002-1 concerning packaging and labelling prior to transfer to consumer, which distinguishes between in store and exit label requirements (Colorado Secretary of State, 2019, p.189-195). It was observed that this situation hinders consumers' ability to identify cannabis grown without the addition of chemical additives. From a public health perspective, this impedes the ability of those in search of organically grown products to make informed decisions, which is a central tenet of A64 and a core justification for legalisation.

Pesticides

In a study [by the author of this book presented in Chapter 8] that examined issues in the implementation and evolution of the CRCM, pesticide related codes were derived from multiple government documents, over 200 media articles, and several transcripts of interviews with key stakeholders. Problems associated with pesticide use and reporting was initially identified in the A64 Task Force Report, which noted there existed "no standards of practice for ensuring product safety in the marijuana industry" (Brohl & Finlaw, 2013, p.66). Definitions of pesticides may include plant growth regulators and other chemical nutrients used during the cultivation process (Subritzky et al., 2017), however this section considers pesticides as primarily chemicals used as protection against insect infestations that can devastate crops. Farmers may have considerable financial exposure in an industry where cannabis plantations are not covered by insurance companies, so there is a reported temptation to resort to nefarious measures (Subritzky et al., 2017). After prominent media coverage of the issue, the public health threat of contaminated cannabis was officially recognised in an Executive Order by Governor Hickenlooper in November 2015, which required state agencies to focus on the problem (Colorado Department of Revenue, 2015a). Examples of this threat were provided in an interview with Seth Wong, President of TEQ Labs in Denver, and included the possibility of pesticides being concentrated in toxicity along with other cannabinoids when concentrated products are manufactured (Subritzky et al., 2017). Additionally, as noted by Wong:

> *We don't know the difference of what that pesticide does to you if it is just ingested or if it is smoked. Some of them have applicable uses and that's a direct application to a plant, but that plant is not necessarily smoked. So if you smoke it, and that's the case with myclobutanil [a chemical compound used in some pesticides] that converts to cyanide once it gets treated with a flame, you've got myclobutanil on your cannabis bud and someone goes to smoke it you have potentially converted that to cyanide and potentially inhaled it" (Subritzky et al., 2017, p.91).*

At the time of writing, over five years since the legal market was implemented, significant progress had been made on how to effectively regulate cultivation standards, and in particular the application of pesticides and other chemical additives such as plant growth regulators. For example, standardised sampling procedures have been developed for flower, edibles, and concentrated products (Colorado Department of Public Health and Environment, 2018b). Furthermore, requirements for the certification of cannabis testing facilities in Colorado have evolved considerably since the first iteration of the RMC in 2013 (Colorado Department of Public Health and Environment, 2018a). After multiple work group meetings among subject matter experts, the reference library for proficiency standards has expanded to cover pesticide residue testing as well as other forms of contamination, sampling procedures, and validation guidelines (Colorado Department of Public Health and Environment, 2018c). Importantly too, it should be noted that the issue is also enforced at the local level, which offers an additional layer of protection. For example, it was reported that the City of Denver had recalled over 28,000 products due to pesticide contamination (Denver Post, 2017,

Apr.20). Reflecting this evolution of pesticide regulations in the State, 17 industry bulletins notifying cannabis businesses of changes relating to testing requirements to be implemented were issued by the State from April 2014 to May 2018 (Colorado Department of Revenue Enforcement Division, 2018b). However, while progress has been made, the issue remains challenging, and development of new regulations is ongoing. Notably, mandatory testing for pesticides in flower and trim products across both medical and recreational markets was not implemented until August 2018.

Part 3 Lessons learned

As a pioneering jurisdiction, Colorado has blazed a trail implementing a commercial approach to legalised cannabis. Regulators developed a comprehensive public health framework, drew on lessons from alcohol and tobacco, and modified rules in a timely fashion as unexpected consequences arose. While regulators should be recognised for their ground-breaking efforts, the Coloradan approach has limitations from a public health perspective and efforts were hindered on a number of fronts. In particular, constitutional constraints of A64 ensured a for-profit model, as opposed to a non-commercial alternative, was implemented. A64 also broadly defined cannabis, which allowed for enormous product diversity. Furthermore, the involvement of the cannabis industry in crafting the regulations that apply to the scheme remains a concern - as was predicted by many, the commercial model has seen the proliferation of widespread advertising and marketing strategies that are excluded from the regulations. In addition, major challenges have arisen regarding cultivation standards, most notably the inability to effectively devise rules and regulate the emerging public health threat of the application of pesticides, particularly in initial years of the market roll out. Furthermore, as previously noted in regard to the accidental ingestion data, the fact there was a well-developed medicinal cannabis market with retail outlets in Colorado for a number of years before recreational cannabis use was legalised has implications when interpreting the impact of recreational cannabis *per se*.

For reader convenience, the recommendations from this chapter have been moved to chapter 12

Chapter 11: Bringing it all together

This chapter brings together the material from across the book. First, a summary of the results is presented. Second, key issues are situated within the harm reduction framework outlined in the Introduction of the book with a focus on price, increased revenue for the state, quality control, and tension between public health and private profit. The issue of commercialism is given further consideration via the CFS as outlined by Stoa (2017) to place the Coloradan commercial model into the context of emerging markets in North and South America, which enabled a more nuanced consideration of the implications of the study.

Summary of results

Chapter 5

In Chapter 5, a 'snapshot' from approximately 20 months post-implementation of the CRCM was presented using the techniques of document analysis and rich description of issues. Issues considered included the regulatory process, tension between public health and private profit, industry and investment, the lack of access to banking services, politics and public opinion, how methods of consumption were evolving (including edibles, dabbing, and vapourisation), challenges associated with quality control, and defining the black market in the Coloradan context.

The analysis concluded that while regulators had established a functioning system within tight deadlines that established a predictable funding mechanism, and that the 'sky had not fallen in' immediately post-implementation, the scheme faced major challenges including the conflict with continued federal prohibition, a growing influence of the cannabis industry, and immature cannabis testing regimes that limited the effectiveness of the regulation to provide a safe product for consumers. Additionally, the uncertainty around the protection of youth due to, for example, the potential for this vulnerable group to be targeted by advertising was noted.

Chapter 6

In Chapter 6, the issue of quality control was examined with a focus on challenges associated with regulating the application of toxic pesticides on commercial cannabis crops. Document analysis, rich description, and thematic analysis techniques were employed. Specific objectives of the book were addressed including the examination of inherent tensions in relationships between public health, consumer protection, and commercial profit-seeking. Specifically, the chapter introduced some of the difficulties associated with defining pesticide, the potential public health threat of contaminated cannabis, basic methodological procedures of testing cannabis for pesticides, and the challenge of developing cultivation and proficiency standards. These real-world challenges for pesticide testing mirrored those outlined in the literature review in regards to potency testing and variation of testing results pertaining to cannabis testing in general (Gieringer & Hazekamp, 2011; Thomas & ElSohly, 2016; United Nations Office on Drugs and Crime, 2009; Vandrey et al., 2015).

In general it was concluded that, while regulators had made significant progress, two years post-implementation the pesticide regulations had yet to be finalised and continued to evolve. Furthermore, the scale of the problem was documented by placing Colorado into the wider context of US cannabis policy and it was noted that other US jurisdictions such as Oregon, Washington, and California were also struggling with the issue. The theme of quality control and consumer protection is further developed later in this chapter within the harm reduction framework both in light of material presented in the literature review and also in the context of recent developments in North America.

Chapter 7

The important issue of youth protection in a jurisdiction with a commercial cannabis market was examined. Document analysis, rich description, and thematic analysis techniques were employed. The Chapter laid out higher risks associated with the consumption of cannabis in adolescence, which can be linked to practical issues outlined in the introduction and literature review of the book (e.g. Fischer et al., 2017; Room et al., 2010; Volkow et al., 2014). In line with Ghosh et al. (2016), it was found that youth protection was a priority for

Coloradan regulators and multiple steps were taken to reduce the risks of harmful impacts.

Key findings included the importance of prevention messaging, an indication that funds for youth protection should be appropriated before the market is implemented as opposed to relying on tax revenue post-implementation, and that data collection is complex, challenging, and needs early consideration by regulators. Chapter 8 also tentatively linked the evolution of prevention messaging campaigns to impact data, which highlighted that no statistically significant increases in consumption in this group had been identified five years after the CRCM was implemented. Despite 'encouraging trends', it was concluded that it was too early to make definitive judgements on the matter, which is in line observations of several scholars (e.g. Kilmer & MacCoun, 2017; Pacula & Sevigny, 2014). The multiple the recommendations that emerged are presented in the recommendations section below to avoid repetition and improve the readability of the book.

Chapter 8

The CG process of policy implementation was addressed. To investigate the issue, the three 'static' data sets including government documents, the media sample, and interviews were drawn on. Documentary analysis, rich description, and thematic analysis techniques were incorporated. The theoretical foundations of CG were described along with a critique of this approach based on lessons from alcohol. Furthermore, the Ansell and Gash (2008) contingency model of CG was incorporated to analyse the data sets, which enabled policy theory to be applied to real-world experience in the Coloradan context. Following the Ansell and Gash model, risks and benefits associated with the CG approach together with several risk mitigation strategies were examined. Specifically, these critical elements relevant to policy implementation in the context of the CRCM were investigated: starting conditions for cannabis policy implementation, facilitative leadership, institutional design, collective learning and the knowledge gap, regulatory paralysis, regulatory capture, and lobbying.

It was concluded that, in line with the findings of Hudak (2015b) on the one hand, the CG process appeared to be largely effective in terms of facilitating initial policy implementation (as opposed to outcomes) in an environment where regulators in a pioneering jurisdiction were challenged by tight deadlines and faced a knowledge vacuum for devising rules for a substance that had previously been illegal. On the other hand, there were indications (based on examples presented of increased lobbying efforts) that as the policy evolved, risks associated with the CG such as regulatory capture persisted and possibly increased.

Chapter 10

Phase 3 of the research program reverted primarily to the continuously updated 'dynamic' data sources and focussed on how the CRCM had evolved in the first five years post-implementation together with practical lessons learned. This is in line with the overall objective of the book to consider both the implementation *and* the evolution of the market. The Chapter consisted of three parts including introduction and background, tension between private profit and public health, and lessons learned. In part 1, latest market insights, emerging literature, and the evolution of the RMC were considered. In general, it was noted that both cannabis sales and related tax revenue had continued to increase since 2014, the market share of high potency products had increased, prices decreased, and there was no evidence of increased consumption among youth or adults in the state. Part 2 considered the CRCM from the perspective of tension between consumer protection, private profit, and public health in line with the book objectives. In particular, the elements of constitutional constraints, marketing and advertising, budtenders and the retail shopping experience, and the challenges associated with the regulation of pesticides were discussed. This tension is further discussed within the harm reduction framework below as a pattern that was identified across the book with implications for other jurisdictions. The multiple practical lessons outlined in Part 3 were moved to the recommendations section below to improve the readability of the book and eliminate unnecessary repetition.

In the following section major public health issues are placed within the harm reduction framework, linked back to the literature review, and implications are considered against recent developments in North American cannabis markets more broadly.

Revisiting harm reduction and the cannabis fragmentation spectrum

In the Introduction of book, harm reduction was outlined as a guiding principle for the study in the broad sense that efforts are directed at minimising the harmful consequences associated with cannabis in a legal market (Crofts et al., 2003). Based on the results presented in the book it is apparent that many regulations developed in the RMC fall into that category. For example, in practical terms it was noted that in commercial cannabis markets regulating product quality, limiting predatory marketing strategies, or allowing a home grow option may be considered harm reduction (Hudak, 2016; Kamin, 2016; Lenton, 2016). Indeed, it can be argued that the CRCM has met the three defining (and still relevant) characteristics of harm reduction as stipulated by Lenton and Single (1998) including having a goal to reduce harm (as opposed to reduced use *per se*), having a range of harm reduction strategies, and a likely net reduction in drug related harm. There are indications that Colorado has achieved the implementation of these harm reduction strategies. However, that is not to say that the outcomes have all been consistent with reduced harm, but rather to highlight that significant resources have clearly been allocated to reduce the potential impacts of the commercial cannabis model in line with core aims stipulated by regulators to incorporate public health lessons from alcohol and tobacco (e.g. Hickenlooper, 2014). Nonetheless, despite this allocation of resources, aspects such as fast product development and the apparent increase in popularity for higher potency products and dabbing represent considerable risk of harm increasing. In the following subsections price, increased revenue for the State, quality control and consumer protection, and tension between public health and private profit are considered from a harm reduction perspective. Additionally, further nuance is provided by situating the Coloradan commercial model within the CFS and considering implications against emerging trends in the wider US and Canadian markets.

Price – an ongoing public health concern

Among the most concerning issues from a public health and harm reduction perspective is that of price. As noted in the literature review, a widely predicted problem was that in commercial markets, economies of scale may result in price collapse that could lead to patterns of increased consumption (Caulkins et al., 2015; Pacula & Lundberg, 2014). This concern was supported by data introduced pointing out that the average price per gram in Colorado had decreased significantly – a trend that appeared to be continuing unabated in late 2019 (Marijuana Policy Group, 2018). While price reductions have been apparent, associated increases in youth consumption or dependency have not been identified in the latest impact assessment data (Brooks-Russell et al., 2019; Brooks-Russell et al., 2018). How lower prices impact on consumption patterns of use are to be addressed by prompt policy modifications with problematic use will require continual monitoring if undesirable patterns of use are to be addressed by prompt policy modifications. As noted, lessons from alcohol demonstrate that price control is an important public health tool to reduce harmful consumption among vulnerable groups, most notably youth and people who depend on the substance (Pacula et al., 2014).

At the time recreational cannabis was legalised in Colorado, statistics generally agreed upon in the literature indicated that approximately 9% of people who have ever used cannabis will meet the criteria of dependence as stipulated by DSM-5 (Lopez-Quintero et al., 2011). The risks increase to almost half of cannabis consumers (at some point in their lives) who initiated consumption before they were 15 (Compton et al., 2013; Hall, 2015). An estimated 1-2% of the adult population is affected by cannabis use-disorders with a reported 2.7 million people in the US, aged 12 and over, reportedly meeting the DSM-5 criteria of dependence (Hall, 2015; Volkow et al., 2014). These statistics have remained constant since the CRCM was implemented, indicating no increase in cannabis use disorders or youth consumption.

As previously noted, while there is currently no evidence that indicates increased instances of cannabis dependency as a result of the CRCM, it would seem logical that, due to marketing techniques and price collapse, at some point there may be. Thus, it remains crucial from a public health perspective to be vigilant in the face of continued price collapse of cannabis products in commercial markets. On the other hand, if prices are kept too high there is the risk that purchasing from the black market will be more attractive (Caulkins et al., 2015). Again, the Uruguay model provides a relevant a comparison point. As stated, a core objective of that approach was to reduce price substantially to effectively eradicate the black market (Pardo, 2014). The public health risk was mitigated in the Uruguayan case by only legalising relatively lower risk, less potent herbal cannabis products (Rolles & Murkin, 2016). In Colorado, where a full range of cannabis products are available, such risk mitigation was not apparent in the face of the ongoing price collapse, and as such the potential public health impacts associated with low priced cannabis remain unclear. The implications of price collapse in the broader North American cannabis market are further discussed from an industry perspective within the CFS later in this chapter.

Increased revenue for the State

It has previously been described that from an harm reduction perspective, the commercial model was the most effective approach for generating revenue for the state that can be used to fund the regulatory mechanism, oversee quality control, and increase services such as drug education, youth prevention, counselling, and treatment programs (Caulkins et al., 2015). This was certainly supported by evidence in Chapter 10 that described increasing tax revenues in Colorado and significant increases in expenditure relating to public health education and access to services such as substance abuse and treatment. To provide perspective on the extent this was achieved in Colorado, by July 2019, the state had received over US$1 billion in fees and taxes from the medical and recreational markets combined from over $6.5 billion in sales (Colorado Department of Revenue, 2019b, 2019c). It was reported that over the five years since the CRCM was implemented, the majority of this revenue had been appropriated to the departments of Human Services (31.7%), Public Health and Environment (20.7%), Education (16.4%), and local affairs (15.5%) (Forbes, 2019, Jun. 12; Joint Budget Committee, 2019). This reportedly led new Coloradan Governor Jared Polis to state "This industry is helping grow our economy by creating jobs and generating valuable revenue that is going towards preventing youth consumption, protecting public health and safety, and investing in public school construction" (Forbes, 2019, Jun. 12).

Nonetheless, as noted by Kamin (2015) it is important not to over-emphasise the potential for increased tax revenue and cost savings associated with enforcement, which may not provide a compelling argument for legalisation *per se*. For context, based on a Rocky

Mountain Economist Quarterly report, it was reported that cannabis revenue in the State accounted for approximately 2.3 % of Colorado's general fund revenue and less than .5% of consumer spending, while employment was estimated at .7% (Cannabist, 2018, Apr.19; Federal Reserve Bank of Kansas City, 2018).

Quality control and consumer safety

The issues of quality control and consumer safety are complex. At the core is one of the central arguments for legalising cannabis, namely that there will be less harm (or public health net gains compared to cannabis prohibition models) if cannabis consumers can make informed choices around products based on potency and purity. According to this view, a legal market should minimally provide cannabis that is contaminant free with additives used during cultivation and potency clearly labelled (Rolles & Murkin, 2016). In theory consumers process this knowledge to make informed choices to consume cannabis in safer (less risky) ways than unregulated scenarios. However, testing cannabis is complicated (Thomas & ElSohly, 2016). When compared against illicit markets, it is apparent that Colorado has achieved this objective to a certain degree, while still falling short of quality control regulations for established legal drugs such as those for alcohol and tobacco.

For example, based on the evidence presented in Chapters 7 and 9, it seems apparent that growing cannabis compliant with regulations is new to an industry that traditionally operated outside of regulated channels. Furthermore, crops are valuable though uninsurable due to federal prohibition, which may further incentivise growers to protect crops by using toxic pesticides. Evidence from field observations noted in Chapter 10 highlighted deficiencies with in-store labelling requirements that restricted the ability of consumers to easily identify product purity. Restrictions on use of the term 'organic', again due to federal prohibition, also appeared to hinder the ability of consumers to make informed choices when purchasing cannabis products. How the focus of CDA changed from creating a banned list to devising an approved pesticide list was noted as a significant step in the process of crafting effective regulations around cultivation standards. This shift of focus evolved from banning thousands of compounds to approving a handful of select pesticide products.

While it is often stated that the advantage of legalising and regulating a cannabis market is ensuring the purity of products (Pacula et al., 2014), from the real-world Colorado experience examined in this book, it is apparent that achieving this goal in practise is rather difficult and takes time. This is reflected by the evolution of quality control regulations, particularly those associated with the application of pesticides as outlined in Chapter 7 compared to Chapter 10. For example, it was not until August 2018 that mandatory testing for pesticides in flower and trim products (which are used to extract cannabinoids for high potency concentrated products) across both medical and recreational markets was implemented, almost five years post-implementation of the CRCM. This progress was also highlighted by interview participant Mitch Yergert, the Director for the Division of Plant Industry at the CDA, who estimated that initially 50-60% of samples tested were found with some form of contamination, which had dropped to approximately 15% within a couple of years. While on the one hand this may be indicative of improved cultivation techniques in line with GACP guidelines that have evolved since the CRCM was implemented, on the other hand, it still represents a significant public health threat in those first five years and beyond.

Relatedly, it was pointed out in the Introduction of the book that vapourisation may be considered a harm reduction method to consume cannabis due to the reduction of carcinogens compared to when cannabis combusts and is smoked (Fischer et al., 2017). Recent developments in the broader US cannabis market however bring that contention into question. For example, recent reports of a mysterious and serious lung disease that has been linked with vapourised products (the so called 'vape pen lung disease') across the US (as opposed to Colorado specifically) are cause for concern. Indeed, a reported 12 people had died and over 800 were seriously injured in August and September 2019 in connection to vaping potentially adulterated nicotine or cannabis products (Centers for Disease Control and Prevention, 2019), which reportedly led the Trump Administration to take action on banning flavoured e-cigarettes (CNBC, 2019, Sep.11). There have been suggestions that the issue may be related to contaminated products. Although conclusive evidence was yet to be found with media reports the only source of information on the issue at time of writing (a public health update that stated the cause was unknown excepted (Centers for Disease Control and Prevention, 2019)), there was speculation that the investigation into the cause of 'vape pen lung disease' was focused on additives such as synthetic vitamin E being used as 'thickeners' in concentrated products (primarily but not exclusively linked to black markets), that reportedly allow for a product to be diluted without appearing any thinner (Leafly, 2019, Sep.12). Vitamin E is known as a safe vitamin as a pill or when applied topically to the skin however may trigger pneumonia when inhaled according to experts cited in the report of this emerging public health threat. This issue points to difficulties associated with regulating and effectively enforcing those regulations on such a diversity of products, which has been a consistent theme throughout the book. It also reinforces the need to ensure that products in regulated markets are contaminant-free as noted by Kilmer (2014), which is a central tenet of many cannabis legalisation debates (Rolles & Murkin, 2016). A final point relates to the variation in cannabis preparations, as there appears to be greater risk with vaping extracted concentrates than dry 'whole-plant' herbal material. This is a level of nuance that is not generally apparent in the academic literature and indicates further research is needed on vapourisation of specific cannabis products such as flower and concentrated oils.

From the evidence presented in this book, it seems apparent that achieving known product potency and purity is challenging and may better be considered as an aspirational goal that can take years to develop - not something automatically achieved on legalisation of the drug as may be argued by legalisation advocates (e.g. Drug Policy Alliance, 2019b). Thus, an apparent lesson for regulators implementing legal cannabis markets is that developing quality standards is complex and involves a significant investment in both time and cost. This needs to be considered in the design of legal cannabis schemes from the outset if reduction in harm is to be maximised.

Tension between private profit and public health

A key objective of the book was to examine the tension between private profit and public health in a real-world commercial model of cannabis regulation. This tension between health and profit built on risks associated with incentivising sales described in Chapters 1 – 3 of the book (e.g. Pacula et al., 2014). For example, as noted in the Introduction, the advanced capitalist structure of American society means that the nature of conducting business with a profit focus is often to the detriment of public health (Caulkins et al., 2016). The potential public health risks associated with cannabis consumption were described in Chapter 2. For example potential acute harms included intoxication and cognitive impairment (National Academies of Sciences Engineering and Medicine, 2017), added risks associated with driving under the influence of cannabis (Asbridge et al., 2012; Rogeberg & Elvik, 2016), and increased risk of accidental poisoning particularly to young children (Caulkins et al., 2015). The potential for chronic harms associated with cannabis consumption included dependency (WHO, 2016), mental health problems (Caulkins et al., 2015), and unclear impacts of cannabis consumption on the developing brain (Volkow et al., 2014).

Multiple illustrations of conflict around the commercial nature of the CRCM emerged from the analysis of the data corpus. For example, advertising and lobbying were identified as the 'coal face' where public health objectives appear to be opposed to those of profit-seeking businesses. Specifically, challenges noted in the chapter related to defining advertising (e.g. are product reviews included?), the role of social media in promoting products, and celebrity branding. Celebrity branding appears to have increased substantially since the publication of Chapter 6[8] and along with other forms of advertising, may further legitimise the consumption of cannabis particularly among youth and other vulnerable groups (Rolles & Murkin, 2016). In terms of implications for other jurisdictions, this relates to options available to regulators to prohibit branded products in legal markets (Caulkins et al., 2015; Rolles & Murkin, 2016). In comparison to the CRCM, the 'blended model' of state monopoly of supply would provide more flexibility to regulators to enact restrictions on product branding (Borland, 2003; Caulkins et al., 2015; Rolles & Murkin, 2016; Zedillo et al., 2019).

The 'tension' issue was crystallised at the macro level by the investigation of how the commercial model was implemented with a CG approach that included industry in discussions on creating regulations. Risks associated with regulatory capture and regulatory paralysis were addressed, while it was also noted that as the market

---

[8] Since the federal legalisation of hemp in 2018 there have been multiple examples of well-known sports stars promoting hemp extracted CBD products. For example, numerous partnerships have recently been announced by CBDMD including with former NFL pros Steve Smith and Jonathon Stewart (CBD MD, 2019).

evolved there was evidence of a shift in lobbying activity towards local jurisdictions. Placing this in the broader US context, it has been reported that lobbying activity in the cannabis space has increased by a factor of 10 in recent years. For example, Justin Strekal, NORML's political director, reportedly stated: "When I started doing this three years ago, there were six paid industry lobbyists working marijuana policy on the Hill. Now there are over 60" (Leafly, 2019, Sep. 12). As noted throughout the book, lobbying remains a major public health concern, although this does not appear to be exclusive to the CG model, but rather a symptom of advanced western capitalist societies that has been observed across industries in the US (e.g. Engdahl, 2007; Nestle, 2013).

When considered against the Colorado specific model outlined in Chapter 4 that stipulated the Coloradan collaborative rulemaking process (Colorado Department of Revenue Enforcement Division, 2017), it may be of interest moving forward to monitor the rate of transition of employees from state regulators to industry executives. Certainly, throughout the course of this research there was a sense that several senior regulators interviewed for the book had moved into the private sector. Whether this has any impact on the ability of industry to impact regulations through lobbying efforts directed through connections from previous professional networks remains to be seen. This obviously raises questions about whether it is appropriate for public servants to go directly into the private sector. As pointed out in a recent study of this 'revolving door' between government and industry (specifically alcohol, gaming, and food industries), such an approach raises a number of public health concerns (Robertson, Sacks, & Miller, 2019). Nonetheless it is worth mentioning recent reports in the US context (not Colorado specific) of corrupt activity reportedly culminating in the arrest of a Massachusetts Mayor for allegedly assisting companies with obtaining limited cannabis licenses in the State in exchange for hundreds of thousands of dollars (USA Today, 2019, Sep.6).

Within the duration of this study, the CG process of cannabis policy implementation appears to have become the default model with prominent examples in California and Canada despite evidence on its effectiveness for enhancing public health outcomes remaining thin. Questions remain as to whether the CG approach was appropriate in the context of policy evolution. For example, is the knowledge void initially faced by regulators as extreme five years after the market has been implemented as it was initially? If not, it is reasonable to question whether the industry needs to remain involved in the process of devising cannabis regulations to the extent that is apparent in the Coloradan model. For other jurisdictions considering legalising cannabis, it is important that they consider the range of policy alternatives to the commercial model such as cannabis social clubs or state monopoly of production approaches that remove profit incentives (Belackova et al., 2016; Rolles & Murkin, 2016).

As noted above, the tension between health and profit was also examined from the structural perspective of constitutional constraints, advertising, and pesticides once again. In addition, the example of budtenders who were shown to be hired on sales ability as opposed to public health credentials, despite being the primary contact point to offer dosing advice for cannabis products, was also presented. A further point is that, as the restrictions to out of state investment have been lifted in Colorado, it may be likely that further financial inducements could potentially tempt regulators. Thus, it remains unclear whether CG approaches to cannabis policy implementation and particularly policy evolution best represent public health objectives.

The cannabis fragmentation spectrum: contextualising the commercial Coloradan model

The CFS provides a theoretical framework that allows stakeholders to consider alternative commercial cannabis market structures including commodification, vertical integration, and appellation designations that aim to protect smaller-scale farmers and create an artisan industry (Stoa, 2017).

Evidence has been presented throughout the book that in the first five years since the CRCM was implemented, the Colorado model has shifted from the middle position of vertical integration on the CFS towards the commodification end of the spectrum. For example, in Chapters 4 and 6 the initial regulatory requirement of the CRCM was described as partial vertical integration whereby retailers were required to cultivate 70% of the produce sold in their stores. Furthermore, the appropriateness of including industry in the regulatory process has been examined. A key finding was that while industry involvement in the implementation of the CRCM was broadly understandable and effective given the knowledge vacuum that existed, as the market matured and the collective learning had increased, the risk of regulatory capture remained. The ending of this 70% cultivation requirement was stipulated as one of the key changes to the CRCM as it evolved. It was also noted that in 2016 the statutory two year residency requirement for investors was removed, while in 2018, a bill that would have further increased flexibility for out-of-state investors by allowing an unlimited number of investors and removing background checks passed through the General Assembly, but was vetoed by Governor Hickenlooper who stated concerns about federal restrictions. Nonetheless, by 2019, under new Governor (Polis), a replacement bill had been passed into law that allowed for greater investment flexibility including the allowance of publicly-traded cannabis companies in the State for the first time (HB19-1090, 2019).

A clear implication of this policy shift to allow out-of-state investment for regulators in other jurisdictions is that as the political landscape changes, there may be associated modifications to the regulatory model that were not initially envisioned when the scheme was conceived. For example, it has been well documented that former Governor Hickenlooper, who oversaw the market implementation as previously described, did not support legalising cannabis initially (although reportedly changed his position to tacit approval some years later), and advocated for a cautious approach that drew on public lessons from other legal drug industries such as alcohol and tobacco (CPR News, 2019, Jan. 7; Hickenlooper, 2014). In contrast, new Governor Polis has reportedly been clear in his support for growing the industry as an economic opportunity for the State (Forbes, 2019, Jun. 12). Thus, at least in part as a result of the change in gubernatorial leadership in Colorado and the potential for increased market concentration, the scheme can now be situated more explicitly in the commodification component of the CFS.

As noted, the Herfindahl-Hirschman Index demonstrated that in Colorado the 10 largest operators controlled approximately 25% of the market although it remained highly competitive in comparison to other industries indicating that a 'big cannabis' style market consolidation had yet to establish itself in the State by 2018 (Marijuana Policy Group, 2018). A central reason for this may have been the protections originally put in place in Colorado to limit out-of-state investment and whether this changes under the new investment laws remains a relevant consideration from a public health perspective.

Considering the implications of commodification in the context of recent developments in North America

As previously discussed, a major concern with the commodification of cannabis regulation is that the industry will morph into a powerful body with significant clout to influence regulations and potentially negatively impact public health. This concern stems from lessons learned from other 'big' industries including alcohol, tobacco, agriculture, and pharmaceuticals (e.g. Pacula et al., 2014). To consider the implications of the commoditisation of the CRCM, it is appropriate to factor in latest developments in wider North American markets. Since Colorado was the first jurisdiction to implement a legal cannabis market in 2014, nine other states, as well as Canada at the federal level had followed suit. Thus, the following subsection considers the issue of commodification against recent reports of increased investment in cannabis from external industries, examples of market consolidation within the US cannabis industry, and the potential of federal legalisation to increase the commodification of cannabis products.

First, some reported examples of the growing investment in the emerging North American markets are helpful to contextualise the commercial CRCM. As legal commercial cannabis models spread across US states and Canada, investment interest appeared to be focused on bigger markets and throughout the study period, larger and larger deals were being reported with regularity in California and Canada in particular, but less so in Colorado. Salient examples include reports of the purchase of 10% of Canada's largest cannabis firm by a US beer distributor for US$ 200m (Wall Street Journal, 2017, Oct. 29), a proposed US$250m investment fund in California (Bloomberg, 2017, Oct. 27), and the $4 billion investment by beer maker Constellation in Canadian cannabis firm Canopy Growth (CNBC, 2018, Aug. 15).

Second, examples of cannabis industry consolidation in US markets have also been reported. For example, Curaleaf's acquisition of Cura Partners in an all-stock deal was reportedly around US$1 billion (Marijuana Business Daily, 2019, May 3). Additionally, reported data relating to Florida indicated that explosive growth would consolidate the medical market share in the hands of the 12 businesses that had obtained operating licenses at the time of writing with a reported 10,000 new patients added to the Floridan medical cannabis register in a single week in 2019 (Marijuana Business Daily, 2019, May 7). In terms of market consolidation, the Floridan model is quite extreme with five licensed businesses reportedly operating 82% of the state's 119 dispensaries (of which the previously mentioned Curaleaf is one of the largest with 24 dispensaries at time of writing) (Marijuana Business Daily, 2019, May 7). It remains unclear how such acquisitions will impact small to medium-sized facilities in the long term, however current conditions appear to favour large and well-resourced entities.

Third, an additional aspect of commodification in the US more broadly relates to whether cannabis is legalised at the federal level, which would presumably impact both banking and interstate (and potentially international) commerce. Although the conflict between federal prohibition and state legalisation was a recurring theme (discussed in more detail in the major themes section below), it was deemed as largely beyond the core objectives of the book. Nonetheless, a brief consideration of the implications if cannabis was (hypothetically) legalised at the federal level in the US is helpful in this context of the commodification of cannabis products.

Challenges relating to cannabis firms not having access to a range of banking services have been described in the book. The issue remained unresolved in mid-2019 with no solution implemented at that time. Federal legalisation would presumably solve the problem of access to banks, and likely incentivise market entry for mega-corporations such as Philip Morris' parent Altria Group, Monsanto, Pfizer, and Walgreens. Comparisons with Uruguay may be insightful in this regard as there have been reports that Monsanto was attempting to corner that cannabis market with genetically modified seeds (Centre for Research on Globalization, 2018, Oct.15). There is no doubt that entry into the market by these types of corporations would likely have an enormous impact and based on publicly available track records of these firms, there is little evidence to suggest that public health would be improved by that outcome. Recent reports also indicate that ownership of cannabis strains is increasingly becoming a battleground in the US between craft growers and corporations (Wired, 2018, Feb.26, 2019, Jul.24).

Placing the CRCM within the context of emerging markets in North America indicates that the noted shift towards commodification in the State is part of a wider pattern in cannabis legalisation. Within that context, the CFS has provided further nuance regarding the nature of commercialism in those markets and may be helpful for regulators in other jurisdictions as they prioritise objectives in the design of their respective schemes, most notably around the establishment of either craft markets or generic, low-price products.

While the commodification of cannabis can have advantages for regulators who seek to enforce compliance regulations (as the comparison between Californian and Floridan regulatory models vividly illustrates), from a public health perspective, very low-cost high potency cannabis is not desirable. While statistically significant increases in harm relating to youth were not identified in the book, the general consensus was that it remained too early to make definitive judgements and that caution is advised in this matter. Furthermore, this lack of increased harm was linked to the Colorado model as it was initially implemented that occupied the middle position of vertical integration, and before looser restrictions on out-of-state investment described above came into force.

On the other hand, by late 2019 it appeared that this downward pressure on price was having a significant impact from the perspective of the cannabis industry in the broader North American context and may result in considerable upheaval of the commercial market structure as large cannabis companies reportedly struggle for profitably. For example, it was reported that Canopy Growth, the world's largest cannabis company by market capitalisation was in 'freefall' over the second and third quarters of 2019 (Equity Guru, 2019, Aug.28). According to the report (p.1) the "cannabis bubble Canopy Growth created is now the tsunami killing everyone". There were similar reports of decreasing market capitalisations for other large cannabis producer companies, ostensibly those head quartered in Canada such as Aurora (Business Insider, 2019, September 12). It remains to be seen how these trends impact on the commercial market structure in North American cannabis markets. Purely speculatively, it does not seem beyond the realms of possibility that companies such as Bayar Monsanto or Phillip Morris may find value in acquiring stock in these recently devalued firms with established distribution, which could represent significant public health threats based on monopolistic activity.

Chapter 12 Major themes & recommendations

In addition to the issues outlined above within a harm reduction framework, multiple themes emerged throughout the book including complexity, evolution and change, political uncertainty, and the entanglement of the recreational and medical cannabis markets.

Complexity

From the analysis in the results it is apparent that regulators faced an extremely steep learning curve when implementing the world's first legal seed-to-sale cannabis market. This reflected the description presented earlier in the book where cannabis was introduced as a complex biological organism that enters the body with pharmacokinetic variation based on variety in preparations, methods of consumption, and consumer tolerance among others (Mechoulam, 2006; Mechoulam & Hanus, 2000; Russo, 2011). Regulatory issues associated with cannabis edible products illustrate the matter. It was found that, on the one hand, edible products may be less harmful to the respiratory system than smoking or vapourisation, while on the other hand, these edible cannabis products may be seen as attractive to children (potentially leading to an increase in accidental ingestions) and/or uncomfortable experiences for novice consumers due to delayed intoxication, often out of state tourists . Most notable was the popularity of edible products that took regulators by surprise with almost half of the market share and requiring regulatory detail around potency testing, labelling, and education (MacCoun & Mello, 2015).

When considered against broader policy options, the issue of unlimited product diversity highlights the stark contrast between the commercial model as implemented in Colorado and other, potentially less risky models available to lawmakers in other jurisdictions. For example there is a clear difference in policy implemented in Colorado and Uruguay in terms of product diversity with the former having near limitless product 'innovation' and the later but a handful of low risk herbal cannabis products (Pardo, 2014). As a result, the breadth of products to regulate contrasts greatly between the two jurisdictions. A notable difference between the two models is that Uruguay took over three years in the pre-implementation phase compared to 13 months for Colorado, which provides an indication of the regulatory complexity for even the limited product options in Uruguay. As noted previously in the book, Coloradan regulators were bound by the constitution as stipulated in A64 to ensure the market was implemented within a relatively short space of time. Furthermore, Uruguay followed the recommended blended model whereby state controls the distribution (marketing) (e.g. Babor, 2010; Borland, 2003; Pacula et al., 2014; Room, 1987). As is discussed further below, nuanced comparisons of the public health outcomes associated with these approaches in Colorado and Uruguay is an area where future research may be beneficial.

Variation in cannabis products as a result of the broad definition of cannabis in Colorado is perhaps the most prominent example of complexity, however evolving methods of consumption, the methodological procedure associated with quality control testing, and challenges related to impact assessment are also testament to the matter. These issues can be linked to, and provide real world examples of, practical issues presented in Chapter 3 as stipulated by, for example, Rolles and Murkin (2016). This has clear implications for regulators in other jurisdictions who are considering legalisation of the drug such as they will need expert input and sufficient time in the pre-implementation phase to come to terms with the required breadth and depth of detail. An obvious recommendation from this (discussed in more detail below in the recommendations sub section), is that defining cannabis in more restrictive terms to limit the range of cannabis products in the rollout phase should be considered as distinct from the broad definition stipulated by A64 in Colorado (Colorado Amendment 64, 2012). The theme of complexity also feeds into the consistent thread of evolution and change, which is now discussed.

Evolution and change

A consistent theme identified throughout the book was the notion of constant change and continuous evolution of policy. Strong evidence has been presented of the evolving nature of the RMC in particular. For example, the so-called 'permanent' version of the RMC was in its 10th iteration by the end of 2018 and consisted of 262 pages, compared with 124 pages in the first iteration in 2013 (Colorado Secretary of State, 2019). A comparison of pesticide regulations as stipulated in chapters 7 and 10 provides more insight. For example, by mid-2018 sampling procedures and proficiency standards had evolved while mandatory testing for pesticides on both flower and trim products had also been implemented. In addition, the initial market requirement of vertical integration being removed, changes to taxation structure, and the 2018 Sunset Review recommendation to unify the two markets further highlighted the theme of constant change. Additionally, there was an estimate of 30-50 legislative bills a year being debated in the Coloradan General Assembly three years post-implementation of the CRCM, which further illustrates the theme.

Beyond the complexity of regulating cannabis outlined above, a number of factors have been noted throughout the book that contributed to the pace of regulatory evolution in the study period including an extensive knowledge gap when the policy was implemented due to Colorado being a pioneering jurisdiction, tight deadlines set by A64 that limited time available for regulators to consider complex matters in the pre-implementation phase, and issues that emerged as a result of the market *per se* such as the increase in hospital admissions of children for accidental ingestions (updates to labelling requirements). These matters posed serious public health risks and required swift intervention by regulators to reduce potential risks.

While it is to be expected that first time regulations for cannabis policy will require updating and finessing (Caulkins et al., 2015), the range of issues that required updates in the Coloradan context was perhaps surprising. For regulators in other jurisdictions, having an established legislative and rulemaking process is paramount for addressing issues promptly. It would seem logical that the pace of regulatory change in Colorado since the market implementation is also linked to the broad definition of cannabis stipulated in A64, which gives weight to the argument that jurisdictions considering implementing a regulated marijuana scheme 'go slow' with the roll-out by initially only legalising a small number of products. This aspect is discussed in more detail below in the recommendations section.

From the description of regulatory change provided above, the evolution of regulations can be seen from a public health perspective as attempts to improve the RMC from original iterations. However, not all changes to the RMC can be viewed through this lens of positive transformation and improvement. For example, a notable change to regulations included HB19-1090, which: "… repeals the provisions that require limited passive investors to go through an initial background check. The bill repeals the provisions that limit the number of out-of-state direct beneficial owners to 15 persons. The bill repeals the provision that prohibits publicly traded corporations from holding a marijuana license" (HB19-1090, 2019, p.1). On the face of it, these changes are concerning from a public health perspective.

As time passed, it has become apparent that the pace of regulatory change related to cannabis is not specific to Colorado. Since Colorado became the first state to implement a legal cannabis market, 10 more states (and the District of Columbia) had followed suit at the time of writing. To place the dynamic nature of the CRCM into the context of reform across the US, it was reported that 1,164 cannabis-related bills were moving through state legislatures and Congress in 2019 (Marijuana Moment, 2019), further emphasising the need for a robust rulemaking process as was apparent in the CRCM (Colorado Secretary of State, 2018a).

Entanglement of the recreational and medical markets

A theme that continuously emerged throughout the research was the entanglement of the recreational and cannabis markets. This perhaps reflects the crossover first identified in Chapter 2 describing how cannabis interacts with the human body via receptors in the ECS regardless of whether that consumption is labelled medical or recreational (e.g. Russo, 2016a). Examples of the entanglement include the establishment of the RMC on existing medical regulations and the co-existence of constitutional amendments A20 and A64, which make changes to cannabis policy problematic as these must be approved by public ballot (Kamin, 2013; Kilmer & MacCoun, 2017). Additionally, there is duplication of regulations, cultivation standards, and testing requirements that further entangle the markets. By 2019 the two codes of regulations were almost completely aligned (Colorado Secretary of State, 2019), leading to the logical recommendation in the 2018 Sunset Review to unify the two markets in 2020 in order to maximise regulatory efficiency and minimise needlessly duplicitous regulation (Colorado Department of Regulatory Agencies, 2018). Unification of the two markets has also been recommended by cannabis policy experts as previously noted (Carnevale et al., 2017).

A unified market would presumably reduce this duplication thereby removing an important barrier to market entry for small businesses and potentially shrink the black-market as a result. It remains to be seen whether the tax structure will be reworked based on this recommendation. On the one hand, given the disparities noted previously in the book regarding how much revenue is generated by each market, there is an opportunity for the CDOR to significantly increase revenues if medical taxes are bought in line with those from the recreational market. On the other hand, increasing taxes on medical cannabis patients may be a hard sell politically in a state that has strict protections against tax increases enshrined in the Constitution, and would seemingly require a ballot measure for approval. While this theme was identified prominently throughout the research, it was deemed largely outside the scope of the book objectives. Nonetheless it warrants further research.

Recommendations, lessons learned, and general suggestions for other jurisdictions

Chapter 6: General considerations for other jurisdictions regarding quality control and the regulation of pesticides

The following considerations may be valuable for jurisdictions seeking to regulate the use of pesticides during cannabis cultivation. First, tobacco and cannabis plants have similar attributes. Regulators might consider using the experience of regulating the cultivation of tobacco around the world as a significant resource for developing pesticide rules. Second, the definition of a pesticide is important, especially in terms of whether (i) it is considered both pre-harvest and post-harvest and (ii) growth regulators are included. Third, allocating resources to implement proficiency standards for pesticide testing including options to validate methods could be considered. Fourth, international accreditations for laboratory methodologies such as ISO 17025 and QuEChERS methodology may provide useful benchmarks for regulators and industry. Fifth, regulators might consider using independent cultivation consultants with no attachment to the specific industry but with documented expertise in producing industrial-sized crops free of pesticides. Sixth, edibles and concentrates have been noted as high-risk products regarding pesticide residues. Considering the legalisation of flower only at phase one of rollout to allow more time to introduce quality control standards for more complex products may reduce exposure to public health harms. Seventh, early identification of acceptable pesticides for use might be encouraged. Finally, development of guidelines for cultivators which include the use of Good Agricultural and Collection Practices (GACP) and Integrated Pest Management (IPM) could be important to provide educational and regulatory direction shaping the adoption of potentially safer cultivation practices appropriate to a legal, regulated cannabis market.

Chapter 7: Recommendations regarding youth protection

Numerous lessons can be learned from the Coloradan experience of implementing a legal, commercial cannabis market allowing recommendations to be made for other jurisdictions. First, developing education material and programs is a multi-department effort that draws on public health, education, human services and public safety departments among others. Leveraging the resources of these departments should be a goal of legalisation regulators.

Second, in Colorado it is apparent that public health initiatives including youth prevention education programs were to be funded in the second round of appropriations, that is, in the second year of implementation. While it is understandable in the context of implementing the world's first adult-use cannabis market that regulators did not want the new industry to be seen as a burden on taxpayers to implement, from a public health perspective and with the benefit of hindsight, pre-funding prevention education programs would seem to warrant further consideration.

Third, in line with previous observations from cannabis scholars (e.g. Caulkins et al., 2015) the ballot led initiative in Colorado appears to have hindered public health best practise as the example of 30% advertising for youth demonstrated. A complete ban on cannabis advertising remains the recommended public health position. This implies that legislative change to cannabis prohibition may better align with public health objectives than ballot measures.

Fourth, prevention messaging campaigns may need to evolve from abstinence-only towards harm reduction.

Fifth, parents and trusted adults play an important role to inform, educate, and ultimately prevent youth consumption. Resources will need to be allocated to this group.

Sixth, data collection needs to begin in advance of any rollout of legal markets to establish baseline consumption rates and how school discipline data is recorded.

Seventh, despite the Mayor of Denver declaring the prevention messaging campaigns "a success", from the perspectives presented in this paper it is still too early to judge youth consumption outcomes.

Chapter 8: Recommendations relating to collaborative governance approaches to cannabis policy implementation

It is apparent that the CG process was helpful to address the knowledge vacuum and build collective learning in a complex and novel policy arena in the context of policy implementation. In this sense, regulators in other jurisdictions considering reform of cannabis policy may find the CG model helpful to address their own knowledge deficiencies given the global history of prohibition.

However, questions remain as to whether the CG approach holds sway in the context of policy evolution several years after initial implementation. For example, it would seem reasonable to conclude that after five years of experience regulating cannabis, policymakers likely have access to substantially more relevant knowledge than previously. As such it is legitimate to ask whether there is the same need to continue consulting the cannabis industry in the same way.

Further, as larger businesses enter the fray there is the potential of creating conditions more fertile for increased investment (and presumably influence) in the cannabis industry (e.g. Subritzky et al., forthcoming). Thus, an annual or biannual review of the CG process may mitigate these risks.

Chapter 10: Lessons learned

The following section outlines some of the major challenges identified from the Coloradan experience and offers some suggestions for regulators in other jurisdictions intending to implement a regulated cannabis market. The list is not exhaustive, however, it draws on examples to highlight key practical difficulties encountered during the first five years of implementation.

First, while the citizen-driven approach to legalisation solves the problem of inactivity at the Federal level, it does not encourage public health best practice (Kleiman, 2018). In the CRCM, an additional complication is that the core market structure was enshrined within the State Constitution via A64. Most notable among these constitutional constraints are the stipulations that cannabis be regulated like alcohol (under a commercial model) and that cannabis is broadly defined, which allowed huge product diversity. Lessons that can be drawn from this seem to be that implementation of more public health-focused legal cannabis models would require proactive legislation by the government and that the definition of cannabis should be strictly defined at the outset. A definition that limited cannabis products to flower only, for example, would potentially reduce risks associated with higher potency concentrates, together with streamlining the initial regulations considerably. The definition could be expanded to include more products at a later date if that was desirable.

Second, the evidence from the CRCM seems to confirm a number of anticipated issues including: that a minority of people with problematic use constitute a majority of total consumption; that these people furthermore are a prime target for cannabis businesses; and that commercial entities will exploit loopholes in the regulations with hopes of increasing opportunities to promote products. From an entrepreneurial perspective this is understandable, while from a public health view it is not. Although information on the risks associated with cannabis dependency is available on the Colorado State Web Portal, more could be done to protect the most vulnerable by: (i) adding explicit warning regarding this issue to cannabis product labels; (ii) artificially increasing prices (as noted above, although this strategy has been suggested within the Coloradan public health framework, prices continue to fall) [9]; (iii) strengthening advertising restrictions, particularly around social media, product reviews, and celebrity branding; and (iv) regulating plain packaging to hinder brand recognition and potentially reduce product appeal.

Third, local jurisdictions have emerged as entities that may provide extra protection around important public health issues such as external signage, opening hours, outlet density, and the application of chemical pesticides during the cultivation stage. This can potentially be seen as a strength of the Coloradan approach if the various levels of government can work harmoniously towards stated goals.

Fourth, regulating cannabis is a complex matter that touches numerous government departments, and from the Coloradan experience, it is apparent that this complexity increases in the first years after market implementation. Unexpected consequences will arise and having the ability to effectively deal with these issues in a timely manner is important. The established rulemaking process in Colorado has been helpful in this regard. Lessons from this include going slow with the initial rollout. In particular, it may be advisable to begin with limited products, such as cannabis flower. This could even be limited to a few well-defined genetic varieties with balanced THC:CBD ratios. Complexity also has implications relating to how long the critical preimplantation phase should be. In Colorado, this was again limited by constitutional restraints in A64 with tight deadlines stipulated. While it is preferable to have sufficient time to develop effective rules, it is also clear that finding perfect policy could be an exercise in perpetuity, so a balance needs to be found. Perhaps an 18 month to two-year period would suffice.

Fifth, funds were not appropriated until after they were received via taxes and fees. This resulted in delays of at least two years after implementation for funding of key public health initiatives such as substance prevention grants, youth education campaigns, roadside driver impairment training, and relevant impact assessment surveys. For other jurisdictions, advanced funding for these issues before tax revenues are generated is recommended.

---

[9] There are reports that increased requirements for product testing introduced in August 2018 will increase prices though the extent of this impact remains unclear (Denver Post, 2018, Aug.26)

Sixth, the issue of quality control that allows buyers to make informed choices is more complex than anticipated, particularly around variability in potency testing due to different testing procedures, lack of proficiency standards for cannabis cultivation, and difficulties in regulating and enforcing restrictions on chemical pesticides and other additives. Furthermore, in-store labelling, particularly for fresh produce, was observed to be insufficient. To resolve these issues, regulators in other jurisdictions need to be aware of the immense challenges and extensive resources required to implement this aspect of legalisation effectively. Prefunding the agricultural component of regulations and authorising state testing labs with standardised testing methodologies may help to resolve the issue. Additionally, more stringent in-store labelling would facilitate more informed purchasing.

Study limitations

The present study has several limitations. First, it is specific to circumstances in Colorado and as such has limited generalisability, however, it does start to build an evidence base of strategy and outcomes. Furthermore, the use of thick description as an analytic technique allows the reader to make judgements on the generalisability of the study findings. Second, the sample size of interviewees was small although this is balanced somewhat by the rich experience and seniority of interviewees in the regulatory process. Third, analysis of the regulations was at the state level and beyond superficial examination, regulations at federal and local levels were not incorporated in the study. Fourth, the entanglement of the medical and recreational cannabis markets in Colorado make it difficult to draw inferences specific to the recreational market. Fifth, the diversity of regulations between local jurisdictions in Colorado make it difficult to generalise conclusions about the Colorado model even within the state, let alone outside it. Sixth, no longitudinal study was undertaken to compare before and after outcomes. Such an approach may have added value to the study. Seventh, the use of visual methods such as incorporating photos or video from the field into the analysis could have been beneficial and may be worth considering in future. Finally, while interviewees were afforded the option of anonymity, the explicit naming of the majority of interview participants as described in the subsection 'Ethics' in Chapter 5 may have impacted on the honesty and candidness of responses from interviewees. As such, there is a possibility that this method might have biased the findings of the book. This point is pertinent in that, as previously noted, interview participants were entitled to review the text to approve it before the findings were published (no changes were made to the book as a result and all texts were approved verbatim). However, as noted in Chapter 5, the alternative in many cases was to not have the interviews. Specifically, as public figures, several interviewees felt that anonymity was akin to speaking off record or whistleblowing and as such they required that their full name and title was associated with the text. Additionally, as also pointed out in Chapter 5, the use of thick description as a method can aid readers to differentiate between apparent and relative truth while also enabling them to make judgements on the suitability of the findings to other contexts and settings (Creswell & Miller, 2000).

Future research

As noted above, cannabis policy in the US is diverse with a broad range of approaches being implemented in real-world contexts. This has meant that there is a wide range of potential issues to research further and some suggestions follow. Moreover, beyond the potential risks and benefits associated emerging methods of consumption such as dabbing or vapourisation outlined in the Results section of the book, the harms associated with cannabis have been well documented and appear to have largely remained consistent over the last century. In this sense future research might be focussed on other factors than simply harmful consequences of cannabis consumption. First, a comparative analysis of varying jurisdictions' policies and impact assessment data is an obvious area where there is a need for further research. For example, as more data points continue to accrue, assessments of impact from the CRCM and the less commercialised Uruguayan model would be useful. Additionally, appropriately defining different models in the US and drawing comparisons between public health outcomes in jurisdictions such as California and Florida would add to the literature.

Second, a potential emerging area of research relates to the quality of consumption experiences. As noted in in the Introduction, controlled cannabis consumption was defined as "regular ingestion ... without escalation to abuse or addiction, and without disruption of daily social functioning" (Waldorf et al., 1991, p.267). The distinction between controlled and not controlled (or non-problematic and problematic) consumption of cannabis has not been clearly articulated in the academic literature and further research is needed, particularly in the context of legal cannabis markets.

Third, there remains a large gap in the academic literature relating to the potential benefits associated with 'controlled' cannabis consumption. As has been described, controlled use can be considered through the paradigm of drug, set, and setting (Weil et al., 1969). While our understanding of the 'drug' element in terms of dosage, pharmacology, and method of consumption has increased substantially in recent years (Clarke & Merlin, 2013; Russo, 2013; Thomas & ElSohly, 2016), the concepts of 'set' and 'setting' that seek to establish what Zinberg (1986) described as a high quality consumption environment in terms of the social setting and mindset of the consumer as a potential harm reduction technique (how, where, when, and with whom the drug is used), remain largely under researched. In practical terms, those who arrange to consume cannabis in a relaxed, safe, and comfortable environment often describe positive effects (Earleywine, 2002). This level of nuance in terms of risk categorisation of how cannabis is used is not generally apparent in the current public health literature.

Fourth, research into beneficial consumption in both medical and recreational contexts continues to evolve and could be the focus for further studies. For example, a recent study concluded that those who consume cannabis for self-reported medical use are more likely to consume regularly and on a daily basis (Dai & Richter, 2019). As has been noted previously in a public health and harm reduction framework daily cannabis consumption increases risks of dependent use, however there is little in the literature that considers regular consumption in the medical context of symptom reduction. Additionally, if the recreational and medical in Colorado are unified as recommended then it may be necessary to consider alternative frameworks that cannabis consumption in the context of beneficial outcomes as opposed to increased risk of harm.

Fifth, while research into the therapeutic potential of CBD is slowly evolving (e.g. Russo, 2017) (particularly in the context that CBD derived from hemp is now federally legal) there remains a paucity of clinically valid studies that have investigated the substance in the specific context of beneficial outcomes for athletes. In this regard studies are beginning to emerge that add to the evidence base such as a recent partnership between Canadian cannabis company Aurora and the Ultimate Fighting Championship (UFC) to test hemp-derived CBD products on elite athletes. According to reports, it is hoped that the partnership "will significantly advance clinical science around how hemp-derived CBD impacts athlete recovery" (CNN Business, 2019, Jul. 25). Considering that CBD was removed from the World Anti-doping Agency (WADA) prohibited list in 2018 (WADA, 2019), it is apparent that similarly focussed research is necessary. The emerging relationship between cannabis consumption and fitness was briefly explored in a paper by the author and can be found in Appendix 1 of the book (Subritzky, 2018).

Sixth, the centrality of the ECS has been outlined. It was noted that, regardless of whether consumption is labelled medical or recreational, cannabis still interacts with the body via endogenous cannabinoid receptors (Mechoulam & Parker, 2013). Despite this, in the academic literature the ECS is almost exclusively linked to the consumption of medical cannabis. In this regard, research that considers the ECS in the context of recreational consumption (or as above in a unified market) would make a needed contribution to the current academic literature. An example could be to examine links between cannabis consumption, the ECS, endocannabinoid deficiency syndrome, and general wellbeing (Russo, 2016b). Relatedly, the ECS is largely not taught in medical schools. Given that cannabis consumption appears to be more prevalent in medical contexts, it is important that cannabis prescribers receive more training in this regard - future research should seek to improve this outcome.

Seventh, the recent Sunset review in Colorado recommended to unify the medical and recreational markets in Colorado. This reflects the closeness of the two sets of regulations (e.g. Kamin, 2013). However, the vast majority of cannabis policy research appears to attempt to distinguish between medical and recreational usage in line with international controls (Mead, 2014). In this sense there is a broad scope for research that realigns the focus to a unified market. Points of interest may include how the unified market cannabis market in

Colorado functions in practise around issues such as price, education, age limits, consumption patterns, and others.

Beyond these potential directions of future research, it was noted previously that the data corpus was coded inductively in the first instance and that this resulted in a codebook of 512 codes. As the research progressed these codes were merged into over 20 major issues or themes. While these issues were relevant to the study, ultimately, they were deemed to be outside the core objectives and culled from the book, primarily due to limited space. In this sense, the research identified multiple avenues for future research. These included (in no particular order): changing definitions of the cannabis industry as hemp derived cannabinoid products such as CBD are sold in large chains across the US; emerging cannabis products and methods of consumption such as high potency concentrates and 'dabbing'; cannabis pharmacology and the endocannabinoid system; the relationship between cannabis legalisation and homelessness; increasing instances of cannabis being consumed in spiritual and religious contexts; the apparent reported increases of the consumption of cannabis consumption for improved fitness and sport; parenting; gun laws as they relate to people who consume cannabis; how stigma is impacted by the normalisation of cannabis consumption; and the complex relationship between cannabis consumption and the potential for creativity.

Considering benefits as well as harms – time for a new paradigm?

Many of the above potential future research topics are related to aspects of cannabis consumption that appear to fall outside the scope of public health and/or harm reduction frameworks. This can be linked to Chapters 1 and 2 of the book where the harm reduction model was critiqued on the basis that it lacked the ability to consider non-harmful consumption of cannabis and the potential benefits associated with cannabis use respectively. In this sense future research could potentially be situated within alternative analytical frameworks that can also consider beneficial consumption. This is most pertinent when considered against the recommendation in Colorado to unify the medical and recreational markets from 2020, which presumably would include beneficial consumption.

In the following section a new paradigm for cannabis research and market structure is suggested. As can be seen in Figure 9, the 3-dimensional cannabis regulatory model is based on a social utilitarian perspective and consists of three main dimensions, namely: (i) the therapeutic 'whole-plant' market (TWPM); (ii) research and innovation; and (iii) public health (2.0).

Caulkins and Reuter (1997, p.5) stated that "most people would exclude the benefits of drug use ..." when devising strategies to reduce harm, although it remains unclear why. In contrast, the 3-D model aligns to a 'social utilitarian perspective', in the mould of Bentham who described utility as "the sum of all pleasure [and other benefits] that results from an action, minus the suffering of anyone involved in the action" (Theory of Knowledge, 2019, p.1).

In general, the 3-D model was conceived from lessons learned from the Coloradan scheme to minimise the risks and harms associated with higher risk cannabis, while also unlocking the potentially beneficial aspects of the drug. In the 3-D model, research and innovation would be incentivised towards finding benefits attributable to the plant - a fundamental shift away from current funding models whereby most public health research on cannabis prioritises establishing causality of harms. Figure 9 shows a conception of the proposed 3-D model. Such an approach may warrant further research.

Figure 9: The 3-Dimensional cannabis regulatory model

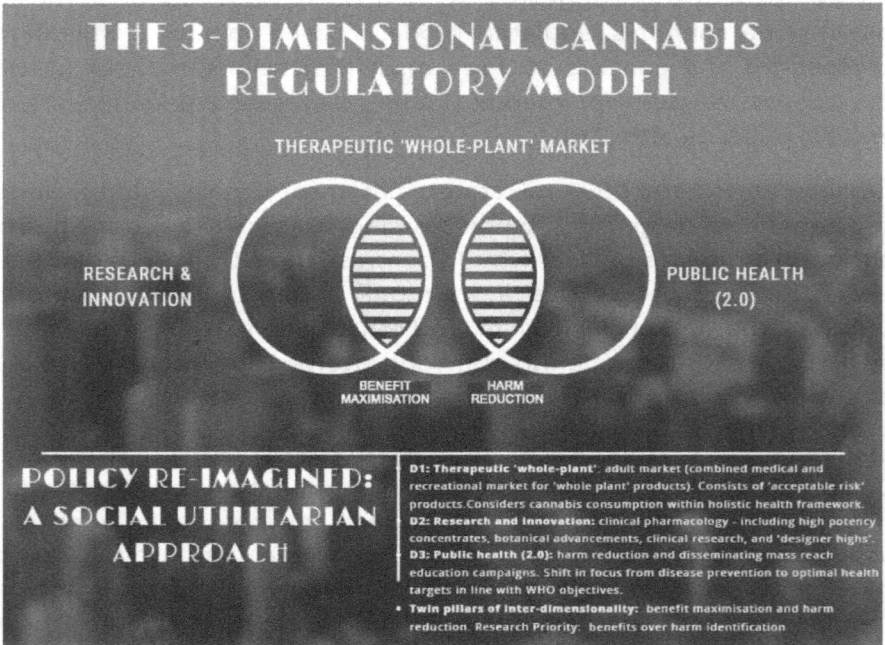

THE 3-DIMENSIONAL CANNABIS REGULATORY MODEL

THERAPEUTIC 'WHOLE-PLANT' MARKET

RESEARCH & INNOVATION

PUBLIC HEALTH (2.0)

BENEFIT MAXIMISATION

HARM REDUCTION

POLICY RE-IMAGINED: A SOCIAL UTILITARIAN APPROACH

D1: Therapeutic 'whole-plant', adult market (combined medical and recreational market for 'whole plant' products). Consists of 'acceptable risk' products.Considers cannabis consumption within holistic health framework.
D2: Research and Innovation: clinical pharmacology - including high potency concentrates, botanical advancements, clinical research, and 'designer highs'.
D3: Public health (2.0): harm reduction and disseminating mass reach education campaigns. Shift in focus from disease prevention to optimal health targets in line with WHO objectives.
• Twin pillars of inter-dimensionality: benefit maximisation and harm reduction. Research Priority: benefits over harm identification

Appendix 1: Considering the spectrum of wellness as an interpretive framework for cannabis consumption

Subritzky, T. (2018). Beyond deficit and harm reduction: incorporating the spectrum of wellness as an interpretive framework for cannabis consumption. International Journal of Drug Policy, 60(10), 18-23. http://dx.doi.org/https://doi.org/10.1016/j.drugpo.2018.07.013

Background

It has been suggested that historically a large body of drug policy research has been informed by the hegemonic pathology, or 'deficit' model of drug use (Barratt, 2011; Karlsson, 2010; Moore, 2002; O'Malley & Mugford, 1991). This view "positions [illicit] drug use as inherently aberrant, as destructive to both health and happiness, and as reflecting some kind of deficit in personality or social position "(Southgate & Hopwood, 1999, p.308). On the face of it, international cannabis controls and prohibition in the US and other countries appear to be informed by the deficit model. Extreme perspectives of the deficit model confer the judgement that all drug use is 'bad' (Zinberg, 1986). To illustrate the point, Caulkins and Reuter (1997) noted that according to this view, even if an adult consumed a psychotropic drug that had zero risk of harm to herself or others, that use is seen as unacceptable because it is morally wrong.

The deficit model has been critiqued on the grounds that it dehumanises people who use cannabis as derelict, or deviant, and as belonging to the margins of society (the so-called 'othering') (Becker, 1963/2008; Lunze, Lunze, Raj, & Samet, 2015). An example of 'othering' is the term 'user', which is perceived as being associated with characteristics such as 'lazy', 'worthless', 'irresponsible', and 'no future' (American Society of Addiction Medicine, 2018; Global Commission on Drug Policy, 2018; International Society of Addiction Journal Editors, 2018).

In part as a response to these concerns a public health framework has evolved. The public health approach, as it pertains to cannabis consumption, moves away from the pathological deficit model of drug use described above, towards a more nuanced recognition that most cannabis related harm is concentrated within a minority of high risk consumer activity (Centre for Addiction and Mental Health, 2014). Public health problems identified in the academic literature associated with cannabis consumption include increased risk of cognitive impairment, added risk of traffic crashes and fatalities and other accidents, dependency, and a greater association with mental health problems among others (Fischer, Rehm, & Hall, 2009; Hall, Renström, & Poznyak, 2016; Room, Fischer, Hall, Lenton, & Reuter, 2010; Szabo, 2014). From the public health perspective, the risk of these harms is amplified by heavy and frequent use of cannabis, long user careers, and initiation of consumption in adolescence, particularly those 15 years or younger (Crépault, Rehm, & Fischer, 2016; Fischer et al., 2009). According to Fischer et al. (2009, p.102) "once these high-risk cannabis users are specified there are two ensuing challenges: (i) ... identifying individuals indicating high risk behaviours; and (ii) offering them appropriate interventions". In other words, according to this view, a public health framework as it relates to cannabis consists of assessment and monitoring (surveillance), and expanding access to treatment and interventions where needed. In this sense, the public health approach appears to operate on the assumption that people who use cannabis lack capacity to make health choices themselves, which aligns with the paternalistic philosophy of drug policy (e.g. MacCoun & Reuter, 2001).

As noted by Fischer et al. (2009), the public health approach has a general focus on reducing harms as opposed to use *per se,* which is very much aligned with the concept of harm reduction. There has long been ambiguity around the term harm reduction as it relates to drug policy (Wodak & Saunders, 1995). In general the concept encompasses a pragmatic approach of "accepting the reality of substance use behaviour, while directing effort at minimising the harmful consequences" (Crofts, Costigan, & Reid, 2003; Erickson, 1995, p.283; Szabo, 2014). Rhodes and Hedrich (2010, p.19) "envisage harm reduction as a 'combination intervention', made up of a package of interventions tailored to local setting and need, which give primary emphasis to reducing the harms of drug use". The Drug Policy Alliance (DPA) among others expanded these definitions to include harms caused by ineffective drug policies including prohibition. An example of harm reduction in a commercial cannabis market might include regulating limits to tetrahydrocannabinol (THC) potency, placing restrictions on predatory marketing strategies, or encouraging the cultivation of products with higher cannabidiol (CBD): THC ratios (Hudak, 2016; Kamin, 2016; Subritzky, Lenton, & Pettigrew, 2016).

A major critique of public health and harm reduction frameworks is that much cannabis consumption appears to take place outside of these realms and that they lack capacity to fully consider: (i) non-problematic use; (ii) the therapeutic nexus of medical and recreational use; and (iii) pleasure.

Person with non-problematic cannabis use

The term 'person with non-problematic cannabis use' recommended by the Global Commission on Drug Policy (2018) report is notable. It appears to introduce a new (or at least under represented) category to the cannabis (academic) literature. Scholars have long pointed out that, while consuming cannabis is not without risk, when considered in the context of burden of disease, most cannabis consumption does not constitute a significant threat to public health at the population level (Caulkins, Kilmer, & Kleiman, 2016; Kleiman, 1992; Room et al., 2010). Attempts to quantify and compare the contribution to the total burden of disease relating to cannabis, other illicit drugs, alcohol, and tobacco provided estimates of 0.2%, 1.8%, 2.3%, and 7.8% respectively (Degenhardt, Ferrari, & Hall, 2017; Room et al., 2010). Indeed, statistics indicate that approximately 90% of people who use cannabis will not reach levels of clinically defined dependence (Caulkins, Hawken, Kilmer, & Kleiman, 2012; Kleiman, 2014). This vast block of people who consume in a manner that is not immediately perceived as harmful, appear to be underrepresented in the cannabis literature generally. While many studies in general do point out most cannabis consumption is in the non-harmful category (in terms of global burden of disease), this contextualisation is often a secondary footnote to central findings. Given that "user" is the term most commonly employed across the literature to describe cannabis consumers, on the face of it the GCDP report appears to insinuate that much of the existing cannabis literature has used stigmatising language when reporting findings that emphasise the harms.

Beyond the general absence of consideration for non-harmful cannabis use, the deficit, public health, and harm reduction frameworks seem to lack the capacity to examine consumption that may be considered beneficial. Indeed, Caulkins and Reuter (1997, p.5) stated that "most people would exclude the benefits of drug use ..." when devising strategies to reduce harm. It remains unclear why this might be the case, although it would seem such views emerge as the result of the hegemonic influence of the deficit model, which is helpful for harm identification purposes. This view appears to illustrate a noteworthy gap in the literature as it pertains to drug consumption generally and cannabis specifically. It seems to discount at least two potential benefits of cannabis consumption, namely: (i) the intersection of cannabis consumption for recreational and medical purposes; and (ii) pleasure.

Overlapping intention of consumption

First, a large portion of cannabis consumption appears to take place in a realm where medical and recreational intent overlap (e.g. Hakkarainen et al., 2017). However, it is generally dealt with as two separate issues. In part this is due to, as Mead (2014) pointed out, international controls that dictate cannabis must be considered separately for medical and recreational use. Colorado is an example of states in the US where the recreational market is built on a separate medical market (Subritzky, Pettigrew, & Lenton, 2016). The similarities and difference between them are beyond the scope of this paper and have been comprehensively reviewed elsewhere (e.g. Kamin, 2013, 2016, 2017).

As an example of this overlap, in a study describing patterns of cannabis use, Pacula, Jacobson, and Maksabedian (2015) found approximately 85% of medical consumers also reported using cannabis recreationally. Furthermore, as part of a global study on cannabis cultivation trends, Dahl and Frank (2016) noted the definitional challenges of medical and recreational consumption of cannabis, and found that cannabis consumers who defined themselves as medical, tended to emphasise the relieving effect over pleasurable outcomes. Chapkis and Webb (2008) identified a group of consumers who refuse to distinguish between recreational and medical consumption. Iversen (2007), moreover, pointed out that the window between an effective medical dose, and one that intoxicates, appears to be quite narrow. Indeed, it has been argued that "defining cannabis consumption as elective recreation ignores fundamental human biology, and history, and devalues the very real benefits the plant provides" DeAngelo (2015, p. 67). Well known cannabis advocate Dennis Peron reportedly stated that all cannabis consumption is medical, with the obvious exception to the rule being misuse (DeAngelo, 2015; Rendon, 2012). This view is illustrative of what Caulkins and Reuter (1997) have called the extreme social utilitarian perspective.

Pleasure

Second, in contrast, several scholars have found that the overwhelming reason for consumption provided by people who use cannabis is pleasure (e.g. Duff, 2008; Webb, Ashton, Kelly, & Kamali, 1998). This is perhaps unsurprising given that an often used description of the effect of cannabis on mood is euphoria (Ashton, 2001). As may be deduced, euphoria is not generally defined as a harm *per se*. In this respect, the harm reduction model has been critiqued for not giving consideration to the concept of pleasure (Houborg, 2010). Moore (2008) pointed out that the term pleasure has become marginalised in discourses that seek to understand drug use. It would not seem unreasonable to conclude that many people who use cannabis may do so with an aim of enjoying it.

Thus, following the cogent logic of the above scholars and studies, these categories of cannabis use (i.e. not significantly harmful, juxtaposed recreational and medical intent, and pleasure) are likely to constitute most consumers in both legalised and illicit markets. It is here where limitations of the dominant frameworks noted above become most salient. For millennia cannabis use has been associated with wellness, particularly at the nexus of mind, body, and spirit. Despite this seemingly obvious match, the literature that incorporates cannabis consumption into wellness conceptions is thin. The following section explores the literature pertaining to the spectrum of wellness and its potential relevance for cannabis scholars.

The Dunn spectrum of wellness as an interpretive framework

The concept of wellness is said to have a history of over 5000 years (Global Wellness Institute, 2017b). In modern times, the spectrum of wellness has evolved as a variant of the psychosomatic health framework, which was conceptually defined as "involving or depending on both the mind and the body as mutually dependent entities" (Lipowski, 1984, p.154). According to several scholars, it developed as a response to changing demographics, existential angst of the modern world, and a critique of disease-based models of health that prioritised funding for treatment as opposed to prevention (Dunn, 1959; Myers, Sweeney, & Witmer, 2000; Steiner & Reisinger, 2006).

The overall goal of a wellness approach to health is for individuals to lead full and rewarding lives, and ultimately maximise their potential (Dunn, 1959; Myers et al., 2000). Therefore health, as conceived within the spectrum of wellness, is considered more than simply being free of disease, or 'unsick' (Ardell, 1979; Dunn, 1959; Schuster, Dobson, Jauregui, & Blanks, 2004). Notions of wellness seek to move from dichotomous conceptions of sickness and health towards a graduated spectrum (Dunn, 1959). This approach is in alignment with World Health Organisation (2017a) principles that state "health is a state of complete physical, mental, and social well-being and not merely the absence of disease or infirmity". To achieve this objective, wellness conceptions are holistic and encapsulate a range of strategies both for disease prevention and enabling of a positive lifestyle (Adler, 1927/2010; Myers et al., 2000). The spectrum of wellness is flexible and has applications both as an analytical framework and a counselling technique with a multi-level healing process (Scholl, McGowan, & Hansen, 2012). In this sense, problematic use of cannabis can be identified within the 'bigger picture' of wellness, and the person with problematic use is empowered to seek support regarding abstinence, harm reduction or counselling (Scholl et al., 2012). Central to this notion is the debate around the capacity, or agency of cannabis consumers to make decisions regarding their own health (e.g. Belackova & Wilkins, 2018; MacCoun & Reuter, 2001).

Philosophically, Heidegger conceived wellness phenomenologically, as encompassing four realms including earth, sky, mortals and divinities - the so-called ringing of the fourfold (Steiner & Reisinger, 2006). Although wellness was initially perceived as largely related to physical health (e.g. Hettler, 1984), Sweeney and Witmer (1991) added a multidisciplinary focus and theoretical grounding through their 'wheel of wellness'. The model included 16 interrelated dimensions of healthy functioning that can be assessed, including creativity, spirituality, nutrition, exercise, pleasure, and stress management among others (Hattie, Myers, & Sweeney, 2004). While historical and first-hand accounts of cannabis use activity have associated its consumption with the enhancement of many of these wheel of wellness components (e.g. Bey & Zug, 2004; Bienenstock, 2016; Pollan, 2002; Sagan, 1971), advocates of consuming cannabis as a tool for achieving wellness tend to frame its use around psychological, physical, and spiritual conceptions (Bello, 2010; Blesching, 2015). In considering wellness lifestyles, Schuster et al. (2004, p.6) contended that wellness is a bio-psychosocial phenomenon that integrates the "... internal and external environment, ranging from physical functioning (ability to deal with disease) to psychologic (emotional, cognitive) and spiritual well-being ... to safety, wealth, freedom, opportunity, and happiness". In relation to drug use in general, these aspects can be linked to, and incorporate the notion of, a stable life structure as an important element for allowing the effective self-regulation of consumption (Decorte, 2001; Grund, 1993).

The motivation or intent for consuming cannabis is seen as a central premise of the spectrum of wellness (DeAngelo, 2015; Dussault, 2017). DeAngelo (2015, p.77), a long-time cannabis legalisation advocate and industry entrepreneur argued that in most cases, cannabis consumption can be categorised as either wellness use, or misuse, and "the difference can only be discerned in the mind of the consumer. When cannabis is ingested with conscious intent, to produce a desired effect that brings some value to life, ... it is being used for wellness purposes". The intent can range from anger management, to enhancing a meal, laughter, or stress relief. According to DeAngelo, it is not the effect that is important, rather, "it is that the consumer be able to honestly identify the value [that consuming cannabis] brings to his or her life" (DeAngelo, 2015, p.77). From this perspective the key to consuming cannabis in a manner that enhances wellness is staying committed to a productive life and accepting responsibility for individual actions.

A key feature of the spectrum of wellness is the prioritisation of self-responsibility for the individual in making conscious health choices (Bello, 2010; Dussault, 2017; Palombi, 1992). This is in alignment with the liberal tradition (MacCoun & Reuter, 2001; Mills, 1859/1985) This aspect relates to the capacity of a cannabis consumer to self-identify when consumption is problematic, and then take steps such as seeking treatment, to address the issue. In this sense, cannabis consumption can be interpreted as a process of self-medication that allows consumers to take greater control in self-assessing their individual requirements (Hazekamp & Pappas, 2014).

Evaluating cannabis use in the spectrum of wellness

There are a range of psychometric instruments available to evaluate individual wellness using the Likert Scale. The concept has traditionally been assessed through: (i) clinical measures that focus on depression, distress, anxiety, or substance abuse (Keyes, 1998); or (ii) the psychological tradition, which follows a subjective evaluation of life satisfaction (Hattie et al., 2004). This is in line with the view of Schuster et al. (2004) who noted that self-perception of health is a strong predictor of subsequent health outcomes. Wellness evaluation tests that have been independently assessed for validity and reliability include: (i) the Five Factor Wellness Inventory that measures almost 100 items (Myers & Sweeney, 2014); and (ii) the Perceived Wellness Survey, which includes physical, spiritual, and psychological dimensions (Adams, Bezner, & Steinhardt, 1997; Kaveh, Ostovarfar, Keshavarzi, & Ghahremani, 2016).

Diagnostic criteria for cannabis dependence can be found in both the Diagnostic and Statistical Manual of Mental Disorders (DSM-5; American Psychiatric Association, 2013), and the International statistical classification of diseases and related health problems (ICD-10; WHO, 1992). While ICD-10 differentiates between dependent and harmful cannabis consumption, DSM-5 classifies level of dependency and associated damage to health as low, moderate or severe (WHO, 2016). DSM-5 has been critiqued for being unidimensional (MacCoun, 2013). Additional tools for evaluating cannabis use patterns specifically include the Severity of Dependence Scale that can provide a 'dependence rating' from 0 - 15 (Copeland, Frewen, & Elkins, 2009), and the Substance Abuse Subtle Screening Inventory (Clements, 2002). Results of these evaluations can then be placed within conceptions of overall health.

At the most fundamental level, DeAngelo (2015, p.78) posits three questions a cannabis consumer could employ to evaluate her or his use: "(i) what effect [is the person who consumes cannabis] seeking ...?; (ii) how will that effect bring value to [the consumer's] life?; and (iii) will cannabis use at this time negatively impact [the person who consumes] or anybody else"?

Cannabis and the wellness industry

According to a report by the Global Wellness Institute (2017a) the wellness industry (not including cannabis) currently contributes US$3.7 trillion to the global economy annually - over three times that of the pharmaceutical industry. The report itemised numerous health aspects under the rubric of wellness, many of which are relevant to the nascent legal cannabis markets currently emerging around the world. For example, several companies have appeared that combine wellness activities such as hiking, infused massage, and art classes with cannabis consumption (e.g. Colorado Cannabis Tours, 2018). The GWI report also identified broader categories in the wellness industry that have an historical association with cannabis including: (i) complementary and alternative medicines (CAM); (ii) mind, body and spirit; and (iii) fitness. These are now discussed.

First, according to Schuster et al. (2004), the concepts of wellness and CAM are closely aligned, with shared underlying beliefs including the prioritisation of a wellness approach to health. While there are numerous CAM categories, the most common are: (i) the use of natural products such as botanicals, probiotics and nutraceuticals as dietary supplements (US Department of Health and Human Services, 2017); (ii) traditional techniques such as acupuncture and aromatherapy (Russo, 2013); and (iii) medicinal plants (World Health Organisation, 2017b). While Mead (2014) noted psychoactive substances in general are not classified as herbal or dietary supplements, several authors have pointed out that this potential exists for herbal cannabis, and advocate for such a classification (Backes, 2014; Dolce, 2016; Small, 2007). Non-psychotropic cannabinoids of cannabis such as CBD and hemp seed oils are widely used in this regard (Small, 2007).

Second, there is a long association between the consumption of cannabis and wellness practices associated with mind-body techniques including yoga, meditation and spiritual exploration. For example Dussault (2017) contended that the use of plant medicines such as cannabis in yogic philosophy dates to the Yoga Sutras (ca. 400 CE). Based on years of self-experimentation, Dussault considers all cannabis consumption, when used in a mindful way, as medicinal (both as treatment and preventative). Furthermore, Dussault (2017, p.2) postulates that when combined with yoga, regular "moderate doses of cannabis, rather than larger amounts less frequently, are a tonic to support a powerful healing system for mental health and wellness". This perspective is in contrast to the public health approach that views all regular and sustained cannabis consumption as high risk (Fischer et al., 2009). Dussault advocates 'microdosing' cannabis to find the minimum effective dose. At time of writing, numerous firms were offering cannabis yoga classes and retreats in states such as Colorado that have legalised cannabis for both recreational and medical purposes (e.g. Cannabis Ganja Yoga Retreat, 2017).

Regarding spirituality, it was noted above this is an important component within the spectrum of wellness (Bello, 2010; Hattie et al., 2004). Spirituality can be defined in many ways. For example, Grof (2016) considered the notion of an expanded consciousness beyond limitations of space and time as spiritual. Myers et al. (2000), in contrast, contended that a feeling of connectedness to the Universe that transcends material aspects of life was an essential component of a spiritual outlook. These definitions are said to be distinct from narrow concepts of religiosity, which refer to institutional beliefs (Steiner & Reisinger, 2006). Descriptions of using cannabis to obtain spiritual states of consciousness (i.e. the entheogenic consumption of cannabis) are numerous with a history that spans millennia (Brown, 2012; Crowley, 2016; Estren, 2017; Gray, 2016). In 2017, a church was established in Denver, Colorado, with the reported aim to allow members to "consume the sacred flower to reveal the best version of self … through ritual and spiritual practice" (International Church of Cannabis, 2017, p.1). The spectrum of wellness may be a useful framework for gaining insights into the consumption of cannabis from this perspective.

Third, an apparently new development that has emerged within the spectrum of wellness is the relationship between cannabis consumption and fitness. Goldstein (2000) has argued there are multiple health related assumptions shared by the fitness movement and the wellness industry including: (i) the notion of taking personal responsibility for health; (ii) the interconnectedness of mind, body and spirit; and (iii) a belief in the positive connotations of 'getting back to nature'. A recent example of fitness and cannabis combining in the modern industry is the opening of the (self-reported) world's first cannabis gym in California. According to their website, Power Plant Fitness (2017) members may consume cannabis at the gym before or after working out "in a full blown health and wellness centre, focused on full body integrative health, wellness and fitness". There is little in the academic literature relating to the consumption of cannabis for fitness purposes beyond a systematic review of fifteen studies by Kennedy (2017), which concluded THC does not enhance exercise performance. However, there appears to be a growing number of anecdotal reports on the benefits of consuming cannabis for fitness purposes, particularly around the notion of increased stamina (e.g. BBC, 2018, May 31; Civilized, 2017, Feb. 20; Guardian, 2016, May 2; The Cannabist, 2017, Jun. 16; Well and Good, 2017, Apr. 3). As noted by Grinspoon (1997), anecdotal evidence and subjective experience can be a valuable source of knowledge regarding both adverse and beneficial effects of consuming cannabis. More research is needed regarding impact assessment of cannabis in this emerging industry, however within the spectrum of wellness, such use may be considered from harmful and abusive consumption, through to potentially beneficial to overall health.

Conclusion

The spectrum of wellness as an analytical framework to conceive cannabis consumption bestows several advantages. First, it offers the possibility of examining broader perspectives of cannabis consumption than the deficit, public health, and harm reduction approaches. Second, the spectrum of wellness is flexible analytically, with the ability to conceptualise both non-harmful cannabis use and high-risk activity. Third, it is complementary to, and can build on practical harm reduction guidelines that aim to reduce risks associated with cannabis consumption. Fourth, there has been a long association between cannabis consumption and wellness, which is reflected in the emerging cannabis wellness industry in the US. Fifth the spectrum of wellness encourages individuals to take responsibility for their own health choices and devise strategies for improving life quality. Sixth the spectrum of wellness is not only useful in the analytical sense, it can also be employed in a counselling environment as a tool to assist the treatment of problematic drug use.

Conversely, the spectrum of wellness is also open to critique on many fronts. First, wellness in general is difficult to measure clinically and relies on subjective interpretation. Second, the spectrum of wellness may seem to down play harms associated with cannabis consumption. Third, beyond the identification of problematic consumption, it lacks the capacity to identify harms, for example early initiation of use careers among young people, driving under the influence, or the consumption of contaminated cannabis (Subritzky, Pettigrew, & Lenton, 2017). Fourth, marginalised and vulnerable people with problematic cannabis use may have difficulty in taking responsibility for their actions or making rational choices around consumption. Fifth, there is a possibility that a tool becomes a crutch, therefore increasing risk of dependency. Sixth, dishonest promotion of benefits is possible (if not likely) (e.g. Voelker, 2017). Seventh, considering any consumption of cannabis as potentially beneficial is likely to be viewed as controversial.

If proponents of the dominant deficit perspective that focuses on harmful drug use were concerned that the harm reduction model was sending the wrong message by pragmatically accepting that people will use cannabis, whether it is outlawed or not, they may be challenged by a theoretical model that can consider potentially beneficial consumption within the context of a wellness approach to health. However, there appears to be broad consensus among the deficit, public health, harm reduction, and wellness models around the notion that cannabis consumption is problematic and harmful for some consumers (Copeland et al., 2009; DeAngelo, 2015; Fox, Armentano, & Tvert, 2009; Hall, 2015). Furthermore, there are broad areas of overlap between the concepts of wellness and harm reduction, particularly around the notions of controlled use (Zinberg, 1986), stable life structures (Decorte, 2001; Grund, 1993), and self-responsibility for health choices (Harm Reduction Coalition, 2017). A key difference between the spectrum of wellness and the public health approach relates to surveillance. In the former, the individual is encouraged to self-monitor, check for harmful consumption patterns and seek help where required, while in the latter, public health professionals oversee survey instruments and guide the most vulnerable to treatment interventions.

At the heart of the matter, the contrasting approaches of the spectrum of wellness and public health framework are informed by the liberal and paternal philosophies respectively, whereby the former will encourage self-ownership of individual health, while the latter may argue cannabis consumers lack capacity to make informed choices. Additionally, the spectrum of wellness differentiates from harm reduction framework in that it can consider some cannabis use as potentially beneficial within broader conceptions of health as opposed to limiting harm. The spectrum of wellness has both advantages and disadvantages compared to existing models and may be useful as a complementary framework that allows for broader coverage of cannabis consumer activity.

Appendix 2: Methodology

The methodology should justify and guide the methods of the study, which in turn produce data and analysis (Carter & Little, 2007; Hesse-Biber & Leavy, 2011). Furthermore, the methodology outlines the strategy or plan of action for the study (Crotty, 1998) or underlying principles (Dew, 2007). Indeed, methodological frameworks can strengthen the rigour of the research (Carpenter & Suto, 2008; Liamputtong, 2013), while the clear classification of the research design has the potential to add value to the knowledge produced (Sandelowski, 2010). The present study aimed to provide a broad descriptive account of the implementation and evolution of the CRCM - a world-first initiative. This approach was necessary due to the gap identified previously in the book concerning the need to understand the implementation and evolution of a fully seed-to-sale, real-world, commercial market for cannabis, which had not previously existed. Accordingly, the research embraced a qualitative descriptive methodology.

As stated by Sandelowski (2000, p.1): "Qualitative descriptive [methodologies] typically are an eclectic but reasonable combination of sampling and data collection, analysis, and re-presentation techniques". Following this, multiple data sources were selected for the study to provide a range of perspectives to examine the phenomenon. A qualitative descriptive methodology seeks to search for patterns or themes across an entire data set or data corpus, rather than within a data item, such as an individual interview or interviews from one person (Braun & Clarke, 2006).

Research design

As stated, the overall objective of the study was to investigate issues both in the implementation *and* the evolution of the CRCM. This required different types of data, which for the sake of clarity were previously described as static or dynamic. The study design encompassed three phases namely document selection and analysis, interviews, and further document analysis (the specific sampling technique for each data set is provided later in the chapter). This allowed for the phenomenon under investigation to be examined from late 2012 through to early 2019.

Phase 1

This phase included an initial document analysis to identify core issues associated with both the implementation and evolution of the CRCM. As has been noted, a broad range of documents was examined including samples of relevant government documents and media articles. Generally, the documents that were examined included specific government documents related to the pre-implementation phase (Nov. 2012 – Dec. 31, 2013) and related mass and niche media articles from 2014 – 2016. As discussed in more detail below, these documents were initially coded inductively, resulting in an initial codebook of 512 codes.

Documents that were being continuously updated throughout the study period were also included in the analyses in phases 1 and 3. These included the RMC, the Colorado Official State Web Portal, and the website of the Coloradan Legislature and Secretary of State. Regular site-wide searches of these online repositories were conducted using the advanced search function for key terms such as marijuana. Major findings from phase one are presented in Chapters 5 and 6 of the book.

Phase 2

Second, a stated objective of the present study was to feedback results from the document analyses to key regulatory, public health, and industry stakeholders. As such, in phase 2, interviews in the field were undertaken in 2016 and 2017. At the heart of the interview is the assumption that participants have specific and essential knowledge about the topic (Liamputtong, 2013). Furthermore, interviews enable a degree of flexibility compared to other data collection strategies such as email surveys (Singleton Jr, 2010). The interview process allows for the extraction of rich information on the topic under investigation from particular individuals with an "insider perspective" (Byrne, 2012; Taylor, 2005, p.39). Additionally, detailed field notes were made immediately after the interviews which, in association with transcription can assist to triangulate the findings, thereby increasing the rigour of the findings (Sands & Roer-Strier, 2006).

Phase 2 also included observations from field trips to Colorado in 2015 (approximately 2 weeks), 2016 (approximately 2 weeks), and 2017 (approximately 6 weeks). Specifically, field notes from tours of cultivation facilities, recreational cannabis dispensaries (sales outlets), trade shows, policy symposiums, and informal discussions with a range of industry and regulatory participants were examined.

According to Mack, Woodsong, MacQueen, Guest, and Namey (2005, p.14), field observations can serve as a check "against participants' subjective reporting of what they believe they do". Further, they enable researchers to develop a nuanced understanding of the context of the study that is only possible through personal experience (Mack et al., 2005). Both the interview transcriptions and field notes were added to the corpus for coding and comparison with results from the first phase of the research. Major findings from phase two are presented in Chapters 7 - 9 of the book.

Phase 3

Third, further document analysis was undertaken in the final phase of the research relating to documents that evolved significantly during the study period as noted above. This allowed for the study to examine the first five years of the CRCM post-implementation. By comparing the results with phases one and two, important lessons learned from that period were synbooked. Major findings from phase three of the study are presented in Chapter 10 of the book.

Methods

Document analysis

According to Bowen (2009) document analysis is a systematic process for examining documents and has several advantages including efficiency, cost-effectiveness, unobtrusive access, and the ability to begin analysis at an early stage. Bowen (2009) further noted that, in combination with other data sources, analysis of documents is useful to achieve triangulation of the research results, which can assist with rigour. Additionally, given that I was based in Australia and the phenomenon under investigation was in the US, document analysis was the most convenient way to access data related to the study objectives, particularly in phases 1 and 3.

Data set 1: Government documents related to the pre-implementation phase Nov. 2012 – Dec. 2013

Data set 1 included important government documents that were related to the pre-implementation phase of the CRCM from Nov. 2012 - Dec. 2013. Comprehensive and targeted searches were conducted on: (i) the Official Colorado Web Portal, which included public records for the CDPHE, CDOR (who oversee the Marijuana Enforcement Division), and CDHS among others; (ii) public online records of the Colorado Secretary of State; and (iii) the Colorado State Legislature (General Assembly). This resulted in a sample of (n=13) government documents that totalled over 600 pages and included Legislative Bills (n=4), Governor Executive Orders (n=2), a Federal Memorandum (n=1), Task Force and General Assembly reports (n=2), a Constitutional Amendment (n=1), and Codes of Regulations (n=3). See Table 10 below for full details of documents by date, title, the number of pages, and document type.

Table 10: Overview of government documents examined in relation to the pre-implementation phase of the recreational cannabis market in Colorado: Nov. 2012 – Dec. 2013

Document ID	Date	Document title	Pages	Document type
A64	Nov. 6, 2012	Amendment 64: Article XVIII, Section 16: Personal Use and Regulation of Marijuana, Colorado Constitution.	12	Initiated constitutional amendment
EO B2012-004	Dec. 10, 2012	Governor's Executive Order B2012-004: Creating a Task Force on the implementation of A64.	4	Governor's Executive Order
A64 Task Force Report	*Dec. 17, 2012 - Feb. 28, 2013	Task Force Report on the Implementation of Amendment 64: Regulation of Marijuana in Colorado.	165	Task Force Report
GA Report	*Mar. 7, 2013 – Apr. 8, 2013	Joint Select Committee Report on the Implementation of the Amendment 64 Task Force Recommendations.	6	General Assembly Report
HB 13-1317	May 28, 2013	House Bill 13-1317 Implement A64	73	Legislative Bill

		Majority Recommendation.		
HB 13-1318	May 28, 2013	House Bill 13-1318 Retail Marijuana Taxes.	19	Legislative Bill
SB 13-283	May 28, 2013	Senate Bill 13-283 Implement A64 Consensus Recommendations.	16	Legislative Bill
HB 13-1325	May 28, 2013	House Bill 13-1325 Inferences For Marijuana And Driving Offences.	18	Legislative Bill
EO D2013-007	Jun. 11, 2013	Governor's Executive Order D2013-007: Directing state agencies to implement Senate Bill 13-283.	2	Governor's Executive Order
RMC 2013 (Temp)	Jun. 28, 2013	Retail Marijuana Code 1 CCR 212-2 (Emergency Rules).	70	Code of Regulations (Retail cannabis)
Cole Memo	Aug. 29, 2013	Cole Memo: Guidance Regarding Marijuana Enforcement.	4	Federal Memorandum (Department of Justice)
RMC 2013 (Perm)	Sep. 9, 2013	Retail Marijuana Code: 1 CCR 212-2 (Updated Permanent Rules).	136	Code of Regulations (Retail cannabis)

MMC 2013 (Perm)	Oct. 15, 2013	Sales, Manufacturing, and Dispensing of Medical Marijuana: 1 CCR 212-1 (Updated Permanent Rules).	88	Code of Regulations (Medical cannabis)

*Denotes period during which participant meetings took place to develop reports as opposed to publication date.

Data set 2: Media articles from Jan. 1, 2014 – Dec. 31, 2016

Data set 2 consisted of samples of mass and niche media articles from Jan. 1, 2014 to Dec. 31, 2016. The final media sample that was thematically analysed included 521 mass and 448 niche media articles. See Table 11 below for full details of publication name, date, and article quantities of final sample uploaded to Nvivo for analysis.

Table 11: Sample of mass and niche media articles by publication and year

Publication	2014	2015	2016	Total
Mass media publications				
Colorado Gazette	102	67	61	230
Denver Post	109	90	92	291
Mass Media Total	211	157	153	521
Niche media publications				
High Times	-	87	65	152
Cannabis Business Times	-	36	-	36
MMJ Business Daily	-	36	74	110
Smart Colorado	-	19	7	26
Learn About SAM	-	17	8	25
Ganjapreneur	-	15	6	21
Cannabis Investing News	-	11	-	11

NORML	-	10	15	25
Canna Law Blog	-	1	-	1
Colorado Cannabis Chamber	-	1	-	1
The Cannabis Industry (NCIA)	-	1	8	9
Marijuana Stocks	-	-	31	31
Niche Media Total		234	214	448
Grand Total	211	391	367	969

Mass media sample (2014 – 2016)

The Denver Post (The Post) and Colorado Gazette (The Gazette) were the two largest newspapers in Colorado at the time of data collection, with daily circulation at approximately 400,000 and 70,000 respectively (Cision, 2012). An online portal, The Cannabist, was established by The Post to focus on cannabis issues in Colorado. Articles were collected via an archival search from the Colorado news section of this portal and by searching for "marijuana" in titles of articles in the Gazette's digital archives over the relevant period. Important to note is that editorial positions of newspapers can influence stories. The resulting sample broadly represented a spectrum of opinion identified in editorials regarding the legalisation of the CRCM ranging from opposed (The Gazette) to advocates (The Post) (e.g. The Cannabist, 2015a; The Gazette, 2015a). Thus, the inclusion of samples from both publications had the potential to reduce reporting bias. Importantly, the two outlets are based in cities with varying laws relating to recreational cannabis. The Post is Denver-based where a fully legal recreational cannabis market is in operation while conversely the Gazette is based in the second-largest city in the state, Colorado Springs, a jurisdiction where only medical cannabis had been sanctioned at the time of sample collection.

There was considerable disparity in the number of articles for each publication. For example, 102 articles were collected from the Gazette in 2014 based on the criterion of searching for "marijuana" in headlines and all were included in the analysis. The Post returned a much larger total over the same period (n=545). To address this disparity, following Altheide (1996), a randomised stratified sampling approach was employed to ensure an equal number of articles was selected from each outlet for analysis. The sample was randomised using Random.org (2016) following these steps: (i) the smallest and largest values of article numbers (e.g. 1 and 545 in 2014) were added at Random.org; (ii) the site then generated a sequence of random numbers; (iii) every 5th article number was selected from the list; and (iv) the final sample of the Post articles (n=109) was reordered chronologically by date of publication. A similar process was undertaken in 2015 and 2016.

Niche media sample (2015 – 2016)
As the CRCM evolved, numerous cannabis industry-specific media outlets were spawned. A news aggregator plugin was set up at marijuanasurveys.org to automatically collate newsfeeds from a wide range of publications. The following niche media were identified as having content potentially representative of a broad range of perspectives: High Times, NORML, Gangapreneur, MJ Business Daily, Cannabis Business Times, Canna Law Blog, Marijuana Investor News, Cannabis Financial Network, Marijuana Stocks, Cannabis Investing News, and National Cannabis Industry Association (NCIA). These media were selected for inclusion in this study to examine perspectives of commercial, advocate, activist, and lobbying groups that were not adequately represented in pilot data collection involving the other data sets. Further, to ensure public health issues and representation of opposition groups, stratified samples of publications from Smart Colorado and Smart Approaches to Marijuana (SAM) were included for coding, which while limited in number provided more balance to the sample.

Over 8000 niche media articles were initially aggregated from 2015 to 2016. To ensure a more manageable sample size, a Prisma style filtering process was employed to ensure only relevant articles were included in the sample frame (Moher, Liberati, Tetzlaff, & Altman, 2009). All article titles were reviewed to judge the suitability for inclusion in the study. It was a requirement that at least one of the following criteria were met:

- Mentioned Colorado specifically
- Related to or could potentially impact the Colorado regulatory model (federal, state, local, international)
- Related to public health issues concerning cannabis generally

- Related to any stage of the cannabis production process (cultivation, manufacturing, extracting, testing, wholesaling, tracking retailing, marketing, or consumption methods)
- Related to any issues regarding commercialism of cannabis markets (e.g. business and stock news)
- Relating to any other issues identified in coding mass media samples (e.g. black market, banking, cannabis migration, environment, medical, and recreational cannabis)
- Where article title was not clear then the actual article was checked to see if it complied with any of the above criteria to be included.

Following this process, the initial sample was reduced from approximately 4000 articles per year to approximately 1000 per year. A similar randomised stratified process to the mass media articles was then undertaken, which further reduced the sample to a more manageable 234 and 214 articles for analysis in 2015 and 2016 respectively.

In total, the final media sample for analysis included 969 mass and niche articles from 2014 – 2016. The sample was sufficient to provide data saturation on a range of issues and perspectives that were examined in phases 1 and 3. Full details of the final media sample are presented in Table 11 above. In addition to the findings presented in the results chapters of the book as published papers, two issues (political uncertainty and public consumption) emerged from the analysis of the media sample. These issues were related to the core objectives of the book, but the analyses were not submitted for publication and therefore excluded from the book body. The results of the analysis of the media samples in relation to these issues are presented in Chapter 9 of the book.

Across both the mass and niche media samples, the articles varied in length from single paragraph notifications to in-depth exposés of several thousand words on specific issues. Most articles were 5 to 15 paragraphs in length and written as informative and descriptive news reports. Around 5% of the sample was coded as editorials. Most articles contained links to other relevant stories within the same publication or other online media. Almost a fifth of the articles quoted or linked to independent cannabis studies, scholars, other experts, or commissioned government reports. These external resources were included in the analysis only to the extent they were described in the coded media stories to confine the scope of the investigation. Many articles contained reader comment sections, which were excluded from the analysis.

Semi-structured face-to-face Interviews 2016 - 2017

Face-to-face interviews can be categorised as in-depth, long, unstructured, and semi-structured (Bryman, 2012; Esterberg, 2002; Liamputtong, 2013). To ensure flexibility in the interview process, while also taking care not to stray too far from the topic under investigation, semi-structured interviews were undertaken (Tong, 2007). The interview procedure undertaken in this study followed Tong (2007) criteria to consider the preparation of interview guides that included open-ended questions to allow participants to expand on their experience, participant selection, and data saturation. In line with Janghorban, Roudsari, and Taghipour (2014), a distinction was not made whether the face-to-face interviews were conducted in the same physical space or by Skype. The interviews were digitally recorded and transcribed for analysis to create written text from verbal dialogue (Liamputtong, 2013), and finally added to NVivo for further analysis.

Participant selection (sampling)

From the document analysis undertaken in phase 1 of the research, the details of several potential interviewees were known to me. This allowed for direct recruitment via. email Selection criteria included having direct experience with the CRCM and availability for interview. Potential interviewees were also identified and recruited at related trade shows and policy symposiums in Colorado. Additionally, a senior cannabis policy scholar based in the US, Professor Beau Kilmer, provided an introduction letter to multiple senior regulators in Colorado. As a result, the initial interview participants were selected by convenience sample (Liamputtong, 2013). Furthermore, these informants had access to networks of interviewees with different expertise, and as such, a snowball technique was also employed to expand the list of potential research participants (Bryman, 2012; Carpenter & Suto, 2008; Hesse-Biber & Leavy, 2011; Liamputtong, 2013). According to Weiss (1995), accessing a network in this manner can add vouching legitimacy to improve success rates of the recruitment process, and this appeared to be the case in the present study where an initial target of 15 key stakeholders was more than doubled. This allowed for data saturation to be achieved on multiple issues examined in the context of interviews.

Data set 3: Description of interview sample

Semi-structured face-to-face interviews were conducted with key stakeholders (n=32) in 2016 and 2017 primarily in Colorado. The interviewees predominantly consisted of senior management level administrators and executive directors from State and local government departments, the cannabis industry, and public health representatives closely involved in developing the world's first Retail Marijuana Code (RMC) in Colorado. 27 face-to-face interviews were conducted including: Individual (n=19); Group (n=3); and Skype (n=5) totalling approximately 16 hours of recorded material. Most interviewees (n=24) participated in the collaborative governance process of implementing cannabis policy in the State – defined in this book as having official involvement in specialist working groups, the Governor's A64 Task Force, or scientific advisory boards (defined as regulatory participant in Table 12). Additional regulatory participation through open public hearings or informal workgroup meetings by interviewees was not stipulated. The majority of interviews took place in Denver, with exceptions being Pueblo, Boulder, Aspen, Colorado Springs, San Francisco, and Skype. Full details of interviewee name role, and interview date, length, and type are available in Table 12 below.

Table 12: Overview of interviews and interviewees

Date	Interviewee	Role	Interview length (mins)	Regulatory participant	Interview Type	Comment
Nov. 2016	Jorge Cervantes	Cannabis Cultivation Author	12	N	I	Cannabis cultivation author. California based.
Nov. 2016	Barbara Brohl*	Executive Director: CDOR	52	Y	G	Participant: A64 Task Force and multiple workgroups.
Nov. 2016	Jim Burrack	Director: MED	52	Y	G	Participant: A64 Task Force and multiple workgroups.
Nov. 2016	Ean Seeb	Industry Pioneer and Lobbyist	27	Y	I	Sold original dispensary to Willie Nelson. Former Chairman of NCIA (largest cannabis industry lobby in the US). Participant: multiple workgroups.
Nov. 2016	Seth Wong	President: TEQ	32	Y	G	First ISO certified cannabis testing lab in Colorado. Member:

Date	Interviewee	Role	Interview length (mins)	Regulatory participant	Interview Type	Comment
		Analytical Labs				Colorado Lab Council and Colorado Leads (a coalition of cannabis business leaders). Participant: multiple workgroups.
Nov. 2016	Eric Ritvo	Business Expansion Manager: TEQ Analytical Labs	32	N	G	
Nov. 2016	Andrew Freedman	Director: OMC (Governor's Office)	27	Y	I	Participant: A64 Task Force and multiple workgroups.
May 2017	Commercial Grow Manager	Cannabis Cultivation Facility Manager	27	N	I	Medium-sized facility (Tier 2). Did not give consent to be named in the interview.
May 2017	Dr. Patricia Winters MD	Medical Marijuana Doctor	10	N	I	California. Mentored by well-known Harvard Professor and cannabis scholar Lester Grinspoon.
May 2017	Dr. Larry Wolk, MD	Executive Director: CDPHE	27	Y	I	Participant: A64 Task Force and multiple workgroups.

Date	Interviewee	Role	Interview length (mins)	Regulatory participant	Interview Type	Comment
May 2017	Hillary Keisar	Analytical Chemist Pharm Labs	19	N	I	California firm.
May 2017	Yogi D	Author and Founder of 420 Yoga Retreats. Cannabis Yogi	35	N	I	Named America's relaxation expert on CNN. Bestselling author.
May 2017	Lexie Potamkin	Philanthropist and Cannabis Youth Education Provider	32	N	I	
May 2017	Maureen McNamara	Founder & Chief Facilitator: Cannabis Trainers	29	Y	S	Participant: responsible vendor workgroup.
May 2017	Mitch Yergert	Director: CDA	30	Y	I	Participant: multiple workgroups.
May 2017	Ryan Medina	Cultivation Manager	27	N	I	Medium-sized facility (Tier 2).
May 2017	Dan Banks	Founder: Next Generation IPM	40	Y	I	Participant: pesticide workgroup.

Date	Interviewee	Role	Interview length (mins)	Regulatory participant	Interview Type	Comment
May 2017	Stephen Goldman, PhD	Lab Director: Phytatech Labs	36	Y	I	Member: Colorado Lab Council. Participant: multiple workgroups.
May 2017	Lee Maloy	Co-Founder: International Church of Cannabis	8	N	I	An 'elevationist'.
May 2017	Industry Executive	CEO: large, vertically integrated, end to end cannabis firm	20	Y	I	Did not give consent to be named in the interview. Participant: multiple workgroups.
May 2017	Shawn Kasseur	Senior Scientist: Neptune & Company	45	Y	I	Participant: multiple workgroups.
May 2017	Jack Reed	Statistical Analyst: CDPS	80	Y	I	Participant: multiple workgroups.
May 2017	Sam Kamin, PhD	Vicente Sederberg Professor: Marijuana Law and Policy,	20	Y	I	Participant: A64 Task Force and multiple workgroups.

Date	Interviewee	Role	Interview length (mins)	Regulatory participant	Interview Type	Comment
		University of Denver				
May 2017	Barbara Brohl*	Executive Director: CDOR	50	Y	G	Participant: A64 Task Force and multiple workgroups.
May 2017	Ron Kammerzell	Senior Director: MED	50	Y	G	Participant: A64 Task Force and multiple workgroups.
May 2017	Mathew Scott	Senior Director: CDT	50	Y	G	Participant: multiple workgroups.
May 2017	Heidi Humphreys	Deputy Director: CDOR	50	Y	G	Participant: multiple workgroups.
May 2017	Ashley Brookes-Russell, PhD	Professor: UC Denver. Project Director: Healthy Kids Colorado Survey	24	Y	I	Member: Colorado Retail Marijuana Public Health Advisory Committee. Participant: A64 Task Force and multiple workgroups.
May 2017	Heath Harmon	Director: Health Programs at Boulder County	54	Y	S	Member: City of Boulder Marijuana Advisory Panel and the Colorado Retail Marijuana Public Health Advisory

Date	Interviewee	Role	Interview length (mins)	Regulatory participant	Interview Type	Comment
						Committee. Participant: A64 Task Force and multiple workgroups.
May 2017	Steve Baugh	Cannabis Chemist and Educator	60	Y	S	Participant: testing licensee workgroup.
May 2017	Colin Bell, PhD	Co-founder and Chief Growth Officer: Growcentia	48	Y	S	Participant: multiple workgroups.
May 2017	Dr. Ken Finn, MD	Pain Medicine Physician	75	Y	S	Member: Colorado Medical Marijuana Scientific Advisory Council. Participant: A64 Task Force and multiple workgroups.

*Key: * Interviewed twice; I = Individual; G = Group; S = Skype*

Abbreviations: CDOR = Colorado Department of Revenue; MED = Marijuana Enforcement Division; CDPHE = Colorado Department of Public Health and Environment; CDA = Colorado Department of Agriculture; CDT = Colorado Department of Taxation; CDPS = Colorado Department of Public Safety; OMC = Office of Marijuana Coordination (Governor's Office); MPG = Marijuana Policy Group; IPM = Independent Pest Management

Qualitative thematic analysis

Given the diversity of material across the data sets under investigation in the book, a thematic analysis (TA) was undertaken to ensure flexibility in the analytic process. TA is a method for identifying, analyzing and describing themes or patterns within data. At the minimum, TA "organizes and describes your data set in (rich) detail ... and frequently [as was the case in this study] ... interprets various aspects of the research topic" (Braun & Clarke, 2006, p.79). TA has several advantages including the flexibility to be applied across different data sets, allowing for interpretations of social data, and the ability to generate insights suitable for informing policy development (Braun & Clarke, 2006). As such TA was considered a natural fit for the present study.

The analytic steps taken were consistent with the six phases of TA stipulated by Braun and Clarke (2006): (i) becoming familiar with the data by reading and re-reading; (ii) generating initial codes and coding consistently across the entire corpus; (iii) collating codes into potential themes; (iv) reviewing the themes; (v) naming and defining themes; and (vi) writing the report. In regards to writing the book, three further steps were taken as outlined by Bazeley (2009) whereby themes were described, compared (both between data sets and at sub-thematic levels within data sets), and finally related back to the literature, with implications drawn for other jurisdictions.

Coding techniques: inductive, deductive, and NVivo

As noted by Miles and Huberman (1994) the coding process is part of the analysis. As noted, TA identifies patterns or themes within data primarily: 'bottom-up' or inductively (e.g. Frith & Gleeson, 2004) or 'top-down' or deductively. Inductive coding generates themes with strong links to the data, while deductive coding tends to be analyst driven with a focus on a detailed analysis of some aspect of the data (Braun & Clarke, 2006). Both techniques were used in the analysis of the three static data sets. First, the data sets were coded inductively to allow for the widest possible range of issues to emerge from the data. As noted above this resulted in an initial codebook in phase 1 of 512 codes. Second, the data sets were coded deductively to facilitate detailed analysis of specific issues of interest (in the case of this study these issues included the regulation of pesticides, youth protection, and collaborative governance, the results of which are presented in chapters 7 – 9 of the book respectively). While colleagues (book supervisors) reviewed the codebook, all texts were coded by myself as a single coder. To verify intracoder reliability, Kondracki, Wellman, and Amundson (2002) were followed in that the same coder recoded a subset of data after the analysis was completed to ensure coding decisions had not altered over time.

The procedure of coding, in essence, reduces large amounts of text to smaller, more manageable representations with the ability to describe the observed phenomenon (Saldana, 2013). By constantly comparing data, the intention is to identify data capable of explicating behaviours of interest. In practical terms, the coding was undertaken with NVivo 11, a data management software application (QSR International Pty Ltd., 2017). According to Bazeley and Jackson (2013), coding qualitative data with Nvivo has several advantages. Nvivo allows great flexibility to merge, rename or move established codes and can, furthermore, improve the validity of a study (Siccama & Penna, 2008). NVivo also allows the flexibility of text searches and matrix analyses to identify relationships between themes and these techniques were also employed in the current study. It is important to note that while Nvivo is useful for organising and comparing text(s), it does not analyse the data for the analyst (Bryman, 2012; Flick & Gibbs, 2007; Liamputtong, 2013). In the present study NVivo was invaluable for data organisation and interrogating the data. Text searches and matrix analyses were employed to both add context and compare findings across the data corpus for a fuller description of the focus of the study.

Thick description

An objective of the book is to provide a thick, multi-dimensional descriptive account of issues that emerged from the implementation and evolution of the CRCM. According to Creswell and Miller (2000), thick description can establish credibility for a study by describing the setting, participants, and themes of a study in rich detail. It aims to provide as much detail as possible around the phenomenon under investigation and allows for the reader to be transported into a setting and feel they have experienced the described events (Creswell & Miller, 2000). Denzin (1989, p.83) distinguished between thick and thin description thus: "thick descriptions are deep, dense, detailed accounts.... Thin descriptions, by contrast, lack detail and simply report fact". Thick description can assist to differentiate between relative and apparent truth, identify the falseness of assertions, and enable readers to make judgements on the suitability to other settings and contexts (Creswell & Miller, 2000). In the present study, thick description was employed in all of the results chapters of the book.

Rigour

Ensuring that research findings are valid and trustworthy is both critical (e.g. Bryman, 2012; Creswell, 2012; Liamputtong, 2013; Rolfe, 2006) and challenging (Whittemore, Chase, & Mandle, 2001). Rigorous studies are credible, dependable, transferable and confirmable, and as such, results can be disseminated with confidence (Liamputtong, 2013; Morse, 2015). Indeed, Tobin and Begley (2004, p. 390) contended that: "Rigour is the means by which we demonstrate integrity and competence ... [and] the legitimacy of the research process". Several scholars have offered criteria for ensuring the quality of qualitative studies (e.g. Green et al., 2007; Liamputtong, 2013; Tracy, 2010). The proposed study embraced four strategies to demonstrate the worth of the findings. First, methodological choices with clear links between the aims of the research and methods of data collection and analysis were made (Carpenter & Suto, 2008). Second, rich description allowed readers to assess the generalisability of the data (Johnson & Waterfield, 2004). Third, the triangulation of various data sets added credibility to the findings (Bowen, 2009; Liamputtong, 2013; Sands & Roer-Strier, 2006). Finally, the potential for bias was minimised by peer review (Creswell, 2012). For this project, colleagues inspected the NVivo files and provided feedback on the coding process. The results of the project have been disseminated in multiple peer-reviewed journal articles and international conferences.

Ethics

Ethics approval was required for the interview phase of the research but was not needed for the document analysis phases of the project. It was granted by Curtin University Human Research Ethics Committee (approval HRE2016-0230) and was implemented in line with the National Health and Medical Research Council (2007) guidelines to ensure participants were asked for informed consent and any potential risk of harm was minimised.

A challenge that became immediately apparent during the interview process of the research was that many of the interviewees did not feel comfortable being interviewed anonymously. As public figures, several interviewees felt that anonymity was akin to speaking off record or whistleblowing. For example, in the very first interview with a senior public official it was made clear that the interview would not proceed unless their full name and title was associated with the text. To address this, an amendment to ethics approval was requested and approved on November 21, 2016 (see amendment request approval number: HRE2016-0230). Thus, for the majority of extracts used in the book, permission to name interviewees was obtained and this is reflected in Table 12 above.

Furthermore, to reduce any risk of professional harm to the interviewees, participants were contacted to review extracts attached to their names with secondary approval granted. A statement reflecting this and noting the interviewee agreed to be named in the study was manually written on hard copies of all participant information statements at the time of interview where the participant has been named. This is in line with the requested amendment to ethics approval for the study. This statement was agreed and signed by both interviewer and interviewee and hard copies of these documents have been retained.

Where permission to name interview participants was not approved, generic labels were attached to the extracts, for example 'industry executive'.

References

Abel, E. (1943/1980). *Marihuana: The first twelve thousand years*. New York, NY: Plenum Press.

Adams, R., Hunt, M., & Clark, J. (1940). Structure of cannabidiol, a product isolated from the marihuana extract of Minnesota wild hemp. *Journal of the American chemical society*,(62), 196 - 200.

Adams, T., Bezner, J., & Steinhardt, M. (1997). The Conceptualization and Measurement of Perceived Wellness: Integrating Balance across and within Dimensions. American Journal of Health Promotion, 11(3), 208-218. http://dx.doi.org/10.4278/0890-1171-11.3.208

Adler, A. (1927/2010). *Understanding human nature*. New York: Blue Ribbon Books.

Alcohol and Tobacco Tax and Trade Bureau. (2006). Federal Alcohol Administration Act. Retrieved 8/11/2017 from Alcohol and Tobacco Tax and Trade Bureau https://www.ttb.gov/pdf/ttbp51008_laws_regs_act052007.pdf.

Alexander, M. (2012). *The New Jim Crow: Mass incarceration in the age of colorblindness*. New York, NY: The New Press.

Algarve Daily News. (2018, Mar.6). Portugal's Social Democratic Party members vote for legalisation of 'personal use' cannabis. Retrieved 9/3/2018 from https://algarvedailynews.com/news/13775-portugal-s-social-democratic-party-members-vote-for-legalisation-of-personal-use-cannabis.

Allen, D. (2016). Survey Shows Low Acceptance of the Science of the ECS (Endocannabinoid System) at American Medical Schools. Retrieved 26/04/2019 from http://www.outwordmagazine.com/inside-outword/glbt-news/1266-survey-shows-low-acceptance-of-the-science-of-the-ecs-endocannabinoid-system.

Allen, E. (2015). *Cannabis in Colorado: Concerns over marijuana edible testing*. Retrieved 30/04/2015 from KRDO.com http://www.krdo.com/news/cannabis-in-colorado-concerns-over-marijuana-edible-testing/32609348. (Archived by WebCite® at http://www.webcitation.org/6YXRdOjz1).

Altheide, D. (1996). *Qualitative Media Analysis. Thousand Oaks, CA: SAGE Publications, Inc.*

Amendment 64 Final Draft. (2012). Amendment 64 Use and regulation of marijuana - revised final draft. Retrieved 12/11/2017 from Colorado General Assembly http://www.leg.state.co.us/LCS/Initiative%20Referendum/1112InitRefr.nsf/d ac421ef79ad243487256def0067c1de/cfa3bae60c8b4949872579c7006fa7ee /$FILE/Amendment%2064%20merged.pdf.

Amendment 64 Task Force. (2013). *Task Force Report on the Implementation of Amendment 64*. Retrieved 24/04/2014 from http://www.colorado.gov/cms/forms/dor-tax/A64TaskForceFinalReport.pdf.

American Herbal Pharmacopeia. (2013). American Herbal Pharmacopeia, 2013. Cannabis inflorescence. In: Upton, R., Dayu, R., Craker, L., ElSohly, M., Romm, A., Russo, E., Sexton, M., (Eds.), Standards of Identity, Analysis, and Quality Control. Scott's Valley, CA.

American Psychiatric Association. (2013). *Diagnostic and statistical manual of mental Disorders, fifth edition*. Arlington (VA)

American Society of Addiction Medicine. (2018). Patients with Addiction Need Treatment - Not Stigma. Retrieved 21/01/2018 from https://www.asam.org/resources/publications/magazine/read/article/2015/

12/15/patients-with-a-substance-use-disorder-need-treatment---not-stigma.

Amirav, I., Luder, A., Viner, Y., & Finkel, M. (2011). Decriminalization of Cannabis–potential risks for children? *Acta Paediatrica, 100*(4), 618-619.

Anastassiades, M., Lehotay, S., Štajnbaher, D., & Schenck, F. (2003). Fast and easy multiresidue method employing acetonitrile extraction/partitioning and "dispersive solid-phase extraction" for the determination of pesticide residues in produce. *Journal of AOAC international, 86*(2), 412-431.

Anderson, D., Hansen, B., & Rees, D. (2013). Medical Marijuana Laws, Traffic Fatalities, and Alcohol Consumption. *Journal of Law and Economics. 56*(2), 333-369.

Ansell, C., & Gash, A. (2008). Collaborative Governance in Theory and Practice. *Journal of Public Administration Research and Theory, 18*(4), 543-571. http://dx.doi.org/10.1093/jopart/mum032

Anthony, J. (2006). The epidemiology of cannabis dependence. *Cannabis dependence: Its nature, consequences and treatment,* 58-105.

Appelboam, A., & Oades, P. (2006). Coma due to cannabis toxicity in an infant. *European Journal of Emergency Medicine, 13*(3), 177-179.

Ardell, D. (1979). High level wellness, an alternative to doctors, drugs, and disease. Cincinnati, Ohio: Bantam Books.

Armentano, P. (2010). Driving under the influence. In Holland, J. (Ed.). *The pot book: A complete guide to cannabis* (pp. 196-201). Rochester, VT: Park Street Press.

Armentano, P. (2017). The Evidence Is Overwhelming: Cannabis Is an Exit Drug for Major Addictions, Not a Gateway to New Ones. Retrieved 13/01/2018 from https://www.alternet.org/drugs/evidence-overwhelming-cannabis-exit-drug-major-addictions-not-gateway-new-ones.

Asbridge, M., Hayden, J., & Cartwright, J. (2012). Acute cannabis consumption and motor vehicle collision risk: systematic review of observational studies and meta-analysis. *The BMJ, 344*, e536. http://dx.doi.org/10.1136/bmj.e536

Ashton, H. (2001). Pharmacology and effects of cannabis: a brief review. *The British Journal of Psychiatry, 178*(2), 101-106.

Aspen Journalism. (2017). The Aspen 50 – Forbes billionaires in Pitkin County. Retrieved 15/11/2017 from Aspen Journalism http://aspenjournalism.org/2012/04/02/the-aspen-50-forbes-billionaires-in-pitkin-county/.

Associated Press. (2014). *Rand Paul on smoking marijuana: 'I made mistakes'.* Retrieved 05/05/2015 from The Washington Post http://www.washingtontimes.com/news/2014/dec/6/rand-paul-says-he-smoked-marijuana-i-made-mistakes/. (Archived by WebCite® at http://www.webcitation.org/6YXXvVVuf). December 6

Associated Press. (2018, Feb.1). Massachusetts cannabis capitalists exploit loopholes by "gifting" before sales start. Retrieved 9/02/2018 from https://www.thecannabist.co/2018/02/01/massachusetts-marijuana-gifts-sales/98014/.

Associated Press. (2018, Jan.22). Kentucky assistant police chief fired for racist messages. Retrieved 23/01/2018 from https://apnews.com/03a85945d1b442acad43e9a470367ce2/Kentucky-assistant-police-chief-fired-for-racist-messages.

Attorney General Order No. 3946-2017. (2017). *Federal Forfeiture of Property Seized by State and Local Law Enforcement Agencies.* Washington, D.C.: Retrieved from http://cannabusinesslaw.com/wp-content/uploads/2017/08/ag_order_3946-2017.pdf

Babor, T. (2010). *Alcohol: No Ordinary Commodity: Research and Public Policy* (2nd ed.). Oxford: Oxford University Press.

Baca, R. (2014a). *Edibles' THC claims versus lab tests reveal big discrepancies.* Retrieved 06/08/2015 from The Cannabist http://www.thecannabist.co/2014/03/09/tests-show-thc-content-marijuana-edibles-inconsistent/6421/ (Archived by WebCite® at http://www.webcitation.org/6bBitpNMW). March 9

Baca, R. (2014b). *Report: More than 15 months in, pot-infused edibles still confound.* Retrieved 08/09/2015 from http://www.denverpost.com/news/ci_27896734/report-more-than-15-months-pot-infused-edibles (Archived by WebCite® at http://www.webcitation.org/6bUSsNPLY). December 4

Baca, R. (2015a). *Colorado pot sales spike in June, top $50 million for first time.* Retrieved 24/08/2015 from The Cannabist http://www.thecannabist.co/2015/08/13/colorado-marijuana-taxes-recreational-sales-june-2015-50-million/39384/ (Archived by WebCite® at http://www.webcitation.org/6bBjuUmDl). August 13

Baca, R. (2015b). *Colorado's pot tax for schools sets record in May, crushes 2014 totals.* Retrieved 24/08/2015 from The Cannabist http://www.thecannabist.co/2015/07/13/may-colorado-pot-school-tax-marijuana/37839/ (Archived by WebCite® at http://www.webcitation.org/6bBk0clBu). August 13

Baca, R. (2015c). *Lab: Edibles' potency more accurate than a year ago, but buyer beware.* Retrieved 06/08/2015 from The Cannabist http://www.thecannabist.co/2015/04/12/colorado-marijuana-edibles-lab-testing/33061/ (Archived by WebCite® at http://www.webcitation.org/6bBkG2r06). April 12

Baca, R. (2015d). *New proposal: Allow more places for pot use in Denver.* Retrieved 08/08/2015 from The Cannabist http://www.thecannabist.co/2015/06/17/denver-marijuana-public-consumption/36261/ (Archived by WebCite® at http://www.webcitation.org/6bBkLgFVa). June 17

Baca, R. (2015e). *New rules in effect for Colorado marijuana edibles Feb. 1.* Retrieved 06/08/2015 from The Cannabist http://www.thecannabist.co/2015/01/29/colorado-marijuana-edibles-fire-sale-regulations-feb-1/28775/ (Archived by WebCite® at http://www.webcitation.org/6bBkpKQ7y). January 29

Baca, R. (2015f). *Pot industry reacts to new Denver scope on pesticide checks.* Retrieved 08/09/2015 from The Cannabist http://www.thecannabist.co/2015/09/07/colorado-pot-industry-denver-pesticide-inspections/40473/ (Archived by WebCite® at http://www.webcitation.org/6bUSxpEcW). September 7

Bachhuber, M., Saloner, B., Cunningham, C., & Barry, C. (2014). Medical cannabis laws and opioid analgesic overdose mortality in the United States, 1999-2010. *JAMA internal medicine, 174*(10), 1668-1673.

Backes, M. (2014). Cannabis Pharmacy: The practical guide to medical marijuana. New York, NY: Black Dog & Leventhal.

Baggio, M., Chong, A., & Kwon, S. (2017). Helping Settle the Marijuana and Alcohol Debate: Evidence from Scanner Data. Available at SSRN: https://ssrn.com/abstract=3063288 or http://dx.doi.org/10.2139/ssrn.3063288.

Baldwin, R., Cave, M., & Lodge, M. (2012). *Understanding regulation: Theory, strategy, and practice. New York, NY: Oxford University Press.*

Ballotpedia. (2017a). Article V, Colorado Constitution. Retrieved 16/11/2017 from Ballotpedia https://ballotpedia.org/Article_V,_Colorado_Constitution#Section_1.

Ballotpedia. (2017b). Ballotpedia: Search the encyclopedia of American politics. Retrieved 15/11/2017 from https://www.ballotpedia.org.

Ballotpedia. (2017c). Colorado Marijuana Legalization Initiative, Amendment 64 (2012). Retrieved 15/11/2017 from Ballotpedia https://ballotpedia.org/Colorado_Marijuana_Legalization_Initiative,_Amendment_64_(2012)#Text_of_the_measure.

Ballotpedia. (2017d). Colorado Medical Use of Marijuana, Initiative 20 (2000). Retrieved 15/11/2017 from Ballotpedia https://ballotpedia.org/Colorado_Medical_Use_of_Marijuana,_Initiative_20_(2000).

Ballotpedia. (2017e). Initiated Constitutional Amendment. Retrieved 16/11/2017 from Ballotpedia https://ballotpedia.org/Initiated_constitutional_amendment.

Ballotpedia. (2017f). Laws governing the initiative process in Colorado. Retrieved 30/10/2017 from Ballotpedia https://ballotpedia.org/Laws_governing_the_initiative_process_in_Colorado

Bard, B. (2014). *40% of Colorado's weed is sold on the black market*. Retrieved 02/05/2015 from Marijuana.com http://www.marijuana.com/news/2014/09/40-of-colorados-weed-is-sold-on-the-black-market/. (Archived by WebCite® at http://www.webcitation.org/6YXRrIsLq). September 3

Barratt, M. (2011). *Beyond internet as tool: A mixed-methods study of online drug discussion* Doctural book Curtin University, Melbourne, Australia.

Barratt, M., Allen, M., & Lenton, S. (2014). "PMA Sounds Fun": Negotiating drug discourses online. *Substance use & misuse, 49*(8), 987-998.

Barry, R., & Glantz, S. (2016a). A Public Health Analysis of Two Proposed Marijuana Legalization Initiatives for the 2016 California Ballot: Creating the new tobacco industry.

Barry, R., & Glantz, S. (2016b). A Public Health Framework for Legalized Retail Marijuana Based on the US Experience: Avoiding a New Tobacco Industry. *PLOS Medicine, 13*(9), e1002131. http://dx.doi.org/10.1371/journal.pmed.1002131

Batalla, A., Bhattacharyya, S., Yücel, M., Fusar-Poli, P., Crippa, J., Nogué, S., . . . Martin-Santos, R. (2013). Structural and functional imaging studies in chronic cannabis users: a systematic review of adolescent and adult findings. *PloS one, 8*(2), e55821.

Baudelaire, C. (1860/1998). *Artificial Paradises: Baudelaire's masterpiece on hashish*. New York, NY: Citadel.

Bazeley, P. (2009). Analysing qualitative data: More than 'identifying themes'. *Malaysian Journal of Qualitative Research, 2*(2), 6-22.

Bazeley, P., & Jackson, K. (2013). *Qualitative data analysis with NVivo*. London: Sage Publications Limited.

BBC. (2014, Jan. 1). Cannabis goes on legal sale in US state of Colorado. Retrieved 13/11/2017 from http://www.bbc.com/news/world-us-canada-25566863.

BBC. (2018, May 31). Cannabis and sport: NBA winner Matt Barnes 'smoked before games'. Retrieved 27/06/2018 from https://www.bbc.com/sport/basketball/43836214.

BDS Analytics. (2017). Marijuana Prices in Denver and Colorado: Spring 2017 Update. Retrieved 15/11/2017 from Colorado Pot Guide https://www.coloradopotguide.com/colorado-marijuana-blog/article/marijuana-prices-in-denver-and-colorado-spring-2017-update/.

Becker, H. (1963/2008). *Outsiders: Studies in the sociology of deviance*. New York, NY: Free Press.

Belackova, V., Brandnerova, M., & Vechet, D. (2018). How Close to the "Honeypot?" A Comparative Analysis of Cannabis Markets Under Two Different Policies Toward Personal Cultivation. *International Criminal Justice Review*, 1057567717744857.

Belackova, V., Maalsté, N., Zabransky, T., & Grund, J. (2015). "Should I Buy or Should I Grow?" How drug policy institutions and drug market transaction costs shape the decision to self-supply with cannabis in the Netherlands and the Czech Republic. *International Journal of Drug Policy, 26*(3), 296-310. http://dx.doi.org/https://doi.org/10.1016/j.drugpo.2014.12.002

Belackova, V., Tomkova, A., & Zabransky, T. (2016). Qualitative research in Spanish cannabis social clubs: "The moment you enter the door, you are minimising the risks". *International Journal of Drug Policy, 34*, 49-57. http://dx.doi.org/https://doi.org/10.1016/j.drugpo.2016.04.009

Belackova, V., & Vaccaro, C. (2013). "A Friend With Weed Is a Friend Indeed" Understanding the Relationship Between Friendship Identity and Market Relations Among Marijuana Users. *Journal of drug issues, 43*(3), 289-313.

Belackova, V., & Wilkins, C. (2018). Consumer agency in cannabis supply–Exploring auto-regulatory documents of the cannabis social clubs in Spain. *International Journal of Drug Policy, 54*, 26-34.

Bell, C., Slim, J., Flaten, H., Lindberg, G., Arek, W., & Monte, A. (2015). Butane hash oil burns associated with marijuana liberalization in Colorado. *Journal of Medical Toxicology*, 1-4. http://dx.doi.org/10.1007/s13181-015-0501-0

Bello, J. (2010). *The Benefits of Marijuana: Physical, psychological and spiritual.* Susquehanna, PA: Lifeservices Press.

Bentsen, K., & Gunton, C. (2014). *There's Money in Marijuana.* Retrieved 17/03/2015 from Opensecrets.org http://www.opensecrets.org/news/issues/marijuana/. (Archived by WebCite® at http://www.webcitation.org/6YXS0ArM6).

Berg, C., Daniel, C., Vu, M., Li, J., Martin, K., & Le, L. (2017). Marijuana use and driving under the influence among young adults: a socioecological perspective on risk factors. *Substance use & misuse*, 1-11.

Best Places. (2017). Best places to live: compare cost of living, crime, cities, schools and more. Retrieved 15/11/2017 from Sperlings Best Places http://www.bestplaces.net.

Bey, H., & Zug, A. (2004). Orgies of the Hemp Eaters: Cuisine, Slang, Literature & Ritual of Cannabis Culture: Autonomedia.

Beyond Pesticides. (2015). *Pesticide Use in Marijuana Production: Safety issues and sustainable options.* Retrieved 17/11/2016 from http://www.beyondpesticides.org/programs/national-watchdog/overview/pesticides-and-cannabis (Archived by WebCite® at http://www.webcitation.org/6m54jZi57). March 11

Bienenstock, D. (2016). How to Smoke Pot (Properly): A highbrow guide to getting high. New York, NY: Penguin Publishing Group.

Blake, D., & Finlaw, J. (2014). Marijuana legalization in Colorado: Learned lessons. *Harvard Law & Policy Review, 8*, 359-380.

Blesching, U. (2015). *The Cannabis Health Index: Combining the science of medical marijuana with mindfulness techniques to heal 100 chronic symptoms and diseases.* Berkley, CA: North Atlantic Books.

Bloomberg. (2015). *For These 55 Marijuana Companies, Every Day is 4/20.* Retrieved 30/04/2015 from http://www.bloomberg.com/graphics/2015-weed-index/ (Archived by WebCite® at http://www.webcitation.org/6YXS6wMUp). April 15

Bloomberg. (2017, Oct. 27). A Former Blackrock Executive Is Raising One Of The Biggest Marijuana Funds Yet. Retrieved 30/10/2017 from Bloomberg https://www.bloomberg.com/news/articles/2017-10-27/pot-fund-s-250-million-target-marks-cannabis-industry-milestone

Blows, S., Ivers, R., Connor, J., Ameratunga, S., Woodward, M., & Norton, R. (2005). Marijuana use and car crash injury. *Addiction, 100*(5), 605-611.

Blue Ribbon Commission on Marijuana Policy. (2015). Pathways Report: Policy Options for Regulating Marijuana in California. Retrieved 31/10/2017 from Blue Ribbon Commission https://www.safeandsmartpolicy.org/wp-content/uploads/2015/07/BRCPathwaysReport.pdf.

Boire, R. G. (2010). The collateral consequences of cannabis convictions. In Holland, J. (Ed.). *The pot book: A complete guide to cannabis* (pp. 219-222). Rochester, VT: Park Street Press.

Bonnie, R., & Whitebread, C. (1974). *The Marijuana Conviction: A history of marijuana prohibition in the United States*. New York, NY: Lindesmith Center.

Bonomo, Y., Norman, A., Biondo, S., Bruno, R., Daglish, M., Dawe, S., . . . Castle, D. (2019). The Australian drug harms ranking study. *Journal of Psychopharmacology, 33*(7), 759-768. http://dx.doi.org/10.1177/0269881119841569

Booth, M. (2005). *Cannabis: A history*. New York, NY: Picador.

Borland, R. (2003). A strategy for controlling the marketing of tobacco products: a regulated market model. *Tobacco Control, 12*(4), 374-382.

Bowen, G. A. (2009). Document analysis as a qualitative research method. *Qualitative Research Journal, 9*(2), 27-40.

Brown, J. (2012). Marijuana and the Bible (Volume 2) CreateSpace Independent Publishing Platform.

Brady, E. (2013). *Humboldt: Life on America's marijuana frontier*. New York, NY: Grand Central Publishing.

Braun, V., & Clarke, V. (2006). Using thematic analysis in psychology. *Qualitative Research in Psychology. 3*(2), 77-101.

British Pharmacopoeia. (2016). Volume IV Appendices Appendix XI L. Pesticide Residues. (Ph. Eur. method 2.8.13). Retrieved 30/06/2016 from https://www.pharmacopoeia.com/bp-2016/appendices/?date=2016-04-01.

Brohl, B., & Finlaw, J. (2013). Task Force Report on the Implementation of Amendment 64. Retrieved 24/04/2014 from https://www.colorado.gov/pacific/sites/default/files/A64TaskForceFinalReport%5B1%5D_1.pdf.

Brohl, B., Kammerzell, R., & Koski, L. (2015a). *MED 2015 Third Quarter Update*. Retrieved 20/06/2016 from https://www.colorado.gov/pacific/sites/default/files/FINAL%20Third%20Quarter%202015%20Update.pdf (Archived by WebCite® at http://www.webcitation.org/6iOrnlNQO).

Brohl, B., Kammerzell, R., & Koski, W. (2015b). *Colorado Marijuana Enforcement Division: Annual Update*. C. D. o. Revenue. Retrieved from https://www.colorado.gov/pacific/sites/default/files/2014%20MED%20Annual%20Report_1.pdf

Brooks-Russell, A., Ma, M., Levinson, A., Kattari, L., Kirchner, T., Anderson-Goodell, E., & Johnson, R. (2019). Adolescent Marijuana Use, Marijuana-Related Perceptions, and Use of Other Substances Before and After Initiation of Retail Marijuana Sales in Colorado (2013–2015). *Prevention Science, 20*(2), 185-193. http://dx.doi.org/10.1007/s11121-018-0933-2

Brooks-Russell, A., Ma, M., Levinson, A., Kattari, L., Kirchner, T., Goodell, E., & Johnson, R. (2018). Adolescent Marijuana Use, Marijuana-Related Perceptions, and Use of Other Substances Before and After Initiation of Retail Marijuana Sales in Colorado (2013–2015). *Prevention science*, 1-9.

Broyd, S., van Hell, H., Beale, C., Yücel, M., & Solowij, N. (2016). Acute and chronic effects of cannabinoids on human cognition—a systematic review. *Biological psychiatry, 79*(7), 557-567.

Bruun, K., Pan, L., & Rexed, I. (1975). *The Gentlemen's Club: International control of drugs and alcohol.* (Vol. 9). Chicago, IL: University of Chicago Press.

Bryman, A. (2012). *Social research methods. 4th edition. Oxford: Oxford University Press.*

Bryson, J., Crosby, B., & Stone, M. (2006). The design and implementation of Cross-Sector collaborations: Propositions from the literature. *Public administration review, 66*(s1), 44-55.

Budney, A., Roffman, R., Stephens, R., & Walker, D. (2007). Marijuana Dependence and Its Treatment. *Addiction Science & Clinical Practice, 4*(1), 4-16. Retrieved from http://www.ncbi.nlm.nih.gov/pmc/articles/PMC2797098/

Buffington, E. J., & McDonald, S. K. (2006). *Pesticide Fact Sheet #141. Banned and Severely Restricted Pesticides.* Denver, CO: Colorado State University. Colorado Environmental Pesticide Education Program. Retrieved 21/06/2016 from http://www.cepep.colostate.edu/Fact%20Sheets/141BannedPesticides.pdf (Archived by WebCite® at http://www.webcitation.org/6iQaGTWIc). June

Burges, E. (2015). *Pot lobby turns its back on 'Cheech & Chong'.* Retrieved 06/05/2015 from Politico http://www.politico.com/story/2015/03/marijuana-lobby-tommy-chong-dropped-116551.html (Archived by WebCite® at http://www.webcitation.org/6YXSMAMyU). March 31

Burns, R., Caulkins, J., Everingham, S., & Kilmer, B. (2013). Statistics on cannabis users skew perceptions of cannabis use. *Frontiers in Psychiatry, 4*(NOV) http://dx.doi.org/10.3389/fpsyt.2013.00138

Business Insider. (2019, September 12). Aurora Cannabis tumbles double digits after saying it won't turn a profit until next year as weed-industry earnings flag. Retrieved 12/9/2019 from https://markets.businessinsider.com/news/stocks/aurora-cannabis-stock-price-drops-on-earnings-miss-delayed-profits-2019-9-1028520590.

Byrne, B. (2012). *Qualitative Interviewing. In C. Seale (ed), Researching Society and Culture 3rd Edn. Sage, London.*

Caba, J. (2014). *Marijuana breathalyzer could help catch pot-smoking motorists.* Retrieved 05/08/2015 from Medical Daily http://www.medicaldaily.com/new-marijuana-breath-test-could-determine-if-driver-under-influence-pot-312648 (Archived by WebCite® at http://www.webcitation.org/6bUT4gfp4). December 1

Campaign to Regulate Marijuana Like Alcohol. (2012). Endorsements and Supporters. Retirieved 13/11/2017 from Wayback machine https://web.archive.org/web/20120904012727/http://www.regulatemarijuana.org/endorsements.

Canna Law Blog. (2015). *Marijuana Taxes: The IRS On Section 280E.* Retrieved 07/05/2015 from http://www.cannalawblog.com/irs-issues-legal-memorandum-discussing-irc-section-280e/ (Archived by WebCite® at http://www.webcitation.org/6YXSUPidZ). January 30

Cannabis Business Law. (2017, Aug. 30). Civil Asset Forfeiture and Commercial Cannabis. Retrieved 12/01/2018 from http://cannabusinesslaw.com/2017/08/civil-asset-forfeiture-and-commercial-cannabis/.

Cannabis Ganja Yoga Retreat. (2017). Weekend Yoga Retreats. retrieved 22/12/2017 from http://www.420yogaretreats.com/

Cannabis Public Media. (2015). *Colorado Cannabis Tax Collections in a Glance.* Retrieved 24/08/2015 from http://www.marijuanapublicmedia.org/colorado-cannabis-tax-collections-

in-a-glance/ (Archived by WebCite® at
http://www.webcitation.org/6bBmTxMLj). August 18

CannabisRehab.org. (2015). *New guy, just quit.* Retrieved 09/05/2015 from
http://www.cannabisrehab.org/forums/showthread.php/3676-New-guy-just-quit (Archived by WebCite® at
http://www.webcitation.org/6YXSscJVb).

CannabisRehab.org. (2018). Cannabis Rehab: Online Cannabis and Synthetic
Marijuana Rehab. Retrieved 3/1/2018 from
https://www.cannabisrehab.org/. Retrieved from
http://www.cannabisrehab.org/forums/showthread.php/3676-New-guy-just-quit

Cannabist. (2017, Jul.18). Legal cannabis sales begin in Uruguay under landmark
2013 law. retrieved 12/3/2018 from
https://www.thecannabist.co/2017/07/18/uruguay-marijuana-pharmacies-sales/83968/.

Cannabist. (2017, Nov.24). A grow of your very own: Nation's capital a hotbed for DIY
cannabis. Retrieved 9/02/2018 from
https://www.thecannabist.co/2017/11/24/home-growing-marijuana-washington-dc/93217/.

Cannabist. (2017, Sep.14). Uruguay setting up dedicated cannabis dispensaries after
banks scare off pharmacies. Retrieved 12/3/2018 from
https://www.thecannabist.co/2017/09/14/uruguay-marijuana-dispensaries-banks/88071/.

Cannabist. (2018, Apr.19). Cannabis industry not king in Colorado economy: new
report. Retrieved 16/9/2019 from
https://www.thecannabist.co/2018/04/19/colorado-cannabis-industry-federal-reserve-economists/103835/.

Cannabist. (2018, Mar.7). Cannabis cultivation a go for giant Canadian tomato
greenhouse. Retrieved 7/3/2018 from
https://www.thecannabist.co/2018/03/05/canada-greenhouse-cannabis-cultivation-approved/100501/.

Cannabist. (2018, Mar. 22). New Sessions memo pushes death penalty for big drug
dealers. That could include legal marijuana business owners. Retrieved
25/03/2018 https://www.thecannabist.co/2018/03/22/jeff-sessions-marijuana-death-penalty/102131/.

Cannabix Technologies Inc. (2015). *THC Breathalyzer.* Retrieved 05/08/2015 from
http://www.cannabixtechnologies.com/thc-breathalyzer.html (Archived
by WebCite® at http://www.webcitation.org/6bBmYPXVR).

Cannasure. (2016). *Cultivation facilities.* Retrieved 02/07/2016 from
http://www.cannassure.com/products/growers-crop/.

CannLabs. (2015). *Potency Testing.* Retrieved 16/03/2016 from
http://cannlabs.com/potency-testing/ (Archived by WebCite® at
http://www.webcitation.org/6g3KVAK74).

Carlini, E. (2004). The good and the bad effects of (−) trans-delta-9-
tetrahydrocannabinol (Δ 9-THC) on humans. *Toxicon, 44*(4), 461-467.
http://dx.doi.org/10.1016/j.toxicon.2004.05.009

Carnevale, J., Kagan, R., Murphy, P., & Esrick, J. (2017). A practical framework for
regulating for-profit recreational marijuana in US states: lessons from
Colorado and Washington. *International Journal of Drug Policy, 42*, 71-85.

Carpenter, & Suto. (2008). *Qualitative Research for Occupational Therapists and
Physical Therapists: A Practical Guide. Oxford: Blackwell Publishing*

Carstairs, S., Fujinaka, M., Keeney, G., & Ly, B. (2011). Prolonged coma in a child due
to hashish ingestion with quantitation of THC metabolites in urine. *The
Journal of Emergency Medicine, 41*(3), e69-e71.

Carter, S., & Little, M. (2007). Justifying knowledge, justifying method, taking action: epistemologies, methodologies and methods in qualitative research. *Qualitative Health Research*, *17*(10), 1316-1328.

Caulkins, J. (2014). Nonprofit Motive: How to avoid a likely and dangerous corporate takeover of the legal marijuana market. *Washington Monthly*. Retrieved 17/03/2015 from http://www.washingtonmonthly.com/magazine/march_april_may_2014/fe atures/nonprofit_motive049293.php. (Archived by WebCite® at http://www.webcitation.org/6YXT2SURt). Mar/Apr/May

Caulkins, J. (2017). A Principled Approach to Taxing Marijuana. Retrieved 14/3/2018 from https://www.nationalaffairs.com/publications/detail/a-principled-approach-to-taxing-marijuana/.

Caulkins, J., Hawken, A., Kilmer, B., & Kleiman, M. (2012a). *Marijuana Legalization: What everyone needs to know*. New York, NY: Oxford University Press.

Caulkins, J., Kilmer, B., & Kleiman, M. (2016). *Marijuana legalization: What everyone needs to know (2nd edition)*. New York, NY: Oxford University Press.

Caulkins, J., Kilmer, B., Kleiman, M., MacCoun, R., Midgette, G., Oglesby, P., . . . Reuter, P. (2015). *Considering marijuana legalization: insights for Vermont and other jurisdictions*. Rand Corporation.

Caulkins, J., Kilmer, B., MacCoun, R., Pacula, R., & Reuter, P. (2012b). Design considerations for legalizing cannabis: lessons inspired by analysis of California's Proposition 19. *Addiction, 107*(5), 865-871. http://dx.doi.org/10.1111/j.1360-0443.2011.03561.x

Caulkins, J., Lee, M., & Kasunic, A. (2012c). Marijuana Legalization: Lessons from the 2012 State Proposals. *World Medical & Health Policy, 4*(3-4), 4-34. http://dx.doi.org/10.1002/wmh3.2

Caulkins, J., Nicosia, N., & Pacula, R. (2014). Economic analysis and policy studies: Special challenges in the prevention sciences *Defining prevention science* (pp. 571-596): Springer.

Caulkins, J., & Reuter, P. (1997). Setting goals for drug policy: harm reduction or use reduction? . *Addiction, 92*(9), 1143-1150.

Cavazos-Rehg, P., Sowles, S. J., Krauss, M. J., Agbonavbare, V., Grucza, R., & Bierut, L. (2016). A content analysis of tweets about high-potency marijuana. *Drug and alcohol dependence, 166*, 100-108. http://dx.doi.org/10.1016/j.drugalcdep.2016.06.034

CBD MD. (2019). Athletes. Retrieved 8/8/2019 from https://www.cbdmd.com/athlete.

CBS Denver. (2018, May 25). State Report: Tougher To Buy Marijuana Underage Than Tobacco And Alcohol. Retrieved 8/4/2019 from https://denver.cbslocal.com/2018/05/25/state-report-tougher-to-buy-marijuana-underage-than-tobacco-and-alcohol/.

Celine. (2011). *Difference Between GC-MS and LC-MS*. Retrieved 04/01/2016 from DifferenceBetween http://www.differencebetween.net/science/difference-between-gc-ms-and-lc-ms/.

Centre for Addiction and Mental Health. (2014). Cannabis Policy Framework. Centre for Addiction and Mental Health.

Center for Disease Control and Prevention. (2018). Opioid Overdose. Retrieved 23/01/2018 from https://www.cdc.gov/drugoverdose/.

Centers for Disease Control and Prevention. (2016a). Data, Trends and Maps. Retrieved 15/11/2017 from Centers for Disease Control and Prevention https://www.cdc.gov/obesity/data/databases.html.

Centers for Disease Control and Prevention. (2016b). Overweight And Obesity. Retrieved 15/11/2017 from Centers for Disease Control and Prevention https://www.cdc.gov/obesity/data/prevalence-maps.html.

Centers for Disease Control and Prevention. (2019). Characteristics of a Multistate Outbreak of Lung Injury Associated with E-cigarette Use, or Vaping — United States, 2019. Retrieved 30/9/2019 from https://www.cdc.gov/mmwr/volumes/68/wr/mm6839e1.htm?s_cid=mm6839e1_w.

Centre for Research on Globalization. (2018, Oct.15). The War on Weed: Monsanto, Bayer, and the Push for "Corporate Cannabis". Retrieved 30/01/2019 from the Centre for Research on Globalization https://www.globalresearch.ca/the-war-on-weed-monsanto-bayer-and-the-push-for-corporate-cannabis/5534771.

Cervantes, J. (2006). *Marijuana Horticulture: The Indoor/Outdoor Medical Grower's Bible*. USA: Van Patten Publishing.

Cervantes, J. (2015). *The Cannabis Encyclopedia: The definitive guide to cultivation & consumption of medical marijuana*. USA: Van Patten Publishing.

Chambers, R. (2013). *What is dabbing and how do dabs work?*. Retrieved 06/08/2015 from Leafly https://www.leafly.com/news/cannabis-101/is-dabbing-good-or-bad-or-both (Archived by WebCite® at http://www.webcitation.org/6bBmbyAUX). October 28

Chapkis, W., & Webb, R. (2008). Dying To Get High: Marijuana as medicine. New York, NY: New York University Press.

Chasteen, J. (2016). *Getting High: Marijuana through the ages* London, UK: Rowman & Littlefield.

Chemerinsky, E., Forman, J., Hopper, A., & Kamin, S. (2015). Cooperative federalism and marijuana regulation. *UCLA L. Rev., 62*, 74.

Cision. (2012). *Top 10 Daily Newspapers in Colorado*. Retrieved 07/03/2016 from http://www.cision.com/us/2012/10/top-10-daily-newspapers-in-colorado/ (Archived by WebCite® at http://www.webcitation.org/6frEzsBIb). October 24

City and County of Denver. (2016). *Search results: Pesticide*. Retrieved 16/03/2016 from https://www.denvergov.org/content/denvergov/en/city-of-denver-home/search-results.html?q=pesticide (Archived by WebCite® at http://www.webcitation.org/6g3LLAlGr).

City of Denver. (2015). *Denver Marijuana Management Symposium 2015*. Retrieved 21/03/2016 from https://dmms2015.com/ (Archived by WebCite® at http://www.webcitation.org/6gAWaY3iS).

City of Denver. (2018). Denver Marijuana Management Symposium. Retrieved 17/12/2018 from https://dmms.website.

City of Denver. (2019a). HIgh costs post campaign survey. Retrieved 7/4/2019 from https://www.thehighcosts.com/wp-content/uploads/2019/03/High-Costs-Post-Campaign-Survey-Results.pdf.

City of Denver. (2019b). The high costs. Retrieved 7/4/2019 from https://www.thehighcosts.com/the-facts/.

Civilized. (2017, Feb. 20). The Cannabis Health Challenge - How To Add Micro dosing To Your Fitness Routine. Retrieved 13/12/2017 https://www.civilized.life/articles/the-cannabis-health-challenge-how-to-add-microdosing-to-your-fitness-routine/.

Clark, J. (2007). *High performance liquid chromatography - HPLC*. Retrieved 04/01/2016 from Chemguide http://www.chemguide.co.uk/analysis/chromatography/hplc.html.

Clarke, R. (1993). *Marijuana Botany An Advanced study: The propagation and breeding of distinctive cannabis (2nd edition)*. Oakland, CA: Ronin Publishing.

Clarke, R., & Merlin, M. (2013). *Cannabis: Evolution and ethnobotany*. Berkley, CA: University of California Press.

Clements, R. (2002). Psychometric properties of the Substance Abuse Subtle Screening Inventory-3. Journal of substance abuse treatment, 23(4), 419-423.

CNBC. (2015). *Green Rush* [video file]. Retrieved 17/03/2015 from http://www.cnbc.com/id/101429121 (Archived by WebCite® at http://www.webcitation.org/6YXTAT3FC). February 26

CNBC. (2018, Aug. 15). Corona beer maker Constellation ups bet on cannabis with $4 billion investment in Canopy Growth. Retrieved 25/07/2019 from https://www.cnbc.com/2018/08/15/corona-maker-constellation-ups-bet-on-cannabis-with-4-billion-investm.html.

CNBC. (2019, Sep.11). Trump administration readies ban on flavored e-cigarettes amid outbreak of vaping-related deaths. Retrieved 16/9/2019 from https://www.cnbc.com/2019/09/11/trump-to-consider-e-cigarette-policy-amid-outbreak-of-lung-disease.html.

CNN. (2014, Jan. 2). Colorado's recreational marijuana stores make history. retrieved 13/11/2017 from http://edition.cnn.com/2013/12/31/us/colorado-recreational-marijuana/index.html.

CNN. (2015, Jul. 31). *Colorado pot bank sues the Fed.* Retrieved 05/08/2015 from CNN Money http://money.cnn.com/2015/07/31/news/marijuana-pot-bank-sues-fed/ (Archived by WebCite® at http://www.webcitation.org/6bBsgAHTV).

CNN Business. (2019, Jul. 25). UFC teams with Aurora Cannabis on CBD study in fighters. Retrieved 8/8/2019 from https://edition.cnn.com/2019/07/25/business/ufc-aurora-cannabis-cbd-study/index.html.

CNN Money. (2015a). *Cannabis Technology Company MassRoots Files Application to Have Its Common Stock Uplisted to the NASDAQ Capital Market.* Retrieved 03/09/2015 From http://money.cnn.com/news/newsfeeds/articles/globenewswire/5923334.htm (Archived by WebCite® at http://www.webcitation.org/6bUTH1hDV). August 31

CNN Money. (2015b). *Colorado pot bank sues the Fed.* Retrieved 06/08/2015 from http://money.cnn.com/2015/07/31/news/marijuana-pot-bank-sues-fed/ (Archived by WebCite® at http://www.webcitation.org/6bBn3AUBa). July 31

CNN Money. (2015c). *The pot effect on Denver's housing market.* Retrieved 31/08/2015 from http://money.cnn.com/2015/06/04/real_estate/marijuana-denver-housing-market/ (Archived by WebCite® at http://www.webcitation.org/6bBmCCQik). June 4

CNN Money. (2018, Apr.10). Celebs are jumping on the marijuana brand wagon. Retrieved 18/08/2018 from https://money.cnn.com/2018/04/10/news/celebrity-marijuana-brands/index.html.

CNN Political Unit. (2015, 07/04/2015). CNN Poll: Support for legal marijuana soaring Re: Political Ticker Retrieved from http://politicalticker.blogs.cnn.com/2014/01/06/cnn-poll-support-for-legal-marijuana-soaring/

Coffey, C. (2015). *Nail Temperatures and Flavor.* Retrieved 04/08/2015 from High Times http://www.hightimes.com/read/nail-temperatures-and-flavor (Archived by WebCite® at http://www.webcitation.org/6bBn6bBrw). August 3

Colorado Amendment 20. (2000). Colorado Medical Use of Marijuana, Initiative 20 (2000). Retrieved 15/11/2017 from Colorado Official State Web Portal https://www.colorado.gov/pacific/sites/default/files/CHEIS_MMJ_Colorado-Constitution-Article-XVIII.pdf.

Colorado Amendment 64. (2012). The Regulate Marijuana Like Alcohol Act. Retrieved 15/11/2017 from City of Fort Collins https://www.fcgov.com/mmj/pdf/amendment64.pdf.

Colorado Cannabis Chamber of Commerce (CCCC). (2015). Retrieved 05/05/2015 from http://www.cocannabischamber.com/#!educate/c18cf%20approx%2018,000. (Archived by WebCite® at http://www.webcitation.org/6YZAFDt8k).

Colorado Cannabis Tours. (2018). Colorado Cannabis Tours, classes, and 420 friendly hotel bookings. Retrieved 23/01/2018 from https://coloradocannabistours.com/.

Colorado Center on Law and Policy. (2012). Rules and Regulations: A primer on formal rulemaking processes and procedures in Colorado. Retrieved 5/4/2018 from http://cclponline.org/wp-content/uploads/2013/12/Rulemaking-Primer-_DOC-11.24.12.pdf

Colorado Department of Agriculture. (2015a). *Criteria for Pesticides Used in the Production of Marijuana In Colorado*. Retrieved 04/01/2016 from https://www.colorado.gov/pacific/sites/default/files/atoms/files/Criteria%20for%20pesticides%20used%20in%20the%20production%20of%20marijuana%20in%20Colorado_0.pdf (Archived by WebCite® at http://www.webcitation.org/6g029u3Ax).

Colorado Department of Agriculture. (2015b). *Criteria for potential pesticide products for SLN Cannabis use*. Retrieved 21/06/2016 from https://www.colorado.gov/pacific/sites/default/files/atoms/files/Criteria%20for%20potential%20pesticide%20products%20%20for%20SLN%20Cannabis%20use.pdf (Archived by WebCite® at http://www.webcitation.org/6iQYv05EG).

Colorado Department of Agriculture. (2015c). *Letter to Colorado marijuana producers and other stakeholders*. Retrieved 04/01/2016 from https://www.colorado.gov/pacific/sites/default/files/atoms/files/letter%20mj%20stakeholders%20SLN%20info.pdf (Archived by WebCite® at http://www.webcitation.org/6kVsHplJn).

Colorado Department of Agriculture. (2015d). *Reference Guide of the Pesticide Applicators' Act. Retrieved 04/01/2016 from http://www.colostate.edu/dept/DIS/PAA.pdf (Archived by WebCite® at http://www.webcitation.org/6g022mytz)*.

Colorado Department of Agriculture. (2015e). *Selected examples of pesticides that cannot be used in marijuana production*. Retrieved 04/01/2016 from https://www.colorado.gov/pacific/sites/default/files/atoms/files/Selected%20examples%20of%20pesticides%20that%20cannot%20be%20used%20in%20marijuana%20production.pdf (Archived by WebCite® at http://www.webcitation.org/6kVsP2xW9).

Colorado Department of Agriculture. (2016a). *Pesticide Advisory Committee*. Retrieved 22/06/2016 from https://www.colorado.gov/pacific/agplants/pesticide-advisory-committee (Archived by WebCite® at http://www.webcitation.org/6iSepEqyb).

Colorado Department of Agriculture. (2016b). *Pesticides allowed for use in cannabis production as of June 16, 2016*. Retrieved 04/01/2016 from https://www.colorado.gov/pacific/sites/default/files/atoms/files/Pesticides%20allowed%20for%20use%20in%20cannabis%20production%206-16-16.pdf (Archived by WebCite® at http://www.webcitation.org/6iQT4L3da).

Colorado Department of Agriculture. (2016c). *Products that have been removed from the list of pesticides that may be used on marijuana*. Retrieved 04/01/2016 from https://www.colorado.gov/pacific/sites/default/files/atoms/files/Products%20that%20have%20been%20removed%20from%20the%20list%20of%20pe sticides%20that%20may%20be%20used%20on%20marijuana.pdf (Archived by WebCite® at http://www.webcitation.org/6kVsvwdvz).

Colorado Department of Agriculture (CDA). (2015). *Criteria for pesticides used in the production of marijuana in Colorado*. Retrieved 02/09/2015 from https://www.colorado.gov/pacific/sites/default/files/atoms/files/Criteria%20for%20pesticides%20used%20in%20the%20production%20of%20marijuana%20in%20Colorado_0.pdf.

Colorado Department of Military and Veterans Affairs. (2015). Report On the Comprehensive Military Value and Economic Impact of Department of Defense Activities in Colorado. Retrieved 15/11/2017 from Colorado Official State Web Portal https://www.colorado.gov/pacific/sites/default/files/CO%20Mil%20Value%20Study%20Unabridged%20Report%20FINAL%202015.pdf.

Colorado Department of Public Health and Environment. (2014). Retail Marijuana Education Program: legislative report. Retrieved 2/2/2019 from the Colorado Official State Web Portal https://www.colorado.gov/pacific/sites/default/files/MJ_RMEP_Legislative-Report_March-1-2015.pdf

Colorado Department of Public Health and Environment. (2015a). *Inspection of retail marijuana testing facilities*. Retrieved 22/12/2015 from https://www.colorado.gov/pacific/cdphe/inspection-retail-marijuana-testing-facilities (Archived by WebCite® at http://www.webcitation.org/6g1ShKb2U).

Colorado Department of Public Health and Environment. (2015b). *Marijuana in Colorado: Know the facts. Learn the laws*. Retrieved 16/04/2015 from Good to Know http://www.goodtoknowcolorado.com/. (Archived by WebCite® at http://www.webcitation.org/6YXTXUQBg).

Colorado Department of Public Health and Environment. (2016a). *Certification of Marijuana Testing Facilities for Pesticide Analysis Working Group Summary. April 11, 2016*. Retrieved 18/06/2016 from https://www.colorado.gov/pacific/sites/default/files/4.11.16%20Pesticide%20Meeting%20Summary.pdf (Archived by WebCite® at http://www.webcitation.org/6iM3IHyeJ).

Colorado Department of Public Health and Environment. (2016b). *Certification of Marijuana Testing Facilities for Pesticide Analysis Working Group Summary. February 19, 2016*. Retrieved 18/06/2016 from https://www.colorado.gov/pacific/sites/default/files/2.19.16%20Pesticide%20Meeting%20Summary.pdf (Archived by WebCite® at http://www.webcitation.org/6iM3UuNKV).

Colorado Department of Public Health and Environment. (2016c). *Certification of Marijuana Testing Facilities for Pesticide Analysis Working Group Summary. January 13, 2016*. Retrieved 18/06/2016 from https://www.colorado.gov/pacific/sites/default/files/01132016_PesticideUseOnMarijuana_Meeting%20Summary.pdf (Archived by WebCite® at http://www.webcitation.org/6iM3f1JIg).

Colorado Department of Public Health and Environment. (2016d). *Certification of Marijuana Testing Facilities for Pesticide Analysis Working Group Summary. March 14, 2016*. Retrieved 18/06/2016 from https://www.colorado.gov/pacific/sites/default/files/3.14.16%20Pesticide%20Meeting%20Summary.pdf (Archived by WebCite® at http://www.webcitation.org/6iM3NiXMD).

Colorado Department of Public Health and Environment. (2016e). *Monitoring trends in marijuana use*. Retrieved 07/03/2016 from The Official Web Portal of Colorado https://www.colorado.gov/pacific/cdphe/monitoring-

trends-marijuana-use (Archived by WebCite® at
http://www.webcitation.org/6frFlo2sg).

Colorado Department of Public Health and Environment. (2016f). *Pesticide Testing Working Group Agenda. January 13, 2016*. Retrieved 18/06/2016 from
https://www.colorado.gov/pacific/sites/default/files/1.13.16%20Pesticide%20
Meeting%20Agenda.pdf (Archived by WebCite® at
http://www.webcitation.org/6iM4NI3Gc).

Colorado Department of Public Health and Environment. (2016g). *Reference Methods for the Testing of Retail and Medical Marijuana*. Retrieved
15/03/2016 from
https://www.colorado.gov/pacific/sites/default/files/Marijuana%20Testing
%20Method%20Reference%20Library.pdf (Archived by WebCite® at
http://www.webcitation.org/6g1STZakI).

Colorado Department of Public Health and Environment. (2017a). Monitoring
health concerns relating to marijuana: 2016. Retrieved 16/08/2018 from
https://www.colorado.gov/pacific/cdphe/marijuana-health-report

Colorado Department of Public Health and Environment. (2017b). Qualifying
medical conditions Medical Marijuana Registry. Retrieved 15/11/2017 from
Colorado Official State Web Portal
https://www.colorado.gov/pacific/cdphe/qualifying-medical-conditions-
medical-marijuana-registry.

Colorado Department of Public Health and Environment. (2017c). Retail Marijuana
Education Program: annual report. Retrieved 2/2/2019 from the Colorado
Official State Web Portal
https://colorado.gov/pacific/sites/default/files/MJ_RMEP_FinalMJReport17.
pdf.

Colorado Department of Public Health and Environment. (2018a). Inspection of
marijuana testing facilities. Retrieved 20/08/2018 from the Colorado
Official State Web Portal
https://www.colorado.gov/pacific/cdphe/inspection-retail-marijuana-
testing-facilities.

Colorado Department of Public Health and Environment. (2018b). Marijuana
inspection: sampling procedures. Retrieved 20/8/2018 from the Colorado
Official State Web Portal
https://www.colorado.gov/pacific/cdphe/marijuana-sampling-procedures.

Colorado Department of Public Health and Environment. (2018c). Marijuana
reference library. Retrieved 20/08/2018 from the Colorado Official State
Web Portal https://www.colorado.gov/pacific/cdphe/marijuana-reference-
library.

Colorado Department of Public Health and Environment. (2018d). Monitoring
health concerns relating to marijuana: 2018. Retrieved 8/4/2019 from
https://drive.google.com/file/d/1cyaRNiT7fUVD2VMb91ma5bLMuvtc9jZy/vi
ew.

Colorado Department of Public Health and Environment. (2019a). Marijuana:
Education and youth prevention resources for community agencies.
Retrieved 2/2/2019 from
https://www.colorado.gov/pacific/cdphe/RetailMarijuanaTA.

Colorado Department of Public Health and Environment. (2019b). Responsibility
grows here. Retrieved 7/4/2019 from
https://responsibilitygrowshere.com/youth-and-marijuana.

Colorado Department of Public Health and Environment. (2019c). Retail Marijuana
Education Program (RMEP). Retrieved 8/4/2019 from the Colorado Official
State Web Portal
https://drive.google.com/file/d/1a96G6zjZMRUd2cbHo3iz8LClakWQU-
0e/view.

Colorado Department of Public Safety Division of Criminal Justice. (2018a). Driving under the influence of alcohol and drugs: A report pursuant to House Bill 17-1315. Retrieved 8/9/2018 from the Colorado Official State Web Portal http://cdpsdocs.state.co.us/ors/docs/reports/2018-DUI_HB17-1315.pdf.

Colorado Department of Public Safety Division of Criminal Justice. (2018b). Impacts of marijuana legalization in Colorado: a report pursuant to Senate Bill 13-283. Retrieved 10/11/2018 from Colorado Officail State Web Portal http://cdpsdocs.state.co.us/ors/docs/reports/2018-SB-13-283_report.pdf.

Colorado Department of Regulatory Agencies. (2018). 2018 Sunset reviews: Colorado medical marijuana code and Colorado retail marijuana code. Retrieved 10/11/2018 from https://drive.google.com/file/d/1QeSxuD7cqil3L5mLuInWze2BsyYpCSQj/view.

Colorado Department of Revenue. (2015a). *Industry-wide bulletin: 15-10. Executive order directing state agencies to address threats to public safety posed by marijuana contaminated by pesticide.* Retrieved 04/01/2016 from https://www.colorado.gov/pacific/sites/default/files/15-10_IB-MJ%20Pesticides_1.pdf (Archived by WebCite® at http://www.webcitation.org/6fzzpJAwp).

Colorado Department of Revenue. (2015b). *Marijuana taxes. Quick Answers.* Retrieved 31/08/2015 from https://www.colorado.gov/pacific/tax/marijuana-taxes-quick-answers (Archived by WebCite® at http://www.webcitation.org/6bBnDAj94).

Colorado Department of Revenue. (2015c). *Retail Marijuana Facilities.* Retrieved 18/09/2015 from https://www.colorado.gov/pacific/enforcement/med-licensed-facilities.

Colorado Department of Revenue. (2016a). *MED Licensed Retail Marijuana Testing Facilities as of June 1, 2016.* Retrieved 21/06/2016 from https://www.colorado.gov/pacific/sites/default/files/Lab%2006012016_1.pdf (Archived by WebCite® at http://www.webcitation.org/6iQSmseri).

Colorado Department of Revenue. (2016b). *Rulemaking - Marijuana Enforcement.* Retrieved 20/06/2016 from https://www.colorado.gov/pacific/enforcement/MEDrulemaking (Archived by WebCite® at http://www.webcitation.org/6iOrKkKaw).

Colorado Department of Revenue. (2019a). Current & Prior Average Market Rates (AMR) for Retail Marijuana Excise Tax. Retrieved 13/08/2018 from Colorado Official State Web Portal https://www.colorado.gov/pacific/sites/default/files/AMR_PriorRates_Jan2019.pdf.

Colorado Department of Revenue. (2019b). Marijuana sales reports. Retrieved 28/07/2019 from Colorado Official State Web Portal https://www.colorado.gov/pacific/revenue/colorado-marijuana-sales-reports.

Colorado Department of Revenue. (2019c). Marijuana Tax Data. Retrieved 28/07/2019 from olorado Official State Web Portal https://www.colorado.gov/pacific/revenue/colorado-marijuana-tax-data.

Colorado Department of Revenue and Marijuana Enforcement Division. (2013). *Permanent Rules related to the Colorado Retail Marijuana Code.* Retrieved 15/03/2015 from https://www.colorado.gov/pacific/sites/default/files/Retail%20Marijuana%20Rules,%20Adopted%20090913,%20Effective%20101513%5B1%5D_0.pdf.

Colorado Department of Revenue Enforcement Division. (2016). Liquor and Beer Codes. Retrieved 22/05/2018 from Colorado Official State Web Portal https://www.colorado.gov/pacific/enforcement/liquor-beer-codes-2016.

Colorado Department of Revenue Enforcement Division. (2017). Rulemaking - Marijuana Enforcement. Retrieved 1/11/2017 from Colorado Official State Web Portal https://www.colorado.gov/pacific/enforcement/MEDrulemaking

Colorado Department of Revenue Enforcement Division. (2018a). Marijuana Enforcement Division (MED) occupational licensing. Retrieved 20/08/2018 from Colorado Official State Web Portal https://www.colorado.gov/pacific/enforcement/med-occupational-licensing.

Colorado Department of Revenue Enforcement Division. (2018b). MED Industry Bulletins. Retrieved 8/8/2018 from Colorado Official State Portal https://www.colorado.gov/pacific/enforcement/med-industry-bulletins-0.

Colorado Department of Revenue Marijuana Enforcement Division. (2014). *Annual Update*. Retrieved 22/12/2015 from Colorado Official State Web Portal https://www.colorado.gov/pacific/sites/default/files/2014%20MED%20Annual%20Report_1.pdf.

Colorado Department of Revenue Marijuana Enforcement Division. (2015). *Retail Marijuana Code*. Retrieved 24/04/2015 from the Colorado Department of Revenue https://www.colorado.gov/pacific/sites/default/files/Retail%20Marijuana%20Rules%20through%2001302015.pdf.

Colorado Department of Revenue Marijuana Enforcement Division. (2017). MED Annual Report. Retrieved 03/08/2019 from Colorado Official State Web Portal https://www.colorado.gov/pacific/sites/default/files/MED2017AnnualUpdate.pdf.

Colorado Department of Revenue. Enforcement Division. (2016). *MED Licensed Facilities*. Retrieved 20/06/2016 from https://www.colorado.gov/pacific/enforcement/med-licensed-facilities (Archived by WebCite® at http://www.webcitation.org/6iOr1fvVR).

Colorado Department of Transportation. (2018). Drugged driving statistics. Retrieved 20/08/2018 from the Colorado Official State Web Portal https://www.codot.gov/safety/alcohol-and-impaired-driving/druggeddriving/safety/alcohol-and-impaired-driving/druggeddriving/statistics.

Colorado House Bill 15-1283. (2015). Marijuana reference library and lab testing access. Retrieved 16/08/2018 from https://openstates.org/co/bills/2015A/HB15-1283/.

Colorado Legislative Council Staff. (2015). Distribution of marijuana tax revenue. Retrieved 15/08/2018 from Colorado General Assembly https://leg.colorado.gov/sites/default/files/15-10_distribution_of_marijuana_tax_revenue_issue_brief_1.pdf.

Colorado Office of Behavioral Health. (2019). Speak Now. Retrieved 8/4/2019 from https://www.speaknowcolorado.org/.

Colorado Office of State Planning & Budgeting. (2017). State of Colorado Marijuana Tax Cash Fund Appropriations and Actual Expenditures updated 26/9/2017. Retrieved from https://indusdictum.com/wp-content/uploads/2018/01/Colorado-Marijuana-Tax-Cash-Fund-Appropriations-and-Expenditure-Report-09-26-2017-PUBLIC.pdf.

Colorado Official State Web Portal. (2018). Official state information on the laws and health effects of retail marijuana. Retrieved 9/9/2018 from the Colorado Official State Web Portal https://www.colorado.gov/pacific/marijuana/.

Colorado Secretary of State. (2013). 1 CCR 212-2: Retail Marijuana Regulations. Retrieved 11/09/2018 from

https://www.sos.state.co.us/CCR/GenerateRulePdf.do?ruleVersionId=5402
&fileName=1%20CCR%20212-2.

Colorado Secretary of State. (2018a). Colorado Revised Statutes: Article 4 Rulemaking and licensing procedures by state agencies. Retrieved 5/4/2018
from
https://www.sos.state.co.us/pubs/info_center/laws/Title24/Title24Article4.
html.

Colorado Secretary of State. (2018b). Emergency Rulemaking Process. Retrieved
5/4/2018 from
https://www.sos.state.co.us/pubs/CCR/files/emer_rulemaking_process_flo
wchart.pdf.

Colorado Secretary of State. (2018c). Permanent Rulemaking Process. Retrieved
5/4/2018 from
https://www.sos.state.co.us/pubs/CCR/files/perm_rulemaking_process_flo
wchart.pdf.

Colorado Secretary of State. (2019). 1 CCR 212-2: Retail Marijuana Regulations.
Retrieved 5/4/2019 from
http://www.sos.state.co.us/CCR/DisplayRule.do?action=ruleinfo&ruleId=317
5&deptID=19&agencyID=185&deptName=200&agencyName=212%20Mariju
ana%20Enforcement%20Division&seriesNum=1%20CCR%20212-2.

Colorado State Government. (2017). Colorado State Government. Retrieved
15/11/2017 from Colorado Official State Web Portal
https://www.colorado.gov/.

Commission on Marihuana Drug Abuse. (1972). *Marihuana, a Signal of
Misunderstanding: 1st Report of the National Commission on Marihuana
and Drug Abuse*. U.S. Government Printing Office.

Community Preventive Services Task Force. (2014). Reducing tobacco use and
secondhand smoke. Retrieved 22/12/2017 from
http://www.thecommunityguide.org/tobacco/index.html.

Compton, W., Dawson, D., Goldstein, R., & Grant, B. (2013). Crosswalk between DSM-
IV dependence and DSM-5 substance use disorders for opioids, cannabis,
cocaine and alcohol. *Drug and alcohol dependence, 132*(1), 387-390.

Coomber, R., Moyle, L., & South, N. (2016). Reflections on three decades of research
on 'social supply'in the UK. In B. Werse & C. Bernard (Eds.), *Friendly
Business: International Views on Social Supply, Self-Supply and Small-
Scale Drug Dealing* (pp. 13-28). Frankfurt, Germany: Springer.

Copeland, J., Frewen, A., & Elkins, K. (2009). Management of cannabis use disorder
and related issues: A clinician's guide. Retrieved 23/11/2017 from
https://cannabissupport.com.au/media/3069/gp-kit_resource-pack.pdf
NCPIC, National Cannabis Prevention and Information Centre.

Corsi, L., Pellati, F., Brighenti, V., Plessi, N., & Benvenuti, S. (2019). Chemical
Composition and In Vitro Neuroprotective Activity of Fibre-Type Cannabis
sativa L. (Hemp). *Current Bioactive Compounds, 15*(2), 201-210.
http://dx.doi.org/10.2174/1573407214666180809124952

Costa, B., & Comelli, F. (2014). Pain. In R. Pertwee (Ed.), *Handbook of Cannabis*. New
York, NY: Oxford University Press.

Council on Responsible Cannabis Regulation. (2014). *Projects*. Retrieved 27/04/2015
from http://www.crcr.org/projects/ (Archived by WebCite® at
http://www.webcitation.org/6bBnH0Fjq).

Cowlishaw, S., & Thomas, S. (2018). Industry interests in gambling research: Lessons
learned from other forms of hazardous consumption. *Addictive behaviors,
78*, 101-106.

CPR News. (2019, Jan. 7). Beyond Cheetos And Goldfish, Hickenlooper's Marijuana
Legacy Is His Cautious Approach. Retrieved 28/07/2019 from

https://www.cpr.org/2019/01/07/beyond-cheetos-and-goldfish-hickenloopers-marijuana-legacy-is-his-cautious-approach/.

Crane, N., Schuster, R., & Gonzalez, R. (2013). Preliminary evidence for a sex-specific relationship between amount of cannabis use and neurocognitive performance in young adult cannabis users. *Journal of the International Neuropsychological Society, 19*(9), 1009-1015.

Crépault, J., Rehm, J., & Fischer, B. (2016). The Cannabis Policy Framework by the Centre for Addiction and Mental Health: A proposal for a public health approach to cannabis policy in Canada. *International Journal of Drug Policy,*

Creswell, J. (2012). *Qualitative inquiry and research design: Choosing among five approaches.* Sage.

Creswell, J., & Miller, D. (2000). Determining validity in qualitative inquiry. *Theory into Practice, 39*(3), 124.

Crofts, N., Costigan, G., & Reid, G. (2003). Manual for reducing drug related harm in Asia. *Melbourne, Australia: The Centre for Harm Reduction,*

Crotty, M. (1998). *The foundations of social research. Meaning and perspective in the research process (pp.1-17).* Sydney NSW: Allen & Unwin.

Crowley, M. (2016). *Secret Drugs of Buddhism: Psychedelic Sacraments and the Origins of the Vajrayāna.* Hayfork, California: Amrita Press.

CVUA Stuttgart. (2016). *QuEChERS.* Retrieved 30/06/2016 from http://quechers.cvua-stuttgart.de/ (Archived by WebCite® at http://www.webcitation.org/6ieF5MvsO).

D'Amato, A. (2015). *Letter to the Colorado Department of Agriculture from Beyond Pesticides.* Retrieved 17/11/2016 from http://www.beyondpesticides.org/assets/media/documents/watchdog/documents/LettertoCDAfromBeyondPesticides.pdf (Archived by WebCite® at http://www.webcitation.org/6m54cjLhr). July 14

D'Souza, D. C., & Ranganathan, M. (2015). Medical marijuana. Is the cart before the horse?. *JAMA, 313*(24), 2431-2432.

D'Amico, E., Miles, J., & Tucker, J. (2015). Gateway to Curiosity: Medical marijuana ads and intention and use during middle school. *Psychology of Addictive Behaviors: Journal of the Society of Psychologists in Addictive Behaviors, 29*(3), 613-619. http://dx.doi.org/http://dx.doi.org/10.1037/adb0000094

Dahl, H., & Frank, V. (2016). Medical Marijuana: Exploring the concept in relation to small scale cannabis growers in Denmark. In T. Decorte, G. Potter & M. Bouchard (Eds.), World Wide Weed: Global trends in cannabis cultivation and its control. London: Routledge.

Dai, H., & Richter, K. (2019). A National Survey of Marijuana Use Among US Adults With Medical Conditions, 2016-2017. *JAMA Network Open, 2*(9), e1911936-e1911936. http://dx.doi.org/10.1001/jamanetworkopen.2019.11936

Daley, P., Lampach, D., & Sguerra, S. (2013). *Testing cannabis for contaminants.* Retrieved 06/08/2015 from Steep Hill http://steephill.com/pdf/uploads/whitepapers/5c5be0247e264b5020a99b669a936362.pdf (Archived by WebCite® at http://www.webcitation.org/6bBnLWPed).

Daniulaityte, R., Nahhas, R., Wijeratne, S., Carlson, R., Lamy, F., Martins, S., . . . Sheth, A. (2015). "Time for dabs": Analyzing Twitter data on marijuana concentrates across the US. *Drug and Alcohol Dependence* (155), 307-311. http://dx.doi.org/10.1016/j.drugalcdep.2015.07.1199.

Danko, D. (2010). Cannabis Grow Revolution. In J. Holland (Ed.), *The pot book: A complete guide to cannabis* (pp. 44 - 51). Toronto, Canada: Park Street Press.

Danovitch, I., & Gorelick, D. (2012). State of the art treatments for cannabis dependence. *The Psychiatric Clinics of North America, 35*(2), 309.

DeAngelo, S. (2015). *The Cannabis Manifesto: A new paradigm for wellness.* Berkeley: North Atlantic Books.

Decorte, T. (2001). Drug users' perceptions of 'controlled' and 'uncontrolled' use. *International Journal of Drug Policy, 12*(4), 297-320.

Decorte, T. (2010). The case for small-scale domestic cannabis cultivation. *International Journal of Drug Policy, 21*(4), 271-275.

Decorte, T. (2015). Cannabis social clubs in Belgium: Organizational strengths and weaknesses, and threats to the model. *International Journal of Drug Policy, 26*(2), 122-130.

Decorte, T. (2018). *Regulating Cannabis: A detailed scenario for a nonprofit Cannabis Market.* Bloomington, IN: Archway Publishing.

Decorte, T., Pardal, M., Queirolo, R., Boidi, M., Avilés, C., & Franquero, Ò. (2017). Regulating Cannabis Social Clubs: A comparative analysis of legal and self-regulatory practices in Spain, Belgium and Uruguay. *International Journal of Drug Policy, 43*, 44-56.

Degenhardt, L., Ferrari, A., Calabria, B., Hall, W., Norman, R., McGrath, J., . . . Vos, T. (2013). The global epidemiology and contribution of cannabis use and dependence to the global burden of disease: results from the GBD 2010 study. *PloS one, 8*(10), e76635-e76635. http://dx.doi.org/10.1371/journal.pone.0076635

Degenhardt, L., Ferrari, A., & Hall, W. (2017). The Global Epidemiology and Disease Burden of Cannabis Use and Dependence. In V. Preedy (Ed.), *Handbook of Cannabis and Related Pathologies: Biology, Pharmacology, Diagnosis, and Treatment.* Cambridge, Massachusetts: Academic Press.

Denver Post. (2012, Dec. 28). The inside story of how marijuana became legal in Colorado. Retrieved 12/15/2017 from Denver Post http://blogs.denverpost.com/thespot/2012/12/28/story-marijuana-legal-colorado/87640/.

Denver Post. (2012, Nov. 10). Colorado marijuana activists buttoned down to win legalization measure. retrieved 13/11/2017 from Denver Post http://www.denverpost.com/2012/11/10/colorado-marijuana-activists-buttoned-down-to-win-legalization-measure/.

Denver Post. (2012, Oct. 20). Breakdowns of Amendment 64 campaign-finance reports. Retrieved 11/11/2017 from Denver Post http://blogs.denverpost.com/thespot/2012/10/21/breakdowns-amendment-64-campaignfinance-reports/84483/.

Denver Post. (2013, Dec. 31). Marijuana in Colorado has a long history and an uncertain future. Retrieved 13/11/2017 from http://www.denverpost.com/2013/12/31/marijuana-in-colorado-has-a-long-history-and-an-uncertain-future/.

Denver Post. (2017, Apr.20). Denver releases 28,000 marijuana products it had recalled for pesticides. Retrieved 20/08/2018 from https://www.denverpost.com/2016/02/02/denver-releases-28000-marijuana-products-it-had-recalled-for-pesticides/.

Denver Post. (2017, Aug.25). Exclusive: Traffic fatalities linked to marijuana are up sharply in Colorado. Is legalization to blame? Retrieved 16/08/2018 from https://www.denverpost.com/2017/08/25/colorado-marijuana-traffic-fatalities/.

Denver Post. (2018, Aug.26). Mandatory testing costly for Colorado marijuana growers. Retrieved 11/09/2018 from https://www.denverpost.com/2018/08/26/colorado-marijuana-mandatory-pesticide-testing/.

Denver Public Health Inspections Division. (2015). *Special Concerns Associated with Marijuana Extractions, Concentrations, Infusions, and Infused Foods. Retrieved 21/12/2015 from* https://www.denvergov.org/Portals/771/documents/Special%20concerns%20with%20marijuana%20extractions%20and%20infusions.pdf::

Denzin, N. (1989). *Interpretive interactionism*. Newbury Park, Calif: Newbury Park, Calif : Sage Publications.

Dew, K. (2007). A health researcher's guide to qualitative methodologies. *Australian and New Zealand journal of public health, 31*(5), 433-437.

Di Forti, M., Marconi, A., Carra, E., Fraietta, S., Trotta, A., Bonomo, M., . . . Murray, R. (2015). Proportion of patients in south London with first-episode psychosis attributable to use of high potency cannabis: a case-control study. *The Lancet Psychiatry, 2*(3), 233-238.

Dolce, J. (2016). Brave New Weed: Adventures into the uncharted world of cannabis. New York, NY: HarperCollins.

Don't Be a Lab Rat. (2015). Retrieved 24/08/2015 from http://dontbealabrat.com/ (Archived by WebCite® at http://www.webcitation.org/6bBni6UMR).

Donoghue, K., Doody, G., Murray, R., Jones, P., Morgan, C., Dazzan, P., . . . MacCabe, J. (2014). Cannabis use, gender and age of onset of schizophrenia: data from the AESOP study. *Psychiatry research, 215*(3), 528-532.

Dowd, M. (2014). *Don't Harsh Our Mellow, Dude*. Retrieved 03/04/2015 from The New York Times http://www.nytimes.com/2014/06/04/opinion/dowd-dont-harsh-our-mellow-dude.html?_r=1 (Archived by WebCite® at http://www.webcitation.org/6bBnlUZOR). June 3

Dowell, C. (2015). *Cannabis trade group hires lobbyist firms to improve bank access*. Retrieved 05/08/2015 from MJI News http://www.mjinews.com/cannabis-trade-group-hires-lobbyist-firms-improve-bank-access/ (Archived by WebCite® at http://www.webcitation.org/6bBnveJpR). August 4

Drug Abuse Resistance Education. (2019). Drug Abuse Resistance Education. Retrieved 7/4/2019 from https://dare.org/.

Drug Enforcement Administration (DEA). (2017). *Marijuana Concentrates*. Retrieved 05/08/2017 from https://www.dea.gov/pr/multimedia-library/publications/marijuana-concentrates.pdf.

Drug Enforcement Administration (DEA). (2018). Controlled Substances Act. Retrieved 8/8/2018 from https://www.dea.gov/druginfo/csa.shtml.

Drug Policy Alliance. (2019a). *Guiding Drug Law Reform & Advocacy*. Retrieved 09/08/2017 from Drug Policy Alliance http://www.drugpolicy.org/. (Archived by WebCite® at http://www.webcitation.org/6YXTjp0PE).

Drug Policy Alliance. (2019b). Marijuana legaization and regulation. Retrieved 28/07/2019 from http://www.drugpolicy.org/issues/marijuana-legalization-and-regulation.

Drug Policy Alliance. (2019c). Protecting Youth. Retrieved 7/4/2019 from http://www.drugpolicy.org/issues/protecting-youth.

Duff, C. (2008). The pleasure in context. *International journal of drug policy, 19*(5), 384-392.

Dunn, H. (1959). High-level wellness for man and society. American Journal of Public Health and the Nations Health, 49(6), 786-792.

Dunt, I. (2015). *Dabbing: the 'cannabis crack' that makes skunk seem weak*. Retrieved 01/09/2015 from The Guardian http://www.theguardian.com/society/shortcuts/2015/aug/31/dabbing-cannabis-crack-concentrated-oil (Archived by WebCite® at http://www.webcitation.org/6bUUmgYet). September 1

Dussault, D. (2017). *Ganja Yoga: A Practical Guide to Conscious Relaxation, Soothing Pain Relief and Enlightened Self-Discovery*. New York, NY: HarperCollins Publishers.

346

Dutch Review. (2018, Jan.15). Dutch councils call for better cannabis laws in the Netherlands. Retrieved 8/3/2018 from https://dutchreview.com/news/dutch/cannabis-laws-in-the-netherlands/.

Earleywine, M. (2002). *Understanding Marijuana: A new look at the scientific evidence.* USA: Oxford University Press.

Earleywine, M. (2010). Pulmonary harm and vaporizers. In Holland, J. (Ed.). *The pot book: A complete guide to cannabis* (pp. 153-160). Rochester, VT: Park Street Press.

Edwards, H. (2014). The Corporate "Free Speech" Racket. *Washington Monthly.* Retrieved 07/05/2015 from http://www.washingtonmonthly.com/magazine/january_february_2014/features/the_corporate_free_speech_rack048355.php. (Archived by WebCite® at http://www.webcitation.org/6YXTpgMkO). Jan/Feb

Ehler, L. (2006). Integrated Pest Management (IPM): Definition, historical development and implementation, and the other IPM. *Pest Management Science, 62*(9), 787-789.

ElSohly, M., & Waseem, G. (2014). Constituents of cannabis sativa. In R. Pertwee (Ed.), *Handbook of Cannabis.* New York, NY: Oxford University Press.

EMCDDA. (2005). EMCDDA thematic papers: Illicit drug use in the EU: Legislative approaches. Lisbon: European Monitoring Centre for Drugs and Drug Addiction.

Emerging Growth LLC. (2014). *Police and Employers May Finally See Cannabis Breathalyzer.* Retrieved 05/08/2015 from Market Watch http://www.marketwatch.com/story/police-and-employers-may-finally-see-cannabis-breathalyzer-2014-09-10 (Archived by WebCite® at http://www.webcitation.org/6bBo5Iy6L). September 10

Emerson, K., Nabatchi, T., & Balogh, S. (2012). An integrative framework for collaborative governance. *Journal of public administration research and theory, 22*(1), 1-29.

ENCOD. (2011). European Coalition for Just and Effective Drug Policies: Code of Conduct for European Cannabis Clubs. Retrieved 12/02/2018 from http://www.encod.org/info/CODE-OF-CONDUCT-FOR-EUROPEAN.html.

Endejan, J. (2015). *Can Puff the Magic Dragon lawfully advertise his wares?* Retrieved 18/09/2015 from http://www.americanbar.org/content/dam/aba/publications/communications_lawyer/summer2015/CL_Sum15_v31n3_Endejan.authcheckdam.pdf.

Engdahl, W. (2007). *Seeds of Destruction: The hidden agenda of gentic manipulation.* Montreal: Global Research.

Engdahl, W. (2014, Mar.2). The Connection Between The Legalization Of Marijuana In Uruguay, Monsanto And George Soros. Retrieved 12/3/2018 from the European Coalition for Just and Effective Drug POlicies (ENCOD) http://www.encod.org/info/The-Connection-Between-The.html.

Equities Canada. (2014). *Cannabix Technologies Inc.'s Marijuana Breathalyzer Test Set to Smoke the Competition.* Retrieved 05/08/2015 from equities http://www.equities.com/spotlight/canadian-spotlight/west-points-marijuana-breathalyzer-test-set-to-smoke-the-competition (Archived by WebCite® at http://www.webcitation.org/6bBo8KpwO). November 24

Equity Guru. (2019, Aug.28). The cannabis bubble Canopy Growth (WEED.T) created is now the tsunami killing everyone. Retrieved 14/9/2019 from https://equity.guru/2019/08/28/cannabis-bubble-canopy-growth-weed-t-created-now-tsunami-killing-everyone/.

Erickson, P. (1993). The law, social control, and drug policy: models, factors, and processes. *International journal of the addictions, 28*(12), 1155-1176.

Erickson, P. (1995). Harm reduction: What it is and is not. *Drug and Alcohol Review, 14*(3), 283-285.

Esterberg, K. G. (2002). *Qualitative Methods in Social Research*: McGraw-Hill.

Estren, M. (2017). *One Toke to God: The entheogenic spirituality of cannabis*. Malibu, CA: Cannabis Spiritual Center.

European Monitoring Centre for Drugs and Drug Addiction. (2017). Portugal: Country Drug Report 2017, Publications Office of the European Union, Luxembourg.

Evanoff, A., Quan, T., Dufault, C., Awad, M., & Bierut, L. (2017). Physicians-in-training are not prepared to prescribe medical marijuana. *Drug and Alcohol Dependence, 180*, 151.

Fawcett, S., Paine-Andrews, A., Francisco, V., Schultz, J., Richter, K., Lewis, R., . . . Fisher, J. (1995). Using empowerment theory in collaborative partnerships for community health and development. *American journal of community psychology, 23*(5), 677-697.

Federal Reserve Bank of Kansas City. (2018). The Economic Effects of the Marijuana Industry in Colorado. Retrieved 16/9/2019 from https://www.kansascityfed.org/en/publications/research/rme/articles/2018/rme-1q-2018.

Feldman, J. (2014-15). *Pesticide Use in Marijuana Production: Safety issues and sustainable options*. Retrieved 17/11/2016 from Beyond Pesticides http://www.beyondpesticides.org/assets/media/documents/watchdog/documents/PesticideUseCannabisProduction.pdf (Archived by WebCite® at http://www.webcitation.org/6m6dIILfS).

Filbey, F., & Yezhuvath, U. (2013). Functional connectivity in inhibitory control networks and severity of cannabis use disorder. *The American journal of drug and alcohol abuse, 39*(6), 382-391.

First Time 5. (2014). *First Time 5*. Retrieved 27/04/2015 from http://firsttime5.com/ (Archived by WebCite® at http://www.webcitation.org/6bBoFdJ2s).

Fischer, B. (2017). Legalisation of non-medical cannabis in Canada: will supply regulations effectively serve public health? *The Lancet Public Health, 2*(12), e536-e537.

Fischer, B., Rehm, J., & Hall, W. (2009). Cannabis use in Canada: The need for a'public health'approach. *Canadian Journal of Public Health/Revue Canadienne de Sante'e Publique*, 101-103.

Fischer, B., Russell, C., Sabioni, P., Van Den Brink, W., Le Foll, B., Hall, W., . . . Room, R. (2017). Lower-Risk Cannabis Use Guidelines: A Comprehensive Update of Evidence and Recommendations. *American Journal of Public Health, 107*(8), e1-e12. http://dx.doi.org/10.2105/ajph.2017.303818

Fisher, R., & Ury, W. (1981). *Getting to Yes: Negotiating agreement without giving in*. New York: PenguinGroup.

Flick, U., & Gibbs, G. (2007). Analyzing qualitative data. *Designing qualitative research,*

Forbes. (2019, Jun. 12). Colorado Has Generated Over $1 Billion In Marijuana Revenue, State Announces. Retrieved 28/07/2019 from https://www.forbes.com/sites/tomangell/2019/06/12/colorado-has-generated-over-1-billion-in-marijuana-revenue-state-announces/#68e445b762d0.

Freisthler, B., & Gruenewald, P. J. (2014). Examining the relationship between the physical availability of medical marijuana and marijuana use across fifty California cities. *Drug and Alcohol Dependence. 143*, 244-250.

Freud, S., & Byck, R. (1975). *Cocaine papers. New York, NY: Stonehill.*

Frith, H., & Gleeson, K. (2004). Clothing and Embodiment: Men Managing Body Image and Appearance. *Psychology of Men & Masculinity, 5*(1), 40-48. http://dx.doi.org/10.1037/1524-9220.5.1.40

Fox, S., Armentano, P., & Tvert, M. (2009). Marijuana is safer so why are we driving people to drink. Vermont, US: Chelsea Green Publishing.

Fuchs, L. (1542/1999). *The Great Herbal of Leonhart Fuchs: De historia stirpium commentarii insignes, 1542 (notable commentaries on the history of plants)*. Stanford, Calif: Stanford University Press

Gable, R. (2004). Comparison of acute lethal toxicity of commonly abused psychoactive substances. *Addiction, 99*(6), 686-696.

Gallahue, P., Gunawan, R., Rahman, F., El Mufti, K., Din, N., & Felten, R. (2012). *The death penalty for drug offences: Global overview 2012.*

Galli, J., Andari Sawaya, R., & Friedenberg, F. (2011). Cannabinoid hyperemesis syndrome. *Current drug abuse reviews, 4*(4), 241-249.

Galston, W., & Dionne, E. (2013). *The New Politics of Marijuana Legalization: Why Opinion is Changing*. Retrieved 25/04/2015 from the Brookings Institute http://www.brookings.edu/~/media/research/files/papers/2013/05/29-politics-marijuana-legalization-galston-dionne/dionne-galston_newpoliticsofmjleg_final.pdf. (Archived by WebCite® at http://www.webcitation.org/6YXU1UQUK). May

Ganjapreneur. (2016, Jul.12). Crafting Your Dispensary's Voice on Social Media: Do's and Dont's. Retrieved 18/8/2018 from https://www.ganjapreneur.com/crafting-dispensarys-voice-social-media-dos-donts/.

Gaoni, Y., & Mechoulam, R. (1964a). Isolation, structure, and partial synbook of an active constituent of hashish. *Journal of the American chemical society, 86*(8), 1646-1647.

Gaoni, Y., & Mechoulam, R. (1964b). Structure and synbook of cannabigerol, a new hashish constituent. *Proceedings of the Chemical Society,*(82)

Gaoni, Y., & Mechoulam, R. (1971). Isolation and structure of. DELTA.+-tetrahydrocannabinol and other neutral cannabinoids from hashish. *Journal of the American Chemical Society, 93*(1), 217-224.

Garcia, A., & Manning, A. (2015). *How legal marijuana is working in Colorado*. Retrieved 03/09/2015 from Reason https://reason.com/reasontv/2015/08/25/how-legal-marijuana-working-colorado (Archived by WebCite® at http://www.webcitation.org/6bUVbXmVJ). August 25

Gautier, T. (1846/1966). The Hashish Club. In D. Solomon (Ed.), *The Marijuana Papers* (pp. 163-178). New York, NY: Signet Books.

Gen Tech Scientific. (2015). *GenTech Cannabis Testing Products*. Retrieved 22/12/2015 from http://gentechscientific.com/cannabis-testing/products.php (Archived by WebCite® at http://www.webcitation.org/6g4MagHLq).

Ghosh, T., Van Dyke, M., Maffey, A., Whitley, E., Erpelding, D., & Wolk, L. (2015). Medical Marijuana's Public Health Lessons — Implications for Retail Marijuana in Colorado. *New England Journal of Medicine, 372*(11), 991-993. http://dx.doi.org/doi:10.1056/NEJMp1500043

Ghosh, T., Van Dyke, M., Maffey, A., Whitley, E., Gillim-Ross, L., & Wolk, L. (2016). The Public Health Framework of Legalized Marijuana in Colorado. *American journal of public health, 106*(1), 21-27.

Gibbs, M., Winsper, C., Marwaha, S., Gilbert, E., Broome, M., & Singh, S. (2015). Cannabis use and mania symptoms: a systematic review and meta-analysis. *Journal of Affective Disorders, 171*, 39-47.

Gieringer, D. (2001). Cannabis "Vaporization": A promising strategy for smoke harm reduction. *Journal of Cannabis Therapeutics, 1*(3/4), 153-170. Retrieved from http://search.ebscohost.com/login.aspx?direct=true&db=rzh&AN=2002026309&site=ehost-live

Gieringer, D., & Hazekamp, A. (2011). How Accurate is Potency Testing? *O'Shaughnessy's*, Autumn 2011, 17-18.

349

Gilboy, C. (2014). *High anxiety: The state of a highly regulated industry.* Retrieved 05/08/2015 from Boulder Weekly http://www.boulderweekly.com/article-13544-high-anxiety-the-state-of-a-highly-regulated-industry.html (Archived by WebCite® at http://www.webcitation.org/6bBoNed92). October 23

Ginsberg, A. (1966). The Great Marijuana Hoax: First manifesto to end the bringdown. In D. Soloman (Ed.), *The Marijuana Papers* (pp. 230-248). New York, NY: Signet Books.

Global Commission on Drug Policy. (2018). *The World Drug Perception Problem: Countering prejudices about people who use drugs.* Geneva: Retrieved from http://www.globalcommissionondrugs.org/wp-content/uploads/2018/01/GCDP-Report-2017_Perceptions-ENGLISH.pdf

Global Wellness Institute. (2017a). Global Wellness Economy Monitor, January 2017. Retrieved 13/11/2017 from Global Wellness Institute https://www.globalwellnessinstitute.org/industry-research/.

Global Wellness Institute. (2017b). The History of Wellness. Retrieved 12/12/2017 from https://www.globalwellnessinstitute.org/history-of-wellness/.

Gobi Analytical. (2015). *Gobi Analytical Inc. - Cannabis Testing.* Retrieved 10/09/2015 from http://www.gobianalytical.net/ (Archived by WebCite® at http://www.webcitation.org/6bUWGgKMh).

Gogtay, N., Giedd, J., Lusk, L., Hayashi, K., Greenstein, D., Vaituzis, A., . . . Toga, A. (2004). Dynamic mapping of human cortical development during childhood through early adulthood. *Proceedings of the National academy of Sciences of the United States of America, 101*(21), 8174-8179.

Goldstein, M. (2000). The culture of fitness and the growth of CAM. Complementary and alternative medicine: Challenge and change, 27-38.

Golub, A., Johnson, B., & Dunlap, E. (2007). The race/ethnicity disparity in misdemeanor marijuana arrests in new york city. *Criminology & public policy, 6*(1), 131-164.

Goode, E. (2012). *Drugs in American Society* (Eighth ed.). New York, NY: McGraw-Hill.

Google Trends. (2015). *Explore. Dabbing.* Retrieved 01.09.2015 from https://www.google.com/trends/explore#q=dabbing (Archived by WebCite® at http://www.webcitation.org/6bUWaG7F1).

Gorelick, D., Levin, K., Copersino, M., Heishman, S., Liu, F., Boggs, D., & Kelly, D. (2012). Diagnostic criteria for cannabis withdrawal syndrome. *Drug and alcohol dependence, 123*(1), 141-147.

Gorski, E. (2014). *Evolving edibles rules: less potency, more education.* Retrieved 27/04/2015, from http://www.thecannabist.co/2014/07/01/marijuana-edibles-downsizing-potency-increasing-education/15164/ (Archived by WebCite® at http://www.webcitation.org/6bBoR0WXP). July 1

Grant, I., Gonzalez, R., Carey, C., Natarajan, L., & Wolfson, T. (2003). Non-acute (residual) neurocognitive effects of cannabis use: a meta-analytic study. *Journal of the International Neuropsychological Society, 9*(5), 679-689.

Gravelle, J., & Lowry, S. (2014). *Federal Proposals to Tax Marijuana: An Economic Analysis, Washington, D.C.: Congressional Research Service, R43785, November 13, 2014. As of December 12, 2014:* http://fas.org/sgp/crs/misc/R43785.pdf.

Gray, B. (1989). *Collaborating: Finding common ground for multiparty problems. San Francisco, CA: Jossey-Bass.*

Gray, S. (2016). Cannabis and Spirituality: *An explorer's guide to an ancient plant spirit ally. Toronto, Canada: Park Street Press.*

Greco, R., Gasperi, V., Maccarone, M., & Tassorelli, C. (2010). The endocannabinoid system and migraine. *Experimental Neurology, 224*(1), 85-91. http://dx.doi.org/10.1016/j.expneurol.2010.03.029

Green, J. (2015). *Colorado Cannabis Chamber Calls For Marijuana Testing Reference Library.* Retrieved 30/03/2015 from The Weed Blog http://www.theweedblog.com/colorado-cannabis-chamber-calls-for-marijuana-testing-reference-library/ (Archived by WebCite® at http://www.webcitation.org/6bBoemLK1). March 28

Green, J., Willis, K., Hughes, E., Small, R., Welch, N., Gibbs, L., & Daly, J. (2007). Generating best evidence from qualitative research: the role of data analysis. *Australian and New Zealand Journal of Public Health, 31*(6), 545-550.

Greenwald, G. (2009). Drug decriminalization in Portugal: lessons for creating fair and successful drug policies.

Griego, T. (2014). *Weed everywhere in Colorado, yet black market for marijuana thriving.* Retrieved 08/08/2015 from The Cannabist http://www.thecannabist.co/2014/07/30/colorado-marijuana-black-market-pot-illegal-marijuana-growing/17245/0/ (Archived by WebCite® at http://www.webcitation.org/6bBoku9B4). July 30

Grinspoon, L. (1997). *Marihuana: The forbidden medicine.* New Haven, CT: Yale University Press.

Grof, S. (2016). Realms of the human unconscious: Observations from LSD research. NY: Souvenir Press Ltd.

Grow HD. (2011). *Strawberry Haze grow video* [video file]. Retrieved 21/03/2016 from https://growhd.tv/video/Strawberry-Haze-grow-video/9cafc103b50583bc792f5428a110c928 (Archived by WebCite® at http://www.webcitation.org/6gAVztYAp). January 7

Grund, J. (1993). *Drug Use as a Social Ritual: Functionality, symbolism and determinants of self-regulation.* Rotterdam: Instituut voor Verslavingsonderzoek.

Grund, J., & Breeksema, J. (2013). *Coffee Shops and Compromise: Separated Illicit Drug Markets in the Netherlands, Global Drug Policy Program, Open Society Foundations.* https://www.opensocietyfoundations.org/sites/default/files/coffee-shops-and-compromise-20130713.pdf.

Guardian. (2016, May 2). Runner's high: *the athletes who use marijuana to improve their training. Retrieved 27/06/2018 from* https://www.theguardian.com/society/2016/may/02/marijuana-athlete-running-performance-enhancing-drug

Gupta, S. (2013). *Why I changed my mind on weed.* Retrieved 16/04/2015 from CNN International http://www.cnn.com/2013/08/08/health/gupta-changed-mind-marijuana. (Archived by WebCite® at http://www.webcitation.org/6YXUDCMyi. August 9

Habermas, J. (1981/2015). *The Theory of Communicative Action: Reason and the Rationalization of Society.* Wiley.

Hakkarainen, P., Decorte, T., Sznitman, S., Karjalainen, K., Barratt, M., Frank, V., . . . Wilkins, C. (2017). Examining the blurred boundaries between medical and recreational cannabis – results from an international study of small-scale cannabis cultivators. *Drugs: Education, Prevention and Policy,* 1-9. http://dx.doi.org/10.1080/09687637.2017.1411888

Hall, W. (2015). What has research over the past two decades revealed about the adverse health effects of recreational cannabis use? *Addiction, 110*(1), 19-35. http://dx.doi.org/10.1111/add.12703

Hall, W., & Degenhardt, L. (2015). High potency cannabis: A Risk Factor for Dependence, Poor Psychosocial Outcomes, and Psychosis. *BMJ : British Medical Journal, 350* http://dx.doi.org/10.1136/bmj.h1205

Hall, W., & Fischer, B. (2010). Harm reduction policies for cannabis. *MONOGRAPHS,* 235.

Hall, W., & Pacula, R. (2003). *Cannabis Use and Dependence: Public health and public policy*. Cambridge, UK: Cambridge University Press.

Hall, W., & Weier, M. (2015). Assessing the public health impacts of legalising recreational cannabis use in the USA. *Clinical Pharmacology & Therapeutics*. *97*(6), 607-615.

Hall, W., Renström, M., & Poznyak, V. (2016). The health and social effects of nonmedical cannabis use. World Health Organization. Retrieved 15/03/2016 from http://www.who.int/substance_abuse/publications/cannabis_report/en/ (Archived by WebCite® at http://www.webcitation.org/6g1TjPH4C).

Harbarger, M. (2016, November 3). *Oregon issues health alert for three marijuana strains with pesticide residue*. Retrieved 20/11/2016 from Oregonlive http://www.oregonlive.com/business/index.ssf/2016/11/oregon_issues_health_alert_for.html.

Harm Reduction Coalition. (2017). *Principles of harm reduction*. Retrieved 20/02/2017 from Harm Reduction Coalition http://harmreduction.org/about-us/principles-of-harm-reduction.

Harm Reduction International. (2017). *What is harm reduction? :A position statement from Harm reduction International. Retrieved 20/02/2017 from Harm Reduction International https://www.hri.global/what-is-harm-reduction*.

Hart, C. (2014). *High Price: A neuroscientist's journey of self-discovery that challenges everything you know about drugs and society*. HarperCollins.

Hatalsky, L. E., Trumble, S., & Diggles, M. (2014). *The Marijuana Middle: Americans Ponder Legalization*. Retrieved 30/04/2015 from Third Way http://www.thirdway.org/report/the-marijuana-middle-americans-ponder-legalization. (Archived by WebCite® at http://www.webcitation.org/6YXUKgchi). December 8

Hattie, J., Myers, J., & Sweeney, T. (2004). A factor structure of wellness: Theory, assessment, analysis, and practice. Journal of Counseling & Development, 82(3), 354-364.

Hawken, A., Caulkins, J., Kilmer, B., & Kleiman, M. (2013). Quasi-legal cannabis in Colorado and Washington: local and national implications. *Addiction, 108*(5), 837-838. http://dx.doi.org/10.1111/add.12156

Hawken, A., & Kulick, J. (2014). Treaties (probably) not an impediment to 'legal'cannabis in Washington and Colorado. *Addiction, 109*(3), 355-356.

Hazekamp, A., & Pappas, G. (2014). Self-Medication With Cannabis. In R. Pertwee (Ed.), Handbook of Cannabis. New York, NY: Oxford University Press.

HB19-1090. (2019). Publicly Licensed Marijuana Companies: Concerning measures to allow greater investment flexibility in marijuana businesses. Retrieved 31/01/2019 from https://leg.colorado.gov/bills/hb19-1090.

HB 15-1283 Working Group. (2015). *HB 15-1283 Implementation Meeting Summary, October 26, 2015*. Retrieved 22/12/2015 from https://www.colorado.gov/pacific/sites/default/files/Policy_Lab_10.26.15%20PT%20Meeting%20Summary.pdf.

HB 18-1011. (2018). Concerning measures to allow greater investment flexibility in marijuana businesses, and, in connection therewith, making an appropriation. Retrieved 5/9/2018 from the Colorado General Assembly http://leg.colorado.gov/sites/default/files/documents/2018A/bills/2018a_1011_signed.pdf.

Healey, P. (1996). Consensus-building across difficult divisions: new approaches to collaborative strategy making. *Planning Practice and Research*, *11*(2), 207-216.

Healey, P. (2003). Collaborative planning in perspective. *Planning Theory*, *2*(2), 101-123.

Herer, J., Conrad, C., & Osburn, L. (2007). *The Emperor Wears No Clothes: Hemp and the marijuana conspiracy* (eleventh ed.). Van Nuys, CA: AH HA Publishing.

Hermes, K. (2011). *Long-banned Alar (Daminozide) Shows Up on Hydroponic Store Shelves Before Being Removed Again.* Retrieved 21/06/2016 from Americans for Safe Access http://www.safeaccessnow.org/long_banned_alar_daminozide_shows_up_on_hydroponic_store_shelves_before_being_removed_again (Archived by WebCite® at http://www.webcitation.org/6iQaLFVB3). September 20

Herodotus. (440 BC/2016). *The History of Herodotus - Volume 1.* New York, NY: Palatine press.

Hesse-Biber, S. N., & Leavy, P. (2011). *The practice of qualitative research* (2nd ed.): Sage.

Hesse, J. (2015). *A divided weed world: Black market growers and legit industry jobs.* Retrieved 02/05/2015 from The Cannabist http://www.thecannabist.co/2015/02/11/black-market-marijuana-growers-legal-jobs-pot-industry/26631/. (Archived by WebCite® at http://www.webcitation.org/6YXUPfcBF). February 11

Hettler, B. (1984). Wellness: encouraging a lifetime pursuit of excellence. Health values, 8(4), 13.

Hickenlooper, J. (2014). Experimenting with Pot: The state of Colorado's legalization of marijuana. *Milbank Quarterly, 92*(2), 243-249. http://dx.doi.org/10.1111/1468-0009.12056

Hickman, M., Vickerman, P., Macleod, J., Lewis, G., Zammit, S., Kirkbride, J., & Jones, P. (2009). If cannabis caused schizophrenia—how many cannabis users may need to be prevented in order to prevent one case of schizophrenia? England and Wales calculations. *Addiction, 104*(11), 1856-1861.

Himes, S. K., Scheidweiler, K. B., Beck, O., Gorelick, D. A., Desrosiers, N. A., & Huestis, M. A. (2013). Cannabinoids in exhaled breath following controlled administration of smoked cannabis. *Clinical Chemistry, 59*(12), 1780-1789.

Hirvonen, J., Goodwin, R., Li, C., Terry, G., Zoghbi, S., Morse, C., . . . Innis, R. (2012). Reversible and regionally selective downregulation of brain cannabinoid CB1 receptors in chronic daily cannabis smokers. *Molecular psychiatry, 17*(6), 642-649.

Holland, J. (2010). Getting busted is not so funny. An interview with Tommy Chong. In *The pot book: A complete guide to cannabis* (pp. 207-218). Rochester, VT: Park Street Press.

Houborg, E. (2010). Regulating intoxication and disciplining pleasure. In T. Decorte & J. Fountain (Eds.), Pleasure, pain and profit: European perspectives on drugs: Pabst, Wolfgang Science.

Houghton, E., & Hamilton, H. (1908). A pharmacological study of Cannabis americana (Cannabis Sativa) Am. *J. Pharma, 80*, 16-20.

House Bill 14-1366 Edibles Work Group. (2014a). *Marijuana Enforcement Division Work Group Announcement - August.* Retrieved 24/04/2015 from the Colorado Department of Revenue https://www.colorado.gov/pacific/sites/default/files/2014-08-01_Announcement.pdf.

House Bill 14-1366 Edibles Work Group. (2014b). *Marijuana Enforcement Division Work Group Announcement - September.* Retrieved 24/04/2015 from the Colorado Department of Revenue https://www.colorado.gov/pacific/sites/default/files/2014-09-11_1366WGAnnouncement%20%281%29.pdf.

House Bill 15-1283. (2015). Marijuana Reference Library And Lab Testing Access 2015 (CO). Retrieved 15/03/2016 from http://www.leg.state.co.us/clics/clics2015a/csl.nsf/fsbillcont2/086093068E8

3958287257DDC005712E6/$FILE/1283hie_01.pdf (Archived by WebCite® at http://www.webcitation.org/6g1RiisaM).

House Bill 15-1305 Unlawful Manufacture Marijuana Concentrate (CO). (2015). Retrieved 07/09/2015 from http://www.leg.state.co.us/clics/clics2015a/csl.nsf/fsbillcont2/3B54532171BA DD6E87257D900078390F/$FILE/1305_enr.pdf.

House Bill 16-1079. (2016). Pesticide-free Cannabis Certification Program (CO). Retrieved 13/03/2016 from http://www.leg.state.co.us/clics/clics2016a/csl.nsf/fsbillcont/0B12AFB56DD AE0B187257F2400644F05?Open&file=1079_01.pdf (Archived by WebCite® at http://www.webcitation.org/6fyOWrcO5).

House Bill 263. (1917). To Declare Unlawful the Planting, Cultivating, Harvesting, Drying, Curing, or Preparation for Sale or Gift of Cannabis Sativa, and to Provide a Penalty Therefor. Retrieved 13/11/2017 from William A. Wise Law Library, University of Colorado Boulder http://lawlibrary.colorado.edu/session-laws-advanced-search?advanced_year_value=1917&advanced_document_type_value=All&f ield_session_title_value=cannabis&field_session_newsubject_value=

House Bill 1284. (2010). Concerning Regulation of Medical Marijuana and Making an Appropriation therefor. Retrieved 15/11/2017 from the Colorado General Assembly http://www.leg.state.co.us/clics/clics2010a/csl.nsf/billcontainers/0C6B6577 EC6DB1E8872576A80029D7E2/$FILE/1284_rer.pdf.

Housenger, J. E. (2015). *Special Local Needs Registration for pesticide uses for legal marijuana production in Colorado. US Environmental Protection Agency letter to the Colorado Department of Agriculture.* Retrieved 21/06/2016 from the Colorado Department of Agriculture https://www.colorado.gov/pacific/sites/default/files/atoms/files/EPA%20let ter%20to%20CDA%205-19-15%20%20SLNs%20%20for%20marijuana.pdf (Archived by WebCite® at http://www.webcitation.org/6iQYiTu4v). May 19

Huang, C., & Stone, A. (2003). Transformation of the plant growth regulator daminozide (alar) and structurally related compounds with cuii ions: Oxidation versus hydrolysis. *Environmental science & technology, 37*(9), 1829-1837.

Hudak. (2018). The Farm Bill, hemp legalization and the status of CBD: An explainer. Retrieved 19/07/2019 from https://www.brookings.edu/blog/fixgov/2018/12/14/the-farm-bill-hemp-and-cbd-explainer/.

Hudak, J. (2015a). *2016 Will Be the Marijuana Election.* Retrieved 07/05/2015 from News Week http://www.newsweek.com/2016-will-be-marijuana-election-315472. (Archived by WebCite® at http://www.webcitation.org/6YXUVAecf). March 22

Hudak, J. (2015b). Colorado's Rollout of Legal Marijuana Is Succeeding. A Report on the State's implementation of legalization. *Case Western Reserve Law Review, 65*(3)Retrieved from http://www.brookings.edu/~/media/research/files/papers/2014/07/colorad o-marijuana-legalization-succeeding/cepmmjcov2.pdf

Hudak, J. (2016). *Marijuana: A short history.* Washington, D.C.: Brookings Institution Press.

Huffington Post. (2018, Jan.3). Less Than 1 Ounce Of Marijuana Leads To Arrests Of More Than 60 Georgia Partygoers. Retrieved 13/01/2018 from http://www.huffingtonpost.com.au/entry/marijuana-ounce-arrests-georgia_us_5a4c5785e4b06d1621bb9898.

Hughes, A., Lipari, R. N., & Williams, M. (2015). *The CBHSQ Report: State estimates of adolescent marijuana use and perceptions of risk of harm from marijuana use: 2013 and 2014*. Rockville, MD: Substance Abuse and Mental Health Services Administration, Center for Behavioral Health Statistics and Quality. Retrieved 23/12/2015 from http://www.samhsa.gov/data/sites/default/files/report_2121/ShortReport-2121.html (Archived by WebCite® at http://www.webcitation.org/6fJRrQNKm).

Hughes, C. (2017). Portuguese drug policy. In R. Colson & H. Bergeron (Eds.), *European drug policies: The ways of reform*. UK: Routledge.

Hughes, C., & Stevens, A. (2007). The effects of decriminalization of drug use in Portugal. Retrieved 9/3/2018 from Beckley Foundation http://www.beckleyfoundation.org/bib/doc/bf/2007_Caitlin_211672_1.pdf

Hughes, C., & Stevens, A. (2010). What Can We Learn From The Portuguese Decriminalization of Illicit Drugs? *The British Journal of Criminology, 50*(6), 999-1022. http://dx.doi.org/10.1093/bjc/azq038

Hughes, C., & Stevens, A. (2012). A resounding success or a disastrous failure: Re-examining the interpretation of evidence on the Portuguese decriminalisation of illicit drugs. *Drug and Alcohol Review, 31*(1), 101-113.

Hughes, T. (2015). *Denver halts some pot sales over bug spray worries*. Retrieved 07/08/2015 from USA Today http://www.usatoday.com/story/news/nation/2015/04/30/marijuana-contamination/26588989/ (Archived by WebCite® at http://www.webcitation.org/6bBoxxykZ). April 30

Huxham, C., Vangen, S., Huxham, C., & Eden, C. (2000). The Challenge of Collaborative Governance. *Public Management: An International Journal of Research and Theory, 2*(3), 337-358. http://dx.doi.org/10.1080/14719030000000021

Incredibles. (2015). *incredibles: High Quality, THC-Infused Marijuana Edibles*. Retrieved 20/04/2015 from https://incrediblescolorado.com/. (Archived by WebCite® at http://www.webcitation.org/6YXUZgvAM).

Indian Hemp Drugs Commission. (1894/2010). *Report of the Indian Hemp Drugs Commission 1893-94 Volume 1 Report*. London, UK: Hardinge Simpole Publishing.

Ingold, J. (2011). *Medical marijuana users in Colorado mostly male*. Retrieved 31/08/2015 from The Denver Post http://www.denverpost.com/ci_17603530 (Archived by WebCite® at http://www.webcitation.org/6bBpBA3XX).

Ingold, J. (2014a). *Children's Hospital sees surge in kids accidentally eating marijuana*. Retrieved 08/09/2015 from The Denver Post http://www.denverpost.com/news/ci_25807342/childrens-hospital-sees-surge-kids-accidentally-eating-marijuana (Archived by WebCite® at http://www.webcitation.org/6bUaBmyjL). May 21

Ingold, J. (2014b). *Colorado marijuana edibles rules group adjourns without a decision*. Retrieved 08/09/2015 from The Denver Post http://www.brushnewstribune.com/entertainment/ci_26958767/colorado-marijuana-edibles-rules-group-adjourns-without-decision (Archived by WebCite® at http://www.webcitation.org/6bUaQSUSb). November 17

Ingold, J. (2014c). *Colorado recreational marijuana industry begins major transformation*. Retrieved 08/09/2015 from The Denver Post http://www.denverpost.com/news/ci_26063902/colorado-recreational-marijuana-industry-begins-major-transformation (Archived by WebCite® at http://www.webcitation.org/6bUaWdRBb). June 30

Ingold, J. (2014d). *Proposed Colorado marijuana edibles ban shows lingering pot discord*. Retrieved 08/09/2015 from The Denver Post http://www.denverpost.com/news/ci_26765732/proposed-colorado-marijuana-edibles-ban-shows-lingering-pot (Archived by WebCite® at http://www.webcitation.org/6bUadaakv). October 20

Ingold, J. (2014e). *Stoned driving cases in Colorado tough to track.* Retrieved 21/12/2015 from The Cannabist http://www.thecannabist.co/2014/02/10/stoned-driving-cases-proving-difficult-track/4265/ (Archived by WebCite® at http://www.webcitation.org/6fJSwll4k). February 10

Innes, J., & Booher, D. (1999). Consensus building and complex adaptive systems: A framework for evaluating collaborative planning. *Journal of the American Planning Association, 65*(4), 412-423.

Innes, J., & Booher, D. (2010). *Planning with complexity: An introduction to collaborative rationality for public policy. Abingdon, UK: Routledge.*

Institute of Medicine. (1999). *Marijuana and Medicine: Assessing the science base.* Washington, D.C.: National Academy Press.

Institute of Medicine. (2011). *Relieving Pain in America: A Blueprint for Transforming Prevention, Care, Education, and Research.* Washington: Retrieved from https://www.nap.edu/read/13172/chapter/1

International Church of Cannabis. (2017). International Church of Cannabis. Retrieved 12/12/2017 https://www.elevationists.org/about.

International Conferences Group. (2015). *ICBC SF 2015.* Retrieved 08/09/2015 from http://internationalcbc.com/ (Archived by WebCite® at http://www.webcitation.org/6bUao3s2K).

International Society of Addiction Journal Editors. (2018). Statements and Guidelines Addiction Terminology. Retrieved 21/01/2018 from http://www.isaje.net/addiction-terminology.html.

Israeli Ministry of Health. (2018). Medical Grade Cannabis – Clinical Guide (Green Book). Retrieved 2/2/2019 from https://www.xn--4dbcyzi5a.com/2018/01/medical-cannabis-official-israeli-clinical-guide/

Iversen, L. (2007). *The Science of Marijuana.* (second ed.). New York, NY: Oxford University Press.

James, A., James, C., & Thwaites, T. (2013). The brain effects of cannabis in healthy adolescents and in adolescents with schizophrenia: A systematic review. *Psychiatry Research - Neuroimaging, 214*(3), 181-189. http://dx.doi.org/10.1016/j.pscychresns.2013.07.012

Janghorban, R., Roudsari, R. L., & Taghipour, A. (2014). Skype interviewing: The new generation of online synchronous interview in qualitative research. *International Journal of Qualitative Studies on Health and Well-being, 9*, 10.3402/qhw.v3409.24152. http://dx.doi.org/10.3402/qhw.v9.24152

Jay, M. (2010). *High society: The central role of mind-altering drugs in history, science and culture.* Rochester, VT Park Street Press.

Johnson, G. (2016, September 16). *Washington to increase testing pot for pesticides.* Retrieved 21/11/2016 from The Cannabist http://www.thecannabist.co/2016/09/16/washingston-pesticides-increase-testing/63316/ (Archived by WebCite® at http://www.webcitation.org/6mBGs69P6). September 16

Johnson, N. (2015). *Are marijuana regulations weeding out family farmers?.* Retrieved 30/04/2015 from Grist http://grist.org/food/are-marijuana-regulations-weeding-out-family-farmers/. (Archived by WebCite® at http://www.webcitation.org/6YXUdsROW). April 23

Johnson, R., & Waterfield, J. (2004). Making words count: the value of qualitative research. *Physiotherapy Research International, 9*(3), 121-131.

Johnston, E., Hicks, D., Nan, N., & Auer, J. (2010). Managing the inclusion process in collaborative governance. *Journal of Public Administration Research and Theory, 21*(4), 699-721.

Johnston, L. D., O'Malley, P. M., Miech, R. A., Bachman, J. G., & Schulenberg, J. E. (2015). *Monitoring the Future. National survey results on drug use, 1975-2015: Overview, key findings on adolescent drug use.* Ann Arbor: Institute for *Social Research, The University of Michigan. Retrieved 07/03/2016 from* http://www.monitoringthefuture.org/pubs/monographs/mtf-overview2015.pdf *(Archived by WebCite® at* http://www.webcitation.org/6frFpquZs*).*

Joint Budget Committee. (2019). Appropriations report Fiscal year 2018-19. Retrieved 28/07/2019 from https://leg.colorado.gov/sites/default/files/fy18-19apprept_0.pdf.

Kalant, H. (2004). Adverse effects of cannabis on health: an update of the literature since 1996. *Progress in neuro-psychopharmacology and biological psychiatry, 28*(5), 849-863.

Kalant, O. (1972). Report of the Indian Hemp Drugs Commission, 1893-94: A Critical Review. *International Journal of the Addictions, 7*(1), 77 - 96.

Kamin, S. (2013). Medical marijuana in Colorado and the future of marijuana regulation in the United States. *McGeorge Law Review, 43*(12), p.147.

Kamin, S. (2015). Marijuana Legalization in Colorado: Lessons for Columbia. *Journal Columbian Institute of Tax Law, 75* http://dx.doi.org/http://dx.doi.org/10.2139/ssrn.2654305

Kamin, S. (2016). Legal Cannabis in the US: Not Whether but How. *UCDL Rev., 50*, 617.

Kamin, S. (2017). Marijuana Regulation in the United States. In E. Savona, M. Kleiman & F. Calderoni (Eds.), Dual Markets: Comparative Approaches to Regulation (pp. 105-119). Cham: Springer International Publishing.

Kamin, S. (2017a). Marijuana Regulation in the United States. In E. Savona, M. Kleiman & F. Calderoni (Eds.), *Dual Markets: Comparative Approaches to Regulation* (pp. 105-119). Cham: Springer International Publishing.

Kamin, S. (2017b). What California Can Learn from Colorado's Marijuana Regulations. *McGeorge L. Rev., 49*, 13.

Kammerzell, R. (2015). *Public testimony to The Colorado Senate Finance Committee* [audio file]. Retrieved 05/08/2015 from http://www.marijuanapublicmedia.org/colorado-medical-marijuana-code-reconsidered/ (Archived by WebCite® at http://www.webcitation.org/6bBq1FMEL).

Karlsson, P. (2010). Alternatives to the deficit model of adolescent drug use. In T. Decorte & J. Fountain (Eds.), *Pleasure, pain and profit: European perspectives on drugs*. Pabst, Wolfgang Science.

Kaufman, H. (1971). *Limits of organizational change*. Tuscaloosa: Transaction Publishers.

Kaveh, M., Ostovarfar, J., Keshavarzi, S., & Ghahremani, L. (2016). Validation of Perceived Wellness Survey (PWS) in a Sample of Iranian Population. The Malaysian Journal of Medical Sciences : MJMS, 23(4), 46-53. http://dx.doi.org/10.21315/mjms2016.23.4.6

Kedmey, D. (2015). *Willie Nelson to launch his own brand of marijuana*. Retrieved 05/09/2015 from Time http://time.com/3829422/willie-nelson-marijuana-brand/ (Archived by WebCite® at http://www.webcitation.org/6bUb536IG). April 21

Kelley, D. (2015). *State marijuana taxes dribble in for a handful of Colorado Springs area school districts*. Retrieved 31/08/2015 from Colorado gazette http://gazette.com/state-marijuana-taxes-dribble-in-for-a-handful-of-colorado-springs-area-school-districts/article/1558384 (Archived by WebCite® at http://www.webcitation.org/6bUbIJJvS). August 31

Kelly, J., & Westerhoff, C. (2010). Does it matter how we refer to individuals with substance-related conditions? A randomized study of two commonly used terms. *International Journal of Drug Policy, 21*(3), 202-207. http://dx.doi.org/10.1016/j.drugpo.2009.10.010

Kennedy, M. (2017). Cannabis: Exercise performance and sport. A systematic review. Journal of Science and Medicine in Sport, 20(9), 825-829. http://dx.doi.org/10.1016/j.jsams.2017.03.012

Ketchum, J. (2012). *Chemical Warfare Secrets Almost Forgotten*. Bloomington, In: AuthorHouse.

Keyes, C. (1998). Social well-being. Social psychology quarterly, 121-140.

Kilmer, B. (2014). Policy designs for cannabis legalization: starting with the eight Ps. *American Journal of Drug and Alcohol Abuse. 40*(4), 259-261.

Kilmer, B. (2015a). The "10 Ps" of Marijuana Legalization. Retrived 19/02/2018 from Berkeley Review of Latin American Studies http://live-clas.pantheon.berkeley.edu/sites/default/files/shared/docs/tertiary/BRLAS Spring2015-KILMER-spreads.pdf.

Kilmer, B. (2015b). *Marijuana regulation: There are many options*. Retrieved 15/12/2015 from El Daily Post http://www.eldailypost.com/news/2015/11/marijuana-regulation-there-are-many-options/ (Archived by WebCite® at http://www.webcitation.org/6frFtLdI9). November 25

Kilmer, B. (2017). *New developments in cannabis regulation. Retrieved 14/11/2017 from EMCDDA http://www.emcdda.europa.eu/system/files/attachments/6232/European ResponsesGuide2017_BackgroundPaper-Cannabis-policy_0.pdf.*

Kilmer, B., & MacCoun, R. (2017). How Medical Marijuana Smoothed the Transition to Marijuana Legalization in the United States. *Annual Review of Law and Social Science, 13*(1), 181-202. http://dx.doi.org/10.1146/annurev-lawsocsci-110615-084851

Kilmer, B., & Pacula, R. (2009). *Estimating the size of the global drug market: A demand-side approach* (Report no. 2). Cambridge: The RAND Corporation.

Kilmer, B., Reuter, P., & Giommoni, L. (2015). What Can Be Learned from Cross-National Comparisons of Data on Illegal Drugs? *Crime and Justice, 44*(1), 227-296. http://dx.doi.org/10.1086/681552

Kleiman, M. (1992). *Against excess: Drug policy for results*. New York, NY: BasicBooks

Kleiman, M. (2013). Cooperative Enforcement Agreements and Policy Waivers: New Options for Federal Accommodation to State-Level Cannabis Legalization. In *Journal of Drug Policy Analysis* (Vol. 6, pp. 41.

Kleiman, M. (2014). A Nudge Toward Temperance. Retrieved 08/03/2015 from Washington Monthly http://www.washingtonmonthly.com/magazine/march_april_may_2014/features/a_nudge_toward_temperance049292.php. (Archived by WebCite® at http://www.webcitation.org/6YXUlwqoj). Mar/Apr/May

Kleiman, M. (2014a). *How not to make a hash out of cannabis legalization*. Retrieved 07/05/2015 from Washington Monthly http://www.washingtonmonthly.com/magazine/march_april_may_2014/features/how_not_to_make_a_hash_out_of049291.php. (Archived by WebCite® at http://www.webcitation.org/6YXUib5kq). Mar/Apr/May

Kleiman, M. (2014b). *A Nudge Toward Temperance*. Retrieved 08/03/2015 from Washington Monthly http://www.washingtonmonthly.com/magazine/march_april_may_2014/features/a_nudge_toward_temperance049292.php. (Archived by WebCite® at http://www.webcitation.org/6YXUlwqoj). Mar/Apr/May

Kleiman, M. (2015). Legal Commercial Cannabis Sales in Colorado and Washington: What can we learn. *Brookings Institution,*

Kleiman, M. (2016). We're Legalising Weed Wrong. Retrieved 23/12/2017 from http://www.slate.com/articles/business/moneybox/2016/11/america_is_legalizing_marijuana_wrong.html.

Kleiman, M. (2018). How to prevent casual pot smokers from slipping into abuse and dependence. Retrieved 9/9/2018 from https://www.vox.com/the-big-idea/2018/4/20/17259032/marijuana-abuse-dependency-risk-policy-420-drug-addiction.

Klein, C. A. (2015). Current state of marijuana and employment issues: A moving target. *Trial Talk*, June/July, 47-54.

Kondracki, N., Wellman, N., & Amundson, D. (2002). Content Analysis: Review of Methods and Their Applications in Nutrition Education. *Journal of Nutrition Education and Behavior, 34*(4), 224-230. http://dx.doi.org/10.1016/S1499-4046(06)60097-3

Korf, D. (2002). Dutch coffee shops and trends in cannabis use. *Addictive Behaviors, 27*(6), 851-866.

Krauss, M., Sowles, S., Mylvaganam, S., Zewdie, K., Bierut, L., & Cavazos-Rehg, P. (2015). Displays of dabbing marijuana extracts on YouTube. *Drug and Alcohol Dependence*, http://dx.doi.org/http://dx.doi.org/10.1016/j.drugalcdep.2015.08.020

Kroll, D. (2015). *Senators Introduce Bill To End Federal Curbs On Medical Marijuana*. Retrieved 07/05/2015 from Forbes http://www.forbes.com/sites/davidkroll/2015/03/11/is-congress-planning-to-legalize-marijuana/. (Archived by WebCite® at http://www.webcitation.org/6YXUpwHcZ). March 11

Labak, A. (2015). *See the two pot ads a Denver TV station didn't air over legal worries*. Retrieved 24/08/2015 from The Cannabist http://www.thecannabist.co/2015/07/22/marijuana-ads-denver-tv-station/38379/ (Archived by WebCite® at http://www.webcitation.org/6bBq4l6hJ). July 22

LaGuardia Committee on Marihuana. (1944). *The Marihuana Problem in the City of New York: Sociological, medical, psychological and pharmacological studies*. New York, NY: Jaques Cattell Press.

Lammers, J., & Happell, B. (2003). Consumer participation in mental health services: looking from a consumer perspective. *Journal of Psychiatric and Mental Health Nursing, 10*(4), 385-392. http://dx.doi.org/10.1046/j.1365-2850.2003.00598.x

Lancaster, K., Seear, K., & Ritter, A. (2017). Making medicine; producing pleasure: A critical examination of medicinal cannabis policy and law in Victoria, Australia. *International Journal of Drug Policy, 49*(Supplement C), 117-125. http://dx.doi.org/https://doi.org/10.1016/j.drugpo.2017.07.020

Laqueur, H. (2010). Uses and Abuses of Drug Decriminalization in Portugal. *Law and Social Inquiry, 40*(3), 746-781.

Larkin, M., Cierpial, C., Stack, J., Morrison, V., & Griffith, C. (2008). Empowerment theory in action: The wisdom of collaborative governance. *Online Journal of Issues in Nursing, 13*(2), 2-2.

Lata, H., Chandra, S., Khan, I., & ElSohly, M. (2010). High frequency plant regeneration from leaf derived callus of high Δ9-tetrahydrocannabinol yielding Cannabis sativa L. *Planta medica, 76*(14), 1629-1633.

Law Atlas. (2016). *Medical Marijuana Product Safety Map*. Retrieved 17/11/2016 from http://www.lawatlas.org/query?dataset=product-safety-medical-marijuana (Archived by WebCite® at http://www.webcitation.org/6m54uGDao).

Leaf Science. (2014). *Does The U.S. Government Own A Patent On Marijuana?*. Retrieved 30/04/2015 from http://www.leafscience.com/2014/07/25/u-s-government-patent-marijuana/. (Archived by WebCite® at http://www.webcitation.org/6YXUuElhT). July 25

Leaf Science. (2015). *What are Cannabinoids?* Retrieved 16/03/2016 from http://www.leafscience.com/2015/10/23/cannabinoids/ (Archived by WebCite® at http://www.webcitation.org/6g3JvOKMo). October 23

Leafly. (2019, Sep.12). Vape Death Pushes Oregon to Call for Cannabis Product Review. Retrieved 12/9/2019 from https://www.leafly.com/news/industry/vape-death-pushes-oregon-to-call-for-cannabis-product-review.

Leafly. (2019, Sep. 12). Could Trump Pull a 'Cannabis Surprise' in 2020? It's Not Impossible. Retrieved 16/9/2019 from https://www.leafly.com/news/politics/could-trump-pull-a-cannabis-surprise-in-2020-its-not-impossible.

Leafly.com. (2018). Explore marijuana strains and infused products. Retrieved 22/12/2015 from https://www.leafly.com/start-exploring.

Lee, M. (2012). *Smoke Signals: A social history of marijuana-medical, recreational and scientific.* New York, NY: Simon and Schuster.

Lenson, D. (1999). *On drugs.* Minneapolis, MN: University of Minnesota Press.

Lenton, S. (2000). Cannabis policy and the burden of proof: is it now beyond reasonable doubt that cannabis prohibition is not working? *Drug and Alcohol Review, 19*(1), 95-100.

Lenton, S. (2004). Pot, politics and the press—reflections on cannabis law reform in Western Australia. *Drug and Alcohol Review,*(23(2)), 223-233.

Lenton, S. (2005). Deterrence theory and the limitation of criminal penalties for cannabis use. In T. Stockwell, P. J. Gruenewald, J. Toumbourou & W. Loxley (Eds.), *Preventing harmful substance use: The evidence base for policy and practice,* (pp. 267-277). Chichester, England: John Wiley & Sons.

Lenton, S. (2012). Drug Policy reform: Moving beyond strict criminal penalties for drugs. *Policy Talk,*(September 2012)

Lenton, S. (2013). Cannabis: A reason to regulate? Look before we leap. *Of Substance.* 11(2), 14-15.

Lenton, S. (2014a). New regulated markets for recreational cannabis: public health or private profit? *Addiction, 109*(3), 354-355.

Lenton, S. (2014b). New regulated markets for recreational cannabis: public health or private profit? *Addiction. 109*(3), 354-355.

Lenton, S. (2016). Reforming laws applying to domestic cannabis production as a harm reduction strategy: a case study. In T. Decorte, G. Potter & M. Bouchard (Eds.), *World Wide Weed: Global trends in cannabis cultivation and its control.* London: Routledge.

Lenton, S., & Allsop, S. (2010). A tale of CIN—the cannabis infringement notice scheme in Western Australia. *Addiction 105(5)*, 808-816.

Lenton, S., Bennett, M., & Heale, P. (1999). The social impact of a minor cannabis offence under strict prohibition-the case of Western Australia.

Lenton, S., Frank, V., Barratt, M., Dahl, H., & Potter, G. (2015). Attitudes of cannabis growers to regulation of cannabis cultivation under a non-prohibition cannabis model. *Int J Drug Policy, 26*(3), 257-266. http://dx.doi.org/10.1016/j.drugpo.2014.08.002

Lenton, S., & Single, E. (1998). The definition of harm reduction. *Drug and Alcohol Review, 17*(2), 213-220. http://dx.doi.org/10.1080/09595239800187011

Lenton, S., & Subritzky, T. (2017). On sentinel samples, sales data and potency. Commentary on Kilmer & Pacula: Greening the Black Market. *Addiction, 112*(7), 1137-1138. http://dx.doi.org/10.1111/add.13756

Levine, H. (2010). Arrest statistics and racism. In Holland, J. (Ed.). *The pot book: A complete guide to cannabis* (pp. 202-206). Rochester, VT: Park Street Press.

Liamputtong, P. (2013). *Qualitative Research Methods, 4th Edition, Melbourne: Oxford University Press. ISBN/ISSN: 9780195518559.*

Liguori, A., Gatto, C., & Jarrett, D. (2002). Separate and combined effects of marijuana and alcohol on mood, equilibrium and simulated driving. *Psychopharmacology, 163*(3), 399-405.

Lipowski, Z. (1984). What does the word" psychosomatic" really mean? A historical and semantic inquiry. Psychosomatic Medicine, 46(2), 153-171.

Linnaeus, C. (1753/2014). *Linnaeus Species Plantarum* (Vol. 1). UK: Scion Publishing Limited.

Lisdahl, K. (2013). Dare to Delay?: The Impacts of Adolescent Alcohol and Marijuana Use Onset on Cognition, Brain Struture and Function. *Frontiers in Psychiatry, 4*(53) http://dx.doi.org/10.3389/fpsyt.2013.00053

Livingston, M. (2008). Alcohol outlet density and assault: a spatial analysis. *Addiction, 103*(4), 619-628.

Loflin, M., & Earleywine, M. (2014). A new method of cannabis ingestion: The dangers of dabs? *Addictive Behaviors, 39*(10), 1430-1433.

Logroño, J. (2014). *In vitro cell culture of Cannabis sativa for the production of cannabinoids.* Universitat Autònoma de Barcelona, Bellaterra. Retrieved 21/06/2016 from https://ddd.uab.cat/pub/tfg/2014/119249/TFG_javierlidoylogrono.pdf (Archived by WebCite® at http://www.webcitation.org/6iQag5m8u).

Lopez-Quintero, C., de los Cobos, J., Hasin, D., Okuda, M., Wang, S., Grant, B., & Blanco, C. (2011). Probability and predictors of transition from first use to dependence on nicotine, alcohol, cannabis, and cocaine: results of the National Epidemiologic Survey on Alcohol and Related Conditions (NESARC). *Drug and alcohol dependence, 115*(1), 120-130.

Lopez, G. (2014). *What if Big Marijuana becomes Big Tobacco?.* Retrieved 02/05/2015 from VOX http://www.vox.com/2014/9/23/6218695/case-against-pot-legalization-big-marijuana. (Archived by WebCite® at http://www.webcitation.org/6YXV8rehS). December 17

Lucas, P., & Walsh, Z. (2017). Medical cannabis access, use, and substitution for prescription opioids and other substances: A survey of authorized medical cannabis patients. *International Journal of Drug Policy, 42*, 30-35.

Lucas, P., Walsh, Z., Crosby, K., Callaway, R., Belle-Isle, L., Kay, R., . . . Holtzman, S. (2016). Substituting cannabis for prescription drugs, alcohol and other substances among medical cannabis patients: the impact of contextual factors. *Drug and alcohol review, 35*(3), 326-333.

Ludlow, F. (1857/2015). *The hasheesh eater.* Los Angeles, CA: Enhanced Media Publishing.

Lunze, K., Lunze, F., Raj, A., & Samet, J. (2015). Stigma and human rights abuses against people who inject drugs in Russia—a qualitative investigation to inform policy and public health strategies. *PloS one, 10*(8), e0136030.

Lynch, M. (2002). The culture of control: Crime and social order in contemporary society. *PoLAR: Political and Legal Anthropology Review, 25*(2), 109-112.

Maccallum, C., & Russo, E. (2018). Practical considerations in medical cannabis administration and dosing. *European Journal of Internal Medicine, 49*, 12-19. http://dx.doi.org/10.1016/j.ejim.2018.01.004

Maccarrone, M. (2005). Endocannabinoids and regulation of fertility *Cannabinoids as Therapeutics* (pp. 67-78): Springer.

MacCoun, R. (2011). What can we learn from the Dutch cannabis coffeeshop system? *Addiction, 106*(11), 1899-1910.

MacCoun, R. (2013a). The Paths Not (Yet) Taken: Lower risk alternatives to full-market legalisation of cannabis. In K. Tate, J. Taylor & M. Sawyer (Eds.), *Something's in the Air: Race, crime, and the legalization of marijuana.* New York, NY: Taylor & Francis.

MacCoun, R. (2013b). The puzzling unidimensionality of DSM-5 substance use disorder diagnoses. *Frontiers in psychiatry, 4*

MacCoun, R., & Mello, M. (2015). Half-Baked — The Retail Promotion of Marijuana Edibles. *The New England Journal of Medicine*, 989-991.

MacCoun, R., & Reuter, P. (1997). Interpreting Dutch cannabis policy: reasoning by analogy in the legalization debate. *Science, 278*(5335), 47-52.

MacCoun, R., & Reuter, P. (2001). *Drug War Heresies: Learning from other vices, times, and places.* Cambridge, UK Cambridge University Press.

Mack, N., Woodsong, C., MacQueen, K., Guest, G., & Namey, E. (2005). *Qualitative research methods: A data collector's field guide.* North carolina, US: Family Health International.

Malchow, B., Hasan, A., Fusar-Poli, P., Schmitt, A., Falkai, P., & Wobrock, T. (2013). Cannabis abuse and brain morphology in schizophrenia: a review of the available evidence. *European archives of psychiatry and clinical neuroscience, 263*(1), 3-13.

Mann, O. (2015). *An Uber for weed: the start-up that's totally dope.* Retrieved 30/04/2015 from The Telegraph http://www.telegraph.co.uk/men/thinking-man/11539955/An-Uber-for-weed-the-start-up-thats-totally-dope.html. (Archived by WebCite® at http://www.webcitation.org/6YXVEtRSu). April 16

Marconi, A., Di Forti, M., Lewis, C., Murray, R., & Vassos, E. (2016). Meta-analysis of the association between the level of cannabis use and risk of psychosis. *Schizophrenia bulletin, 42*(5), 1262-1269.

MacCoun, R. (2013). The puzzling unidimensionality of DSM-5 substance use disorder diagnoses. Frontiers in psychiatry, 4

MacCoun, R., & Reuter, P. (2001). Drug War Heresies: Learning from other vices, times, and places. Cambridge, UK Cambridge University Press.

Marijuana-Anonymous.org. (2018). Marijuana Anonymous. Retrieved 2/1/2018 from https://www.marijuana-anonymous.org/.

Marijuana Business Daily. (2016, Jul. 27). The famous marijuana memos: Q&A with former DOJ Deputy Attorney General James Cole. Retrieved 15/11/2017 from https://mjbizdaily.com/the-famous-marijuana-memos-qa-with-former-doj-deputy-attorney-general-james-cole/.

Marijuana Business Daily. (2019, May 3). Curaleaf's $1B buy, cannabis brews, social use progress & more of the week's top news. Retrieved 28/07/2019 from https://mjbizdaily.com/marijuana-acquisition-nearly-1b-canadian-brewer-takes-cannabis-plunge-social-use-colorado-las-vegas/.

Marijuana Business Daily. (2019, May 7). Chart: Florida medical cannabis market surges ahead, with five companies dominating. Retrieved 28/07/2019 from https://mjbizdaily.com/chart-florida-medical-cannabis-market-companies-dominating/.

Marijuana Enforcement Division. (2014a). *R 1503 – Retail Marijuana Testing Program – Potency Testing.* Retrieved 29/04/2015 from the Colorado Department of Revenue https://www.colorado.gov/pacific/sites/default/files/Adopted%20Rules%20Regarding%20the%20Retail%20Marijuana%20Code%20%20%28R103%2CR231%2CR234-235%2CR407%2CR604-605%2CR712%2CR1004-1004.5%2CR1006-1006.5%2CR1204%2CR1501-1503%29%2C%20Adopted%2009242014.pdf.

Marijuana Enforcement Division. (2014b). *Retail Marijuana Product Potency and Serving Size Working Group Announcement - April.* Retrieved 06/05/2015 from http://archive.9news.com/assetpool/documents/140428051349_2014-04-30_MjEdiblesANNOUNCE.PDF.

Marijuana Index. (2015). *Measuring the Marijuana Market. An Introduction to the World's First Marijuana Investment Index. Retrieved 05/08/2015 from http://marijuanaindex.com/reports/MJIC_special_report_012715.pdf (Archived by WebCite® at http://www.webcitation.org/6bBqNY6p0).*

Marijuana Moment. (2019). Marijuana Legislation Tracking. Retrieved 25/07/2019 from https://www.marijuanamoment.net/bills/.

Marijuana Moment. (2020, Feb. 10). Trump Again Applauds Death Penalty For Drug Offenses. Retrieved 14/02/2020 from https://www.marijuanamoment.net/trump-again-applauds-death-penalty-for-drug-offenses/.

Marijuana Moments. (2019, Mar. 19). Denver's Teen Marijuana Education Campaign Seems To Be Working, Survey Finds. Retrieved 7/4/2019 from https://www.marijuanamoment.net/denvers-teen-marijuana-education-campaign-seems-to-be-working-survey-finds/.

Marijuana Policy Group. (2015). *Marijuana Equivalency in Portion and Dosage*. Report prepared for the Colorado Department of Revenue. Retrieved 22/12/2015 from https://www.colorado.gov/pacific/sites/default/files/MED%20Equivalency_Final%2008102015.pdf (Archived by WebCite® at http://www.webcitation.org/6fJSKermn).

Marijuana Policy Group. (2018). Market size and demand for marijuana in Colorado 2017 market update (prepared for Colorado Department of Revenue). Retrieved 13/8/2018 from Colorado Official State Web Portal https://www.colorado.gov/pacific/sites/default/files/MED%20Demand%20and%20Market%20%20Study%20%20082018.pdf.

Marijuana Policy Project. (2014). *Consume Responsibly*. Retrieved 27/04/2015 from http://www.consumeresponsibly.org/ (Archived by WebCite® at http://www.webcitation.org/6bBqQ2vTt).

Marijuana Policy Project. (2015). *Marijuana Policy Project*. Retrieved 09/05/2015 from http://www.mpp.org/. (Archived by WebCite® at http://www.webcitation.org/6YXVfzbo4).

Marijuana Policy Project. (2017). *Marijuana Policy Project. Retrieved 13/11/2017 from https://www.mpp.org/our-mission-vision/* Retrieved from http://www.mpp.org/

Marijuana Stock News. (2015). *$DIGP Well Positioned to Take Advantage of $850M Cannabis Testing Market*. Retrieved 05/08/2015 from Marijuana Stocks http://marijuanastocks.com/digp-well-positioned-to-take-advantage-of-850m-cannabis-testing-market/ (Archived by WebCite® at http://www.webcitation.org/6bBqWAdxq). July 16

MassRoots. (2015). *MassRoots*. Retrieved 08/09/2015 from http://massroots.com/landing-desktop (Archived by WebCite® at http://www.webcitation.org/6bUbIUXV3).

McCambridge, J., Kypri, K., Miller, P., Hawkins, B., & Hastings, G. (2014). From tobacco control to alcohol policy. *Addiction, 109*(4), 519-524.

McCarthy, D., Lynch, A., & Pederson, S. (2007). Driving after use of alcohol and marijuana in college students. *Psychology of Addictive Behaviors, 21*(3), 425.

McCloskey, M. (1999). Problems with using collaboration to shape environmental public policy. *Valparaiso University Law Review, 34*(2), 423-434.

McDaniel, P., Solomon, G., & Malone, R. (2005). The tobacco industry and pesticide regulations: Case studies from tobacco industry archives. *Environmental health perspectives, 113*(2), 1659-1665.

McDonough, E. (2015). *Colorado Edibles Makers React to New Rules*. Retrieved 27/04/2015 from High Times http://www.hightimes.com/read/colorado-edibles-makers-react-new-rules. March 30

McGuire, M. (2006). Collaborative public management: Assessing what we know and how we know it. *Public administration review, 66*(s1), 33-43.

McKenna, T. (2010). *Food of the Gods: The search for the original tree of knowledge: a radical history of plants, drugs, and human evolution*. New York, NY: Bantam Books.

McLaren, J., Silins, E., Hutchinson, D., Mattick, R., & Hall, W. (2010). Assessing evidence for a causal link between cannabis and psychosis: a review of cohort studies. *International Journal of Drug Policy, 21*(1), 10-19.

McLaren, J., Swift, W., Dillon, P., & Allsop, S. (2008). Cannabis potency and contamination: a review of the literature. *Addiction, 103*(7), 1100-1109.

McPartland, J., Clarke, R., & Watson, D. (2000). *Hemp Diseases and Pests: Management and biological Control : an advanced treatise*. Oxford, UK: CABI Pub.

McPartland, J., Guy, G., & Di Marzo, V. (2014). Care and feeding of the endocannabinoid system: a systematic review of potential clinical interventions that upregulate the endocannabinoid system. *PloS one, 9*(3), e89566-e89566. http://dx.doi.org/10.1371/journal.pone.0089566

McPartland, J., & Russo, E. (2014). Non Phytocannabinoid Constituents of Cannabis and Herbal Synergy. In R. Pertwee (Ed.), *Handbook of Cannabis*. New York, NY: Oxford University Press.

Mead, A. (2014). *International Control of Cannabis*. In R. Pertwee (Ed.), *Handbook of Cannabis*. New York, NY: Oxford University Press.

Mechoulam, R. (2006). Cannabinoids as Therapeutics *Milestones in Drug Therapy*. Basel, Switzerland: Birkhäuser Basel.

Mechoulam, R., Fride, E., & Di Marzo, V. (1998). Endocannabinoids. *European Journal of Pharmacology, 359*(1), 1-18. http://dx.doi.org/10.1016/S0014-2999(98)00649-9

Mechoulam, R., & Hanus, L. (2000). Historical overview of chemical research on cannabinoids. *Chemistry and Physics of Lipids, 108*, 1-13.

Mechoulam, R., & Parker, L. (2013). The Endocannabinoid System and the Brain. *Annual Review of Psychology, 64*(1), 21-47. http://dx.doi.org/10.1146/annurev-psych-113011-143739

Mechoulam, R., Peters, M., Murillo-Rodriguez, E., & Hanuš, L. (2007). Cannabidiol– recent advances. *Chemistry & biodiversity, 4*(8), 1678-1692.

Medicine Man Denver. (2015). *Medicine Man Denver. Marijuana dispensary*. Retrieved 08/09/2015 from http://www.medicinemandenver.com/ (Archived by WebCite® at http://www.webcitation.org/6bUbyg1tl).

MedicineNet.com. (2018). Medical Definition of Toxicity. Retrieved Jan 3, 2018 from https://www.medicinenet.com/script/main/art.asp?articlekey=34093.

Meier, M., Caspi, A., Ambler, A., Harrington, H., Houts, R., Keefe, R., . . . Moffitt, T. (2012). Persistent cannabis users show neuropsychological decline from childhood to midlife. *Proceedings of the National Academy of Sciences, 109*(40), E2657-E2664.

Meier, M., Caspi, A., Cerdá, M., Hancox, R., Harrington, H., Houts, R., . . . Moffitt, T. (2016). Associations between cannabis use and physical health problems in early midlife: a longitudinal comparison of persistent cannabis vs tobacco users. *JAMA psychiatry, 73*(7), 731-740.

Meier, M., Caspi, A., Danese, A., Fisher, H., Houts, R., Arseneault, L., & Moffitt, T. (2017). Associations between Adolescent Cannabis Use and Neuropsychological Decline: A Longitudinal Co-Twin Control Study. *Addiction,*

Meier, M., Schriber, R., Beardslee, J., Hanson, J., & Pardini, D. (2019). Associations between adolescent cannabis use frequency and adult brain structure: a prospective study of boys followed to adulthood. *Drug and Alcohol Dependence,* http://dx.doi.org/https://doi.org/10.1016/j.drugalcdep.2019.05.012

Meijer, E. (2014). The chemical phenotypes (chemotypes) of cannabis. In R. Pertwee (Ed.), *Handbook of Cannabis*. New York, NY: Oxford University Press.

Mendoza, M. (2015). *Colorado's senators back bill calling for marijuana banking services*. Retrieved 05/08/2015 from Denver Business Journal http://www.bizjournals.com/denver/blog/finance_etc/2015/07/colorado-senators-call-for-marijuana-banking.html (Archived by WebCite® at http://www.webcitation.org/6bBqa6odD). July 9

Mergel, M. (2011). *Myclobutanil*. Retrieved 21/11/2016 from Toxipedia http://www.toxipedia.org/display/toxipedia/Myclobutanil (Archived by WebCite® at http://www.webcitation.org/6mBH6NUsQ). March 23

Merlin, M. (1973). *Man and Marijuana: Some aspects of their ancient relationship.* . New York, NY: A. S. Barnes and Company.

Metrc. (2015). *Metrc: Secure end-to-end effective reporting*. Retrieved 11/05/2014 from http://www.metrc.com/. (Archived by WebCite® at http://www.webcitation.org/6YXVM7IWr).

Metro Denver. (2017). Population. Retrieved 15/11/2017 from Metro Denver from http://www.metrodenver.org/do-business/demographics/population/.

Migoya, D., & Baca, R. (2015). *Investigation: Denver Post tests find pesticides in pot products*. Retrieved 10/09/2015 from The Cannabist http://www.thecannabist.co/2015/09/07/denver-marijuana-pesticides-concentrates-colorado-pot-testing/40493/ (Archived by WebCite® at http://www.webcitation.org/6bUc7xL68). September 7

Mikuriya, T. H. (2007). *Marijuana: Medical papers, 1839-1972.* (Vol. one). Nevada City, CA: Symposium Publishing.

Miles, M., & Huberman, A. (1994). *Qualitative data analysis. An expanded sourcebook. Thousand Oaks, California: Sage Publications Inc.*

Miller, D., & Harkins, C. (2010). Corporate strategy, corporate capture: food and alcohol industry lobbying and public health. *Critical social policy, 30*(4), 564-589.

Millican, R. (2015). *Firing employees for medical cannabis: Colorado Supreme Court says that's okay*. Retrieved 05/08/2015 from Canna Law Blog http://www.cannalawblog.com/firing-employees-for-medical-cannabis-colorado-supreme-court-says-thats-okay/ (Archived by WebCite® at http://www.webcitation.org/6bBqczSGE). June 17

Millman, G. (2015). *SEC allows marijuana dealer to register stock*. Retrieved 09/05/2015 from Market Watch http://www.marketwatch.com/story/sec-allows-marijuana-dealer-to-register-stock-2015-01-28. (Archived by WebCite® at http://www.webcitation.org/6YXVa2RHi). January 28

Mills, J. (1859/1985). On Liberty. Harmondsworth, England: Penguin Books.

Mills, J. (2003). *Cannabis Britannica: Empire, trade, and prohibition, 1800-1928*. Oxford: Oxford University Press.

Mitchell, B. (2005). Participatory partnerships: Engaging and empowering to enhance environmental management and quality of life? *Quality-of-Life Research in Chinese, Western and Global Contexts*, 123-144.

Mitchell, T. (2015). *Marijuana and women: Will industry set a new standard for gender equality?*. Retrieved 31/08/2015 from Westword http://www.westword.com/news/marijuana-and-women-will-industry-set-a-new-standard-for-gender-equality-6586793 (Archived by WebCite® at http://www.webcitation.org/6bBqgPEpI). March 3

MJ News Network. (2016). *Putting Pesticides In Their Place*. Retrieved 21/03/2016 from http://mjnewsnetwork.com/business/putting-pesticides-in-their-place/ (Archived by WebCite® at http://www.webcitation.org/6gAW9sSd1). March 11

Moher, D., Liberati, A., Tetzlaff, J., & Altman, D. (2009). Preferred Reporting Items for Systematic Reviews and Meta-Analyses: The PRISMA Statement. *PLoS Med, 6*(7), e1000097. doi:10.1371/journal.pmed1000097.

Montemayor, S. (2015). *After woman's death, overdoses, Minn. officials raise alarm over marijuana wax*. Retrieved 04/08/2015 from StarTribune http://www.startribune.com/after-woman-s-death-overdoses-state-raises-alarm-over-marijuana-wax/297518631/ (Archived by WebCite® at http://www.webcitation.org/6bBqkovgX). March 26

Moodie, R., Stuckler, D., Monteiro, C., Sheron, N., Neal, B., Thamarangsi, T., . . . Lancet NCD Action Group. (2013). Profits and pandemics: prevention of harmful effects of tobacco, alcohol, and ultra-processed food and drink industries. *The Lancet, 381*(9867), 670-679.

Moore, D. (2002). Opening up the cul-de-sac of youth drug studies: A contribution to the construction of some alternative truths. *Contemporary Drug Problems, 29*(1), 13-63.

Moore, D. (2008). Erasing pleasure from public discourse on illicit drugs: On the creation and reproduction of an absence. *International Journal of Drug Policy, 19*(5), 353-358.

Moore, T., Zammit, S., Lingford-Hughes, A., Barnes, T., Jones, P., Burke, M., & Lewis, G. (2007). Cannabis use and risk of psychotic or affective mental health outcomes: a systematic review. *The Lancet, 370*(9584), 319-328. http://dx.doi.org/10.1016/S0140-6736(07)61162-3

Moreau, J. (1845/1973). *Hashish and mental illness (H. Peter & GG Nahas, Eds., GJ Barnett, Trans.)*. New York, NY: Raven Press.

Moreno, I. (2015). *Stricter Colorado law for home hash oil extraction goes into effect July 1*. Retrieved 04/08/2015 from The Cannabist http://www.thecannabist.co/2015/06/30/colorado-marijuana-laws-hash-oil-extraction/37165/ (Archived by WebCite® at http://www.webcitation.org/6bBqoG7uM). June 30

Morgan, C., & Curran, V. (2008). Effects of cannabidiol on schizophrenia-like symptoms in people who use cannabis. *The British Journal of Psychiatry, 192*(4), 306-307. http://dx.doi.org/10.1192/bjp.bp.107.046649

Morse, J. M. (2015). Critical analysis of strategies for determining rigor in qualitative inquiry. *Qualitative Health Research, 25*(9), 1212-1222.

Motel, S. (2015). *6 facts about marijuana*. Retrieved 10/09/2015 from http://www.pewresearch.org/fact-tank/2015/04/14/6-facts-about-marijuana/ (Archived by WebCite® at http://www.webcitation.org/6bUcG2SZ4). April 14

MSNBC. (2014). Pot Barons Of Colorado Season 1 Episode 1. The Grand Experiment [video file]. Retrieved 05/05/2015 from YouTube https://www.youtube.com/watch?v=T5-ogOmY_-U. (Archived by WebCite® at http://www.webcitation.org/6YXVki3Sm).

Murray, J. (2015). *Social pot use: Denver ballot initiative gets 10K signatures*. Retrieved 24/08/2015 from The Cannabist http://www.thecannabist.co/2015/08/10/denver-social-pot-use-initiative-signatures/39217/ (Archived by WebCite® at http://www.webcitation.org/6bBqttFZH). August 10

Myers, J., Sweeney, T., & Witmer, J. (2000). The wheel of wellness counseling for wellness: A holistic model for treatment planning. Journal of Counseling & Development, 78(3), 251-266.

National Academies of Sciences Engineering and Medicine. (2017). *The health effects of cannabis and cannabinoids: the current state of evidence and recommendations for research*. US: National Academies Press.

National Cannabis Industry Association (NCIA). (2014). *National Cannabis Industry Association: The Voice of The Cannabis Industry*. Retrieved 30/04/2015 from https://thecannabisindustry.org/ (Archived by WebCite® at http://www.webcitation.org/6YXVqMJgI).

National Health and Medical Research Council. (2007). *National statement on ethical conduct in human research (Updated May 2013). Canberra, Australia: National Health and Medical Research Council, Australian Research Council, Australian Vice-Chancellors' Committee.:*

National Highway Traffic Safety Administration. (2018). National Highway Traffic Safety Administration. Retrieved 9/9/2018 from National Highway Traffic Safety Administration https://www.nhtsa.gov/research-data/fatality-analysis-reporting-system-fars.

National Institue on Drug Abuse. (2019). Marijuana: Facts for Teens: Letter to Teens. Retrieved 7/4/2019 from https://www.drugabuse.gov/publications/marijuana-facts-teens/letter-to-teens.

National Pesticide Information Center. (2016). *Home Page.* Retrieved 29/03/2016 from http://npic.orst.edu/ (Archived by WebCite® at http://www.webcitation.org/6gMogm713).

Native Roots. (2018). Medical & recreational budtender needed – Denver, Co. Retrieved 18/08/2018 from https://jobs.lever.co/nativeroots/e4b10217-f6b9-4e5f-8ae2-a7d50c181bf6

Nestle, M. (2013). *Food Politics: How the Food Industry Influences Nutrition and Health.* Berkerley: University of California Press.

NORML. (2017a). *NORML.org - Working to reform marijuana laws.* Retrieved 09/05/2017 from http://norml.org/. (Archived by WebCite® at http://www.webcitation.org/6YXW7zIIp).

NORML. (2017b). State Info. Retrieved from http://norml.org/states

NORML. (2018). Principles of Responsible Cannabis Use. Retrieved 3/1/2018 from http://norml.org/principles.

Nutt, D. (2012). *Drugs Without the Hot Air. Minimising the harms of legal and illegal drugs.* Cambridge UIT Cambridge Ltd.

O'Malley, P., & Mugford, S. (1991). The Demand for Intoxicating Commodities: Implications for the" War on Drugs". *Social Justice, 18*(4 (46), 49-75.

O'Shaughnessy, W. B. (1843). On the preparations of the indian hemp, or gunjah: Cannabis indica their effects on the animal system in health, and their utility in the treatment of tetanus and other convulsive diseases. *Provincial Medical Journal and Retrospect of the Medical Sciences, 5*(123), 363.

O.penVAPE. (2015). *O.penVAPE.com - Open Vape.* Retrieved 30/04/2015 from http://www.openvape.com/. (Archived by WebCite® at http://www.webcitation.org/6YXWChW0Y).

Oddi, S., & Maccarrone, M. (2014). Phytocannabinoids and skin disorders. In R. Pertwee (Ed.), *Handbook of Cannabis.* New York, NY: Oxford University Press.

Office of Attorney General. (2018). Memorandum to United States Attorneys: Guidance regarding use of capital punishment in drug-related prosecutions. retrieved 15/02/20 from https://web.archive.org/web/20200212050502/https://www.justice.gov/file/1045036/download.

Office of the Attorney General. (2017). *Sessions-Hickenlooper-July-24-2017-Letter. Retrieved 21/01/2018 from https://assets.documentcloud.org/documents/3913305/Sessions-Hickenlooper-July-24-2017-Letter.pdf.*

Office of the Attorney General. (2018). Memorandum for all United States Attorneys. Retrieved 21/01/2018 from http://www.documentcloud.org/documents/4343688-AG-Marijuana-Enforcement-1-4-18.html#document/p1.

Ogden, D. (2009). *Memorandum for Selected United States attorneys. Investigations and Prosecutions in States Authorizing the Medical Use of Marijuana*. Washington D.C., U.S. Department of Justice, Office of the Deputy Attorney General. Retrieved 20/11/2016 from https://www.justice.gov/opa/blog/memorandum-selected-united-state-attorneys-investigations-and-prosecutions-states.

Oglesby, P. (2015). Questionable objections to marijuana monopoly — Updated July 28, 2015. Retrieved 10/11/2017 from the Center for New Revenue https://newrevenue.org/2015/04/27/questionable-objections-to-marijuana-monopoly/.

Oglesby, P. (2018). The Center For New Revenue. Retrieved 14/3/2018 from https://newrevenue.org/.

Olson, B. (2015). *Chart of the Week: 1,292 Marijuana Banking Relationships Terminated in 12 Months*. Retrieved 30/04/2015 from Marijuana Business Daily http://mjbizdaily.com/chart-of-the-week-financial-institutions-terminated-1292-marijuana-business-relationships-in-12-months/. (Archived by WebCite® at http://www.webcitation.org/6YXWHVdS3). April 27

Open States. (2017). Open States: Discover politics in your state. Retrieved 15/11/2017 from https://openstates.org/.

Pacula, R., Jacobson, M., & Maksabedian, E. (2015). In the weeds: a baseline view of cannabis use among legalizing states and their neighbours. *Addiction,* http://dx.doi.org/10.1111/add.13282

Pacula, R., Kilmer, B., Wagenaar, A., Chaloupka, F., & Caulkins, J. (2014). Developing public health regulations for marijuana: Lessons from alcohol and tobacco. *American Journal of Public Health, 104*(6), 1021-1028. http://dx.doi.org/10.2105/AJPH.2013.301766

Pacula, R., & Lundberg, R. (2014). Why changes in price matter when thinking about marijuana policy: A review of the literature on the elasticity of demand. *Public Health Reviews. 35*(2), 1-18.

Pacula, R., MacCoun, R., Reuter, P., Chriqui, J., Kilmer, B., Harris, K., . . . Schäfer, C. (2005). What does it mean to decriminalize marijuana? A cross-national empirical examination *Substance Use: Individual Behaviour, Social Interactions, Markets and Politics* (pp. 347-369): Emerald Group Publishing Limited.

Pacula, R., & Sevigny, E. (2014). Marijuana liberalization policies: why we can't learn much from policy still in motion. *Journal of Policy Analysis and Management, 33*(1), 212-221.

Paley, D. (2014). *Drug war capitalism*. Oakland, CA: AK Press.

Palombi, B. (1992). Psychometric properties of wellness instruments. Journal of Counseling & Development, 71(2), 221-225.

Pardo, B. (2014). Cannabis policy reforms in the Americas: a comparative analysis of Colorado, Washington, and Uruguay. *Int J Drug Policy, 25*(4), 727-735. http://dx.doi.org/10.1016/j.drugpo.2014.05.010

Parés, Ò., & Bouso, J. (2015). *Cannabis social clubs innovation born of necessity*. New York:

Payá, P., Anastassiades, M., Mack, D., Sigalova, I., Tasdelen, B., Oliva, J., & Barba, A. (2007). Analysis of pesticide residues using the Quick Easy Cheap Effective Rugged and Safe (QuEChERS) pesticide multiresidue method in combination with gas and liquid chromatography and tandem mass spectrometric detection. *Analytical and bioanalytical chemistry, 389*(6), 1697-1714.

PBS Frontline. (1997-1998). *Interviews - Mark Kleiman. Busted - America's War on Marijuana*. Retrieved 06/05/2015 from PBS http://www.pbs.org/wgbh/pages/frontline/shows/dope/interviews/kleima

n.html. (Archived by WebCite® at
http://www.webcitation.org/6YXWQn3kD). December
Pearson, J. (2015). *Marijuana Investors Lost $23.3 Billion in Penny Stocks Last Year*.
Retrieved 30/04/2015 from Motherboard
http://motherboard.vice.com/read/marijuana-investors-lost-billions-in-
penny-stocks-last-year. (Archived by WebCite® at
http://www.webcitation.org/6YXWV4rP8). February 26
Pérez-Parada, A., Alonso, B., Rodríguez, C., Besil, N., Cesio, V., Diana, L., . . . Heinzen,
H. (2016). Evaluation of Three Multiresidue Methods for the Determination
of Pesticides in Marijuana (Cannabis sativa L.) with Liquid
Chromatography-Tandem Mass Spectrometry. *Chromatographia*. doi:
10.1007/s10337-016-3029-9.
Perry, C. (2005). *The Haight-Ashbury: A History*. Wenner.
Pertwee, R. (2008). The diverse CB1 and CB2 receptor pharmacology of three plant
cannabinoids: Δ9-tetrahydrocannabinol, cannabidiol and Δ9-
tetrahydrocannabivarin. *British journal of pharmacology, 153*(2), 199-215.
Pertwee, R., & Cascio, M. (2014). Known pharmacological actions of delta-9
tetrahydrocannabinol and of four other chemical constituents of cannabis
that activate cananbinoid receptors. In R. Pertwee (Ed.), *Handbook of
Cannabis*. New York, NY: Oxford University Press.
Pesticide Action Network. (2016). *PAN Pesticide Database*. Retrieved 21/06/2016
from http://pesticideinfo.org/Docs/data.html (Archived by WebCite® at
http://www.webcitation.org/6iQZaoXDv).
Pesticide Advisory Committee. (2015). *Pesticide Advisory Committee Meeting
Minutes. October 26, 2015*. Retrieved 21/06/2016 from the Colorado
Department of Agriculture
https://www.colorado.gov/pacific/sites/default/files/atoms/files/PAC%20Mi
nutes%2010-26-2015.pdf (Archived by WebCite® at
http://www.webcitation.org/6iQTRL9Ik).
Pesticide Advisory Committee. (2016). *Pesticide Advisory Committee Meeting
Minutes. February 1, 2016*. Retrieved 21/06/2016 from the Colorado
Department of Agriculture
https://www.colorado.gov/pacific/sites/default/files/atoms/files/2016%20Fe
bruary%20PAC%20Meeting%20Minutes.pdf (Archived by WebCite® at
http://www.webcitation.org/6iQTLkaF9).
Phillips, J., Holland, M., Baldwin, D., Meuleveld, L., Mueller, K., Perkison, B., . . .
Dreger, M. (2015). Marijuana in the workplace: Guidance for occupational
health professionals and employers. *Journal of Occupational and
Environmental Medicine, 57*(4), 459-475.
Phillips, N. (2015). *Aurora considers tighter limit on pot plants for home growers*.
Retrieved 08/08/2015 from The Cannabist
http://www.thecannabist.co/2015/07/07/aurora-marijuana-laws-plant-
limits/37648/ (Archived by WebCite® at
http://www.webcitation.org/6bBrLc0vm). July 7
Phylos. (2019). Phylos Galaxy: the world's largest database of cannabis DNA.
Retrieved 25/07/2019 from https://phylos.bio/galaxy.
Pickert, K. (2015). *Pot Kids*. Retrieved 07/05/2015 from Time http://time.com/pot-
kids/. (Archived by WebCite® at http://www.webcitation.org/6YXWZsEw7).
Pinto, C. (2010). The 'resounding success' of Portuguese drug policy: the power of
an attractive fallacy. *Lisboa: Associação para uma Portugal livre de
drogas,*
Pollan, M. (2001). *The botany of desire: A plant's eye view of the world. New York,
NY: Random House.*
Pollan, M. (2002). The Botany of Desire: A Plant's-Eye View of the World. . New York,
NY: Random House Trade Paperbacks.

Popper, N. (2015). *Banking for Pot Industry Hits a Roadblock*. Retrieved 05/08/2015 from The New York Times http://www.nytimes.com/2015/07/31/business/dealbook/federal-reserve-denies-credit-union-for-cannabis.html?_r=2 (Archived by WebCite® at http://www.webcitation.org/6bBrQRySa). July 30

Potter, G., Barratt, M., Malm, A., Bouchard, M., Blok, T., Christensen, A., . . . Klein, A. (2015). Global patterns of domestic cannabis cultivation: Sample characteristics and patterns of growing across eleven countries. *International Journal of Drug Policy, 26*(3), 226-237.

Powell, D., Pacula, R., & Jacobson, M. (2015). *Do medical marijuana laws reduce addictions and deaths related to pain killers? (No. w21345). National Bureau of Economic Research.*

Power Plant Fitness. (2017). About Power Plant Fitness. retrieved 23/12/2017 from http://powerplantgym.com/about-power-plant-fitness/.

Preedy, V. (2017). *Handbook of Cannabis and Related Pathologies: Biology, pharmacology, diagnosis, and treatment.* San Diego: Academic Press.

Prichard, R. (2015a). *Concentrates 101: How to consume them — dabbing, vaping and more.* Retrieved 04/08/2015 from The Cannabist http://www.thecannabist.co/2015/06/19/concentrates-how-to-consume-them-dabbing-vaping-hash-pipe-vaporizer/36402/ (Archived by WebCite® at http://www.webcitation.org/6bBrSnn0D). June 19

Prichard, R. (2015b). *Concentrates 101: What's on the market, from kief and CO2 oil to BHO.* Retrieved 04/08/2015 from The Cannabist http://www.thecannabist.co/2015/06/19/marijuana-concentrates-kief-bho-water-hash-co2-oil-wax-shatter/36386/ (Archived by WebCite® at http://www.webcitation.org/6bBrWuade). June 19

Prichard, R. (2015c). *Concentrates 101: Why try them? Potency, flavor & other factors.* Retrieved 04/08/2015 from The Cannabist http://www.thecannabist.co/2015/06/19/cannabis-concentrates-vaping-potency-flavor/34104/ (Archived by WebCite® at http://www.webcitation.org/6bBraRHRR). June 19

Proal, A., Fleming, J., Galvez-Buccollini, J., & DeLisi, L. (2014). A controlled family study of cannabis users with and without psychosis. *Schizophrenia research, 152*(1), 283-288.

Proposition 19. (2010). California Proposition 19, the Marijuana Legalization Initiative (2010). Retrieved 11/11/2017 from Ballotpedia https://ballotpedia.org/California_Proposition_19,_the_Marijuana_Legalization_Initiative_(2010).

Protect What's Next. (2015). Retrieved 20/08/2015 from http://protectwhatsnext.com/ (Archived by WebCite® at http://www.webcitation.org/6bBreKe4I).

Purdy, J. (2012). A framework for assessing power in collaborative governance processes. *Public Administration Review, 72*(3), 409-417.

QSR International Pty Ltd. (2017). NVivo qualitative data analysis software [computer software]. Version 11. Doncaster, VIC: QSR International Pty Ltd.

Quah, D., Collins, J., Atuesta Becerra, L., Caulkins, J., Csete, J., Drucker, E., . . . Mejia, D. (2014). Ending the drug wars: report of the LSE Expert Group on the economics of drug policy.

Queirolo, R., Boidi, M., & Cruz, J. (2016). Cannabis clubs in Uruguay: The challenges of regulation. *International Journal of Drug Policy, 34*, 41-48. http://dx.doi.org/https://doi.org/10.1016/j.drugpo.2016.05.015

Quora. (2013). *What are the negative health impacts, if any, to consuming marijuana via a vaporizer?.* Retrieved 04/08/2015 from http://www.quora.com/What-are-the-negative-health-impacts-if-any-to-consuming-marijuana-via-a-vaporizer (Archived by WebCite® at http://www.webcitation.org/6bBri9zL8).

Radhakrishnan, R., Wilkinson, S., & D'Souza, D. (2014). Gone to pot–a review of the association between cannabis and psychosis. *Frontiers in psychiatry, 5*

Ramaekers, J., Berghaus, G., van Laar, M., & Drummer, O. (2004). Dose related risk of motor vehicle crashes after cannabis use. *Drug and alcohol dependence, 73*(2), 109-119.

Random.org. (2016). *Random.org - True Random Number Service.* Retrieved 07/03/2016 from https://www.random.org/.

Rappold, R. S. (2015). *Metals, Fungus Found in Colorado's Marijuana.* Retrieved 25/03/2015 from Web MD http://www.webmd.com/brain/news/20150324/colorado-marijuana-metals-fungus (Archived by WebCite® at http://www.webcitation.org/6bBrkyqcY). March 24

Rätsch, C. (2001). *Marijuana Medicine. A World Tour of the Healing and Visionary Powers of Cannabis.* Rochester, VT: Haworth Integrative Healing Press.

Rätsch, C. (2005). *The Encyclopedia of Psychoactive Plants: Ethnopharmacology and its applications* Rochester, VT: Park Street Press.

Reason. (2018, Jan.8). GOP State Rep. Steve Alford of Kansas Says Marijuana Was Outlawed Because 'the African Americans...Responded the Worst...Just Because of their Character Makeup, Their Genetics'. Retrieved 21/01/2018 from http://reason.com/blog/2018/01/08/gop-state-rep-steve-alford-of-kansas-say

Rehm, J., Taylor, B., & Room, R. (2006). Global burden of disease from alcohol, illicit drugs and tobacco. *Drug and Alcohol Review, 25*(6), 503-513. http://dx.doi.org/10.1080/09595230600944453

Reichard, Z. (2013). *Lab-Testing Cannabis: What You Should Know.* Retrieved 16/03/2016 from Medical Jane http://www.medicaljane.com/2013/02/11/lab-testing-cannabis-prescription-meds-list-dosage-information-concentration-levels-why-not-cannabis/ (Archived by WebCite® at http://www.webcitation.org/6g3KoJ0Fm).

Reiman, A., Welty, M., & Solomon, P. (2017). Cannabis as a substitute for opioid-based pain medication: Patient self-report. *Cannabis and cannabinoid research, 2*(1), 160-166.

Rendon, J. (2012). Super Charged: How outlaws, hippies, and scientists reinvented marijuana. Portland, OR: Timber Press.

Rhodes, T., & Hedrich, D. (2010). Harm reduction and the mainstream. Retrieved 23/11/2017 from EMCDDA http://www.drugs.ie/resourcesfiles/ResearchDocs/Europe/Research/2010/EMCDDA-monograph10-harm_reduction_final.pdf#page=21 *EMCDDA Monographs,*

Rittel, H., & Webber, M. (1973). Dilemmas in a general theory of planning. *Policy Sciences, 4*(2), 155-169. http://dx.doi.org/10.1007/bf01405730

Rizzo, T. (2015). *Colorado pilot pleads guilty to flying marijuana into Kansas.* Retrieved 08/08/2015 from The Kansas City Star http://www.kansascity.com/news/local/crime/article28330954.html (Archived by WebCite® at http://www.webcitation.org/6bBtt6abF). July 22

Roberts, M. (2015). *Reader: Stoned driving blood tests are a violation of human rights.* Retrieved 08/08/2015 from Westword http://www.westword.com/news/reader-stoned-driving-blood-tests-are-a-violation-of-human-rights-6940351 (Archived by WebCite® at http://www.webcitation.org/6bBsEDUk1). July 22

Robertson, N., Sacks, G., & Miller, P. (2019). The revolving door between government and the alcohol, food and gambling industries in Australia. *Public Health*

*Research & Practice,*Retrieved from
http://www.phrp.com.au/issues/september-2019-volume-29-issue-3/the-revolving-door-between-government-and-the-alcohol-food-and-gambling-industries-in-australia/

Rock, E., Goodwin, J., Limebeer, C., Breuer, A., Pertwee, R., Mechoulam, R., & Parker, L. (2011). Interaction between non-psychotropic cannabinoids in marihuana: effect of cannabigerol (CBG) on the anti-nausea or anti-emetic effects of cannabidiol (CBD) in rats and shrews. *Psychopharmacology, 215*(3), 505-512. http://dx.doi.org/10.1007/s00213-010-2157-4

Rocky Mountain High Intensity Drug Trafficking Area. (2013). *The Legalization of Marijuana in Colorado: The Impact. Volume 1.* Retrieved 22/12/2015 from http://www.rmhidta.org/html/FINAL%20Legalization%20of%20MJ%20in%20Colorado%20The%20Impact.pdf.

Rocky Mountain High Intensity Drug Trafficking Area. (2014). *The Legalization of Marijuana in Colorado: The Impact. Volume 2.* Retrieved 22/12/2015 from http://www.rmhidta.org/html/August%202014%20Legalization%20of%20MJ%20in%20Colorado%20the%20Impact.pdf.

Rocky Mountain High Intensity Drug Trafficking Area. (2015). *The Legalization of Marijuana in Colorado: The Impact. Volume 3 Preview.* Retrieved 22/12/2015 from http://www.rmhidta.org/html/2015%20PREVIEW%20Legalization%20of%20MJ%20in%20Colorado%20the%20Impact.pdf.

Rocky Mountain High Intensity Drug Trafficking Area. (2016). *The Legalization of Marijuana in Colorado: The Impact. Volume 4.* Retrieved 03/12/2016 from http://www.rmhidta.org/html/2016%20FINAL%20Legalization%20of%20Marijuana%20in%20Colorado%20The%20Impact.pdf.

Rocky Mountain High Intensity Drug Trafficking Area. (2017). *The Legalization of Marijuana in Colorado: The Impact. Volume 5.* Retrieved 20/08/2018 from https://www.rmhidta.org/html/FINAL%202017%20Legalization%20of%20Marijuana%20in%20Colorado%20The%20Impact.pdf.

Rogeberg, O., Bergsvik, D., Phillips, L., van Amsterdam, J., Eastwood, N., Henderson, G., . . . Nutt, D. (2018). A new approach to formulating and appraising drug policy: A multi-criterion decision analysis applied to alcohol and cannabis regulation. *International Journal of Drug Policy,* http://dx.doi.org/10.1016/j.drugpo.2018.01.019

Rogeberg, O., & Elvik, R. (2016). The effects of cannabis intoxication on motor vehicle collision revisited and revised. *Addiction, 111*(8), 1348-1359.

Rolfe, G. (2006). Validity, trustworthiness and rigour: quality and the idea of qualitative research. *Journal of Advanced Nursing, 53*(3), 304-310.

Rolles, S. (2012). *The Alternative World Drug Report: Counting the Costs of the War on Drugs.* Retrieved 30/04/2015 from https://www.unodc.org/documents/ungass2016//Contributions/Civil/Count-the-Costs-Initiative/AWDR.pdf. (Archived by WebCite® at http://www.webcitation.org/6Z3zGSBxI).

Rolles, S., & Murkin, G. (2013). *How to regulate cannabis: A practical guide.* Retrieved 02/05/2015 from Transform Drug Policy Foundation http://www.tdpf.org.uk/resources/publications/how-regulate-cannabispractical-guide. (Archived by WebCite® at http://www.webcitation.org/6YXWzKcL0).

Rolles, S., & Murkin, G. (2016). *How to regulate cannabis: a practical guide* (2nd ed.). London: Transform Drug Policy Foundation.

Rolles, S., Murkin, G., Kushlick, D., Blickman, T., Zwitser, G., Barra, A., & Sanchez, L. (2014). Cannabis policy in the Netherlands-moving forwards not backwards. Retrieved 8/3/2018 from Transform Drug Policy Foundation http://www.tdpf.org.uk/blog/cannabis-policy-netherlands-moving-forwards-not-backwards.

Rolling Stone. (2018, Jun.12). How mapping marijuana DNA could change the future of pot. Retrieved 18/08/2018 from https://www.rollingstone.com/culture/culture-features/how-mapping-marijuana-dna-could-change-the-future-of-pot-629606/.

Room, R. (1987). Alcohol monopolies in the US: Challenges and opportunities. *Journal of Public Health Policy, 8*(4), 509-530.

Room, R. (2012). *Roadmaps to reforming the UN Drug Conventions. Retrieved 28/11/2017 from https://www.unodc.org/documents/ungass2016/Contributions/Civil/Beckl ey_Foundation/Roadmaps_to_Reform_Report_w_Foreword_110915.pdf.pdf* . Beckley park, Oxford, UK: Beckley Foundation.

Room, R. (2014). Legalizing a market for cannabis for pleasure: Colorado, Washington, Uruguay and beyond. *Addiction. 109*(3), 345-351.

Room, R., Fischer, B., Hall, W., Lenton, S., & Reuter, P. (2010). *Cannabis Policy: Moving beyond stalemate.* Oxford: Oxford University Press.

Rosenbloom, D., & Gong, T. (2013). Coproducing "clean" collaborative governance: Examples from the United States and China. *Public Performance & Management Review, 36*(4), 544-561.

Rosenthal, E. (2010). *Marijuana Grower's Handbook: Your complete guide for medical and personal marijuana cultivation* Oakland, CA: Quick American Publishing.

Rosenthal, E., & Imbriani, K. (2012). *Marijuana Pest and Disease Control: How to protect your plants and win back your garden.* Piedmont, CA: Ed Rosenthal.

Russo, E. (2008). Clinical endocannabinoid deficiency (CECD): can this concept explain therapeutic benefits of cannabis in migraine, fibromyalgia, irritable bowel syndrome and other treatment-resistant conditions? *Neuro endocrinology letters, 29*(2), 192-200.

Russo, E. (2011). Taming THC: potential cannabis synergy and phytocannabinoid-terpenoid entourage effects. *British Journal of Pharmacology, 163*(7), 1344-1364.

Russo, E. (2013). *Cannabis and cannabinoids: Pharmacology, toxicology, and therapeutic potential.* London, UK: Routledge.

Russo, E. (2014). The pharmacological history of cannabis. In R. Pertwee (Ed.), *Handbook of Cannabis* (pp. 23-43). Oxford, UK: Oxford University Press.

Russo, E. (2016a). Beyond Cannabis: Plants and the Endocannabinoid System. *Trends in Pharmacological Sciences, 37*(7), 594-605. http://dx.doi.org/https://doi.org/10.1016/j.tips.2016.04.005

Russo, E. (2016b). Clinical endocannabinoid deficiency reconsidered: current research supports the theory in migraine, fibromyalgia, irritable bowel, and other treatment-resistant syndromes. *Cannabis and cannabinoid research, 7*(1), 154-165.

Russo, E. (2017). Cannabidiol Claims and Misconceptions. *Trends in Pharmacological Sciences, 38*(3), 198-201. http://dx.doi.org/10.1016/j.tips.2016.12.004

Ryan, C. (2001). Leadership in collaborative policy-making: An analysis of agency roles in regulatory negotiations. *Policy Sciences, 34*(3), 221-245.

Sagan, C. (1971). An essay. In L. Grinspoon (Ed.), Marihuana Reconsidered (pp. 109 - 116). Mambridge, Massachusetts: Harvard University press.

Saldana, J. (2013). *The coding manual for qualitative researchers. London: Sage.*

Salomonsen-Sautel, S., Min, S., Sakai, J., Thurstone, C., & Hopfer, C. (2014). Trends in fatal motor vehicle crashes before and after marijuana commercialization

in Colorado. *Drug and Alcohol Dependence, 140*(0), 137-144.
http://dx.doi.org/http://dx.doi.org/10.1016/j.drugalcdep.2014.04.008

Sandelowski, M. (2000). Whatever happened to qualitative description? *Research in Nursing & Health, 23*(4), 334-340. http://dx.doi.org/10.1002/1098-240X(200008)23:4<334::AID-NUR9>3.0.CO;2-G

Sandelowski, M. (2010). What's in a name? Qualitative description revisited. *Research in Nursing & Health, 33*(1), 77-84.
http://dx.doi.org/10.1002/nur.20362

Sands, R. G., & Roer-Strier, D. (2006). Using data triangulation of mother and daughter interviews to enhance research about families. *Qualitative Social Work, 5*(2), 237-260.

SB 16-040. (2016). Concerning changes to the requirements for owners of a licensed marijuana business, and, in connection therewith, making an appropriation. Retrieved 5/9/2018 from the Colorado General Assembly https://leg.colorado.gov/sites/default/files/documents/2016a/bills/2016A_040_rer.pdf.

Schlossarek, S., Kempkensteffen, J., Reimer, J., & Verthein, U. (2016). Psychosocial determinants of cannabis dependence: a systematic review of the literature. *European addiction research, 22*(3), 131-144.

Scholl, M., McGowan, A., & Hansen, J. (2012). Humanistic Perspectives on Contemporary Counseling Issues: Routledge.

Schrader, M. (2015). *Crackdown on pot caregivers likely to pass Colorado Senate*. Retrieved 08/08/2015 from The Gazette http://gazette.com/crackdown-on-pot-caregivers-likely-to-pass-colorado-senate/article/1549697 (Archived by WebCite® at http://www.webcitation.org/6bBsJ1CTh). April 14

Schreck, B., Wagneur, N., Caillet, P., Gérardin, M., Cholet, J., Spadari, M., . . . Serre, A. (2018). Cannabinoid hyperemesis syndrome: Review of the literature and of cases reported to the French addictovigilance network. *Drug & Alcohol Dependence, 182*, 27-32.

Schreiner, A., & Dunn, M. (2012). Residual effects of cannabis use on neurocognitive performance after prolonged abstinence: a meta-analysis. (American Psychological Association).

Schroyer, J. (2014). *Colorado's Emerging Wholesale Marijuana Market: Q&A With Cannabase CEO Jennifer Beck*. Retrieved 04/08/2015 from Marijuana Business Daily http://mjbizdaily.com/colorados-emerging-wholesale-marijuana-market-qa-with-cannabase-ceo/ (Archived by WebCite® at http://www.webcitation.org/6bBsMNytT). October 1

Schuermeyer, J., Salomonsen-Sautel, S., Price, R., Balan, S., Thurstone, C., Min, S., & Sakai, J. (2014). Temporal trends in marijuana attitudes, availability and use in Colorado compared to non-medical marijuana states: 2003-11. *Drug Alcohol Depend, 140*, 145-155.
http://dx.doi.org/10.1016/j.drugalcdep.2014.04.016

Schultes, R., & Hofmann, A. (1992). *Plants of the Gods: their sacred, healing, and hallucinogenic powers*. Rochester, VT: Healing Arts Press.

Schuster, T., Dobson, M., Jauregui, M., & Blanks, R. (2004). Wellness lifestyles I: A theoretical framework linking wellness, health lifestyles, and complementary and alternative medicine. The Journal of Alternative & Complementary Medicine, 10(2), 349-356.

Schwabe, A., & McGlaughlin, M. (2017). Weeding out the Truth behind Cannabis Strain Names: Genetic analyses confirm Cannabis strain names are inconsistent and need regulation *Institute of Cannabis Research Conference (1st : 2017 : Colorado State University-Pueblo) held in Pueblo, Colorado,*

Scientific American. (2017). High Hopes Ride on Marijuana Amid Opioid Crisis. Retrieved 17/01/2018 from https://www.scientificamerican.com/article/high-hopes-ride-on-marijuana-amid-opioid-crisis/.

Scott, J., Grigg, J., Barratt, M., & Lenton, S. (2017a). Social capital and cannabis supply. *Journal of Sociology, 53*(2), 382-397.

Scott, J., Slomiak, T., Jones, J., Rosen, A., Moore, T., & Gur, R. (2018). Association of Cannabis With Cognitive Functioning in Adolescents and Young Adults: A Systematic Review and Meta-analysis. *JAMA Psychiatry, 75*(6), 585-595. http://dx.doi.org/10.1001/jamapsychiatry.2018.0335

Scott, J., Wolf, D., Calkins, M., Bach, E., Weidner, J., Ruparel, K., . . . Gur, R. (2017b). Cognitive functioning of adolescent and young adult cannabis users in the Philadelphia Neurodevelopmental Cohort. *Psychology of Addictive Behaviors, 31*(4), 423.

Scriber, A. (2014). Marijuana Legalization in Colorado: A Nursing Student's Perspective. *Colorado Nurse. 114*(2), 14.

Senate Bill 15-260. (2015). Medical Marijuana Product Testing (CO). 70th Gen. Assem., First Regular Session. Retrieved 15/03/2016 from http://www.leg.state.co.us/clics/clics2015a/csl.nsf/fsbillcont2/E7163AC3243269A787257E0E005FB897/$FILE/260_01.pdf (Archived by WebCite® at http://www.webcitation.org/6g1Rpjbcp).

Senate Bill 16-015. (2016). Rules For Allowed Marijuana Pesticides (CO). Retrieved 29/03/2016 from http://www.leg.state.co.us/clics/clics2016a/csl.nsf/fsbillcont3/0B2E48F8E01263DD87257F240064FA92?Open&file=015_enr.pdf (Archived by WebCite® at http://www.webcitation.org/6gMosebI7).

Sexton, M., & Ziskind, J. (2013). *Sampling cannabis for analytical purposes. Retrieved 06/08/2015 from Steep Hill http://steephill.com/pdf/uploads/whitepapers/1ceb1b244f042c2bd5f36422a9f3b8c2.pdf*:

Shontell, A. (2014). *Peter Thiel's Fund Is Leading A $75 Million Round In Marijuana Startup Privateer At A Whopping $425 Million Valuation.* Retrieved 09/05/2015 from Business Insider http://www.businessinsider.com.au/weed-startup-privateer-raises-75-million-at-425-million-valuation-2014-12. (Archived by WebCite® at http://www.webcitation.org/6YXX5J1MR). December 16

Shulgin, A., & Shulgin, A. (1991). *Pihkal: A chemical love story.* Berkley, CA: Transform Press.

Siccama, C. J., & Penna, S. (2008). Enhancing validity of a qualitative dissertation research study by using NVivo. *Qualitative research journal, 8*(2), 91-103.

Siegel, R. (1989). *Intoxication: Life in pursuit of artificial paradise.* New York, NY: Dutton.

Single, E. (1997). The concept of harm reduction and its application to alcohol: The 6th Dorothy Black lecture. *Drugs: education, prevention and policy, 4*(1), 7-22.

Singleton Jr, R. A., and Straits, B. C. (2010). *Approaches to social research fifth edition:* Oxford University Press.

Sirius, J. (2016, January 26). *What Are PGR's and Why Are They In My Weed?.* Retrieved 22/06/2016 from http://www.hightimes.com/read/what-are-pgrs-and-why-are-they-my-weed (Archived by WebCite® at http://www.webcitation.org/6iSayqwwH).

Slusarkiewicz-Jarzina, A., Ponitka, A., & Kaczmarek, Z. (2005). Influence of cultivar, explant source and plant growth regulator on callus induction and plant regeneration of Cannabis sativa L. *Acta Biologica Cracoviensia. Series Botanica, 2*(47)

Small, E. (2007). Cannabis as a source of medicinals, nutraceuticals, and functional foods. Adv Med Plant Res, 2007, 1-39.

Smiley, A. (1999). Marijuana: on the road and driving simulator studies. In H. Kalant, W. Corrigall, W. Hall & R. Smart (Eds.), *The Health Effects of Cannabis* (pp. 171-191). Toronto: Centre for Addiction and Mental Health.

Smith, M. (2012). *Heart of Dankness: Underground botanists, outlaw farmers, and the race for the cannabis cup.* New York, NY: Broadway.

Solinas, M., Goldberg, S., & Piomelli, D. (2008). The endocannabinoid system in brain reward processes.Vol. 154, pp. 369-383 Oxford, UK.

Solomon, D. (1970). *The Marijuana Papers:* Panther Books.

Solomon, D. (2015). *Using Integrated Pest Management To Reduce Pesticide Usage.* Retrieved 16/03/2016 from https://medmen.com/blog/using-integrated-pest-management-to-reduce-pesticide-usage/ (Archived by WebCite® at http://www.webcitation.org/6g3LXXk26). July 23

Sommer, I., & Van Den Brink, W. (2019). High-potency cannabis and incident psychosis: correcting the causal assumption. *The Lancet Psychiatry, 6*(6) http://dx.doi.org/10.1016/S2215-0366(19)30178-6

Southgate, E., & Hopwood, M. (1999). Mardi Gras says 'be drug free': Accounting for resistance, pleasure and the demand for illicit drugs. *Health, 3,* 303-316.

Spencer, A. (2016). *Pest control for cannabis growing without chemicals.* Retrieved 21/03/2016 from How to Grow Marijuana http://howtogrowmarijuana.com/pest-control-without-chemicals/ (Archived by WebCite® at http://www.webcitation.org/6gAViJREh).

Squibb, S. (2015). *Ask The Cannabist, 4/20 edition: How to get around Denver without driving.* Retrieved 16/02/2016 from The Cannabist http://www.thecannabist.co/2015/04/13/ask-the-cannabist-denver-transportation-420-edition/32787/ (Archived by WebCite® at http://www.webcitation.org/6frGc7sct). April 13

Stancik, A. (2015). *Testing standards must rein in inflated potency.* Retrieved 13/03/2016 from Marijuana Venture http://www.marijuanaventure.com/testing-standards/ (Archived by WebCite® at http://www.webcitation.org/6fyNpNSKy). July 20

State of Alaska. (2017). *Re: Marijuana regulation and criminal prosecustions in Alaska. Retrieved 21/01/210 from https://assets.documentcloud.org/documents/3933419/08-14-17-Jeff-Sessions-Marijuana-Regulation-and.pdf.*

State of Colorado. (2012). B 2012-004 Executive Order. Creating a Task Force on the implementation of Amendment 64. Retrieved 8/8/2018 from the Office of Governor https://www.colorado.gov/governor/sites/default/files/executive_orders/b_2012-004.pdf.

State of Colorado. (2017). *HIckenlooper-Coffman Letter, August 24, 2017. Retrieved 21/01/2018 from https://s3.amazonaws.com/big.assets.huffingtonpost.com/Hickenlooper-Coffmanletter.pdf.*

State of Colorado. (2018). Letter to members of the Colorado House of Representatives. Retrieved 5/9/2018 from the Colorado Official State Web Portal https://www.colorado.gov/governor/sites/default/files/1011_letter.pdf.

State of Oregon. (2017). *Oregon Governor Kate Brown Letter to Jeff Sessions. Retrieved 21/01/2018 from https://www.documentcloud.org/documents/3943774-8-22-17-Sessions.html.*

State of Washington. (2017). *Inslee Fergusen Letter to Sessions Re Marijuana. Retrieved 21/01/2018 from https://assets.documentcloud.org/documents/3933420/Inslee-Ferguson-Ltr-to-Sessions-Re-Marijuana-Aug.pdf.*

Steep Hill. (2016, October 19). *Steep Hill Launches New High Detection Cannabis Pesticide Testing in California*. Retrieved 21/11/2016 from PR Newswire http://www.prnewswire.com/news-releases/steep-hill-launches-new-high-detection-cannabis-pesticide-testing-in-california-300347811.html (Archived by WebCite® at http://www.webcitation.org/6mBGm1HSl). October 19

Steep Hill Labs. (2017). Cannabinol (CBN): a sleeping synergy. Retrieved 5/19/20129 from https://www.steephill.com/blogs/34/Cannabinol-(CBD):-A-Sleeping-Synergy.

Steiner, C., & Reisinger, Y. (2006). Ringing the fourfold: A philosophical framework for thinking about wellness tourism. Tourism Recreation Research, 31(1), 5-14.

Stigler, G. (1971). The theory of economic regulation. *The Bell journal of economics and management science*, 3-21.

Stoa, R. (2017). Marijuana Agriculture Law: Regulation at the Root of an Industry. *Fla. L. Rev., 69*, 297.

Stogner, J. M., & Miller, B. L. (2015). Assessing the Dangers of "Dabbing": Mere Marijuana or Harmful New Trend? *Pediatrics, 136*(1), 1-3. http://dx.doi.org/10.1542/peds.2015-0454

Stone, D. (2014). Cannabis, pesticides and conflicting laws: The dilemma for legalized States and implications for public health. *Regulatory Toxicology and Pharmacology, 69*(3), 284-288. http://dx.doi.org/http://dx.doi.org/10.1016/j.yrtph.2014.05.015

Storr, M., Yüce, B., Andrews, C., & Sharkey, K. (2008). The role of the endocannabinoid system in the pathophysiology and treatment of irritable bowel syndrome. *Neurogastroenterology & Motility, 20*(8), 857-868.

Stout, D., & Moore, S. (2009, October 19). *U.S. Won't Prosecute in States That Allow Medical Marijuana*. Retrieved 22/11/2016 from New York Times http://www.nytimes.com/2009/10/20/us/20cannabis.html.

Strain Hunters. (2016). Strain Hunters Youtube Channel. Retrieved 7/3/2018 from https://www.youtube.com/user/strainhunters.

Stroup, K. (2015). The Loss of Innocence: Follow the Money [blog post]. Retrieved 27/03/2015 from NORML Blog http://blog.norml.org/2015/03/16/the-loss-of-innocence-follow-the-money/. (Archived by WebCite® at http://www.webcitation.org/6YXXjGiOM). March 16

Subbaraman, M. (2016). Substitution and Complementarity of Alcohol and Cannabis: A Review of the Literature. *Substance use & misuse*, 1-16.

Subritzky, T. (2018). Beyond deficit and harm reduction: incorporating the spectrum of wellness as an interpretive framework for cannabis consumption. *International Journal of Drug Policy, 60*(10), 18-23. http://dx.doi.org/https://doi.org/10.1016/j.drugpo.2018.07.013

Subritzky, T., Lenton, S., & Pettigrew, S. (2016). Legal cannabis industry adopting strategies of the tobacco industry. Drug and Alcohol Review, 35(5), 511-513.

Subritzky, T., Pettigrew, S., & Lenton, S. (2016). Issues in the implementation and evolution of the commercial recreational marijuana market in Colorado. International Journal of Drug Policy, 27, 1-12. http://dx.doi.org/10.1016/j.drugpo.2015.12.001

Subritzky, T., Lenton, S., & Pettigrew, S. (2016a). Legal cannabis industry adopting strategies of the tobacco industry. *Drug and Alcohol Review, 35*(5), 511-513. http://dx.doi.org/https://doi.org/10.1111/dar.12459

Subritzky, T., Lenton, S., & Pettigrew, S. (2019). Cannabis and youth protection in Colorado's commercial adult-use market: a qualitative investigation. *International Journal of Drug Policy, 74*, 116-126. http://dx.doi.org/https://doi.org/10.1016/j.drugpo.2019.09.007

Subritzky, T., Lenton, S., & Pettigrew, S. (forthcoming). Practical lessons learned from the first years of the regulated recreational cannabis market in Colorado. In T. Decorte, S. Lenton & C. Wilkins (Eds.), *Legalizing cannabis. Experiences, lessons and scenarios*. London: Routledge.

Subritzky, T., Pettigrew, S., & Lenton, S. (2016b). Issues in the implementation and evolution of the commercial recreational cannabis market in Colorado. *International Journal of Drug Policy, 27*, 1-12. http://dx.doi.org/10.1016/j.drugpo.2015.12.001

Subritzky, T., Pettigrew, S., & Lenton, S. (2017). Into the void: Regulating pesticide use in Colorado's commercial cannabis markets. *International Journal of Drug Policy, 42*(4), 86-96. http://dx.doi.org/http://dx.doi.org/10.1016/j.drugpo.2017.01.014

Sullivan, N., Elzinga, S., & Raber, J. (2013). Determination of pesticide residues in cannabis smoke. *Journal of Toxicology, 2013*

Surna. (2016). *Surna. Water-Chilled Climate Control Systems*. Retrieved 02/07/2016 from http://surna.com/.

Susskind, L., & Cruikshank, J. (1987). *Breaking the impasse: Consensual approaches to resolving public disputes*. New York, NY: Basic Books.

Sweeney, T., & Witmer, J. (1991). Beyond social interest: Striving toward optimum health and wellness. Individual Psychology: Journal of Adlerian Theory, Research & Practice,

Szabo, B. (2014). Effects of phytocannabinoids on neurotransmission in the central and peripheral nervous systems. In R. Pertwee (Ed.), *Handbook of Cannabis*. New York, NY: Oxford University Press.

Sznitman, S., & Lewis, N. (2015). Is cannabis an illicit drug or a medicine? A quantitative framing analysis of Israeli newspaper coverage. *International Journal of Drug Policy. 26*(5), 446-452.

Sznitman, S., & Zolotov, Y. (2015). Cannabis for therapeutic purposes and public health and safety: a systematic and critical review. *International Journal of Drug Policy, 26*(1), 20-29.

Tart, C. (1971). *On Being Stoned: A psychological study of marijuana intoxication*. Palo Alto, CA: Science and Behavior Books.

Tate, K., Taylor, J., & Sawyer, M. (2013). *Something's in the Air: Race, crime, and the legalization of marijuana*. New York, NY: Taylor & Francis.

Tax Policy Centre. (2017). Statistics: Alcohol Rates 2000 - 2010, 2013 - 2017. Retrieved 4/11/2017 from Tax Policy Centre Urban Institutue & Brookings Institution http://www.taxpolicycenter.org/statistics/alcohol-rates-2000-2010-2013-2017.

Taylor, M. (2005). 'Interviewing'. In I. Holloway (Ed.), *Qualitative Research in Health Care*. Maidenhead, UK: Open University Press.

Tewdwr-Jones, M., & Allmendinger, P. (1998). Deconstructing communicative rationality: a critique of Habermasian collaborative planning. *Environment and planning A, 30*(11), 1975-1989.

The Cannabist. (2015a). *The Cannabist Show: 'She makes edibles; He reviews marijuana' (episode No. 4)* [video file]. Retrieved 30/04/2015 from http://www.thecannabist.co/2015/04/10/420-colorado-prep-marijuana-edibles-cannabis-cup-jake-browne-lindsay-topping/32914/ (Archived by WebCite® at http://www.webcitation.org/6YXXoOjU3). April 22

The Cannabist. (2015b). *The Cannabist Show: Colorado pot czar Andrew Freedman gives report card on first year of sales* [video file]. Retrieved 30/04/2015 from http://www.thecannabist.co/2015/03/27/cannabist-show-andrew-freedman-ean-seeb-interviews-marijuana-news/32258/. (Archived by WebCite® at http://www.webcitation.org/6YXXoOjU3). March 27

The Cannabist. (2015c). *Rand Paul's Denver fundraiser taps marijuana industry and more*. Retrieved 04/08/2015 from The Cannabist http://www.thecannabist.co/2015/07/01/sen-rand-paul-denver-campaign-fundraiser-marijuana-industry/37301/ (Archived by WebCite® at http://www.webcitation.org/6bBt2AoTe). July 1

The Cannabist. (2015d). *The White (marijuana review)*. Retrieved 24/08/2015 from http://www.thecannabist.co/category/reviews/strain-reviews/ (Archived by WebCite® at http://www.webcitation.org/6bBt6DlRF).

The Cannabist. (2015e). *Women in weed need to make a mark before industry becomes a 'boy's club'.* Retrieved 24/08/2015 from http://www.thecannabist.co/2015/06/09/women-cannabis-industry/35914/ (Archived by WebCite® at http://www.webcitation.org/6bBt9rQrA). June 9

The Cannabist. (2017, Jun. 16). Cannabist Show: She's a fit cannabis girl breaking stigmas. Retrieved 12/12/2017 http://www.thecannabist.co/2017/06/16/s03e09-cannabist-show-jennessa-lea-break-the-stigma-fitness/81728/

The Cannabist. (2018). Strain reviews archive - The Cannabist. Retrieved 18/08/2018 from https://www.thecannabist.co/strains/.

The Denver Post Editorial Board. (2014). *Marijuana edibles must be distinguishable*. Retrieved 27/04/2015 from The Denver Post http://www.denverpost.com/editorials/ci_26985545/marijuana-edibles-must-be-distinguishable Archived by WebCite® at http://www.webcitation.org/6bUcRgNqV). November 22

The Denver Post Editorial Board. (2015). *Editorial: Edibles 'stop sign' symbol wrong way to go, but other rules work*. Retrieved 01/09/2015 from The Cannabist http://www.thecannabist.co/2015/08/22/colorado-marijuana-edibles-rules-stop-sign-overkill/39766/ (Archived by WebCite® at http://www.webcitation.org/6bUcaAvDD). August 22

The Gazette. (2015a). *Clearing the Haze - A perspective series by The Gazette*. Retrieved 30/04/2015 from The Gazette http://gazette.com/clearingthehaze. 2015. (Archived by WebCite® at http://www.webcitation.org/6Z3wouZmv).

The Gazette. (2015b). *Regulation still ineffective*. Retrieved 03/09/2015 from The Gazette http://gazette.com/regulation-still-ineffective/article/1548296 (Archived by WebCite® at http://www.webcitation.org/6bUclazkB). March 22

The Marijuana Policy Group. (2014). *Market size and demand for marijuana in Colorado*. Report prepared for the Colorado Department of Revenue. Retrieved 22/12/2015 from https://www.colorado.gov/pacific/sites/default/files/Market%20Size%20and%20Demand%20Study%2C%20July%209%2C%202014%5B1%5D.pdf.

The Telegraph. (2017, Feb.21). Dutch MPs vote in favour of regulated cannabis cultivation. retrieved 8/3/2018 from https://www.telegraph.co.uk/news/2017/02/21/dutch-mps-vote-favour-regulated-cannabis-cultivation/.

Theory of Knowledge. (2019). Key Ethics Ideas. Retrieved 16/9/2019 from https://www.theoryofknowledge.net/areas-of-knowledge/ethics/key-ethics-ideas/.

Thomas, B., & ElSohly, M. (2016). *The Analytical Chemistry of Cannabis: Quality Assessment, Assurance, and Regulation of Medicinal Marijuana and Cannabinoid Preparations*. Amsterdam, Netherlands: Elsevier.

Thomson, M., Poulton, R., Broadbent, J., Moffitt, T., Caspi, A., Beck, J., . . . Hancox, R. (2008). Cannabis smoking and periodontal disease among young adults. *Jama, 299*(5), 525-531.

Tobin, G. A., & Begley, C. M. (2004). Methodological rigour within a qualitative framework. *Journal of advanced nursing, 48*(4), 388-396.

Tong, A. (2007). Consolidated criteria for reporting qualitative research (COREQ): a 32-item checklist for interviews and focus groups. *International Journal for Quality in Health Care, 19*(6), 349–357.

Tracy, S. J. (2010). Qualitative quality: Eight "big-tent" criteria for excellent qualitative research. *Qualitative Inquiry, 16*(10), 837-851.

Trofin, I., Dabija, G., Vaireanu, D., & Filipescu, L. (2012). Long-term Storage and Cannabis Oil Stability. *Revista de Chimie, 63*(3), 293-297.

Turtinen, M. (2015). *Skydiving planes used in $12M Colorado-Minnesota drug ring, charges say*. Retrieved 08/08/2015 from Bring Me the News http://bringmethenews.com/2015/03/26/mn-skydiving-planes-used-in-multi-million-dollar-colorado-minnesota-drug-ring-charges-say/ (Archived by WebCite® at http://www.webcitation.org/6bBtlDTGl). March 26

Unger, P., Brauninger, R., Hudalla, C., Holmes, M., & Sherman, B. (2014). *Standards for Cannabis Testing Laboratories*. Eugene, OR: Cannabis Safety Institute. Retrieved 04/01/2016 from http://cannabissafetyinstitute.org/wp-content/uploads/2015/01/Standards-for-Cannabis-Testing-Laboratories.pdf (Archived by WebCite® at http://www.webcitation.org/6g02iNGyj).

United Nations. (1961). *Single Convention on Narcotic Drugs*. Retrieved from: http://www.unodc.org/pdf/convention.1961.en.pdf.

United Nations. (1988). United Nations Convention Against Illicit Traffic in Narcotic Drugs and Psychotropic Substances. Retrived from UNODC https://www.unodc.org/pdf/convention_1988_en.pdf.

United Nations Office on Drugs and Crime. (2009). *Recommended Methods for the Identification and Analysis of Cannabis and Cannabis Products. Manual for use by national drug analysis laboratories. New York, NY: United Nations. Retrieved 16/03/2016 from https://www.unodc.org/documents/scientific/ST-NAR-40-Ebook.pdf (Archived by WebCite® at http://www.webcitation.org/6g3KME6dj)*.

United Nations Office on Drugs and Crime. (2016). *World Drug Report. Retrieved 13/11/2017 from UNODC https://www.unodc.org/doc/wdr2016/WORLD_DRUG_REPORT_2016_web.pdf*. New York:

United Nations Office on Drugs and Crime, (UNODC). (2014). *World Drug Report 2014*. Vienna: UNODC:

US Department of Health and Human Services. (2017). National Center For Complementary and Integrative Health: Complementary, alternative, or integrative health what's in a name? Retrieved 20/12/2017 from https://nccih.nih.gov/health/integrative-health#types.

US Department of Justice. (2017). US Department of Justice. Retrieved 30/10/2017 from US Department of Justice https://www.justice.gov/.

US Environmental Protection Agency. (2014). *Label Review Manual. Chapter 2: What Is a Pesticide?*. Retrieved 21/06/2016 from https://www.epa.gov/sites/production/files/2015-03/documents/chap-02-apr-2014.pdf (Archived by WebCite® at http://www.webcitation.org/6iQZUoea7).

US Environmental Protection Agency. (2016a). *Minimum Risk Pesticides Exempted from FIFRA Registration*. Retrieved 17/11/2016 from https://www.epa.gov/minimum-risk-pesticides (Archived by WebCite® at http://www.webcitation.org/6m552qxGU). January 4

US Environmental Protection Agency. (2016b). *Pesticide Use on Marijuana*. Retrieved 21/06/2016 from https://www.epa.gov/pesticide-registration/pesticide-use-marijuana (Archived by WebCite® at http://www.webcitation.org/6iQYG7Ulm).

US Food and Drug Administration. (2016). *FDA and Marijuana*. Retrieved 10/06/2016 from http://www.fda.gov/NewsEvents/PublicHealthFocus/ucm421163.htm

(Archived by WebCite® at http://www.webcitation.org/6i9n9NS2Z).
February 9

US Health Map. (2014). All Causes, both sexes, age-standardized, 2014. Retrieved
15/11/2017 from Institute for Health Metrics and Evaluation
https://vizhub.healthdata.org/subnational/usa.

USA Today. (2015, Jul. 31). *Federal bankers: No account for Colo. cannabis credit
union.* Retrieved 05/08/2015 from USA Today
http://www.usatoday.com/story/money/business/2015/07/31/federal-
bankers-no-account-colo-cannabis-credit-union/30943749/ (Archived by
WebCite® at http://www.webcitation.org/6bBp3PlBL).

USA Today. (2019, Sep.6). Massachusetts mayor arrested for extorting marijuana
vendors for 6-figure bribes. Retrieved 14/9/2019 from
https://www.usatoday.com/story/news/nation/2019/09/06/massachusetts-
mayor-arrested-extorting-marijuana-vendors/2231423001/.

Valença, M., Medeiros, F., Martins, H., Massaud, R., & Peres, M. (2009).
Neuroendocrine dysfunction in fibromyalgia and migraine. *Current Pain
and Headache Reports, 13*(5), 358-364. http://dx.doi.org/10.1007/s11916-
009-0058-1

Vandrey, R., & Haney, M. (2010). How real is the risk of addiction?. In Holland, J. (Ed.).
The pot book: A complete guide to cannabis (pp. 187-195). Rochester, VT:
Park Street Press.

Vandrey, R., Raber, J., Raber, M., Douglass, B., Miller, C., & Bonn-Miller, M. (2015).
Cannabinoid dose and label accuracy in edible medical cannabis
products. *JAMA, 313*(24), 2491-2493.

Viveros, M., de Fonseca, F., Bermudez-Silva, F., & McPartland, J. (2008). Critical Role
of the Endocannabinoid System in the Regulation of Food Intake and
Energy Metabolism, with Phylogenetic, Developmental, and
Pathophysiological Implications. *Endocrine, Metabolic & Immune
Disorders - Drug Targets(Formerly Current Drug Targets - Immune,
Endocrine & Metabolic Disorders), 8*(3), 220-230.
http://dx.doi.org/10.2174/187153008785700082

Voelker, R., & Holmes, M. (2015). *Pesticide Use on Cannabis.* Eugene, OR: Cannabis
Safety Institute. Retrieved 04/01/2016 from
http://cannabissafetyinstitute.org/wp-content/uploads/2015/06/CSI-
Pesticides-White-Paper.pdf (Archived by WebCite® at
http://www.webcitation.org/6g02bASnX).

Voelker, R. (2017). News from the Food and Drug Administration: FDA Pursues
Unproven Cancer Claims. Retrieved 22/01/2018 from
https://jamanetwork.com/journals/jama/article-
abstract/2666486?redirect=true

Volkow, N., Baler, R., Compton, W., & Weiss, S. (2014). Adverse health effects of
marijuana use. *New England Journal of Medicine, 370*(23), 2219-2227.

Vox. (2017, Mar. 16). Jeff Sessions: "stupid" to say marijuana can fight opioid
epidemic. Research: it may be a good idea. Retrieved 17/01/2018 from
https://www.vox.com/policy-and-politics/2017/3/16/14945064/jeff-sessions-
marijuana-opioids.

WADA. (2019). Cannabinoid. Retrieved 8/19/2019 from https://www.wada-
ama.org/en/questions-answers/cannabinoid.

Waldorf, D., Reinarman, C., & Murphy, S. (1991). *Cocaine Changes: The experience of
using and quitting* (Vol. 49). Philadelphia: Temple University Press.

Wall Street Journal. (2014, Jan. 2). Colorado's Pot Experiment. Retrieved 13/11/2017
from https://www.wsj.com/articles/colorado8217s-pot-experiment-
1388707110.

Wall Street Journal. (2017, Oct. 29). Big Brewer Makes a Play for Marijuana
Beverages. Retrieved 31/10/2017 from Wass Street Journal

https://www.wsj.com/articles/big-brewer-makes-a-play-for-marijuana-beverages-1509300002

Wallace, A. (2015). *Colorado Supreme Court: Employers can fire for off-duty pot use.* Retrieved 05/08/2015 from The Cannabist http://www.thecannabist.co/2015/06/15/colorado-drug-testing-laws-marijuana-use-coats-vs-dish-network/36110/ (Archived by WebCite® at http://www.webcitation.org/6bBtLoce6). Jun 15

Wang, G., Le Lait, M., Deakyne, S. J., Bronstein, A. C., Bajaj, L., & Roosevelt, G. (2016). Unintentional pediatric exposures to marijuana in colorado, 2009-2015. *JAMA Pediatrics, 170*(9), e160971. http://dx.doi.org/10.1001/jamapediatrics.2016.0971

Wang, G., Roosevelt, G., & Heard, K. (2013). Pediatric marijuana exposures in a medical marijuana state. *JAMA Pediatrics, 167*(7), 630-633. http://dx.doi.org/10.1001/jamapediatrics.2013.140

Warren, G. (2014). Regulating pot to save the polar bear: Energy and Climate Impacts of the Marijuana Industry. *Columbia Journal of Environmental Law. 40*(3), 385-432.

Watts, L. (2015). *Denver may ban large non-commercial pot grows; growers would be limited to 36 plants.* Retrieved 04/08/2015 from ABC 7 News Denver http://www.thedenverchannel.com/news/local-news/marijuana/denver-may-ban-large-non-commercial-pot-grows-growers-would-be-limited-to-36-plants03032015 (Archived by WebCite® at http://www.webcitation.org/6bBtVcMzc). March 10

Webb, E., Ashton, C., Kelly, P., & Kamali, F. (1998). An update on British medical students' lifestyles. *Medical education, 32*(3), 325-331.

Weible, C., & Sabatier, P. (2006). A Guide to the Advocacy Coalition Framework. *Handbook of public policy analysis*, 123.

Weible, C., & Sabatier, P. (2009). Coalitions, science, and belief change: Comparing adversarial and collaborative policy subsystems. *Policy Studies Journal, 37*(2), 195-212.

Weil, A. (2004). *The Natural Mind: A Revolutionary Approach to the Drug Problem.* New York, NY: Houghton Mifflin.

Weil, A., Zinberg, N., & Nelsen, J. (1969). Clinical and psychological effects of marijuana in man. *International Journal of the Addictions, 4*(3), 427-451.

Weiss, R. (1995). *Learning from strangers: The art and method of qualitative interview studies.* Simon and Schuster.

Werner, C. (2011). *Marijuana, Gateway to Health: How Cannabis Protects Us From Cancer and Alzheimer's Disease.* San Francisco, CA: Dachstar Press.

Westword. (2012a). The history of cannabis in Colorado...or how the state went to pot. Retrieved 15/11/2017 from http://www.westword.com/news/the-history-of-cannabis-in-coloradoor-how-the-state-went-to-pot-5118475.

Westword. (2012b). Marijuana criminalized in Colorado 95 years ago today: Unhappy anniversary? Retrieved 15/11/2017 from http://www.westword.com/news/marijuana-criminalized-in-colorado-95-years-ago-today-unhappy-anniversary-5845807.

Westword. (2012, Sep. 25). Marijuana: Amendment 64 opponents, backers fueled by controversial out-of-state money. Retrieved 15/11/2017 from http://www.westword.com/news/marijuana-amendment-64-opponents-backers-fueled-by-controversial-out-of-state-money-5864448.

Westword. (2017, June 28). Want a Say in Colorado's Marijuana Enforcement? Here's Your Chance. Retrieved 6/15/2019 from https://www.westword.com/marijuana/colorado-marijuana-enforcement-division-wants-stakeholder-input-9201935.

Whittemore, R., Chase, S. K., & Mandle, C. L. (2001). Validity in qualitative research. *Qualitative Health Research, 11*(4), 522-537.

WHO. (1992). *The ICD-10 classification of mental and behavioural disorders. Clinical descriptions and diagnostic guidelines.* Geneva:

WHO. (2016). *The health and social effects of nonmedical cannabis use.* Geneva:

Wilkins, C. (2018). A "not-for-profit" regulatory model for legal recreational cannabis: Insights from the regulation of gaming machine gambling in New Zealand. *International Journal of Drug Policy, 53*, 115-122. http://dx.doi.org/https://doi.org/10.1016/j.drugpo.2017.12.002

Wired. (2018, Feb.26). Why its so hard to dose weed. retrieved 31/01/2019 from https://www.wired.com/story/why-its-so-hard-to-dose-weed/.

Wired. (2019, Jul.24). High Drama: A Cannabis Biotech Company Roils Small Growers. Retrieved 28/07/2019 from https://www.wired.com/story/high-drama-cannabis-biotech-company-roils-small-growers/.

Wodak, A., Reinarman, C., Cohen, P., & Drummond, C. (2002). Cannabis control: costs outweigh the benefits. For. *BMJ (Clinical research ed.), 324*(7329), 105-106.

Wodak, A., & Saunders, B. (1995). Harm reduction means what I choose it to mean. (Taylor & Francis).

Wood, E., Brooks-Russell, A., & Drum, P. (2015). Delays in DUI blood testing: Impact on cannabis DUI assessments. *Traffic Injury Prevention.* doi: 10.1080/15389588.2015.1052421.

Wood, R. (2015). *Chris Christie Says Marijuana Taxes Are Blood Money. Is He Right?.* Retrieved 30/04/2015 from Forbes http://www.forbes.com/sites/robertwood/2015/03/27/chris-christie-says-marijuana-taxes-are-blood-money-is-he-right/. (Archived by WebCite® at http://www.webcitation.org/6YXY5DB1j). March 27

World Health Organization. (2003). *WHO guidelines on good agricultural and collection practices (GACP) for medicinal plants retrieved from http://apps.who.int/iris/bitstream/10665/42783/1/9241546271.pdf.* Geneva: World Health Organization.

Wyatt, K. (2015a). *Colorado bill seeks to standardize marijuana lab testing.* Retrieved 05/08/2015 from The Cannabist http://www.thecannabist.co/2015/03/26/colorado-marijuana-testing-lab-standards-review-lawmakers/32194/ (Archived by WebCite® at http://www.webcitation.org/6bBtZ8pf3). March 26

Wyatt, K. (2015b). *Colorado may ban 'candy' label on weed edibles.* Retrieved 24/08/2015 from Time Magazine http://time.com/3993569/colorado-marijuana-edibles-candy/ (Archived by WebCite® at http://www.webcitation.org/6bBtccReK). August 11

Wyatt, K. (2015c). *Colorado medical pot: New caregiver limits, MMJ in schools OK'd by gov.* Retrieved 08/08/2015 from The Cannabist http://www.thecannabist.co/2015/05/18/colorado-medical-pot-new-caregiver-limits-mmj-in-schools-okd-by-gov/35084/ (Archived by WebCite® at http://www.webcitation.org/6bBtft1av). May 18

Wyatt, K. (2015d). *Colorado pulls in $76M in marijuana taxes and business fees for 2014.* Retrieved 05/05/2015 from The Cannabist http://www.thecannabist.co/2015/02/10/colorado-pot-tax-44-million-recreational-taxes-2014/29510/. (Archived by WebCite® at http://www.webcitation.org/6YXY9SfE9). February 10

Zalesky, A., Solowij, N., Yücel, M., Lubman, D., Takagi, M., Harding, I., . . . Pantelis, C. (2012). Effect of long-term cannabis use on axonal fibre connectivity. *Brain, 135*(7), 2245-2255.

Zedillo, E., Pérez-Correa, C., Madrazo, A., & Alonso, F. (2019). Drug Policy in Mexico: The cause of a national tragedy. A Radical but Indispensable Proposal to Fix it. *University of Pennsylvania Journal of International Law,*

Zimmer, L., & Morgan, J. (1997). *Marijuana Myths, Marijuana Facts: A review of the scientific evidence*. New York, NY: Lindesmith Center.

Zinberg, N. (1986). *Drug, Set, and Setting: The basis for controlled intoxicant use*. Binghampton, NY: Yale University Press.

Zuardi, A., Crippa, J., Hallak, J., Moreira, F., & Guimarães, F. (2006). Cannabidiol, a Cannabis sativa constituent, as an antipsychotic drug. *Brazilian Journal of Medical and Biological Research, 39*, 421-429. Retrieved from http://www.scielo.br/scielo.php?script=sci_arttext&pid=S0100-879X2006000400001&nrm=iso

Every reasonable effort has been made to acknowledge the owners of copyright material. I would be pleased to hear from any copyright owner who has been omitted or incorrectly acknowledged.

Bonus Material

Ownership of this book provides discount codes for the book and lecture series. Get access to lectures, field notes, full interview transcripts, quizzes and a certificate on completion of course

Find more details here https://www.cannabis-education.online/courses/regulating-cannabis/

Use Discount Code: RCBOOK65 for 65% discount off the course

www.ingramcontent.com/pod-product-compliance
Lightning Source LLC
Chambersburg PA
CBHW060020030426
42334CB00019B/2117